Women and Democracy in Iraq

Women and Democracy in Iraq

Gender, Politics and Nation-Building

Huda Al-Tamimi

I.B. TAURIS
LONDON • NEW YORK • OXFORD • NEW DELHI • SYDNEY

I.B. TAURIS
Bloomsbury Publishing Plc
50 Bedford Square, London, WC1B 3DP, UK
1385 Broadway, New York, NY 10018, USA
29 Earlsfort Terrace, Dublin 2, Ireland

BLOOMSBURY, I.B. TAURIS and the I.B. Tauris logo are
trademarks of Bloomsbury Publishing Plc

First published in Great Britain 2019
Paperback edition first published 2021

Copyright © Huda Al-Tamimi 2019

Huda Al-Tamimi has asserted her right under the Copyright,
Designs and Patents Act, 1988, to be identified as Author of this work.

For legal purposes the Acknowledgements on p. viii constitute
an extension of this copyright page.

Cover design: Adriana Brioso
Cover image: Iraqi voter Safi a Taleb al-Suhail during the State of the Union address,
Washington, DC, 2005. (© PAUL J. RICHARDS/AFP/Getty Images)

All rights reserved. No part of this publication may be reproduced or
transmitted in any form or by any means, electronic or mechanical,
including photocopying, recording, or any information storage or retrieval
system, without prior permission in writing from the publishers.

Bloomsbury Publishing Plc does not have any control over, or responsibility for,
any third-party websites referred to or in this book. All internet addresses given
in this book were correct at the time of going to press. The author and publisher
regret any inconvenience caused if addresses have changed or sites have
ceased to exist, but can accept no responsibility for any such changes.

A catalogue record for this book is available from the British Library.

A catalog record for this book is available from the Library of Congress.

ISBN: HB: 978-1-7883-1280-6
PB: 978-0-7556-4122-2
ePDF: 978-1-7883-1622-4
eBook: 978-1-7883-1623-1

Series: Library of Modern Middle East Studies

Typeset by Newgen KnowledgeWorks Pvt. Ltd., Chennai, India

To find out more about our authors and books visit
www.bloomsbury.com and sign up for our newsletters.

This book is dedicated to the women of Iraq: may their voices be heard.

Contents

Acknowledgments		viii
1	Introduction: Impetus behind the Parliamentary Gender Quota in Iraq	1
2	Historical Context for Iraqi Women's Political Participation	13
3	Gender Quotas and Women's Political Mobilization in Iraq and the Middle East	35
4	Descriptive Representation: Quota Effects on Numbers of Women in Office	59
5	Case Studies: Twelve Iraqi Female Members of Parliament since 2005	89
6	Substantive Representation: How Have Women Affected Public Policy?	143
7	Symbolic Representation: Legitimacy and Media Treatment of Women as Political Agents	183
8	The Iraqi Political Situation and Women's Representation Post-2014: An Update on Case Study MP Activities since 2014	209
9	Conclusion	225
Notes		231
Bibliography		281
Index		309

Acknowledgments

This book would have not been possible without the support and encouragement from those who have contributed directly or indirectly to my work. I am especially grateful to my husband, Dr. M. Al-Hindawi; my daughters, Dr. Zain Al-Hindawi and Dr. Yasmeen Al-Hindawi; my son, Dr. Ahmed Al-Hindawi; and my granddaughter, Sara Hindawi Thompson.

I also owe much to my mentor and colleague Professor James Piscatori, who took an interest in the book from early on and gave me encouragement and support through its various stages.

I am fundamentally indebted to I.B. Tauris, particularly Dr. Sophie Rudland and the readers to whom the publisher sent my manuscript and whose comments, both critical and appreciative, helped clarify and refine my thinking. I am grateful to Lisa Vera, whose meticulous editing improved the manuscript in numerous ways and whose dedication and enthusiasm certainly made labor preparing the manuscript for press far more enjoyable than it might have been.

1

Introduction: Impetus behind the Parliamentary Gender Quota in Iraq

Ever since the region that is now modern Iraq first came under Ottoman rule in the sixteenth century, the fortunes of Iraqi women have waxed and waned in step with fluctuations in the country's political climate. Throughout contemporary history, Iraqi women have struggled simply to gain and hold basic rights. Amid shifts in the political landscape that have included monarchies, dictatorships, armed conflict, international sanctions and civil unrest, women's ability to have a measurable impact on Iraq's public policy has remained minimal across time. It may be argued that the opportunity for women to exert a viable influence on the country's future through formal election to, and participation in, public office has only very recently become possible. This situation was brought about largely by the political and institutional reconstruction following the United States' invasion of Iraq in 2003. The expressed primary aim of the invasion was to locate and destroy weapons of mass destruction (WMD). As these claims were repudiated,[1] the rationale turned to the need to depose the Iraqi president Saddam, whose Ba'athist regime was accused of state-sponsored violence and political persecution of the Iraqi people for more than two and a half decades.

While the regime change sparked by US-allied forces in Iraq was met with outrage among certain segments of the Iraqi and international communities,[2] it gave many Iraqi people hope for the possibility of moving to a democratic government. The invasion and the nation-state's subsequent moves toward democratization have led to mixed results for Iraqi women in politics as well as across the domestic, religious, legal and employment sectors. Reforms to the judicial, legislative and executive governing powers under the political transition post-2003 aimed to establish more liberal discourses in Iraq, particularly relating to Iraqi women's role in government. Although the hopes of instituting more gender-egalitarian trends have been dampened by factors including lack of security and ongoing contentions between political parties and religious factions, Iraq's transition to democracy has indeed shaped new processes by which women may potentially mobilize, become active and seek political influence.[3]

As the post-invasion reconstruction of Iraq has unfolded, the potential for Iraqi women to participate actively and visibly in the country's political structure has been one of its most notable results. Increased opportunities for women to engage in public policy-making can be attributed to the redrafting of the Iraqi Constitution in 2005.[4] Specifically, a quota for female Members of Parliament (MPs) became embedded within the Elections Law, legislating that women should achieve "not less than one-quarter of the Council of Representatives members" (Article 47, Section 4).[5]

The 2005 Constitution granted women at least nominal equality with men, retaining an article that has been in place since the Ba'athist Provisional Constitution was adopted in 1970: "Iraqis are equal before the law without discrimination based on gender, race, ethnicity, origin, color, religion, creed, belief or opinion, or economic and social status" (Article 14). The 2005 Constitution extended this formalized statement of gender equality into the political sphere: "The citizens, men and women, have the right to participate in public affairs and to enjoy political rights including the right to vote, to elect and to nominate" (Article 20). Although the transition to democracy has been characterized by sectarian conflict and increased violence toward women, the new constitution also has offered the promise of an unprecedented formal political role for women in the Iraqi Parliament.

After the new constitution was ratified, parliamentary elections in 2005, 2010 and 2014 resulted in 31.5 percent, 26.1 percent and 25.3 percent of parliamentary seats being awarded to women, respectively.[6]

While those statistics suggest great strides for women's political participation, the current literature is largely silent about the extent to which Iraqi female politicians have been empowered by greater representation. The study of gender quotas stipulates that the inclusion of women in governing institutions is critical, as gaining parliamentary seats is not an end in itself, but rather a means for participating in authoritative decision-making that determines how a society functions. The achievement of gender impartiality in post-conflict countries and insuring democracy in the long term depend on many elements comprising the progress of a democratic political culture, the level of mobilization of women in civil society, and the clearness and reliability of democratic establishments.[7]

In this sense, quota scholars Ballington and Dahlerup differentiate between the descriptive and substantive representation of women in politics: from simple increases in numbers of female representatives in the elected body to evaluations of those women's efficacy and achievements as political agents.[8] Childs and Krook extend this distinction by urging researchers to consider "how the substantive representation of women occurs" and discerning "what specific actors do," in recognition of the diversity of women's voices.[9] In this way "substantive representation" can be understood not simply as those who "initiate policy proposals," but also those who "embolden others to take steps to promote policies for women, regardless of the number of female representatives."[10]

A further distinction may be drawn in the form of symbolic representation, a term that refers to the legitimacy of political institutions and their representatives as perceived by the constituencies being represented.[11] The extent to which women gain symbolic capital and ability to influence public policy determines in part the degree to which democratic processes develop and function adequately. For this reason, it is recommended to explore public opinion, including media discourses, surrounding the implementation of gender quotas to understand quota effects comprehensively.[12]

Given that multiple schools of thought align gender justice with democracy, it is important to delineate the difference between Western democracy and the notions of reformers in the Arab world. This distinction must by definition take into account the influences of Islam, as religion has been highly politicized and deeply ingrained into Iraqi social and cultural frameworks. Any articulation of Islamic democracy must be premised on the acceptance of *tawhid*; that is the conviction and witness that "there is no God but God" and at "the core of the Islamic religious experience ... stands God Who is unique and Whose will is the imperative and guide for all."[13] Within this framework lie the Islamic notions of consultation, consensus and *ijtihad*.[14] Contributing to the debate about Islam and democracy, Fatema Mernissi acknowledges the importance of institutions and concepts of Western representative democracy such as "constitution," "parliament" and "universal suffrage";[15] however, she asserts that for Arab women, democracy is a mark of modernity that presents "an unhoped-for opportunity to construct an alternative to the tradition that weighs so heavily ... [to find] new worlds where freedom is possible."[16] Although in the Iraqi context greater opportunity now exists for women to influence public policy via the political process, the formal gender equality of political engagement remains elusive. That aside, Iraqi women have a long tradition of political activism and participation in their country's affairs, even though their mobilization in formal political roles has languished throughout history.

This book aims to explicate the avenues by which Iraqi women gain and hold parliamentary positions under the electoral gender quota, the extent to which they do influence policy change and their personal experiences while serving as public agents. By illuminating the processes by which Iraqi women are mobilized in Parliament and the subsequent outcomes for women, this research responds to the challenge promulgated by Childs and Krook. The book evaluates Iraq's progress toward eroding gender-based discrimination and considers its potential to identify future opportunities for women to engage effectively in the political and social advancement of their gender.

The role of women in politics is important to consider when characterizing a country's developmental and gender-egalitarian status because social change comes about in large part through political action.[17] How women become motivated and recognized as political actors can be understood only in the context of their particular cultures and histories, and analyzing this context may reveal both possibilities for and limitations on women's public influence in a given state.[18] At the same time, social forms such as gender status and political representation cannot be entirely isolated from regional and global influences.[19] Women across the Middle East share patterns of political participation, with shifts in their public roles mirroring larger political changes that have occurred across the region.[20] Throughout history, the role of Middle Eastern women in politics has tended to be inconsistent, informal and organized in support of men with whom they have socially accepted connections. The avenue through which women's political activism becomes legitimized (i.e., the state, religious authorities or primordial political units such as tribes or clans) affects both the potential for women to become active political agents and the forms their political influence takes.[21]

Both men and women in the Middle East have become increasingly politicized since the beginning of the twentieth century.[22] Factors such as population growth, urbanization, economic development and globalization, education and labor force expansion have contributed to these increases in political activism among people across all social classes.[23] Some of the twenty-first-century discourse on globalization and democracy has posited that global influence on developing countries has a gender dimension, as noted by leading feminist scholars such as Valentine Moghadam, Sylvia Walby and Laurel Weldon who argue that democracy cannot be achieved unless women become full participants in the political process—whether through formally elected public office or through social movements.[24] Democratization has been problematical across the Middle East due to the region's engagement in generations-long cultural conflicts between traditionalists and modernists, fundamentalists and liberalists, proponents of equality of citizenship and those who support the politics of national identity and so-called authenticity.[25] These ideological clashes bear heavily on gender relations as traditionally patriarchal societal systems are challenged by increasingly vigorous women's movements advocating for democratization as well as demanding the full participation of women in the political, economic, labor and conflict resolution systems.[26] This process has been addressed in several bodies of literature and has formed the theme of a number of international conferences. For example, in 1995, the Fourth World Conference on Women in Beijing acknowledged the underrepresentation of women at most governmental levels, the central role of gender in the development of nations and the need to empower women as decision-makers to achieve transparent and accountable government.[27]

Deniz Kandiyoti postulates that, despite the widely differing trajectories of evolution of their states and societies, all Middle Eastern countries have struggled with similar challenges in establishing modern nation-states and developing new notions of sovereignty and citizenship.[28] She further argues that an adequate analysis of women's status in predominantly Muslim societies must be "grounded in a detailed examination of the political projects of contemporary states and of their historical transformations."[29] The representation of women in political discourses, levels of formal emancipation they have reached and forms of economic and political participation they have achieved are inextricably linked to state-building processes. The question of Middle Eastern women's experience has emerged as a hotly debated issue where the treatment of women comes either to symbolize ideologies formed to legitimize new forms of state power or to support the cultural authenticity of conservative Islam. The nature of a country's formative experiences, then, must be analyzed to clarify the roles of its women in sociopolitical processes. The degree to which women are integrated into civic and political life has come to serve as one barometer for the nation-state's level of modernization.[30]

Specific to the Iraqi situation, several variables and combinations thereof have contributed to fluctuations in women's rights, position and political participation across history. These contributing factors have included tribal segmentation and traditions, patriarchal structures, religiosity, wars, political agendas and party ideologies, the socioeconomic climate, globalization and international pressures. Overwhelmingly across history, Iraqi society was patriarchal with male authority permeating every institution from the family to the echelons of government, and women were conditioned from birth for obedience. Early measures to encourage the emancipation of Iraqi women were taken during a repressive authoritarian regime, rather than as part of a gradual evolution toward democratization and the autonomous representation of gender interests.[31] The tyrannical nature of the state that emerged in the 1970s and the international sanctions imposed in the 1990s disintegrated Iraqi society and traumatized its citizens. Factors that should have been assets to women, such as increased education, employment, suffrage and multiculturalism, had the potential to become liabilities as the state manipulated the notion of Iraqi identity to suit its political agenda and exert control over societal institutions.[32] The same government that granted women new rights simultaneously eradicated all independent women's organizations, and instead set up state-sponsored women's groups that were allowed only to reflect and support the stances of the ruling party.[33]

After the 2003 invasion by the United States and its allies, relationships between state power and the citizenry underwent a forced renegotiation in the context of internationalized (globalized) reconstruction of the nation-state.[34] The fall of Saddam's regime and eradication of most national institutions were followed by a series of administrative decisions undertaken by the US-led Coalition Provisional Authority (CPA)—decisions that many scholars and political analysts have considered misguided.[35] These administrative actions sparked violent responses by armed factions, resulting in the assassination of academics and scientists, causing healthcare and educational systems to crumble and leading to dramatic shortages in water, electricity and public services. Women struggled with the severe lack of security as economic support and opportunities for employment were eroded. Iraq was already experiencing societal cleavages along ethnic and religious lines, which were further exacerbated by the occupation and subsequent invention of new governmental institutions. This segmentation included conflicts between secular and religious affiliations, separation between Islamic groups and the rift between those who supported the US occupation and those opposed to Western interference.[36]

It was from within this multilayered context of conflict and strife that negotiations ensued for drafting the new constitution, a process further complicated by US pressures to transition toward a regional order that was conducive to long-term American interests.[37] Consequently, the constitution was drawn up in such a way that it accentuated, rather than eliminated, sectarianism. Further, the 2005 Constitution is centered on *shari'a* (Islamic law), with Article 2 stating "Islam is the official religion of the state and is a basic source of legislation" and that "no law can be passed that contradicts the undisputed rule of Islam." While—as Coleman points out—*shari'a* may be open to a wide range of interpretations and its centrality in the Iraq Constitution does not automatically point toward erosion in women's participation in society and reconstruction,[38] the reinforcement of sectarian identities in Iraqi society brought about by the constitutionalization of *sharia* law has had damaging consequences for women in politics. Female politicians and activists endure relentless security threats that circumscribe their capacity to embrace a legitimate role in Iraq's political processes.[39]

The constitution reflected some influence by women's activism in the inclusion of the electoral gender quota for Parliament. In a 2000 article, Sylvia Walby presents evidence that the institution of democratically elected assemblies in itself increases women's political representation.[40] Walby's analyses were based on data reported by the Inter-Parliamentary Union,[41] the United Nations Development Program[42] and the International Labour Organization,[43] indicating that increases in women elected to Parliaments have overlapped with a rise in global democratization over the past 70 years.[44] Further, modern international norms appear to be trending toward promoting greater inclusion of women in politics.[45] Thus global influences, particularly during the transition to a new government and social structures after an invasion and armed conflict, have served to strengthen the call for the introduction of gender quotas into the governing bodies of developing nations.[46]

Whether implementation of the parliamentary quota has achieved meaningful evolution of participatory levels by women in public office in Iraq is moot. Three nationwide elections have taken place since the 2005 Constitution went into effect. While the first parliamentary election under the new constitution yielded greater women's representation than demanded by the quota, those results were not repeated in ensuing elections wherein women were elected to only the quota-mandated 25 percent of seats. In more recent years, Iraq has witnessed the intensification, rather than the diminution, of sectarian strife following the withdrawal of US troops in 2011. The Shi'a-dominated administration led by Prime Minister Nouri al-Maliki suffered significant criticism for its marginalization and persecution of opposing Sunni, Kurdish and Sadrist blocs, only just surviving a vote of no confidence in 2012. Despite this interim reprieve, the government's failure to uphold the tenets of the 2010 Erbil power-sharing accord, allegations of government corruption, deep flaws in the political process and the inability of the US-orchestrated constitutional order to establish fair distribution and balance of power led to Maliki's demotion to the position of vice president in 2014.[47] The resurgence of radical militants in Iraq and neighboring Syria has been a further consequence of this failure and all Iraqis suffer under such conditions. Against the backdrop of such a complex and dynamic political landscape and its subsequent insecurity, this book seeks to elucidate the extent to which women have achieved effective participation in Iraq's public sphere.

The overall aim of this research is to examine the efforts made, both by Iraqis as a whole and by individual women and women's organizations, toward political mobilization of Iraqi female parliamentarians and their emerging role in the country's politics and decision-making processes post-2003. The study explores the extent to which the 2005 constitutional gender quota measures have given women a political voice in light of prevailing temporal, religious, political, sectarian and cultural constraints since the 2003 invasion. There are three overarching objectives to the research. The first is to analyze thoroughly the recent evolution of women's civic and political voice in Iraq through electoral representation. Second is to identify and explore the processes and outcomes of the political mobilization of Iraqi female MPs in the post-2003 period. The final goal is to describe the primary barriers and supportive factors encountered by the female MPs in their efforts to become elected and to introduce, enact and implement policy change.

In addition, this book attempts to discern whether Iraqi women's political representation imposed by the quota has enhanced or undermined the ability of female MPs to influence policy-making. This objective entails the discovery of the relative strategies employed by female Iraqi MPs to exert their political influence and their subsequent effectiveness, together with an examination of "lawmaker" as a gendered identity. The objectives were pursued through the analysis of televised and print interviews with Iraqi female leaders and interviews with scholars of Iraqi politics and gender relations, accompanied by extensive secondary research.

A broad approach was taken to analyze the contemporary situation of Iraqi women with respect to political mobilization since 2003, with particular emphasis on the female MPs elected as a result of the parliamentary quota established by the 2005 Constitution. The research questions probed the contributions of female MPs to the decision-making process of policies affecting the social, economic and political futures of Iraqi women, as well to instituting policies that are not specific to women's rights and status (likely representing most parliamentary experiences). The experiences of the female MPs—in both the political and personal arenas—from the 2003 transitional government, through the establishment of a permanent authority and the complex influences affecting present-day Iraqi politics, were comprehensively examined.

Two approaches informed the analytical frame. The first was a model advanced by Sabbagh in a contribution to the 2007 *Arab Quota Report* (prepared by the International Institute for Democracy and Electoral Assistance). Sabbagh suggests that this model can be employed to address four areas of parliamentary work. The first is institutional, which is intended to make the institution more woman-friendly; the second is representation by increasing women's election to higher positions; the third is discourse in order to shift public attitudes and the fourth is the impact on enhancing women's influence on legislation that takes women's concerns and recommendations into account.[48] This book focuses on the second point, representation: specifically, women's representation in Iraq's Parliament.

The second guidance came from scholars examining gender quota electoral systems who have called for research to explore the effects of such systems on women's political representation across three dimensions: *descriptive* representation, *substantive* representation and *symbolic* representation.[49] Descriptive representation involves questions regarding the sheer numbers of women elected to political office and their demographic characteristics. Substantive representation refers to the effect of quotas on the performance and effectiveness of female politicians. Symbolic representation concerns the effect of a quota on the legitimacy of the polity, voters' conceptions of their elected representatives and the symbolic frames employed by the media and their agents to depict women in politics. Using these three types of representation as outcome measures, this analysis aimed to realistically delineate the levels of representation women have gained in Iraq since implementation of the parliamentary gender quota in 2005.

The findings suggest that, to date, Iraqi women have achieved formally acknowledged (descriptive) representation in Parliament as a result of the quota in the form of sheer numbers of women filling parliamentary seats. However, they have not yet accomplished full substantive and symbolic representation. Most—if not all—Iraqi female MPs remain marginalized and their voices minimized by a variety of internal and external factors. Women in public office continue to lean upon their relations with influential men within their affiliative political blocs to achieve election and reelection to Parliament. The patriarchal dominance that has cemented its place in Iraqi societal norms continues to influence the experiences and status of women in public life up until the present day. Women's security and physical safety remain severely compromised as a consequence of their participation in political roles.

On the other hand, the analysis also illuminates the fact that Iraqi female politicians do believe they have made some strides toward social, political and economic empowerment. The case studies of individual Iraqi female MPs serve to outline possible steps toward increasing such empowerment of women as substantive social and political influencers. Women in Iraq have been able to introduce and affect at least a modicum of policy change by exerting influence upon legislative agendas, changing sociopolitical norms and attitudes, expressing political views through available media outlets and interacting effectively with their constituencies. They have done so by becoming active members of parliamentary committees, contributing to parliamentary sessions and debate, drafting and amending laws that serve the country and improve the lives of all Iraqi citizens, most particularly its women.

Further, this research explicates the barriers and supports to Iraqi women's mobilization as parliamentary actors, encountered since institution of the gender quota. Examples of supportive factors include backing from constituents and women's nongovernmental organizations (NGOs); connections with influential male figures; aid from international interventionists and educational supports. Illustrations of barriers to women's political mobilization include the devolving security situation, sectarian political power struggles, a tradition toward women's exclusion and governmental corruption. Certain factors such as economics, the gender quota and international influences serve as both supports and barriers to Iraqi women in parliamentary seats. In addition, the Iraqi media play a complex and equivocal role in the quest of Iraqi women to establish legitimacy as political actors. Levels of symbolic capital gained by women pursuing political office are closely tied to processes toward democratization, and the media has powerful potential to frame the public conversation in ways either supportive or detractive from attaining such symbolic legitimacy. Moreover, media outlets emerging since the 2003 invasion have contributed to, rather than lessened, the sectarian schisms that have escalated the violence experienced by all Iraqis, particularly by Iraqi women, and freedom of the press remains largely unrealized. Thus the Iraqi media offer prime examples of supportive and obstructive factors influencing women's parliamentary success.

This research draws upon the theoretical bases of democratization, feminism and the study of gender quotas. Popular support for gender equality and an environment where the importance of basic political liberties is recognized are important cultural factors underpinning the development of a functioning democracy. Democratization theory also conjectures that advanced economic development, ethnic homogeneity (however challenging given the complex social demography of Iraq), efficient state institutions and prior experience with meaningful democratic processes are necessary precursors to shaping enduring democratic outcomes in a transitional nation-state.[50] Both democratic and feminist theories have indicated that the foundational preconditions required for successful transition to democracy were lacking in Iraq at the time of occupation and remain so today.[51] Postcolonial feminist theory posits that democratization contributes to women's ability to succeed in public policy-making roles, and that the converse also is true—full participation by women in the political process contributes to democratization.[52] This book analyzes the effects of adopting a constitutional gender quota by examining the quota impact on women's descriptive, substantive and symbolic representation, in concert with an investigation of the country's progress toward democratization in the context of feminist theoretical perspectives.

Following this introduction, Chapter 2 offers a brief historical context within which to place the evolution of women's role in Iraqi politics over the years, followed by a Chapter 3 which reviews previous literature surrounding sociopolitical evaluations of electoral gender quotas and comparative studies of women's representation in Middle Eastern countries neighboring Iraq. The four chapters that follow cover the sources of representation and mobilization of female MPs in Iraq. Chapter 4 explores the political and sociocultural representation of women from 1920 to the present within the context of the political and societal environments and influences of the times, with emphasis on the outcomes of parliamentary elections relating to gender issues and policies. Chapter 5 lays out case studies of 12 Iraqi women leaders about whom televised interview and print media data were collected. Chapter 6 discusses levels of substantive representation Iraqi women have achieved as a result of election to parliamentary seats. Chapter 7 examines the symbolic representation Iraqi female MPs have accomplished post-2003.

The bulk of these data were gathered in 2012 and 2013. Therefore, Chapter 8 provides a brief update tracking the political movements of the case study MPs from 2014 through the time of this publication. Finally, a short conclusion draws together the key arguments, provides some closing thoughts to tie together prevailing themes and presents an outlook for the future.

2

Historical Context for Iraqi Women's Political Participation

It is important to contextualize Iraqi women's political mobilization historically to provide a basis for comparison with their status post-2003. While this book is not historic in nature, the progressive struggle by Iraqi women for equal rights and attaining a political voice acts as an important backdrop for more recent efforts toward political mobility. In fact, as stated by the Iraq Legal Development Project (ILDP) group formed by the American Bar Association, throughout history women's rights, roles and status in Iraq have been employed as a "largely political tool to be reduced or expanded to suit the political, social and economic interests of the ruling party."[1] Their assessment indicated significant progress since 2003 on particular women's rights issues; however, insecurity and lack of political will to place women in leadership positions have prevented many of those gains from being realized.[2]

The Ottoman Empire

Although the modern state of Iraq was founded in the 1920s, the region is an ancient land with a history going back thousands of years. A comprehensive historical account will not be undertaken here; rather, this historical background section will begin with the Ottoman legacy, which heavily influenced the shaping of modern Iraq. From the sixteenth century until 1831, nomadic and pastoral tribes occupied much of southern Iraq while urban settlement was mostly concentrated in the north.[3] Noted class and religious schisms emerged between Iraq's urban residents and Ottoman and Islamic law governed agricultural populations, while rural Arabs were largely governed by ancient tribal customs only somewhat influenced by Islam.[4] The divide between urban and tribal control had notable implications for women, as the urban sectors tended toward governance by *shari'a* law whereas the tribes made their own laws, which varied substantively by tribe.[5] Thus, the laws governing personal status, which particularly affected the treatment of women and the extent to which women had a voice in their own affairs, varied widely by region and by religious, tribal or kinship affiliation.[6] The Ottoman era also marked a deepening of the division between the Shi'a and Sunni sects of Islam in Iraq, a schism which originated from the major impact of the Safavid-Ottoman conflict in 1638[7] and which continues through present times.

The year 1831 was an important turning point in Iraq's history, marking the region's transition from a medieval to an international structure; this year also marked the end of decentralized rule and the beginning of centralized Ottoman governance.[8] In 1839, the Ottoman Empire underwent the Tanzimat Reforms, a restructuring and improvement of the empire's military, legal and socioeconomic systems.[9] These reforms led to the establishment of Ottoman police and army posts in Iraq; improved military and political strategy, in concert with the introduction of the telegraph, allowed Ottoman leaders to extend rule across the Iraqi provinces.[10] Increased control by the Ottomans over the Iraqi regions should be viewed within the context of growing European interest in the area and Iraq's economic shift from agricultural subsistence to international trade.[11]

In 1869, the Ottoman envoy Midhat Pasha assumed governorship of Baghdad and introduced a centralized administrative system into the provinces that formed the roots of contemporary Iraqi governance.[12] While the Ottoman political structure did not recognize equal rights between women and men, it instituted a series of reforms favorable to women, such as increased access to the legal system.[13] The establishment of a secular public-school system was particularly important, providing an avenue of mobility for children and youth of both genders and from all social classes.[14] The Ottomans also introduced a wide variety of subjects new to the Iraqi populace including Western languages, mathematics and sciences (subjects previously not taught in Iraq's religious schools).[15] In 1908, a new ruling clique, the Young Turks, took power in Istanbul. They reintroduced the 1876 Constitution (this Ottoman Constitution set forth the rights of the ruler and the ruled, but it derived from the ruler and has been called at best an "attenuated autocracy"), held elections throughout the empire and reopened Parliament. Although the Iraqi delegates represented only the well-established families of Baghdad, their parliamentary experience in Istanbul proved to be an important introduction to self-government.[16]

Most important to Iraq history, the Ottomans aggressively pursued a "Turkification" policy that alienated the emerging Iraqi intelligentsia and set in motion a new Arab nationalist movement. Several secret nationalist societies were formed,[17] the most important of which was Al Ahd (the Covenant), whose membership was drawn almost entirely from Iraqi officers in the Ottoman army. Membership spread rapidly in Baghdad and Mosul, growing to 4,000 by the outbreak of World War I. Despite the existence of Al Ahd and of other, smaller nationalist societies, Iraqi nationalism was still mainly the concern of educated Arabs from the upper and middle classes.[18]

When characterizing the influence of the Ottoman legacy on Iraq's history, it is important to recall that the Ottoman reforms were designed to recast the Iraqi people into an Ottoman mold.[19] Although a new intelligentsia emerged from the expanded educational system,[20] that intelligentsia was in essence an Ottoman elite trained in the Ottoman form of rule—namely authoritarian paternalism, which neither sought consultation from the citizens it governed nor recognized equal rights for women.[21] Further, these internal elites were drawn from only one segment of Iraq society, the Sunnis. It is hardly surprising that the Shi'as and the rural tribes, whose power had been thus systematically eroded, spearheaded efforts toward governmental opposition in the early twentieth century.[22]

British Invasion and Colonization

In 1917, the Ottoman Empire collapsed as British troops invaded Mesopotamia and occupied the city of Baghdad. British colonization became increasingly oppressive over time, sparking ongoing resistance primarily from tribal leaders.[23] This resistance culminated in the 1920 armed uprising against the British. Political historian Hanna Batatu suggests that the tenuous bond formed between the Sunnis and Shi'as as they resisted British occupation may have heralded the birth of a new sense of Iraqi national identity.[24] In order to combat this resistance and avoid having to maintain a sizeable military presence in Iraq, the British adopted a tactic of slowing detribalization and exacerbating growing conflicts between the rural and urban communities.[25] This included giving official recognition to tribal customs through the Tribal Criminal and Civil Disputes Regulations (TCCDR), which excluded the rural areas from jurisdiction under national law. In 1925, the British exerted pressure to ensure that the TCCDR were written into the 1925 Iraq Constitution.[26] Reversion to tribal law represented a step back for women's rights; the British blocked education for girls and reversed many Ottoman reforms that had been more favorable toward women with the argument that, to maintain these, women would have been disadvantaged within the tribal system that provided a strategy of efficient rule.[27]

The difficulty of imposing British-style governance on Iraq is illustrated by the fact that it took four years to accomplish.[28] Following patterns used to colonize and rule India, the British instituted several fundamental state structures: a monarch as figurehead of the central government; a bureaucracy to govern the country; an army to maintain order and a constitution patterned after Western examples, including provisions for indirect elections and a Parliament.[29] The first Iraqi Constitution was ratified in 1925, establishing the state as a "constitutional monarchy." Table 2.1 offers a comparison between the Iraqi constitutions established to date, from 1925 to 2005. Article 13 of the 1925 Constitution stipulated that Islam was the official religion of the State; all sects had freedom of practice and there was no differentiation between Sunnis and Shiʻas. However, most of the native Iraqis who were given leadership roles by the British were Ottoman-educated Arab Sunnis.[30] Therefore, although the 1920 revolution ultimately failed to achieve Iraqi independence, it did serve to slow down imposition of the Indian political model and to secure wider representation of Iraqi nationals in their own government.[31]

Noga Efrati's 2012 book provides a well-researched documentary of the treatment of Iraqi women from the onset of the British Mandate in 1914 through present times. Efrati draws parallels between British state-building efforts during British occupation and the British-backed Hashemite Monarchy (1917–58), and the return to religious law and tribal influence post-2003. Her assessment of the situation of Iraqi women after the US-led occupation—in comparison to the period of British influence—points to dramatic similarities between the two eras in the way women have been constructed in public treatment and discourses as second-class citizens.[32] Despite the inherent difficulties for women during the period of British involvement, this era witnessed the rise of Iraqi women leaders such as Asma' al-Zahawi, who advocated for women's rights to education and employment during the late 1920s and early 1930s.[33] Al-Zahawi, president of Nadi al-Nahda al-Nisaiyya, explained how women were treated in that time when she was invited to send a delegation of Iraqi women to participate in the 1929 Arab Women's Congress held in Cairo. She was forced to decline, writing, "The government is unable to help women against the reactionary forces which flex their muscles to threaten our progress and terrorize the club so that we are unable to name even one woman to attend the conference."[34] This reflected the strength of conservative and reactionary opposition to change, albeit three years

Table 2.1 Comparison of Iraqi Constitutions, 1925–present

Provision	1925 Constitution	1970 Interim Constitution	2005 Constitution
State Form	Constitutional Monarchy	Sovereign People's Democratic Republic	Single, independent federal state with full sovereignty; system of government is republican, representative parliamentary and democratic
Head of State	King	President of the Revolutionary Council	President of the Republic
Legislature	Senate—20 members Chamber of deputies (CD)—1 deputy for every 20,000 male Iraqis	Revolutionary Command Council (RCC)—12 members National Council (NC)—representatives from various political, economic and social sectors	Council of Representatives (CoR)—1 representative per 100,000 Iraqis Federation Council (FC)—representatives from regions and governorates not organized in a region
Council of Ministers	Prime minister plus no more than 9 and no less than 6 ministers of state appointed by the king	Competent ministers selected by the president	Prime minister—nominee of the CoR bloc with largest number Council of ministers appointed and directed by the prime minister
Parliamentary Term	Senate—8 years Chamber of deputies—4 ordinary sessions (1 per year)	RCC—no term specified NC—no term specified	4 calendar years

Provision	1925 Constitution	1970 Interim Constitution	2005 Constitution
Selection of Parliamentarians	Senate—appointed by king Chamber of deputies—elected by secret ballot of male Iraqis	RCC—selected by the body itself NC—specified by National Council Law	COR—elected by secret general ballot FC—selected by the COR
Qualifying Criteria for members of Parliament (MPs)	Iraq national 30+ years of age (CD) 40+ years of age (Senate) Not adjudicated bankrupt or interdicted Has not lost civil rights Has not been sentenced to imprisonment Has no material interest with a public department of Iraq Not a lunatic or idiot Not related to the king	RCC—Iraqi by birth, born of two Iraqi parents also Iraqi by birth; membership in Regional Leadership of the Socialist Arab Ba'ath Party NC—specified by National Council Law	A candidate to the CoR must be a fully eligible Iraqi. The CoR shall decide by a two-thirds majority the membership authenticity of its members within 30 days from the date of filing an objection.
Parliamentary Gender Quota	None; no female suffrage	None; no female suffrage	The citizens, men and women, have the right to participate in public affairs and to enjoy political rights including the right to vote, to elect and to nominate.

Provision	1925 Constitution	1970 Interim Constitution	2005 Constitution
Judiciary	Judges appointed by the king Three classes of courts: 　Civil 　Religious 　Special	Independent and subject to no other authority save that of the law The law determines court formation, levels, jurisdiction and conditions for appointment of judges	The judiciary is independent and no power is above the judiciary except the law. Federal Judicial Authority comprised of Higher Juridical Council, Supreme Federal Court, Federal Court of Cassation, Public Prosecution Department, Judiciary Oversight Commission
Personal Status Jurisdiction	*Shari'a* courts (Muslims) Spiritual Councils (Jews and Christians)	Specified by Law 188 of 1959	Specified by Law 188 of 1959
Religion	Islam is the official religion of the state; freedom to practice various forms of worship guaranteed to all Iraqis as long as such forms "do not conflict with the maintenance of discipline or public morality."	Freedom of religion, faith and the exercise of religious rites are guaranteed, "in accordance with the rules of constitution and laws and in compliance with morals and public order."	Islam is the official religion of the state and is a fundamental source of legislation. This constitution guarantees the Islamic identity of the majority of the Iraqi people and guarantees the full religious rights of all individuals to freedom of religious belief and practice such as Christians, Yazidis and Mandi Sabeans.

later, the Arab Women's Congress was held in Baghdad in 1932, reflecting the tidal force of historical change sweeping through Iraq.[35]

Paulina Hassun was the publisher of the first Iraqi women's magazine, *Layla*, published in October 1923 to express views on the issue of women's reform and to contribute to the awakening of the Iraqi woman.[36] It promoted education for girls, gave voice to the women and urged members of the Iraqi Constituent Assembly to work toward improving the status of women, to support women's issues and to recognize their democratic rights.[37] The magazine's last issue was on August 15, 1925 when Hassun declared its liquidation and left Iraq.[38]

A stronger women's movement began to take shape and other women's journals appeared despite attempts to suppress them later in the 1930s and 1940s. These included: *al-Mara al-Haditha* (Modern Woman, 1936), *Fatat al-Iraq* (Young Iraqi Woman, 1936), *Fatat al-Arab* (Young Arab Woman, 1937), *Sawt al-Mara* (Women's Voice, 1943), *al-Rihab* (1946), *al-Umm wa-l-Tifl* (Mother and Child, 1946), *Tahrir al-Mara* (Women Liberation, 1947), *Bint al-Rashid* (al-Rashid's Daughter, 1948) and *al-Ittihad al-Nisai* (Women Union, 1949). Women were involved with these periodicals as proprietors, publishers, editors and writers.[39] Sabihah al-Shaikh Daud, the first to chronicle the women's movement in Iraq and one of the first women to receive a public education, observed that the 1920s' revolution destroyed the major barrier that impeded women's development and laid the foundation for their march.[40] She also noted that, at the beginning of the 1920s, the Women's Awakening Club in Iraq was influenced by the Egyptian Feminist Union (al-Ittihad al-Nisai al-Misri) established and led by Huda Sha'arawi in 1923.[41]

During the British occupation period, Iraqi women continued to protest their marginalization and exerted political influence by supporting male politicians and men's parties and by taking part in riots and demonstrations.[42] Women leaders of these groups (who come from educated, urban, upper and middle class families, and were often related to politicians or high-ranking officials) were active in promoting democracy, national freedom, welfare for children and women's rights across the next three decades.[43]

The Hashemite Monarchy

In 1932, Iraq gained independence as a monarchy under Hashemite King Faisal I, although the British continued to maintain military bases in Iraq and exercise substantial influence in the country. During this time, much of the gender discourse involving citizen disputes (mostly relating to Personal Status laws) remained in the hands of tribal leaders[44] and the TCCDR in particular remained in force until the monarchy was overthrown in 1958 by the "Free Officers" led by Abd al-Karim Qasim.[45] The complete exclusion of women from the formal political sphere was legitimized under the Constitution and Electoral Law set down during the British Mandate, which prevented female citizens from voting or holding public office.[46]

The Hashemite monarchy weakened over the last decade of its rule as new social groups formed to challenge establishment policies.[47] These groups, like their predecessors in the 1920s, came from educated, middle- to upper-class families.[48] Although the oil trade had brought wealth to a few, poverty remained widespread.[49] The growing generation of young intelligentsia was split between the liberals increasingly influenced by the West who sought a more egalitarian society, and the young Arab nationalists who advocated Arab unity and independence from Western influence.[50] The emerging educated middle class and the new working class began exerting greater influence through demonstrations, riots and strikes.[51] The Istiqlal (Independence) Party, the National Democratic Party and most notably the Iraq Communist Party (which functioned underground at this time) evolved into powerful forces against British alliance. The king, who had tied himself increasingly closely to the British and the tribal sheikhs, became vulnerable in the face of growing leftist opinion fuelled by the scarcity and deprivations caused by World War II.[52] Violent urban uprisings in 1948, 1952 and 1956 further weakened the ability of the monarchy to play a unifying role in Iraq's political and social structure.[53]

During the 1940s and 1950s, female groups began organizing in Iraq to promote women's suffrage and political rights. The Iraqi Union for Women's Rights, established in 1952, was most prominent at this time, and became officially recognized by the government in 1958. Despite its legitimacy, calls for greater political rights for women were largely ignored, opposed by political, scholarly and religious interests alike. While opposition parties to the government (such as the Iraq Communist Party) publicly supported women's suffrage, that support was couched in rhetoric that actually posed further obstacles to the process, exemplified by prevailing discourses suggesting that women must receive further education in political systems and processes before they would be "ready" to vote.[54] Iraqi women continued to struggle in vain to gain suffrage throughout the monarchy and into the early years of Ba'athist rule.

Although it did not support the development of opportunities for women, the Hashemite kingdom successfully established a professional military force, provided the infrastructure for a large bureaucracy and laid the foundation for modern economic development.[55] However, these achievements were not enough to prevent revolutionaries from gaining a political foothold in the country. As historian Phebe Marr suggests, the greatest failure of the Hashemite regime may have been its inability to build sustainable political institutions to support its monarchical rule.[56] Rather than recognizing and offering adequate political representation to Iraq's emerging urban middle class, the monarchy instead relied upon the army and martial law to enforce its political positions. Further, the monarch tended to neglect domestic affairs in favor of pursuing greater involvement in foreign policy, thereby alienating elected members of Parliament who felt important issues at home were being overlooked.[57] Thus, opponents of the regime garnered vital support from the expanding middle and lower-middle classes, disenfranchised by the monarchy.[58]

The Qasim Regime and Ba'athist Secular Rule

On July 14, 1958, the Hashemite monarchy was overthrown in a military coup spearheaded by the Free Officers' Movement, which had formed within Iraq's army. The revolution transformed Iraq from a monarchy into a republic, and ranking Brigadier General Abd al-Karim Qasim became its prime minister.[59] The new governmental council established a cabinet representing the National Democratic Party, the Istiqlal Party, the Ba'athists and the Marxists, which factions all had supported the coup. A temporary constitution was drafted, which notably contained no provision for elections or a representative assembly. One of the most significant achievements of the early revolutionary regime was to end the overwhelming influence of the wealthy landed class on Iraqi politics and place greater power into the hands of the emergent middle classes.[60] Between 1958 and 1960, policies introduced by civilian leftist and reformist leaders trended toward greater egalitarianism and more even distribution of wealth. Unfortunately, however, military officers gradually edged the civilian reformists out of the political arena and Iraq's governance moved closer to oligarchy and military dictatorship.[61]

In 1952, Dr. Naziha al-Dulaimi founded the League for Defence of Women's Rights, which was later called the Iraqi Women's League. Al-Dulaimi was later appointed Minister of Municipalities, becoming the first woman in the Arab world to be awarded such responsibility.[62] She inspired women to join the league and work together toward gender equality. The league promoted women's rights by implementing educational programs, social services, and lobbying.[63]

It had members from all social, economic, ethnic and religious strata. During the 1960s and prior to the Ba'athist regime, membership reached over 42,000 members, and 7,502 registered women and 605 volunteer teachers worked in the 78 literacy centers around the country.[64] The league's greatest contribution was the drafting of the 1959 Personal Status Law, an attempt to elevate the status of women that was supported by Qasim.

Urban Iraqi women and girls during this time generally felt unrestricted in their political and social activities as they had access to education and social outlets that allowed interaction with men.[65] Furthermore, Sunni/Shi'a sectarianism did not expressly control Iraqi politics or social lives, and elites of both sects were "Westernizing" their dress and culture in the hope of being associated with modernism.[66] Accomplished men who welcomed advancement perceived the *abaya*[67] as a symbol of tradition and backwardness and by the 1960s, prior to the first Ba'athist coup in 1963, Baghdadi women wore miniskirts and were not veiling.[68] However, patriarchal roles and tribal customs continued to be predominant in rural parts. Rural women, hindered by economic hardship and patriarchy, were restricted in all spheres.[69]

There were four regime changes between 1958 and 1968, when the Ba'athist Party finally seized leadership naming Ahmad Hasan al-Bakr (former military leader and member of the Free Officers) as president.[70] Al-Bakr had achieved prominence during the coup that overthrew the Hashemite monarchy and led the Iraq division of the Ba'athist Party, which at that time represented an ideological mixture of Arab Nationalism and Arab Socialism mainly in Syria and Iraq.[71] The Ba'athist regime was confronted by economic and social problems that hindered the party's goal of creating a strong, unified Iraq.[72] Ba'athist officials believed these problems stemmed from the previous regime's policies.[73] The Ba'athist Party was determined to eliminate what it called "harmful pre-revolutionary values and practices" among the people and replace them with Ba'athist ideology.[74] The regime used the state educational system, youth organizations and social programs to indoctrinate the masses in Arab nationalist principles such as patriotism, national loyalty, participation and civic responsibility. It was during this inception period that women began to formulate opinions about the Ba'athists. The party perceived political activists as a threat, especially women active in the Communist Party, and women experienced political violence and hostility at the hands of the regime.[75] However, women with no previous political affinity found the state-sponsored programs empowering and referred to the first decade of the Ba'athist rule as the "golden age" of economic boom, women-oriented state policies and a liberal social climate.[76]

Although the military revolution of 1958 was popular at its outset because it reduced the political power of the wealthy landowners and increased opportunities for a broader base of Iraq's population to participate in its governance,[77] the intense battles for power destabilized Iraq politically, socially and ideologically.[78] After 1968, Bakr and his ostensible deputy Saddam asserted even greater control as the Ba'athist Party gradually supplanted the army as the central state institution in Iraq. Yet by the late 1970s, not only the military but also the Ba'athist Party were gradually ceding their power to Saddam's personal security services, which he had come to view as essential in the context of ongoing power struggles and both real and ostensible plots against the state.[79] The ubiquitousness of these security forces stifled independent civil society, thereby paving the way to a totalitarian dictatorship, with sole control of the country's oil revenues.[80]

How did women's rights and women's political influence fare under the Ba'athist secular authoritarian regime? The United Nations Development Fund for Women (UNIFEM), which has now dissolved and been replaced by a suborganization of UN Women called the Entity for Gender Equality and the Empowerment of Women, maintained an Iraq country profile, covering the history of gender rights and representation in Iraqi politics. The profile was most recently updated in 2007.[81] Here it is explained that the Ba'athist secular rule of the late 1960s and early 1970s marked the first era in which the status and rights of women were formally recognized within the country's treaties and legislation. During the initial ruling years, the liberation of women was central to efforts to transform society.[82] In theory, women were the vehicles to indoctrinate future generations with the Ba'athist ideology. Saddam articulated this point during an address in 1971: "An enlightened mother, who is educated and liberated, can give the country a generation of conscious and committed fighters."[83] Women's "emancipation" was also intended to replace women's loyalty to extended families and tribal society with party allegiance.[84]

The Iraqi Provisional Constitution, drafted in 1970, contained the legal underpinning for women's equality. Article 19 declared all Iraqi citizens equal before the law regardless of sex, blood, language, social origin or religion.[85] These reforms, laws and programs created a unique combination of contradictions that would expand women's rights in some areas, but severely restrict them in others. While Ba'athist *ideology* included some provisions for gender equality,[86] pressure from religious groups led the regime to amend the section of the 1959 Personal Status Law that had granted women equal inheritance rights.[87]

The General Foundation of Iraqi Women (GFIW) was formed in 1972 as part of a national move to consolidate civil institutions under the control of the state while nominally encouraging Iraqi women's participation in the country's politics.[88] While the 1970 Interim Constitution contained articles proclaiming—at least *de jure*—equal rights for women, the regime allowed only one women's organization, the GFIW, to exist and it was significantly restrained by strict government supervision. Membership in any other women's group was considered a crime. The formerly powerful organization Union for Women's Rights was disbanded and some of its leaders arrested, although they were later released in response to international pressure.[89] The GFIW played a significant role in Iraqi politics by influencing state policy and legal reforms and lobbying for women's rights, although the group has also been criticized as lacking true representation of Iraqi women and even serving against women's empowerment during this era in Iraq's history.[90]

Iraq experienced economic difficulties in 1972 during the nationalization process of the oil industry followed by a period of great economic expansion.[91] Unlike Saudi Arabia and other neighboring countries,[92] the Iraqi state did not rely on foreign workers. Instead, it mobilized its own citizens for skilled labor and encouraged women to enter the labor market. There was an awakening and recognition of the important role of women in the development and modernization of the country.[93] Among the first reforms exclusive to women were free childcare, generous maternity benefits and transportation to and from work. Iraq's Maternal Law of 1971 provided women working in the public sector with generous maternity entitlements.[94] Under this law, women received six months paid maternity leave and could opt to take an additional six months leave with half pay.[95] On-site nurseries and flexible scheduling were also available to accommodate women with families. More importantly, women were able to work under safe conditions because they were ensured protection from harassment in the workplace.[96] The regime ran industries and trade unions that worked closely with the GFIW to provide a full range of occupational training for all women including peasants.[97] These training programs in conjunction with educational assistance encouraged women from all backgrounds to find their role in the labor market, and in 1974, all higher education graduates were promised employment by government decree.[98]

The Regime of Saddam Hussein

When Saddam became President in 1979, having forced al-Bakr out, the outcomes for Iraqi women were diverse. The Iraq National Assembly was established at the time of the 1980 elections, in which Iraqi women were finally allowed to vote for the first time and in which women landed 16 of 250 seats on the National Council. Yet while female candidates were allowed to stand for the Iraq Parliament, only those affiliated to the Ba'athist Party could be elected.[99] Under these conditions, while the 1985 election did show an increase of women elected to Parliament (33 council seats; 13 percent), female representation decreased dramatically over the next 18 years to only 8 percent of parliamentary seats just prior to the 2003 US-led invasion.[100] This decline is the likely result of the Ba'athist Party's curtailment of women's political involvement to the party-sanctioned GFIW.[101] Although the GFIW did make some strides toward advancing women's rights through community programs focused on literacy, education and job training, political participation by women was only nominally supported by the state. Activists who sought to advocate against the ruling regime's policies were likely to be subjected to harassment or severe punishment, which could include rape, torture and/or public beheading.[102]

While the Ba'athist Party did not disappear, its independence did deteriorate as Iraq transitioned from a one-party state to an oligarchy completely subservient to Saddam, his close family members and trusted associates responsible for both security and public policy.[103] During this period, particularly in the Kurdish North, women still engaged in political activism. The Kurds have a long history of political struggle in their fight for autonomy and ethnic rights. Saddam had initially offered them autonomy when he became president, in the most comprehensive offer ever put forth by an Iraqi government to date.[104] However, negotiations broke down when the regime refused to relinquish Kirkuk. Once armed conflicts between Kurdish and Iraqi forces began, many individuals in the North fled their homes. Those who remained suffered arbitrary arrests and violent persecution at the hands of Iraqi state security personnel. Despite tribal customs that were prevalent in Kurdish society, women were politically active alongside men. Many women assumed responsibilities that crossed traditional gender boundaries. These activities included providing logistical support, passing covert messages, working as couriers, distributing leaflets and providing political leadership.[105]

Women became tools used by the Ba'athists against any opposition; the regime used systematic rape and sexual assault against women to extrapolate information from dissidents and pressure expatriate opposition.[106] The regime sent videotapes that showed female family members being raped to the Iraqi oppositionists, a tactic to intimidate and blackmail Iraqi men into cooperating with the regime.[107] The regime became more efficient as it institutionalized methods to torture, murder and arrest women whether they were dissidents or merely related to one. Imprisoned women were subjected to brutal beatings, systematic rape, electrical shocks and branding.[108]

Iraq at War

During the Iran-Iraq war (1980–88),[109] the regime's priorities shifted from domestic modernization and party indoctrination to military strategy and security. The Ba'athist Party relied on certain groups of women to be a vital part of the country's survival. This period was characterized by conflict and economic crisis that led to labor shortages and sparked women's expansions into nontraditional spheres of work and increased their mobility, education and political expression.[110] Employment for women in the public sector reached approximately 40 percent.[111] At the same time, these factors restricted women's rights in areas of family, health and sexual control, and cultural expression. Other aspects such as sectarianism, religion and ethnicity influenced changes in these fields differently depending on the woman's background. The experiences of Shi'a and Kurdish women differed greatly from those of Sunni women, who were affiliated with the ruling elite.[112] In addition to running the bureaucracy, women played a crucial role in running government ministries as well as being producers in the private sector.[113]

The government wanted to protect females in the workplace to prevent any further losses to Iraq's economy as military conflict escalated. To encourage women to participate in the work force, laws were passed against discrimination and sexual harassment. Article 2 of the Unified Labour Code of 1987 guaranteed the right to work for each capable citizen with equal opportunities without discrimination based on sex, race, language or religion.[114] This law also granted every citizen equal opportunity for technical or vocational training in each sector.[115] Vocational training increased and continued even after the war was over. For example, according to a UN report, women's employment in the industrial sector went from 13 percent in 1987 to 21 percent in 1993.[116] Yet besides working at full capacity, women were still expected to produce more children to compensate for losses on the battlefield. Therefore, labor laws protected unborn children from harm. Article 82 of the Unified Labour Code of 1987 prohibited women from doing extra work that could be harmful to their pregnancy.[117] Although women gained employment that provided income, the regime had asked the population to endure fiscal austerity by requesting donations of gold and jewelry,[118] which traditionally served as sources of economic security for women in times of crisis.[119] The state reduced imports, curbed development programs, and borrowed heavily from surrounding nations.[120]

Eventually, Iraqi women were expected to do more tasks with fewer resources and many were left permanently on their own upon losing husbands or fathers to the war. In 1980, an amendment was added that allowed a man to marry more than one wife without the court's permission, if the woman was a widow.[121] Amnesty International reported that half a million Iraqi soldiers died in the Iran-Iraq war, and thousands of men had been executed or had "disappeared."[122] Men who returned home with severe disabilities had to be cared for by their families—a task that generally fell on women.[123]

Soldiers' morale quickly diminished as promises of swift victory turned instead into a long, violent war. The Ba'athist communication strategy moved away from images of men and women together working toward progress to depictions of men protecting their land and women's honor against the enemy.[124] This new gender-biased war propaganda reversed men's perceptions of women being equal and capable, rather reinforcing images of male heroism and superiority, women's frailty, ideals of virility and practices of male bonding.[125] This image of women reinforced patriarchal family structures and increased gender conservatism. As a result, female public and private workers saw a dramatic decrease in salaries and work opportunities, and rising inflation.[126] These conditions compelled many women to leave the formal workforce altogether. Prior to 1991, 23 percent of Iraqi women worked outside the home, which was the highest percentage in the Arab region; by 1997, the rate had fallen to 10 percent.[127]

Two years after the end of the Iran-Iraq war, the Ba'athist Party invaded Kuwait; its political platform reverted from Arab Nationalism to tribalism and Islamization from 1990 to 2002.[128] The Ba'athist Party was inundated by financial and legitimacy crises, and hence this shift in rhetoric served to appeal to the conservative patriarchal and religious establishment.[129] The United Nations imposed comprehensive economic sanctions on Iraq after Saddam refused to withdraw his troops. Security Council Resolution 661 mandated a complete ban on trade to and from Iraq, exempting only "supplies intended strictly for medical purpose, and in humanitarian circumstances" (Para. 3c) such as foodstuffs, including baby's milk powder.[130] International banking ceased to operate, air travel was banned and seaports were blocked; all Iraqi assets abroad were frozen.[131] Any personal or private business transfers were illegal. The intense bombing by coalition forces destroyed most of the country's infrastructure, including electrical grids, factories, storage facilities and buildings.[132] The Ba'athists used women as bargaining chips to gain their support and accepted tribal practices and customs, such as honor killings, in exchange for loyalty.[133] This radical move led to increased social conservatism and sectarianism against women throughout Iraq, in addition to the severe economic hardship of war and sanctions they already had to endure.[134]

After the 1991 Gulf War, Iraq sought to reestablish relations with neighboring countries (severely problematic given the invasion of a Gulf country) and Muslim traditionalists within Iraq. Saddam publicly acknowledged Islam's moral authority in the country[135] and this led to a further reduction of women's rights previously gained under the 1959 Personal Status Law.[136] In 1990, Saddam introduced Article 111 into the Iraqi Penal Code, reducing penalties for honor crimes; murders of women for alleged prostitution or on suspicion of dishonoring their families by sexual misbehavior rose dramatically.[137] The Iraqi woman became a symbol of the nation as Saddam employed discourses of political and national belonging that expressed concerns about sexual morality, possibly as part of an effort to maintain power in both external and domestic fields of conflict.[138] As the regime sought to forge stronger alliances with Islamic and tribal leaders in a bid to unite the ethnically and religiously diverse population, its propaganda became infused with references to women as the repositories of national identity and symbols of moral order.[139] Among most of Iraq's Arab population, the Iran-Iraq war and the deployment of these strategic discourses seemed to have succeeded in generating a greater sense of national community and patriotism.[140] However, while Saddam's regime generally could count on Sunni support, significant rifts in loyalty were appearing among the Shi'as and Kurds, who identified less closely with the nationalist vision.[141]

Objectification of Women as Political Tools

Much has been written about the brutality and oppression experienced by all Iraqis—not just women—under Saddam's dictatorship.[142] For example, Smiles describes how sex trafficking, violence, brutal imprisonment, deprivations and executions were commonplace events.[143] Brown and Romano point out that while Western rhetoric sometimes describes Saddam's rule (especially during its early years) as favorable to women, in reality the rights women gained under his regime were more token than actual.[144] Although the Iraqi government endorsed the UN's Convention to End All Forms of Discrimination against Women (CEDAW), the signature was provided conditionally. Specifically, the endorsement excluded Article 2, Paragraphs f and g, thus refusing to state that Iraq agreed: "(f) To take all appropriate measures, including legislation, to modify or abolish existing laws, regulations, customs and practices which constitute discrimination against women"; and "(g) To repeal all national penal provisions which constitute discrimination against women."[145] The Iraq endorsement also excluded Article 9, Paragraphs 1 and 2, which granted women equal rights with men to acquire, change or retain their nationality and assured women equal rights with men in regards to the nationality of their children.[146] Further evidence suggested that Saddam did not necessarily respect or observe the articles of the convention.[147] While Saddam pledged verbal support to women's rights, at the same time women continued to be exploited as instruments to elicit information from real or suspected dissidents.[148]

Saddam's regime manipulated gender constructs in its nationalist propaganda and political discourses not only during the Iran-Iraq war, but also throughout Iraq's invasion of Kuwait and the US-Iraq Gulf War.[149] In all cases, the sexual objectification of women proved a powerful tool. Saddam sought to institute a uniform moral code that focused public attention on the sexual behavior of women to reunite the diverse Iraqi population and reinvigorate support for the regime during this time of extreme political threat and upheaval. Honor crimes against women became cathartic—designed to pull Iraqi citizens together with a sense of national identity and meaning.[150] From the perspective of most Iraqi women, this strategy became a living nightmare, where males went unpunished for killing female relatives who had allegedly engaged in unsanctioned sexual activity. Signs placed on doors and nighttime raids by a militia known as the Feda'iyye ("loyal fighters") led by Saddam's eldest son Uday, a notorious sexual predator himself, preceded public executions.[151] While Saddam may not have necessarily known or approved of the extent of his eldest son's brutality, the Feda'iyye became officially recognized as part of his security apparatus and the crimes against women committed by that force were largely overlooked by the state.[152]

Nongovernmental organizations published accounts of extrajudicial killings wherein dozens of women were seized from their homes and decapitated in public by the Feda'iyye.[153] Although these women were allegedly killed for prostitution, there is evidence that at least some were not prostitutes but were executed for political reasons. For example, Najat Mohammad Haydar, a Baghdad obstetrician, was killed after she criticized corruption within the health services.[154] In addition, those women executed who were indeed prostitutes may have been forced into that role by poverty.[155]

War and sanctions provided further devastation to Iraqi women as poverty became widespread; many women were widowed, left without husbands; the ranks of marriageable men were depleted; and basic services collapsed.[156] Girls were kept out of school as families struggled financially and could afford to educate only their male children. The literacy rate among Iraqi women dropped from 75 percent in 1987 to 25 percent in 2000.[157] Rising unemployment pushed women out of public sector jobs and back into more traditional roles in the home, a result not uncommon in post-conflict societies.[158] Even today, Iraqi women without husbands struggle to run households and are frequently marginalized by society.[159] Iraqi women experienced increased freedoms and rights when Iraq enjoyed economic prosperity, and relative oppression and subjugation during economic recession—again not uncommon in a post-conflict nation.[160] It is important to remember this observation when exploring the contemporary participation of Iraqi women in public life, since such a lack of security and economic downturn accompanied the 2003–11 US occupation as well.[161]

In sum, Saddam's tenure resulted in a climate of political and domestic threat that was particularly detrimental to women.[162] The 35 years of the Ba'athist regime comprised different periods with different political, social and economic conditions. Ultimately, these had varying outcomes on women's rights and female representation in societal and political structures. Saddam's brutality toward all Iraqis and particularly toward the country's women, however, does not tell the entire story. His regime also undertook land reforms that helped uplift the peasantry, established welfare state benefits for the poor and working classes, made strides toward free education, and granted women rights to pursue careers and participate in civic activities.[163] During Saddam's early years, Iraqi women became the most educated in the region, and were quite active in the country's labor force. However, Iraqi women were not granted full suffrage until 1980. Until then their ability to mobilize politically and exert political influence was achieved only by acting in supportive roles to their male counterparts or by working at the grassroots level. Wars, sanctions and changes in policy over time had various impacts on women's status and their options for political mobilization.

Evolution of the Iraqi Personal Status Law

A good deal of the historical rhetoric surrounding women's rights in Iraq has centered upon the Personal Status Law No. 188 that was introduced in 1959 shortly after Iraq became a republic.[164] Prior to 1959, Iraq had no civil law governing matters of personal status and such decisions rested primarily with the *ulama*, Muslim legal scholars responsible for administering *shari'a* law; Law No. 188 was widely regarded as ground-breaking for its inherent reforms in favor of women.[165] Its stipulations granted equal inheritance for both genders; accorded women unilateral recourse to divorce; restricted forced marriage; provided child support and custody; and placed limits on polygamy. Women were recognized as full citizens with the power to negotiate family issues on their own behalf. In addition, the Personal Status Law provided a framework within which women activists had more power to formulate and propose public policy.[166]

Among those responsible for this milestone was Naziha al-Dulaimi, the first Arab woman to occupy a post in the Iraq cabinet.[167] The Union for Women's Rights presented the first draft of the law to the Ministry of Interior and this body was instrumental in obtaining inclusion of the most innovative of the law's provisions.[168] The legislation underwent several revisions during the next two decades, amendments largely sparked by criticisms raised by women's groups. In 1978, the age of full capacity for women to marry was raised to 18 (although the minimum age at which a girl could be granted legal permission to marry by a judge was simultaneously lowered to 15). This amendment also nullified forced marriages if they were unconsummated and permitted divorce in cases where the marriage had been consummated, where a forced marriage was defined as *one or both parties not consenting* to the marriage, with people being *forced into marriage against their will*.[169] It is important to note, however, that this is *not the same as an arranged marriage. Arranged marriages have worked well in society for many years. An arranged marriage is when families of both spouses take a leading role in arranging the marriage, but the choice whether to accept the arrangement remains with the prospective spouses*. Forced marriage is an *abuse of human rights*. Both physical and emotional abuse may be used to coerce people into the marriage. The 1978 amendment was supported and acclaimed by the Ba'ath Party-backed GFIW.[170]

During the 1980s and 1990s, Saddam's regime used Personal Status Law divorce provisions as a weapon by encouraging women to divorce husbands who the regime condemned as military deserters, political defectors or traitors.[171] Some headway was made by the GFIW when, in 1983, Resolution 77 allowed a divorced woman to continue living without her husband in his home for a period of three years unless she had been the cause of the separation. In 1985, an amendment provided for financial compensation to divorced wives if the divorce was found to be arbitrary and harmful to the woman.[172] This was difficult to prove; hence, the improvements were only superficial, thereby reinforcing the way in which women were manipulated not only by the patriarchy but also by state laws.[173]

Iraqi women's activism toward enacting and amending the Personal Status Law clearly illustrates their commitment to becoming full civic participants. When the US invasion toppled Saddam's regime in 2003 and the transitional government seemed poised to abolish the law, the protests of female activists were instrumental in excluding those clauses from the permanent constitution. The history and controversy surrounding the Personal Status Law, as well as its evolution going forward, are important considerations in the study of Iraqi women as a political force.

Long-term Impact of War and Sanctions on Women

How the 1980s–90s wars and ensuing UN sanctions affected women in Iraq has been addressed in several studies.[174] The ostensible goals of the sanctions—which remained in effect for the 13 years leading up to the US invasion[175]—were to eliminate alleged weapons of mass destruction (WMD) and to force Saddam to withdraw from Kuwait and comply with international laws surrounding terrorism and repayment of foreign debt.[176] This meant Iraq was subject not only to three decades of dictatorship and brutality under Saddam's Ba'ath regime, but also to years of armed conflict and international sanctions. These conditions served to impair all Iraqi society and, along with it, the position and rights of women.[177]

Yasmin Husein al-Jawaheri opines that the sanctions were a resounding failure in terms of the regime capitulating to foreign demands, and it was women who bore the primary brunt of their impact.[178] The sanctions resulted in dramatic increases in poverty, and women and children generally suffered most poignantly under such conditions.[179] Women struggled to hold their families together in the face of violence, hunger, hardship and disease. Girls from financially stressed families were first to be kept back from school, and women were the first to be pushed out of jobs in the public sector. Many of the residual effects remain: illiteracy among Iraqi women is more than double the rate among men; one in three girls aged 12 to 14 is not enrolled in school; only 14 percent of all women in Iraq are either employed or seeking work; one in ten households is female-led, and nine of ten female heads of households are widows.[180] Violence against women including domestic violence, honor killings, rape and sex trafficking remain rampant.[181]

Subjecting a country to a series of wars builds a culture of violence that spills over into public life, especially in a society where conservative and patriarchal factions oppose the inclusion of women in politics.[182] The history of sanctions and war, up to and including the US invasion, has created a discourse that instrumentalizes the status of women as justification for political action.[183] The implications of how this applies to the current status of women, and in particular, female parliamentarians, are discussed in later chapters.

Summary

Many of the political and social structures underpinning modern Iraq have their roots in legacies left by the Ottoman Empire. Systems of political governance, education, law and economic policy found their beginnings during this era, and a foundation for the personal status law was established. However, Ottoman attempts to "Turkify" Iraqi society led to the emergence of a Sunni elite, forming the basis for the sectarian schisms persistent throughout Iraq's modern history. The period of British influence in Iraq was characterized by a return to tribalization in rural areas; however the British also established some fundamental political structures that brought Iraq onto the international stage. The Hashemite monarchy built professional military forces, created a bureaucratic infrastructure and laid the foundation for modern economic development. During this time, the complete exclusion of women from participation in formal policy-making was legitimized, although women succeeded in organizing informally around specific issues such as suffrage. Early Ba'athist rule represented the first time women's rights and status became formally recognized in Iraqi treaties and legislation, as the liberation of women became central to the attempt to transform society after the 1968 coup.

During the early stages of the Saddam regime, a modernization process was fostered that led Iraqi women to be perceived as enjoying some of the most progressive conditions in the Middle East. However, Saddam's subsequent internal and foreign policy decisions resulted in wars and economic sanctions with profoundly negative results for Iraq's female population, across multiple dimensions of existence. The extension of the formal right to vote in 1980 was hardly an advance in women's rights considering the negative effects generated by conflict and authoritarianism in this period. By the time of the 2003 invasion, women were ready for change and eager to play a substantive role in Iraq's reconstruction; but here, too, adverse social and political conditions vitiated, in part, the effect of electoral advances.

3

Gender Quotas and Women's Political Mobilization in Iraq and the Middle East

Essential to the research of how the gender quota has contributed to the mobilization of Iraqi female MPs is an analysis of the extent to which gender quotas have increased the political representation of women in the various regions of the Middle East. A review of the history behind electoral gender quotas, the different types of quotas and the various international, political and women's rights bodies that advocated for their adoption is central to this discussion. Studies investigating the efficacy of gender quotas in achieving descriptive, substantive and symbolic representation are limited. However, this chapter outlines some of the research available regarding how a quota may empower women in their struggle to gain a political voice, as well as the barriers and obstacles faced by women in politics.

This chapter analyzes historical, sociopolitical and feminist literature in order to assess the degree of political representation achieved by women in Iraq as well as Jordan, Sudan, Iran and Lebanon. Specifically, this literature review seeks to elaborate how the presence—or absence—of a gender quota has affected the abilities of females to navigate the complex political and social context of their respective countries. This is in part determined by analyzing the degree of influence achieved by such women in Jordan and Sudan, which employ gender quotas, compared to Iran and Lebanon, where no formal gender quotas exist.

Electoral Gender Quotas

Electoral gender quotas are a relatively new and controversial phenomenon whose success and sustainability is not yet well documented; although some racial (affirmative action) quotas had been introduced earlier,[1] most gender quotas have been instituted since 1991.[2] Gender quotas were proposed at the

Fourth World Conference on Women held in Beijing in 1995 as a mechanism to address the underrepresentation of women in global politics.[3] During post-conflict transition and reconstruction, quotas are typically facilitated by international intervention as transformation of the ruling class opens the way for groups formerly lacking representation to enter the political sphere. Thus quotas are often viewed as a form of compensation for previous political injustice.[4] From the feminist perspective, they are also seen as a means of imposing "Western" or "modern" views on what have traditionally been patriarchal societies.[5] That is, an identifiable marginalized group (such as women or a minority), which has historically been underrepresented in public roles given its proportional presence in the population, is granted a political quota as evidence of the society's attempt to correct that underrepresentation and integrate the group into the decision-making process.[6]

Types of Gender Quotas

Policies that ensure women's representation currently exist in more than 100 countries worldwide.[7] This figure includes three types of gender quotas recognized by the quotaProject, an organization which maintains a global database[8] reporting on quotas for women's parliamentary representation (www.quotaproject.org): (1) reserved seats (constitutionally and/or legislatively mandated); (2) legal candidate quotas (constitutional and/or legislative); and (3) political party quotas (voluntary).[9] Gender quotas have been effective at increasing the number of women in political assemblies;[10] examples of large, immediate boosts in the percentage of women politicians attributable to gender quota policies may be found in Rwanda, Costa Rica and South Africa.[11] Electoral quotas take various forms. Rwanda, for instance, is the only country where the constitution stipulates a percentage of political seats reserved for women.

Iraq's 2005 Constitution, like those in Argentina, Belgium, Costa Rica and Guiana, requires elections to achieve a minimum quota of 25 percent female representation in the Council of Representatives (Article 49). However, it remains silent regarding representation at the executive, provincial or district levels. In 2009, the Parliament of the Kurdistan Region of Iraq increased the quota to 30 percent for its regional elections. The national 2009 provincial electoral laws set a 25 percent quota for women candidates, and this practice has become a norm.[12] In 2013, the Election Commission introduced reduced fees for registration of women-only political entities to encourage women standing for elected office. However, these measures have not been permanently institutionalized; each round of elections has generated a new election law as Iraqi legislators experiment with electoral mechanisms and systems. The absence of a political parties' law, which has been in draft form since 2004, makes it difficult to ensure that women play a greater formal role in political institutions as party activists and not just as figureheads comprising the mandated gender balance on a ballot paper.[13] Voluntary quotas at the political party level represent a third type of gender quota policy, which can be found, for example, in Australia, Austria, Denmark, Finland, Germany and the Netherlands.[14] Voluntary party-level quotas are the most prevalent type of gender quota policy.[15]

Forces Behind Gender Quota Adoption

The fact that both developing and developed countries have adopted electoral quotas raises questions about the conditions under which such policies gain acceptance. Political scientist Lisa Baldez suggests that gender quotas have a democratizing effect and are most likely to be adopted during periods when electoral outcomes are uncertain.[16] This notion mostly applies to Western countries, but the quota adoption in Iraq was considered a step toward transitioning to democracy. International influences may stimulate gender quota adoption; for example, the United Nations Convention to End All Forms of Discrimination against Women (CEDAW), to which Iraq is a conditional signatory, places stress on accelerating processes that give women an equal voice in political decision-making.[17] Lovenduski and Norris support the influence of political culture on gender quotas, arguing that countries with relatively egalitarian political cultures—such as a strong tradition of group rights—are more likely to implement quota laws.[18] Thus democratic states, or those transitioning to democracy such as Iraq, may be more likely to adopt a gender quota as part of the democratization process. As policy analyst Patrick Basham states in a 2004 report for the Cato Institute, "Political culture shapes democracy far more than democracy shapes political culture."[19] Finally, the institution of gender quotas often is influenced by pressure from women's organizations and female politicians.[20] This certainly was the case in Iraq where women's nongovernmental organizations (NGOs), headed by figureheads such as Safia al-Suhail, lobbied heavily both for the parliamentary gender quota (demanding 40 percent representation) and against the erosion of the Personal Status Law.[21]

In 2003, the International Institute for Democracy and Electoral Assistance (IDEA) and Stockholm University spearheaded the quotaProject. As of 2016, the quotaProject places the total representation of women in parliaments around the world at 22 percent.[22] They further note that quotas are becoming increasingly prevalent, with half of the countries in the world currently using some type of electoral gender quota.[23] Gender quotas are fairly equally dispersed among both developing and developed countries.[24]

Effects of Gender Quotas on Women's Representation

Dahlerup and Freidenvall make a strong case stating the need for rigorous empirical and longitudinal research on the effects of gender quotas, which to date is lacking.[25] They identify the three key dimensions of women's political representation that should serve as outcome measures for such research: (1) *descriptive* representation, (2) *substantive* representation and (3) *symbolic* representation.[26] Extant evaluations of the effects of gender quotas[27] have primarily focused on what these scholars define as descriptive representation, with little discussion of the impact of quota systems on the substance and quality of women's political roles. Research is needed to provide qualitative analysis of women's representation in countries with gender quotas, and the effects of quotas on women's actual political empowerment.

Dahlerup and Freidenvall also note that quotas do not remove all barriers to women in politics.[28] Despite the global rise of gender quotas over the past two decades, obstacles to women's full political participation remain even in countries where quotas are in effect. For example, women in public office still face the dual burden of career and family. This dual burden poses a major issue in the Middle East[29] and particularly in Iraq, where the 2003 occupation appears to have increased the extent to which men overshadow women as they strive to gain a political voice.[30] In addition, Iraqi women face obstacles posed by a gender imbalance in campaign financing, and female politicians who gain their posts because of a quota may become stigmatized by cultural, societal and patriarchal challenges.[31] Certainly, these challenges encountered by female politicians may be more pronounced in societies that have been traditionally patriarchal, such as Iraq.[32] Interestingly, Krook and O'Brien[33] discuss that while politicians from racial, ethnic or religious minority groups may face the same types of stigma, oppression and threats of violence under a quota system, most countries recognize *either* women *or* minorities when considering laws guaranteeing political representation to groups. In support of that view, as of 2008, 34 countries had quota provisions for women only; 21 had passed policies applying only to minorities and 16 employed measures for both groups, a situation which may apply to Iraq's heterogeneous demography.[34]

Dahlerup and Freidenvall distinguish between quotas on what they term the "fast track" to equal gender representation as opposed to what they call the "incremental track" which has been demonstrated, for example, in the Scandinavian countries Denmark, Norway and Sweden.[35] The incremental track employs quotas (usually at the party level) to progressively empower women over time in regions where women already have a strong power base in the Parliament and political parties. Along the fast track, in contrast, a gender quota is introduced in a country where women have so far achieved only a small minority of representatives in Parliament, and that country sees an immediate and substantial jump in women's representation (e.g., from 19 percent to 35 percent in Costa Rica in 2002, or from 8 percent to nearly 32 percent in Iraq in 2006).[36] The incremental track favors equal *opportunity* for women whereas the fast track favors equal *results*. Women who are elected on the fast track may be at higher risk of marginalization, regarded as token representatives rather than actively empowered. This occurs in situations where quota initiatives lack broad support, comparative evaluation of performance and/or capacity-building efforts for the newly elected women by women's organizations.[37] Examples may be found in Bangladesh, Pakistan and India in which quotas resulted in the election of large numbers of uneducated women.[38] In a later article, Dahlerup suggests that in Iraq and Pakistan, for example, the motive behind male leaders passing the quota law was to get loyal women elected who would support the leader or the party.[39] In this context Dahlerup and Freidenvall call for empirical analyses to illuminate which groups of women become involved in promoting quotas in their countries and how their alliances with men may be characterized. They also call for qualitative evaluations of quota regulations in terms of women's ability to perform their jobs and achieve actual influence on changes in public policy.[40]

Electoral gender quotas have been employed in many countries worldwide, usually in an attempt to level the political "playing field" upon which women must compete with men. Increased representation in public office is an important step toward empowering women to work toward equal rights and contribute to policies that promote and improve their socioeconomic condition.[41] Electoral quotas may be constitutionally or legislatively mandated, or may be adopted by individual political parties. Effectively promoting women's representation in policy-making bodies requires well-informed strategies that must include accurate measurement and comparison with methods that have worked in other countries.[42] Although there is no guarantee that methods which prove effective in one country will work in another, such comparative analysis is useful to illuminate the social, cultural and political characteristics that influence the effectiveness of gender quotas to increase women's political empowerment. It also may be noted that introducing a gender quota presents difficulties even in a country with a functional political system; and the Iraqi Parliament has yet to become fully functional as a legislative body. The patronage politics of the Saddam era, coupled with a lack of education and awareness of political process among many MPs, have contributed to a political environment without well-established democratic norms and protocols. These conditions further challenge the ability of the women elected parliamentarians to become immediate, effective policy-makers as they need time and experience to evolve and mature in their legislative roles.

The Gender Quota in Iraq

While a good deal of literature describes the evolution of women's rights in Iraq across time, there is a dearth of studies focusing on the experience of Iraqi women as participants in the political sphere. Scholars including al-Ali and Pratt, Ballington and Dahlerup, Brown and Romano, and Isobel Coleman have described the processes via grassroots efforts, lobbying and influences from the diaspora by which the gender quota succeeded in reaching the 2005 Iraq Constitution.[43] However, research describing how women have fared politically since the institution of the quota remains scant. The quality, not just the quantity, of female empowerment in policy-making roles must be examined on a deeper level. Research is needed to illuminate processes by which female parliamentarians come to understand both the written and the unwritten rules of parliamentary function, learn to use those rules to their advantage, and eventually become able to actively influence policy change.

Coleman notes that Western pundits often point to the sheer increase in the numbers of female Iraqi parliamentarians after the quota as an indicator of the quota's success.[44] Indeed, the quota does give Iraqi women one of the highest levels of representation in the world (ranking 45th in terms of the percentage of female representation in Parliament out of the 125 countries with gender quotas).[45] Yet the seats in Iraq's Parliament are just as likely to be filled by conservative women who simply toe the patriarchal line of their political party platforms. Success in making strides toward progressive legislation for Iraqi women may depend on politicians such as Salama al-Khafaji,[46] a former dentist and member of the Interim Governing Council (IGC) who has brought a strong

Shi'a background to her political stance. Al-Khafaji is a self-described moderate with a noted ability to facilitate the collaboration of both secular and Islamic parties together for the common good.[47]

Al-Khafaji is currently a member of the High Commission for Human Rights (HCHR), an entity first introduced to Iraq in Article 102 of the Constitution, confirmed in law in 2008 (Law 53) and finally established in 2012 with the support of the UN Office of the High Commissioner for Human Rights. The HCHR does not report to the government and is struggling with a controversial 2010 Supreme Court decision[48] that places "independent" commissions such as the Communications and Media Commission under executive control. Iraq also has a Ministry for Human Rights and a parliamentary Committee on Human Rights and yet, according to a February 2014 report by the international NGO Human Rights Watch, Iraqi security forces, government and militia still routinely rape and torture women with impunity—pointing to the overarching and prevailing attitude toward women as being second-class citizens.[49]

With the United Nations pressing for the representation of women and minority communities as in any new constitution, the process of constitutional design drew on advice from many international experts, including agencies such as the International Foundation for Electoral Systems (IFES), the National Endowment for Democracy (NED) and the United States Agency for International Development (USAID). The process stimulated considerable debate within Iraq. Prior to the enactment of the Transitional Administrative Law (TAL), public meetings were held around the country in 2004 to debate the proposed contents, including the role of women's rights in the document.[50] In the aftermath of the 2003 invasion, several new women's organizations were formed in Iraq to lobby for both the rights of women in general and political representation in particular. Many of these organizations initially focused seriously on promoting the issue of quota adoption.[51] Iraqi women's activists lobbied for the quota in 2004 by staging demonstrations and sit-ins, with women in civil society playing an important role in the quota debates.[52] They also lobbied strongly through a series of meetings, conferences and workshops, debating the level of quota to adopt and whether the number of elected positions to be allocated to women should be set at 20, 30 or 40 percent. For example, in January 2004, women in Hilla, Diwania, Karbala and Najaf organized a major conference in Basra, attended by 400 delegates. The Iraqi Higher Women's Council, a body containing a diverse cross-section of Iraqi women, presented US Ambassador Paul Bremer with a letter supporting a 40 percent quota for women in legislative bodies. The US-led coalition was divided on the issue. Tony Blair and the British representative in

Baghdad favored introducing gender quotas for Iraqi elections,[53] while Bremer and the Coalition Provisional Authority (CPA) preferred equal opportunity policies over quotas, although it was hard to argue against them for Iraq after reserved seats had been adopted in Afghanistan.[54]

The Transitional Provisional Authority, the Iraqi entity hand-picked by the US government to succeed the CPA in 2004, also was split on the issue of gender quotas as the new constitution was being drafted.[55] The CPA spokesman said: "There are no plans for quotas, but we are planning on empowering women through ... women's organizations, democracy trainings, and involving them in the political process."[56] Al-Ali and Pratt quote an Iraqi woman who was part of a civil society delegation that visited CPA head Bremer in the spring of 2004 to lobby for a quota. She describes Bremer's response: "... Bremer told us: 'We don't do quotas.'"[57] US Labour Secretary Elaine Chao also spoke out against the idea of a quota in 2004, asserting that "... a just Iraq is built on talent and ability of the people. So people should be chosen based on their abilities and not quotas ... It is an issue that you, as Iraqis, have to come to resolve and come to an understanding."[58] Hunt and Posa argue that the United States rejected quotas as representing a contradiction to its own affirmative action policy.[59] Indeed, the United States offers an interesting point of comparison as there is no gender quota in the United States and levels of female political participation are relatively low compared to other countries in the world (18 percent of the US Congress were women in 2012).[60]

Various Iraqi women's organizations were also divided on whether a quota would empower or limit true female representation and mobilization in Parliament. The Women's Alliance for a Democratic Iraq, the Iraqi Women's Network and the Organization for Women's Freedom in Iraq (all formed by women returning from the diaspora) were vocal in support of a quota because they believed it would ensure women's voice in formal decision-making.[61] Other groups, such as the Iraqi Women's League, were not in favor of the quota because they felt it would "close the door" on some highly qualified women by restricting representation to a percentage.[62] Other noted activists, including Safia al-Suhail and Nasreen Barwari, expressed disappointment after the quota was enacted because the women who entered Parliament as a result of the 2005 elections were not those supported by women's rights activists.[63] These differences of opinion and approach are examined in more detail in later chapters.

The 2005 Iraq electoral law, which introduced a closed list system of voting for the national parliamentary elections,[64] required that at least one-third of the candidates on each party list be women (no fewer than one in the first three, no fewer than two out of six and so on). Thus in the 2005 elections the result was greater than the minimum quota requirement—31.5 percent of candidates elected were women.[65] However, by the time of the 2010 elections the election law was based on an open list system, meaning that for each winning list, the candidates with the highest number of votes would be elected rather than the candidates listed first. Ensuring that each third candidate on a list was female did not necessarily ensure that one-third of those elected would be women. To compensate, a corrective mechanism was to be applied only if fewer than 25 percent of elected candidates were women. The amendment led to a lower level of female representation (85 seats; 26 percent) in the Iraqi Parliament in 2010 than in 2005.[66]

It is undeniable that female politicians in Iraq face numerous obstacles in achieving representation in governance.[67] Their participation has been limited by the assumption that women's proper sphere is the "private" sphere. Whereas the "public" domain is one of political authority and contestation, the "private" realm is associated with family and the home. By relegating women to the private sphere, their ability to enter the political arena is curtailed.[68] Maysoun al-Damaluji, an MP for the largely secular Iraqiya list led by former prime minister Ayad Allawi, argues that female candidates elected to Parliament are placed in a very critical position[69] with a double duty of [serving] women and the community.[70] Female candidates hoped that the new quota would give them a foot in the door of provincial politics. Some maintain it is generally harder for women to penetrate provincial politics than national politics, as local leaders are often chosen by tight-knit communities where men dominate.[71] While female candidates say that they do not run solely as women's activists, many intend to raise women's issues while in Parliament. For example, Suhaila Oufi, a 35-year-old veterinarian who ran in the 2009 provincial elections with the al-Dawla Party led by former Basra governor Wael Abdul-Latif (now an MP), said she was campaigning to improve women's rights and public services. Oufi said she wanted to serve "to be a voice for women who have lived under an unjust system and who are always marginalized."[72] According to the Independent High Electoral Commission of Iraq, all political parties seeking office have complied with the requirement that one out of every four of their candidates be female. However, Oufi and others have complained that many men oppose the role of women in public office.[73] Indeed, while many political leaders and parties in Baghdad have publicly backed women's rights, some parliamentarians rejected the women's quota when they first voted on the provincial election law in 2005.[74]

Even women's advocates who pressed for the quota admit that women in Parliament are not necessarily powerful, arguing that the final wording of the law, which vaguely states that there must be "a woman at the end of every three winners," could prevent women from gaining Provincial Council seats.⁷⁵ Other factors also hinder opportunities for female candidates to hold seats in Parliament. For example, prior to the 2009 provincial elections, Halima Abdul Jabber Ismail, a candidate in the largely Shiʻa province of Karbala southwest of Baghdad, said she enjoyed popular support. However, she feared she would not be able to win one of the seven seats allotted to women in Karbala because she lacked adequate funds and the backing of clerics. Women in Karbala "are well-known for their political consciousness, and the people here are quite confident in many of us," Ismail said.⁷⁶ That said, not everyone agrees; some believe that women elected to office as a result of a quota will serve on Provincial Councils as figureheads only. "I think that the women's quota might help women who are not active and productive," said Abdul Hasan al-Furati, a member of Karbala's Provincial Council. "Being on a strong list will pave the way for unqualified women to become provincial council members."⁷⁷

Women's advocates and politicians also say, despite skepticism about their work, that women may have greater impact by serving on Provincial Councils than in Parliament, where many serve but do not necessarily have power. "Women play more active roles [on Provincial Councils] than in Parliament," said Khawal al-Hasani, a member of Baghdad's Provincial Council and chair of the Legal Committee. Al-Hasani said that, locally, women serve on a wider variety of committees than they do at the national level, enabling them to have a stronger impact on local issues. Female Provincial Council members can tackle problems relating to sewage services, education and the displaced, she added.⁷⁸

In past elections, voters chose political lists, which then appointed leaders to serve. In the 2010 parliamentary elections, however, the names of the candidates were made public and voters could elect individuals. These public lists were criticized initially for endangering candidates, but Jenan al-Obeidi, an MP from the Shiʻa-led United Iraqi Alliance, said the system enables women to "be in a heated competition with men."⁷⁹ Lists must guarantee their women candidates' seats if they win, which empowers women, Obeidi asserted. "The women are now challenging the men on the public list because the female candidate who has more votes will have a seat in the council," she added. However, Azhar al-Sheikhli, who was Minister for Women's Affairs at that time, argued that, even with the women's quota, Iraq has "a long way to go" in bringing women to power. She noted that India, Pakistan, Indonesia and Bangladesh have had female heads of state, but in Iraq, "we cannot see women becoming leaders of a major political party."⁸⁰

Krook et al. compare the effects of the US military invasions in Iraq versus Afghanistan on women's political representation.[81] They postulate that it is difficult to predict the extent to which the Iraq parliamentary quota will lead to enduring gains in women's representation that are both substantive and symbolic in nature. Furthermore, because male politicians in Iraq still do not consider female representation to be a significant concern, additional research is important to reveal a deeper understanding of how female policy-makers work to achieve legitimate political agency in a post-conflict society.[82]

Only a comprehensive study of female Iraqi politicians' experiences—both individual and political—will provide a complete picture of how women have fared in the Iraq political arena since the parliamentary quota was established. It may be interesting to compare the election of women MPs to the Iraq Parliament in Baghdad with Iraq's female provincial and district councilors elected without benefit of a gender quota. This book examines the experiences of women politicians within the new emerging hierarchies of power during the Iraqi transition to democracy, through the establishment of a permanent government, and to the phasing out of US occupation and decreased dependence on Western influence. In Iraq's April 2014 elections, 22 women MPs were elected on their own merits, without the necessity of relying upon the quota. This research explores how many of these women had served as MPs previously and the platforms upon which they ran for office in 2014.

Today many countries in the Middle East and North Africa, such as Iran, Iraq, Jordan, Lebanon, Morocco, Sudan, Tunisia and Turkey, are transitioning to regimes based on elections and parliamentary democracy of varying kinds.[83] Many of these reforms and transitions were triggered by the 2010–12 revolutionary movements known as the Arab Spring, where a wave of protests and demonstrations—both violent and nonviolent—were staged with the goal of toppling authoritarian regimes. Despite the proximity of these countries' varied histories, governmental and economic structures, it can be argued that the challenges posed by a transition to adequate political representation for women are very similar across the Arab region.[84]

Comparative Studies: Women in Regional Politics

Moghadam posits that major social change in a given state cannot take place outside of the regional and global context.[85] Describing the conditions with which women must contend in differing political environments demonstrates that gender quotas by themselves do not necessarily result in effective political mobilization and influence for female politicians. Rather, quotas are one factor, whose degree of influence remains moot, among many elements that affect women's capacity to engage with political systems. Other important factors include prevailing war zones, ideology, patriarchy and degree of democratization. This research seeks to elaborate on the case of Iraq by describing the challenges women encounter in public office and the role played by the gender quota in helping women navigate the complex political context. To provide cases for comparison, the following are brief descriptions of women's parliamentary representation in Jordan, Sudan and Morocco (where gender quotas have been formalized); in Iran and Lebanon (which have no quotas); and in Tunisia (which has a gender parity mandate on party candidate lists).

Jordan

Jordan, as a parliamentary monarchy, has allowed women to stand for and be elected to office since 1974, but women have been drastically underrepresented until only recently.[86] In 1993, Jordan adopted a "one person, one vote" electoral system which has been highly contested by Islamists, trade unions and the Jordanian media as producing essentially loyalist MPs who fail to represent the people. Islamists protested calling for sweeping reforms including a new electoral law to ensure some "fair" representation of women. In 2003, Jordan's King Abdullah, under pressure from the women's rights lobby, introduced a gender quota for the Jordanian Parliament to encourage representation of women in this conservative country. In 2009, Jordan approved an electoral system that eliminated the contested "one person, one vote" system and increased the parliamentary quota for women. Efforts leading up to the quota's adoption spanned ten years and involved multiple seminars, opinion polls, tireless efforts by women's NGOs to gather petition signatures and the eventual establishment of a committee to draft recommendations.[87]

Further electoral reform was instituted in 2012. Now in Jordan's complex mixed-member proportional electoral system are 108 members elected from 45 single or multimember districts, with 15 seats reserved for women from 12 governorates and 3 Bedouin districts (as part of the 2012 electoral law reform), and 27 members elected through a proportional representation system. For the allocation of the 15 reserved seats for women, the Election Commission calculates the percentage of votes for unsuccessful female candidates in district elections by dividing the number of votes they obtain by the total number of votes cast in their constituency. The 15 female candidates who obtain the highest percentage of votes nationwide are declared elected on the condition that no governorate obtains more than one reserved seat for women (Article 51 of Law No. 25, 2012 on parliamentary elections). These reforms in favor of increasing the number of female politicians resulted in a rise in female representation in the Jordanian Parliament from 1.3 percent in 2001 to 10.8 percent in 2012.[88]

Although the processes by which the Jordanian gender quota arrived into public debate appear similar, the Jordanian situation contrasts with Iraq in several ways. First, Jordan remains a monarchy which can be likened to the system of governance present in 1930s–50s Iraq (with the difference that Jordanian women have the right of suffrage); Jordan is not progressing toward democratization at this time. Second, the complex Jordanian electoral law provides fewer opportunities for women to gain descriptive representation than does the Iraqi quota. Finally, the power of Islam within the political systems differs between these two countries—while Iraqi politics are largely underpinned by *shari'a*, Islamists are striving to achieve greater representation and power in Jordan. As discussed in later chapters, religiosity has had a major impact on the sectarian schisms and political strife in Iraq since the US occupation— developments which heavily influence the results of the parliamentary gender quota.

Sudan

Sudanese women have been involved in public life at the NGO level since the end of World War I; they gained suffrage in 1955 and the right to stand for election in 1965, heralding the first female parliamentarian the same year. In 1983, Sudan instituted an interpretation of Islamic *shari'a* law that resulted in increased discrimination against women and a setback to their political involvement.[89] The Sudanese Constitution of 1993 placed all issues related to women in the preamble, with no article in the main constitutional body providing for women's rights or gender equality. Just as in Iraq, the treatment of Sudanese women deteriorated during the 1990s with reports of harassment, torture and imprisonment.

Like many countries in the Middle East, Sudan was torn by internal conflict in the 1990s. With the signing of the Comprehensive Peace Agreement between the ruling Islamist National Congress Party (NCP) and the Sudan People's Liberation Movement (SPLM), the longest-running civil war in African history ended in 2005.[90] In the interim constitution adopted that year, equal rights between men and women were acknowledged in the preamble.[91] The Peace Agreement built a framework for reinstating multiparty elections that had been absent in Sudan for nearly 20 years. Women activists in northern Sudan viewed the Peace Agreement as representing a critical moment in efforts toward mobilizing for a women's quota in Sudan's Parliament. These efforts by women's NGOs contributed to the enactment of Sudan's electoral gender quota, legislated under the country's National Election Law of 2008, which provides that 25 percent of seats in the National Assembly are reserved for women.[92] According to Sudan's 2008 electoral law, the gender-quota seats are filled through separate, closed lists of women candidates. Voters may vote for only one women's list of their choice and only parties whose women's lists clear the 4 percent threshold are eligible to access seats reserved for women. Women's seats are allocated proportionately among qualifying parties.[93] These changes facilitated increased proportion of Sudanese women in Parliament from 5.3 percent in 1997 to 24.6 percent in 2012, with a high of 25.6 percent in 2010.[94]

In 2011, the Republic of South Sudan gained independence from Sudan. South Sudan's transitional government instituted stronger gender quota provisions than the Sudanese government; its 2011 Constitution states that "All levels of government shall: promote women's participation in public life and their representation in the legislative and executive organs by at least twenty-five per cent as an affirmative action to redress imbalances created by history, customs, and traditions" (Constitution of South Sudan, 2011, Article 16 (4:a).[95] South Sudan legislated quotas for the Single/Lower Parliamentary House, the Upper House, and at the subnational level, compared to Sudan's quota which is legislated only at the Single/Lower Parliamentary House level.[96] Following the 2011 elections, 27 percent of South Sudan's parliamentary seats (88 of 332) were held by women.

However, Tønnessen observes that, while the implementation of the quota may have carved out a space for more Sudanese women to enter the country's political arena, several factors need to work together in order to build a political environment that enables women's representation to have substantive impact.[97] In addition to sheer numbers of women in Parliament, a critical presence of women's rights activists is required to translate those numbers into policy outcomes favorable to Sudanese women.[98] Tados states that a women's quota "should not be seen as a proxy for assessing a country's commitment to democratization or principles of gender equality."[99] Superficially, the Sudanese electoral gender provisions and their sheer impact on women's political representation seem to approximate those of Iraq. Both countries endured similar civil and international conflicts within a parallel temporal frame in their histories, with comparable effects on their progress toward gender equality. However, Sudan did not suffer the international sanctions imposed upon Iraq in the 1990s, nor have the Sudanese experienced the depth of religious and sectarian conflicts that divide Iraq.

Morocco

In a country where they were once secluded in the enclosed households known as *harems*, from which they could not emerge without male permission, women in Morocco have made astonishing strides toward achieving political voice in the past two decades.[100] Although Morocco remains a monarchy where the king and his elite coterie enjoy enormous power, a series of reforms have been introduced since 1990 that have freed political space and improved human rights conditions for Moroccan women. Women first entered Moroccan government in 1997, when a woman was named Secretary of State.[101]

Morocco's political landscape was dramatically affected by the Arab Spring. The movement spurred many of these top-down reforms as the monarch Mohammed VI swiftly reacted to the overthrow of authoritarian regimes in neighboring countries.[102] In 2011, a revised constitution was approved by referendum, instituting an elected government, judicial independence and equality for all citizens, including women. Morocco also introduced Law No. 59-11 that year, creating a quota system allocating one-third of seats in the Lower House of Parliament to women. In the Moroccan elections held November 2011, the moderate, nonviolent Islamist Party of Justice and Development (PJD) came into power for the first time.[103] This development had paradoxical results for women; even as constitutional reforms preserved their equality, Islamist politics opposed progress toward women's rights.[104] However, there is evidence that women are gaining political authority through Islamic institutions. Politically oriented female Islamist activists leverage Islam to gain power, while in other cases women religious figures gain leadership within religious institutions.[105]

In the Moroccan Parliament, women have steadily gained ground since 2000, when they occupied less than 1 percent of all parliamentary seats. In 2007, they won 11 percent representation; and by 2014, the proportion of women MPs had reached 17 percent. Although the rise of the Islamist government led to a setback in women's governmental representation in 2012–13, when only one minister was female, the current government has six women ministers.[106] This increased voice in Moroccan politics has led to improved outcomes for women. For example, fertility rates are now among the lowest in the region; maternal mortality fell by two-thirds in the past 20 years; enrolment of girls in primary school rose from 52 percent in 1991 to 112 percent in 2012 (over 100 percent due to reenrolment); and women represent nearly 23 percent of the formal workforce.[107]

Iran

In the Islamic Republic of Iran, women's roles in politics have fluctuated with the political and religious climates.[108] During the rule of the Pahlavi Shahs between 1925 and 1979, several women's rights reforms were introduced, some of which were even coercive; an example was an edict issued in 1936 by Mohammad Reza Shah that required women to unveil and which Iranian police enforced.[109] Women were allowed to attend university beginning in 1937,[110] and the Shah granted women suffrage in 1963. Soon after earning the right to vote, women were elected to the Majlis (Parliament) and were appointed to serve as judges and cabinet ministers.[111] Farrokhroo Parsawas became the first woman appointed as Iran's Minister of Education in 1968 and Mahnaz Afkhami as Minister for Women's Affairs in 1976.[112]

The establishment of the current Islamic Republic following the 1979 revolution has had mixed results for women's status. Large numbers of women from conservative religious backgrounds had participated in demonstrations supporting the revolution, and after the monarchy was overthrown, Ayatollah Khomeini reimposed the wearing of hijab and reinstated more gender-discriminatory laws and state policies, which sanctify motherhood and emphasize every woman's domestic duty.[113] Yet despite these conservative trends, the culture of women's education remains ingrained and many women have gained entry into the civil service and higher education arenas.[114]

In 1996, 14 women were elected to Iran's Islamic Consultative Assembly, including Taherej Saffarzadeh, Masumeh Ebtekar, Azam Taleghani, Fatemeh Javadi, Marzieh Dabbag and Zahra Rahnavard.[115] Other Iranian women, such as Goli Ameri and Farah Karimi, have taken prominent positions in Western countries.[116] Shirin Ebadi, the first woman to become a judge during Pahlavi rule, was awarded the Nobel Peace Prize in 2003 for her efforts to promote the rights of Iran's women, children and political prisoners.[117] In more recent years, activist women in Iran have also achieved important media visibility while conducting peaceful protests for women's rights, making use of the Internet to promote activist causes.[118]

At present, while Iranian women retain the right to stand for and hold public office, that provision excludes some of the top governmental bodies including the Office of the Supreme Leader, Assembly of Experts, Guardian Council, Expediency Council, judicial branch and presidency. Female candidates encounter substantial gender-based obstacles—such as the segregation of public spaces—which make reaching male voters extremely difficult.[119] In the absence of a gender quota, the World Bank reports proportions of women in the Iranian Parliament at an average of 3.64 percent between 1990 and 2012, with highs of 4.9 percent from 1997 to 1999 and lows of 2.8 percent from 2008 to 2011.[120] These figures may reflect the presidency of Mahmoud Ahmadinejad, who espoused a conservative, patriarchal ideology. How women in political roles fare under Hassan Rouhani, who succeeded Ahmadinejad in 2013, remains to be seen.

A comparison and contrast between Iran and Iraq reveals similarities in the development of the two countries' Islamist-influenced sociopolitical and cultural ideologies, institutionalization of patriarchal gender relations and fluctuations in personal status laws. After Ahmadinejad assumed the presidency in 2005, human rights and especially gender rights violations intensified, as did censorship and restrictions on women's dress, freedom of assembly and ability to advocate or participate in economic activity.[121] The largely Shi'a Islamic Republic of Iran had significant influence on Iraq's al-Maliki government which was essentially hand-picked by the US CPA in 2005. Women in Iran play a considerable role in the public sphere, perhaps more visibly and with more influence than do Iraqi women. However, Iranian female candidates face more gender-specific obstacles than their Iraqi counterparts while campaigning, such as the gender-based segregation of public spaces and the near impossibility of holding mixed-gender assemblies. Clearly, the absence of a gender quota in Iran to date has impeded the numbers of women being elected to the country's Parliament as contrasted with Iraq.

Lebanon

Lebanon closely neighbors Iraq and its political structure is evolving in similar ways. Lebanese laws governing personal status may be more similar to Iraq than to any country in the Arab region; yet Lebanon has no parliamentary gender quota. Thus a comparison between Iraq and Lebanon in terms of political gender representation has particular significance in terms of a regional and sociopolitical perspective.[122]

Lebanese women are often perceived to enjoy a higher degree of freedom than other Middle Eastern countries, and Lebanon is seen as being relatively politically progressive. The paradox is that Lebanon has one of the lowest rates of women elected or appointed to public office in the world. Furthermore, Lebanon has instituted fewer reforms for gender equality than many countries with more conservative regimes.[123] Although women fought for and gained the right to political representation and suffrage in 1952, they have not become fully integrated into the political system, perhaps mainly due to Lebanon's longstanding sectarian electoral system.[124] There is no formalized gender quota for the Lebanese Parliament, and Lebanese women who gain parliamentary seats remain highly marginalized.[125] The World Bank indicates that the average of Lebanese women in Parliament from 1997 to 2004 is 3.1 percent, with lows of 2.3 percent from 1997 to 2004 and highs of 4.7 percent from 2005 to 2008.[126]

While (like Iraq) post-conflict Lebanon is undergoing a transition to democracy, some political scientists such as Arend Lijphart, Imad Salomey and Rhys Payne have suggested that the current Lebanese government—while formally acknowledged as democratic—falls into a transitional model of democracy known as consociationalism.[127] This model of government was imposed on the Lebanese during the French Colonial Mandate, and although it was meant then to be a temporary system, it has prevailed for more than six decades. Consociationalism, which has been defined as "government by elite cartel designed to turn a democracy with a fragmented political culture into a stable democracy," has been recommended for plural societies such as Lebanon where the schisms between sects are deep.[128] The Lebanese electoral system is organized to provide representation by religious affiliation, which forces citizens to vote based on their religious, rather than their civic, identities. In this system designed to institutionalize the sharing of power, political influence is divided among religious sects according to the size of their populations.[129]

A comparison between the role of Iraqi women in politics and the fate of women's representation in neighboring Lebanon provides some of the regional context advocated by Moghadam.[130] Paul Kingston summarizes the experience of women as members of political parties in Lebanon.[131] Women's participation in public life has been mainly relegated to membership on women's subcommittees attached to political parties, a role which has afforded them a very limited degree of influence. It is interesting that, whereas Kingston calls for political party and personal status reforms to increase participation of Lebanon's women in politics, he does not mention instituting a gender quota as a possible step forward.[132] According to Marguerite Helou, Lebanon may appear on the surface to have been more progressive than its Middle Eastern neighbors on political gender balance. Lebanese women gained suffrage 28 years earlier than Iraqi women who did not earn the right to vote until 1980.[133] However, the

Lebanese Constitution was formulated in 1926 while Lebanon was under French Mandate, and this constitution has changed little over time, continuing to reflect the more egalitarian French ideals. This point is germane to Lovenduski and Norris's contention that egalitarian political structures are more likely to breed electoral gender quotas.[134]

Although some women joined political parties during the 1970s and were instrumental in communicating the party message during the Lebanese civil war (1975–91),[135] women did not begin to represent significant numbers of political party membership until the 1990s, and there remain very few women in higher party roles today. Since political parties are the primary institutional vehicles by which individuals advance to Parliament, the lack of female party-political representation in Lebanon remains significant. As such, Helou calls for political parties in Lebanon to adopt gender quotas as an important stride toward promoting election of women to public office.[136]

Lina Khatib describes the perception that women in Lebanon are more liberalized than their sisters in neighboring countries as a "glossy facade" behind which lies gender exclusion, political marginalization and patriarchal discrimination.[137] Women are still highly discriminated against within the letter of Lebanese law. While the Lebanese government did ratify CEDAW in 1997, it did so only after expressing reservations around articles dealing with personal status—rendering the ratification essentially meaningless.[138] Here a parallel may be drawn with Iraq; Saddam conditionally ratified CEDAW in the 1990s, making noteworthy exclusions that permitted women's rights violations, violence and honor crimes to continue unabated.

Some scholars, such as Schulze et al.,[139] have suggested that the ongoing low numbers of women in Lebanese politics may serve as an indicator not only of the reluctance of a patriarchal society to accept women as politically equal to men, but also of the failure of women to demand such equality.[140] Patrimony is firmly rooted in Lebanese society and Lebanon has no civil personal status code; decisions of marriage, divorce, child custody, domestic violence and alimony rest within the jurisdiction of the religious court system. This means that laws governing personal status in Lebanon are different based on the religious group to which one belongs: Christian women have different rights to Muslim women, and even within Islamic jurisprudence, Shiʻa women follow different laws than do Sunni women. Essentially, this means that Lebanese women are not only unequal to men, but they are not even equal among themselves.[141]

That said, Lebanese women do play significant roles in civil society as social service advocates and workers. Yet, women's NGOs in Lebanon since the civil war have tended to focus on activism toward women's rights in the private, rather than the public, sphere—dealing with charity and social welfare rather than political representation.[142] Any gains by women in Lebanese politics have tended to be temporary and often result from personal or family connections rather than from widespread improvements in gender equality.[143] The first woman in Lebanon to gain public office was Mirna Boustany in 1963, who earned her seat only upon the death of her father whom she was elected to replace. There were no women in the Lebanese cabinet to follow until 2005 when Leila Solh Hamadeh, Waafa Diqa Hamzeh and Nayla Moawad were appointed to the Ministries of Industry, State, and Social Affairs, respectively. The number of women MPs elected in 2005 was the highest in Lebanese history, but women still made up only 4.7 percent of the Parliament (6 out of 128 seats). The subsequent cabinet (2008) included only one woman.[144] In 2009, 12 of 587 (2 percent) parliamentary candidates and 4 of 128 Deputies (3.1 percent) were women. And as of 2012, no women have held seats in the Lebanese cabinet.[145]

As in the case of Iraq, war has had significant impact on the status of women and their subsequent election to public positions in Lebanon.[146] The Lebanese civil war ravished Lebanon economically, politically and socially. Like the aftermaths of the Iran-Iraq war and the 2003 invasion of Iraq by the United States and its allies, the Lebanese civil war had deleterious effects on women by reinforcing patriarchal mores, inhibiting progress toward women's rights, and creating conditions of extreme economic deprivation. Any activities toward gender equality were suspended as citizens struggled simply to survive. However, some feminists have suggested that the war did open new avenues for women to join the political arena, a position possibly taken due to the increased post-conflict presence of women in the Lebanese workforce.[147]

Naila Nauphal calls for research on women's potential contribution to the development of Lebanese civil society, stating that women may have a crosscutting organizational role in vital decisions around employment and civil and political freedoms.[148] She notes that the post-war economic state has differentially affected the genders and placed the primary burden of poverty upon women, especially those who live in rural settings. Furthermore, the unequal and marginalized status of women in politics is reinforced by legal premises that "define and confine women in a state of subordination."[149] Thus while the civil code in Lebanon grants equal rights to all citizens regardless of gender, no article or clause prohibits gender discrimination. In fact, Lebanese personal status laws contradict the basic legal principles of gender equality and nondiscrimination.

When examining the underlying causes of women's representation in Lebanese politics,[150] Sofia Saadeh notes that the state cannot intervene for the advancement of women's rights because the constitution explicitly prohibits it from doing so. The lack of opportunity for upward mobility for women in political and decision-making positions is highlighted. She describes a weak state in Lebanon, which contributes to a mixture of divided sectarian communities that, in turn, discriminate against women each in its own way. Saadeh further calls for the institution of a quota to promote the advancement of women's political agency.[151]

Fatima Sbaity Kassem conducted a series of interviews with Lebanese female politicians as part of her doctoral dissertation.[152] She notes that, in the absence of a formalized gender quota for the Lebanese Parliament, the few Lebanese female MPs who do become elected remain highly marginalized and generally serve to represent only those political views held by their male kin. Kassem theorizes that the confessional affiliation of Lebanon's political parties in large part determines party recruitment, nomination and promotion of women to positions of leadership. In addition, she posits that parties tend to apply higher standards to women candidates than to men. Kassem suggests that the study of female representation in Middle Eastern countries might usefully move beyond looking at the cultural and religious influences on the entire society. Her analyses looked at variation in these influences at the party level, hypothesizing an inverse correlation between party religiosity and women's nomination to public office. She found that her hypothesis was upheld at the municipal, but not at the parliamentary, level.[153] Her research suggests that municipal politics may offer a breakthrough opportunity for women to enter the Lebanese political sphere in larger numbers.[154]

Tunisia

The 1956 Tunisian Personal Status Code profoundly reformed laws related to marriage, divorce and custody, and it abolished polygamy. When Tunisian women gained suffrage the following year, Tunisia stood in the forefront of the Middle East and North Africa (MENA) region in terms of gender legislation.[155] This relatively progressive approach to women's rights was initially spearheaded by Habib Bourguiba, Tunisia's first president after gaining independence from France in 1956. Bourguiba's successor, Zine El Abidine Ben Ali, continued the tradition of top-down gender-related reforms, but arguably with less intent to improve women's rights than to divert international attention away from rampant human rights abuses and restrictions on political freedom.[156] Steps by Ben Ali to restrict the public space placed stringent limitations on the role of women's organizations that had emerged in the 1980s and 1990s. As Ben Ali moved along the trajectory toward dictatorship, independent human rights groups including Amnesty International documented repeated violations of basic human rights and severe constraints on the Tunisian press.[157]

The December 2010–January 2011 Arab Spring uprising in Tunisia saw women from diverse backgrounds take to the streets in the protests that eventually led to the fall of Ben Ali's regime. Women in large numbers also participated in the ensuing October 2011 National Constituent Assembly (NCA) elections—as campaigners, as candidates and as voters.[158] There was strong representation of women on the Constitution Drafting Committee, and their influence prompted the adoption of a relatively innovative electoral principle designed to promote gender parity—the vertical parity provision.[159] Under this system, parties had to alternate male and female candidates in order for their party lists to be valid. However, although this provision enabled some 5,000 women to stand for NCA election in October 2011, it did not result in equal female representation because many parties failed to nominate women as heads of candidate lists—and heads of lists are substantially more likely to become elected. Thus a total of 59 women gained NCA seats in the 2011 election (27 percent of the 217 seats). The vertical parity procedure also ruled that deputies who resigned or died would be replaced by the next candidate named on the electoral list, so several women gained seats in that way, for a final total of 67 (31 percent). This 31 percent of women in Tunisia's Parliament was upheld in the most recent 2014 elections, placing Tunisia at the top of the countries in the MENA region for having the highest number of female MPs. Yet while this achievement may seem impressive, women's representation in other areas—such as parliamentary committee leadership and cabinet posts—has not kept pace. Some research has suggested that this result may be attributed to women's comparative lack of access to financial resources, since campaign funding apparently plays a significant role in determining which candidates are placed first on candidate lists.[160] While the new language describing women's rights in the Tunisian Constitution has served to encourage the state to support and extend those rights, it appears—similar to the case of Iraq—that women in Tunisian politics also face major challenges and obstacles to effective campaigning and rewarding parliamentary experiences.

Summary

Electoral gender quotas take various forms and reach policy agendas through various mechanisms. Most of the 125 countries with quotas have institutionalized the systems since 1991, and research exploring the longitudinal effects of gender quotas on women's political agency—particularly on their substantive and symbolic representation—remains scarce. A comparative examination of six countries across the MENA reveals that Iraq's quota has increased women's political representation (at least descriptively) to a level higher than that of most countries in the region. Among the countries discussed here, only Sudan and Tunisia have achieved greater parliamentary representation than Iraq by instituting gender quota or gender parity systems.

Indeed, relevant to a comparison with Sudan, the somewhat lower percentage of women MPs in Iraq at the 2010 and 2014 elections may have been an indicator that women's empowerment is eroding rather than increasing. However, it is important to note the 22 Iraqi women MPs who were elected outside quota influence in 2014. Insight into how many of these MPs had served previously in Parliament could provide further evidence regarding the effectiveness of quotas in achieving female representation, in both the short and long term.

The experience of Lebanese women in politics is particularly interesting as a comparative point with Iraq. The absence of a gender quota for Lebanon's Parliament, combined with low levels of women's political representation in the country appears, when compared to other cases such as Iraq, to make a prima facie case for at least the partial success of gender quotas—that is, securing parliamentary seats. However once in Parliament, the difficulties encountered by Iraqi female MPs may be similar to those of Lebanese women in public office and thus suggest that gender quotas may be more important for electability rather than effectiveness of representation. Moreover, should sectarianism continue to prevail and evolve in Iraq as it has in Lebanon there is a chance that the quota system may be undermined by failures in building the capacity of women to *exercise* political influence.

Chapter 4 addresses the question of descriptive representation achieved by women in Iraq's Parliament in the context of the political and societal developments of each relevant historical period, from the time when women were granted suffrage in 1980 until the elections in 2014.

4

Descriptive Representation: Quota Effects on Numbers of Women in Office

The first aspect of women's political representation to be analyzed in this evaluation of the effects of an electoral gender quota is *descriptive* representation. Descriptive representation is nominal representation only; it does not qualify the success of the quota in helping women influence actual policy-making, nor does it outline the barriers and supports encountered by female politicians while campaigning or as members of the legislative body.[1] Due to its purely quantitative nature, descriptive representation has a potential reductionist effect on the interpretation of quota results for women in politics. However, quantification of women elected to Parliament, situated within the historical and sociopolitical context of each relevant period, remains an important first step toward determining the comparative success of women in Iraqi politics before and after quota implementation.

This chapter first discusses the levels at which women participated in Iraq's political processes during the period from 1920 (the onset of the Hashemite monarchy) through 1979 (the year in which Saddam assumed the presidency). Despite lacking suffrage at this time, women made strides toward achieving enfranchisement and found other ways to express themselves politically. The second section analyzes the presence of women in the Iraqi Parliament since women were granted the right to vote and stand for office in 1980 and up through 2000 (the last elections held prior to the toppling of Saddam's regime, and the drafting and adoption of the 2005 Constitution). Each election is placed in context of the important sociopolitical and historical events occurring at the time. The third section addresses the efforts of women's activist groups and other individuals and organizations through the phases of interim government and leading up to the drafting of the 2005 Constitution, describing the strategies that succeeded in obtaining the adoption of the parliamentary gender quota. The final section discusses the gains of women candidates in parliamentary elections held after the new constitution went into effect, also embedded within the relevant sociopolitical context.

Representation of Women in Iraqi Politics, 1920–79

Iraqi women have been involved in public activities—including political participation, pursuing secondary and higher education and working in governmental or public sector positions—at various levels across Iraq's history in line with changes in the country's political climate.[2] From the recognition of the modern Iraqi state in 1920 until receiving the right to vote in 1980, women found ways to contribute to Iraq's political agenda by becoming active in women's organizations and political parties, and participating in demonstrations and public debates.[3] This section summarizes the presence of women in the Iraqi polity during this timeframe.

Hashemite Monarchy

Iraq became a political entity recognized by the League of Nations in 1920. During the Iraqi Hashemite Monarchy (1921–58), regular parliamentary elections were held, but those elections were not competitive and Parliament had no actual role in the political process.[4] Although the British found the parliamentary system conducive to achieving its goal of encouraging the involvement of urban Iraqi intellectuals in state processes, they also felt safeguards were needed to circumvent any threats to the British-backed Hashemite government.[5] At least partly for that reason, the 1920 Constitution and electoral system were designed to pose significant obstacles to achieving parliamentary election for most Iraqi men, while completely barring women from becoming elected officials.[6]

Although Iraq's first constitution was drafted in 1920 and redrafted in 1921, its provisions were not implemented until 1925. The monarch retained enormous power, including the power to select and dismiss the prime minister and to appoint and dissolve the cabinet and the bicameral Parliament. The monarch had further authority to approve all governmental decisions and was entitled to rule by decree.[7] While Iraq was ostensibly designated to function as a constitutional monarchy with a king, cabinet, two legislative chambers and democratic rights for all citizens, in practice Iraqi politics were governed and controlled by the British, the royal family and the (primarily Sunni) former

Ottoman officers.[8] Women were even further marginalized as they were excluded altogether from any type of participation in formal politics, including the right to vote.[9] In addition, men of lower classes and those under the age of 30 were also prohibited from election because some regions of the country were experiencing anarchy, with violent conflicts between tribes, and British governance was not yet established in the regions.[10] The electorate was divided into three electoral circles heavily weighted to represent rural regions, effectively excluding any urban politicians who opposed the government from serving in Parliament. As this highly exclusive electoral system naturally met with widespread protest, the issue of women's political enfranchisement tended to be pushed aside in the face of the more broadly based controversy.[11] Criticism of electoral law due to its exclusivity of various groups continued throughout the 1930s and into the mid-1940s.[12]

The barriers Iraqi women encountered during their battle toward enfranchisement, as well as the more generally discriminating exclusivity of electoral provisions during Hashemite rule, illustrate the kinds of sociopolitical, cultural, legal and economic transformations that are necessary in the transition to postcolonial development.[13] As sociopolitical theorist Ayad al-Qazzaz suggests, changes in political and social structure were closely tied to fluctuations in the role and function of the power elite.[14] The political elite of the monarchical period primarily resided in the cabinet body; after the monarch and his regent, the cabinet—not Parliament—held greatest power to influence national politics and structure.[15] The two-step electoral procedure whereby the government provided lists of candidates to the electors and subverted any attempts to oppose its nominees was instituted and upheld by the cabinet.[16] Discourses employed by emerging women's movements at the time reflect the intersection between feminist and democratization theory as they called for electoral reform that did not overlook the inclusion of women in the polity, a prerequisite for democratization and a fundamental principle of gender rights.[17]

Starting in the 1940s, women began to secure some modicum of political influence by establishing formal political parties with the purpose of furthering women's rights and status in Iraq.[18] One influential party was the Iraqi Communist Party, out of whose ranks was formed an executive committee called "Women's Society for Combating Fascism and Nazism." This society later changed its name to the Association of Iraqi Women and finally the Iraqi Women's League (IWL). The IWL attained membership of 42,000 in the 1950s out of a total Iraqi population of eight million at the time and achieved many gains for women, particularly the institution of the 1959 Personal Status Law.[19] As noted previously, in 1959, Naziha al-Dulaimi, an IWL member and full member of the Iraqi Communist Party since 1948, was appointed Minister of Municipal Affairs, becoming the first female minister both in Iraq and across the entire Arab region,[20] and she was the only woman to have contributed to drafting the 1959 Personal Status Law.[21]

In the same year, Zakia Hakki, a Faylee Kurd from Baghdad, was appointed Iraq's first female judge. Her personal story is emblematic of the vicissitudes of modern Iraqi history, especially for a Kurd. Hakki holds a bachelor of science degree in business administration from the International Labour Union in Switzerland and a Ph.D. in international law from the University of Baghdad. As the first female judge in Iraq, she served as expert legal advisor in the government's Ministry of Agriculture and with the Ministry of Justice in the enforcement court of family and Islamic law. She is also the originator and the president of the Kurdish Women's Federation from 1958 until 1975 and the only woman elected to a leadership position in the Kurdish Democratic Party in 1970. She was placed under provisional arrest for two decades in 1976 because of her stand against Saddam's aggression toward Kurds. She migrated to the United States in 1996 and practiced as a lawyer in northern Virginia in addition to serving as vice president of the Iraqi American Council. She was a strong activist for minority and women's rights. After the US invasion of Iraq in 2003, Hakki participated in several working group sessions on Iraq at the US Department of State, including a project on transitional justice. She was appointed advisor to the Ministry of Justice from the Iraqi Reconstruction Development Council in 2003. In 2004, she was appointed a member of the committee that drafted the 2005 Iraq Constitution, contributed to the rewriting of the judicial and political system and gained a parliamentary seat in the first elections held under that constitution.[22] At around the same time, the Ministry of Labour and Social Affairs employed her as its inspector general. Hakki created two local nongovernmental organizations (NGOs) to provide shelter for homeless Iraqi women and children and was a board member of the Women's Alliance for Democratic Iraq.[23]

The political instability and multiple regime changes that followed the downfall of the Hashemite monarchy during the 1958 revolution by the Free Officers Movement unraveled any strides the monarchy had made toward a representative Western-style political system. Certainly, this had backward consequences for the descriptive representation of females in both the political and social arenas in the decade that followed.

Early Ba'athist Regime

In the early years of Ba'athist rule (1968–79), the party labored to establish state-sponsored organizations representing all facets of society, to indoctrinate and subordinate the entire citizenry into the Ba'ath Party.[24] The "reign of terror ... reminiscent of the Stalin era—that became a hallmark of the regime"[25] did not bypass women. No grassroots organizations independent of the Ba'ath Party were permitted to form or operate, and the severity of punishment for maintaining such organizations resulted in the dissolution of many Communist-backed women's groups, including the Iraqi Women's League.[26] As the regime consolidated its power more strongly, Iraqis faced increasing pressure to become party members and declining to join was treated as an act of political defiance.[27]

The Ba'athists pursued strategies of rule that included attempts to court the allegiance of the citizenry away from its traditional affiliation to large familial/kinship, tribal and ethnic groups.[28] After 1958, relations between Iraqi citizens had become less and less governed by kinship and birth considerations and moved more toward being determined by holdings of private property.[29] Agriculture had begun to decline as the primary contributor to Iraq's economy even prior to the Ba'athist coup; afterwards the Ba'ath government placed increasingly greater emphasis on industry and services in its extensive economic growth and urbanization programs.[30] In the 1950s, 1960s and 1970s, around the region, there was a movement to educate women and involve them in the labor force. This process was quicker in Iraq because of the 1970s oil boom. In response to the need for increased labor resources despite the shift of Iraq's population to urban areas,[31] the Ba'ath leadership developed a complex set of programs, including general, vocational and political education programs, aimed at mobilizing women to become "resocialized" into more active roles in the Iraqi economy and polity.[32] On the flip side, pressures to join the Ba'ath Party increased particularly for women, because certain professions (notably predominately female fields such as education) were available only to those who swore loyalty to the party.[33]

The nationalization of Iraqi oil resources in 1972 helped to fund extensive public programs for promoting not only education, but also social and commercial services, agriculture and industry. These programs lasted through the early 1980s.[34] The massive and sudden influx of oil revenues served to strengthen the elitist government, enable its economic autonomy from the society and increase its potential to realize absolute authority.[35] Numerous schools and universities were built in the 1970s, and many postgraduate and higher degree scholarships abroad were made available to women. There were systems in place that allowed women, mainly urban ones, both to have children and to work. For example, childcare was free, as was transportation to work and school.[36] Literacy campaigns in the countryside educated illiterate women, and the General Federation of Iraqi Women (GFIW) was responsible for implementing some of the state's modernizing policies regarding the mobilization of its female population. For instance, it launched a big campaign to raise awareness about health and hygiene, programs on how to feed children and implemented a highly successful literacy campaign. At the end of the 1970s, Iraq received a prize from UNESCO for being the country that managed to raise its female literacy levels the quickest.[37]

To place any gains women made during this period toward enfranchisement and political empowerment into perspective, it is useful to recall that British influence in Iraq had planted the seeds of democratization—such as the constitutional and parliamentary frameworks—while failing to lead an actual transition to democracy. When Iraq became a republic under Ba'athist rule, these strides toward democratization were undermined and the stage was set for the brutal oppressions and profound sectarian schisms that were to follow.

Representation of Women in Iraqi Politics under Saddam

The increased wealth of the state from oil revenues allowed the ruling elite—by the mid-1980s monopolized by Saddam and many of his consanguineal or affinal relatives—to set themselves apart in a class of their own, independent of other social classes and institutions.[38] Over time, the Ba'ath Party became less a powerful, independent party and more an appendage and vehicle of Saddam's personal regime.[39] The growing autocracy demanded of its citizenry the prioritization of state and party above other loyalties such as family.[40] The push to educate women, bring them into the labor market and integrate them into the polity served as a process by which women became symbols to which the leadership could point as evidence of Iraq's success at building a modern nation-state.[41] One of the major vehicles for conducting the so-called resocialization process for women was the GFIW, which had been created by the Ba'ath Party immediately after the 1968 coup. As stated earlier, GFIW leaders were Ba'ath Party members hand-selected by the party; all GFIW funding and programs were state-directed.[42] Any political power achieved by women was channeled through this organization and determined entirely by the closeness of their ties with the ruling class.[43] By the time Iraqi women gained suffrage in 1980, the GFIW claimed more than 177,000 members and was working through 256 centers across Iraq to conduct educational and service programs, collaborate with trade unions and help implement changes to the personal status law.[44]

Iraqi women first received the right to vote and stand for public office in 1980, one year after Saddam assumed the presidency. Between that year and the 2003 US-led invasion, five elections took place in Iraq (including those conducted in June 1980). Figure 4.1 presents the percentage of parliamentary seats gained by women in each of these election years. The remainder of this section summarizes election results and places each election in historical and sociopolitical context. This analysis is central to evaluating the results of the 2005 gender quota in relative comparison to women's descriptive representation achieved in elections prior to quota adoption.

As noted by Nohlen et al.,[45] electoral data and election details from Iraq during Saddam's regime are not easily available, as official documentation was

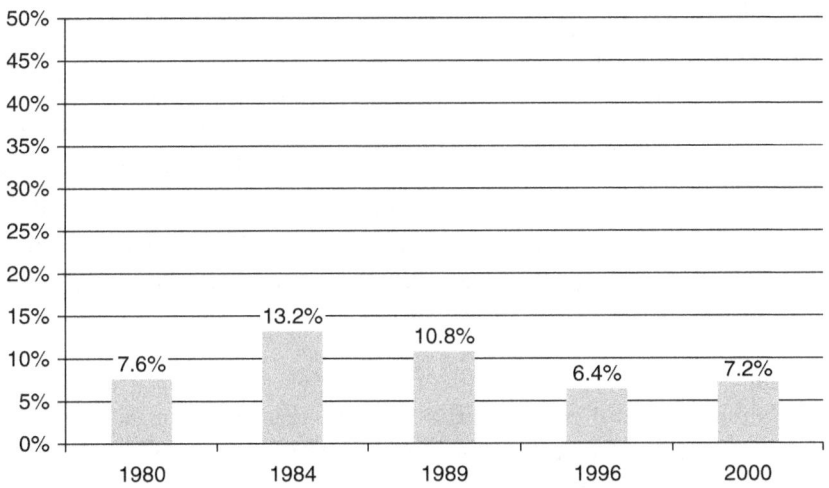

Figure 4.1 Percentage of elected women in Iraqi Parliament, 1980–2000

Sources:

Inter-Parliamentary Union. "Iraq: Council of Representatives of Iraq." Geneva: Inter-Parliamentary Union, October 10, 2014.

quotaProject: Global Database of Quotas for Women. "About Quotas | quotaProject: Global Database of Quotas for Women." Accessed October 5, 2013. http://www.quotaproject.org/aboutQuotas.cfm.

The World Bank, "Middle East and North Africa—Middle East and North Africa : Gender Equality and Empowerment," accessed June 26, 2013, http://go.worldbank.org/PWOKKK10B0.

never published. The figures shown here represent a compilation of the most reliable available data.

The 1980 and 1984 Elections in Light of the Iran-Iraq Conflict

In 1980, shortly after Saddam assumed the presidency, a unicameral Parliament was reestablished under the provisions of a new electoral law. At the time, general elections had not been held in Iraq since 1958, when the military coup d'état overthrew the British-backed monarchy and the National Assembly was dissolved. In 1968, supreme governing authority had been vested in the Revolutionary Command Council (RCC), an 18-member body whose chair was also the president of the Iraqi Republic. Under the ruling of Saddam, in December 1979, the RCC invited political parties, trade unions and popular NGOs to draft and debate an electoral law which would reinstate a 250-member National Council (Parliament) whose members would hold office for a four-year term. This law was adopted on March 16, 1980.

1980 elections. Elections were held for all the members of Parliament provided for under the new electoral law of 1980, which granted suffrage to all Iraqis aged 18 years or above of either gender. In addition, the law required all candidates for the Iraqi Parliament to be literate, at least 25 years of age and an Iraqi national (from Iraqi parents by birth or from an Iraqi father by birth and a mother from one of the Arab countries). A further stipulation required that candidates must have

> upheld the principles and aims of the July 1968 progressive and socialist revolution; completed military service or been exempted from it; not been expropriated landowners from whom land was taken under the Agrarian Reform Law No 117 of 1970, or whose properties were nationalised or confiscated by the State; not been convicted of crimes related to the State's internal or external security after the July 1968 revolution; not been convicted for violating public confidence, harming the national economy and the State's financial confidence, violating public morality, or misdemeanour; and not have had a record of imprisonment for murder for a period not less than 15 years.[46]

These rules in effect restricted candidacy to membership in the Ba'ath Party or in a party which had pledged its allegiance to the Ba'athists (e.g., both the Kurdistan Revolutionary Party and the Democratic Party had pledged support to the Ba'ath-led National Progressive Patriotic Front).[47] Although it was possible to run as an independent without stated party affiliation, very few candidates did so. A total of 860 candidates—19 of whom were women—ran for parliamentary seats in this election. During parliamentary campaigning, Saddam was often seen alongside women candidates during their public appearances, particularly Manal Younis al-Alousi, the general secretary of the GFIW.[48] Very high voter turnout was reported for the 1980 election; nearly 85 percent of the six million eligible voters were said to have gone to the polls.[49] Being personally present at this election, which was the first to grant women the right to vote, meant that I witnessed firsthand the very large turnout of women at the polls. The Ba'ath Party won 187 of the 250 contested seats (75 percent), much higher than the 126 required for a majority. Furthermore, all 19 of the Ba'athist female candidates were elected to parliamentary seats, representing 7.6 percent of the total governing body.

It has been noted that very little information has been published about the 1980 parliamentary campaign and elections in Iraq.[50] However, drawing upon the example of neighboring Arab countries, it may be possible to make a reasonable inference that many women, especially those residing in rural areas, may have felt constrained to vote as their husbands or tribal groups wished.[51]

1984 elections. As noted, women became increasingly visible in the advent of the Iran-Iraq war in the 1980s as they came to take over many of the men's roles in the labor force, state bureaucracy and administration. However, it was also during this time that women became instruments of the regime against any opposition. Rape and sexual assault of wives and female relatives were routinely used to blackmail and extract information from nonconformists and burden opposition members abroad.[52] Women were endangered, incarcerated, executed and raped to build control within an Iraqi political system that has been dubbed a "republic of fear."[53] Yet, even under these horrific conditions, women in opposition to Saddam's regime still engaged in political activism (if little formal political participation), particularly Kurdish women.[54] For example, female activists provided logistical support, passed along covert messages, distributed literature and advocated for the release of prisoners.[55] It was within this sociopolitical and economic climate that the 1984 parliamentary elections took place.

The elections scheduled to be held in June 1984 were postponed, but only until October 20. The Inter-Parliamentary Union characterizes these elections as marked by a great deal of campaign propaganda and garnering much attention from the Iraqi press.[56] Saddam flaunted the fact that the elections were held in the midst of wartime as an indicator of Iraq's adherence to democratic procedures and a sense of normalcy in the country.[57] He was quoted in the *al-Thawra* newspaper as saying, "Millions of Iraqi men and women flocked to the polls to participate in the election operation ... with enthusiasm and maturity."[58]

A total of 782 candidates competed for the 250 seats in the National Assembly, of which 46 were women. As in 1980, the vast majority of candidates and electees were members of the Ba'ath Party. The remaining candidates either were independents or represented a group of minor blocs that together comprised the National Progressive Patriotic Front (which paid allegiance to the Ba'ath Party). Ba'ath Party members were elected to 183 parliamentary seats (73 percent) and 33 women were elected (13.2 percent). The same electoral laws were applied as in 1980, including the requirement that the Ba'athist-run Electoral Commission vet all candidates. There is evidence to suggest that the 1984 election was less an example of democratic process than a mechanism by which the Ba'ath Party rewarded candidates for their contributions to the war effort.[59] Therefore the doubled proportion of female MPs in Parliament over the 1980 election likely reflected the enhanced roles of women in society since the war's outbreak, rather than campaign results or widespread voter preference.[60] From the standpoint of women's participation, it is noteworthy that the Parliament elected in 1984 became responsible for ratifying—albeit with several reservations—the United Nations Convention on the Elimination of all Forms of Discrimination against Women in 1986.[61]

1989, 1996 and 2000 Elections: The Sanctions Era

Iraq experienced less than two years of tenuous peace after the terminus of its war with Iran, and one parliamentary election took place during this unstable peacetime. Although the four-year term set forth by the 1980 electoral law would have originally required elections to be held in August 1988, the poll was postponed several times due in part to uncertainty over the course and outcome of the war. Ultimately the election date was set for April 1, 1989. Of the 921 candidates who contested the 250 parliamentary seats, it was reported that approximately 25 percent were members of the Ba'ath Party and the remainder were either independents or members of the National Progressive Patriotic Front. A total of 65 candidates in 1989 were women, approximately 26 percent, and as before, all Ba'athists. All candidates again were screened by the Election Committee, which was headed by Izzat Ibrahim al-Douri, vice chairman of the

RCC. The committee issued a statement that the government had "embarked on a course of democratization and liberalization to redraft the Constitution and pave the way for multi-party elections."[62] The Parliament elected in 1989 was regarded as governing in transition until the new constitution could be drafted and adopted. Although the Ba'ath Party retained the parliamentary majority in 1989, winning 207 (83 percent) of seats, it has been suggested that by that time the elections served more to generate a popular base for Saddam's supreme leadership than to demonstrate party support.[63] A total of 27 women were elected in 1989 representing 10.8 percent of the assembly. During this phase in Saddam's regime, the Parliament held no real legislative authority, although the elections did provide a voice for the citizenry that extended beyond the Ba'ath Party.[64]

After the 1991 *Sha'aban Intifada* (uprising),[65] a series of public uprisings against the Ba'ath regime in northern and southern Iraq, the allied Gulf War troops established a "safe haven" in northern Kurdistan to protect Kurdish refugees fleeing Iraqi government forces.[66] Although the Baghdad-based regime maintained sovereignty over this area, the allied protection set the stage for a political separation between the Kurdistan region and southern Iraq.[67] In addition to the UN sanctions, the Iraqi government imposed internal trade restrictions on Kurdistan effectively placing the region under double embargo.[68] Amid this climate of persistent economic hardship and ongoing conflicts, both internal and international, Iraq's parliamentary elections were postponed and the legislature's four-year term extended twice (in 1993 and 1995).[69]

1996 elections. By the time elections finally took place in 1996, the Saddam regime deemed several changes to the electoral law necessary. For the first time, 30 of the 250 parliamentary seats were set aside to represent the provinces located in the now semiautonomous Kurdistan region. Rather than elected, the 30 Kurdish MPs were to be government-appointed and approved by the Minister of Justice. Masoud Barzani was leader of the Kurdistan Democratic Party (KDP) at that time and his party won three seats.[70] A further amendment formalized the reward system for participation in the Iran-Iraq war effort. Now not only were candidates required to uphold the principles and aims of the 1968 revolution, but also to "have participated in the 'sacred battle against the Iranian aggression,' to have faith that Saddam's *Qadissiyah* (war against Iran) has strengthened the glory of Iraq, and to believe in the 'eternal Mother of all Battles' (the 1991 war against Kuwait)."[71]

All candidates were screened and approved by a government-appointed Election Commission chaired by the Minister of Justice. There were 689 candidates competing for 220 available seats (excluding the 30 appointed to represent Kurdistan). Very high voter turnout (93.5 percent of approximately eight million eligible registered voters) was reported for the 1996 election.[72] Although independents for the first time greatly outnumbered Ba'ath Party candidates in 1996, all 161 of the Ba'ath Party members were elected. Sixteen women gained seats for a historical low of 6.4 percent parliamentary representation. This reduction in women's representation reflects the political effects of sanctions which disproportionately affected women and children by restricting their access to food, healthcare and education, and the regime's ideological shift back toward patriarchal domination, by which women were forced out of the public sphere and back into the home management arena in the atmosphere of long-term hardship and impoverishment.[73]

2000 elections. By the 2000 elections, any regime-sponsored support for women's participation in politics had been essentially eliminated. The GFIW, despite its growth in ranks to nearly a million members by this time, had seen its role in providing a presence for women in public life completely marginalized; its focus had then turned primarily toward providing humanitarian aid and healthcare.[74] At the same time, the semiautonomy of the Kurdistan governorates allowed some women to establish associations in civil society and become more involved in party politics at the regional level; however, Kurdish female political participation still met with substantial opposition by conservative male politicians and influencers.[75] The substantial numbers of Iraqi women in the diaspora became strong advocates for women's political mobilization at this time, seeking to raise awareness about the plight of Iraqi women between the sanctions and the oppression of Saddam's regime.[76] Several diasporic women's NGOs were formed which provided social and economic support to Iraqi refugees and lobbied for the lift of the UN sanctions.[77]

General elections were held on March 27, 2000 at the normal expiry of the four-year parliamentary term. As in 1996, 30 seats were appointed by the government to represent the northern Kurdish provinces. In 2000, 522 candidates (25 of whom were women) vied for the 220 available seats. All candidates were either members of the Ba'ath Party or independents loyal to the party. This poll was viewed as a demonstration of solidarity with Saddam in support of conflict over the UN trade embargo.[78] Due to the ongoing embargo, severe restrictions were placed on parliamentary candidates' ability to conduct political campaigns. Any discussion of the UN sanctions during campaigning was prohibited, as were campaign rallies and election manifestos, and candidates were allowed very little media access. The ruling Ba'ath Party won 165 seats while 55 went to independent candidates. Saddam's eldest son Uday, making his political debut, was elected to

Parliament with the highest number of votes received by any candidate that year. Of the 25 women who ran for Parliament, 18 were elected (7.2 percent total representation), representing very little gain in women's political representation as the extreme economic conditions and patriarchal suppression continued.

In addition to the women who achieved parliamentary seats, two other women notably attained influential positions during the late years of Saddam's presidency. Dr. Huda Salih Mahdi Ammash, a professor of microbiology at Baghdad University, became the only female in the Iraq Command Council (RCC), the 18-member council that ran the Ba'ath Party, as well as a party regional commander.[79] Ammash, born in 1953, is from a second generation of Iraqi leaders—her father Salih Mahdi Ammash was a prominent Iraqi revolutionary during the 1960s. However, he disappeared under mysterious circumstances in the 1970s when Saddam came to power, prompting rumors that the new Iraqi president had ordered him killed. Ammash was one of the few women in Saddam's inner circle and the only one on the US list of 55 most wanted Iraqi leaders, and is best known for her alleged involvement with the "weapons of mass destruction" program which the United States claimed Iraq pursued. Dubbed "Mrs. Anthrax" by Washington, US intelligence services say Ammash masterminded the reconstruction of Iraq's biological weapons facilities after the 1991 Gulf War.[80]

The second prominent woman was microbiologist Dr. Rihab Rashid Taha, dubbed "Dr. Germ" by UN weapons inspectors. She helped develop weapons-grade anthrax and botulinum and led the Iraq biological weapons development program from 1988 to 1995. She was particularly recognized by British intelligence for her role in the manufacture of anthrax and other agents of biological warfare.[81] Taha, born in 1957, was married to General Amir Mohammad Rashid al-Ubaydi, Saddam's Oil Minister, sometimes called "Missile Man" in reference to his expertise with weapons delivery systems.[82] In recognition of her service, Saddam presented Taha with an award for her work in biological weapons at a special "Science Day" celebration.[83] Taha condemned the weapons inspections process introduced by the UN in Iraq after the 1991 Gulf War and defended Iraqi scientists' right to refuse to cooperate. Despite her alleged involvement in illegal weapons development, she was not on the US list of 55 most wanted Iraqi officials.[84]

Saddam's repressive rule highlights the uncertain linkage between democratization and the advancement of women's rights. First, while enfranchisement is considered both a consequence of and a stimulus to greater democratization, it was in this period a by-product of authoritarianism. The regime was undeniably undemocratic, without an autonomous civil society that could advance women's interests. But some agency, however limited and minimal, was granted to women nonetheless. As has been discussed previously, women have found ways to advance political agency under such autocratic rule, even Islamist women progressing from within the context of *sharī'a*. To the extent that this created a measure of female empowerment, it represented the paradox of undemocratic regimes being at least formally "progressive" on women's issues. Kandiyoti has shown this to be a feature of authoritarian Middle Eastern regimes.[85]

Second, in the liberal concept of citizenship in most Western states, the unit of society is the individual citizen, not the family or any other collective; and the individual is the bearer of rights and responsibilities to the state.[86] Individual citizens have equal access and rights to a neutral state, which does not differentiate among its members based on race, gender, class, ethnicity or religion.[87] In the Middle East, however, citizenship is socially constructed differently from the Western notion because citizens are understood to be members of family units, religious sects, ethnic, tribal or other subnational groups.[88] Therefore, although women in Iraq during Saddam's regime gained the right to vote and stand for political office, the regime's singular control and reversion to patriarchal traditions encouraged social support for female subordination regardless of constitutional rights, even instilling a culture of violence against women.[89]

Third, democratization theory tends to privilege internal processes over exogenous and externally induced factors such as have been important in the Iraqi case. The most prominent of these external impediments are war and international sanctions. As we have shown, the wars with Iran and over Kuwait created a particularly bleak environment for two decades that worked—to put it mildly—to the disadvantage of citizen rights. Under conditions of severe economic hardship, military losses, territorial fragmentation and a complete lack of plurality in the political system, no progress toward democracy and/or the representativeness of women in the Iraq polity was possible.

Post-2003 Invasion: Strategies to Increase Iraqi Women's Political Representation

At the end of Saddam's regime, the GFIW remained the only legally recognized women's NGO in Iraq. Yet prior to the 2003 invasion, Iraqi women living in the diaspora had been organizing from afar for several years with the goal of raising international awareness about the human rights violations in Iraq.[90] Although official US discourse often justified war as a means of ending the regime's crimes against Iraqi women, the organizations of women in exile were divided in terms of support or opposition for the invasion.[91] While some saw it as a key opportunity to further the human rights agenda, others took a more skeptical view, citing American and British interests in Iraq's oil market as the West's primary motivators for war.[92] When the 2002 Iraqi opposition prewar conference was convened in London, only 5 of the 300 invited delegates were women; and just 3 women were named to the 65-member follow-up committee.[93]

Women in the Interim Government

Following the 2003 invasion and Saddam's fall, the US administration engaged in minimal efforts to formally mobilize women in Iraq's public policy-making processes as the country embarked upon an ostensible transition toward democracy. Much of the discourse employed by the intervening authorities—led by American diplomat L. Paul Bremer—centered primarily on Iraqi women's "empowerment," focusing on allowing them a role in rebuilding a "new Iraq."[94] In particular Paul Wolfowitz, an administrator with a central role in US policy-making regarding Iraq, was vocal about giving women "an equal role" and including more women "in Iraqi governing bodies and ministries."[95] Wolfowitz, along with the American NGO Women Waging Peace, brought several Iraqi women leaders to the United States for a workshop to support their involvement in post-conflict reconstruction and to increase the number of women in Parliament.[96]

Analysts Foust and Haring have criticized the focus of Western governments and NGOs on goals such as trying to increase the number of women in Parliaments, arguing that there are other useful measures for women's representation in politics, and Parliament is not one of them.[97] However, enhancing women's representation remains a central objective of many international democracy promotion efforts in the Arab world, and this was evident in Iraq after the 2003 invasion.[98] The impact of these efforts is more complex than it might appear, according to Lila Abu-Lughod's views on this notion. She challenges what she refers to as a Western "moral crusade to rescue oppressed Muslim women from their cultures and their religion that has swept the public sphere."[99] She notes that international, and especially United States, pressure on Muslim governments to improve on certain measures of gender equality could actually undermine the local legitimacy of the feminist cause.[100]

The Coalition Provision Authority (CPA) appointed Nasreen Barwari—a prominent Kurdish-Iraqi woman—as Minister of Public Affairs; Barwari, who had served in a ministry post prior to the invasion, was the only female minister selected among 25 ministries.[101] The CPA governed Iraq on an interim basis until July 2003 when it hand-picked the Iraqi Governing Council (IGC), a body 25 strong whose members were primarily selected from among affiliates of the Saddam opposition in exile.[102] No gender quota was implemented for IGC membership and the inclusion of women was therefore dependent solely upon the authority's willingness to appoint them.[103] Three women were selected to the IGC: Sondul Chapouk, a Turcoman and head of the Iraqi Women's Organization (IWO); Raja Habib al-Khuzaai, an MD and former member of the Iraq National Assembly; and Aqila al-Hashimi, who had served in Saddam's Ministry of Foreign Affairs. Al-Hashimi (who had a PhD in French literature from the Sorbonne) had been a diplomat and French translator to former deputy prime minister Tariq Aziz and ran the Oil-for-Food program in the Foreign Ministry. Although she was an active member of the Ba'ath Party and close associate of former foreign minister Naji Sabri (who in turn had close ties to Qusay Saddam), al-Hashimi switched allegiance after Saddam's fall in order to stand for and become elected to office.[104] Her role in the IGC has been described as "puppet minister."[105] Insurgents assassinated al-Hashimi in September 2003.[106] Salama al-Khufaji, a professor of dentistry at Baghdad University, replaced al-Hashimi on the IGC. The female IGC members later became subject to criticism from some Iraqi women leaders, who pointed to their lack of experience in the political arena.[107]

In 2004, the IGC was replaced by the Iraqi Interim Government (IIG), which included five female ministers and six female deputy ministers out of 31 total ministers/deputy ministers.[108] The female ministers were as follows:[109]

- Sawsan al-Sharifi, Minister of Agriculture
- Pascale Isho Warda, Minister of Displacement and Migration
- Mishkat Moumin, Minister of Environment
- Layla Abd al-Latif al-Tamimi, Minister of Labour and Social Affairs
- Nasreen Barwari, Minister of Public Works
- Narmin Othman, Minister of State for Women

The female ministers in the IIG appeared at least on the surface to be highly qualified for their ministerial roles. Sharifi holds a doctorate in animal breeding and was editor of the *Iraqi Journal of Agriculture*. Warda was president of the

Assyrian Women's Union in Baghdad and cofounded the Iraqi Society for Human Rights. Moumin was a law professor at Baghdad University, where she lectured on human rights, fundamental rights, international and constitutional law as well as being speaker and facilitator at several conferences on women's issues in Iraq. Tamimi was an engineer; Barwari studied government at Harvard University and was formerly the Minister of Reconstruction and Development for Kurdistan. Othman was formerly the Minister of Social Affairs in Kurdistan and had been a member of the peshmerga (Kurdish militia). However, the ministries awarded to women were relatively low-profile in comparison to the six most important and influential ministerial posts. The powerful Ministries of Defence, Foreign Affairs, Oil, Interior, Finance and Justice in the interim government were all headed by men.[110]

Female Representation in Iraqi Parliament Post-occupation, 2005–14

As discussed in Chapter 3, the proliferation of gender quota provisions in countries around the world has built new routes by which women may strive toward achieving a more equal balance of political representation.[111] The expansion of gender quota systems in the past 20 years has attracted a sizeable number of scholars to begin conducting empirical research on the relative successes and failures of those provisions. This section presents the electoral results for Iraqi women in the four parliamentary elections since 2004, with the quota in effect—that is, the results of descriptive representation.

January 2005 Transitional Elections

The IIG announced in November 2004 that elections would be held on January 30, 2005 for 275 seats in the Transitional National Assembly. The electoral system originally adopted in 2004 met the gender quota by requiring that at least one-third of the candidates on each party list were to be women (no fewer than one in the first three, no fewer than two out of six and so on). Following this announcement, an influential group of Sunni clerics, the Association of Muslim Scholars, publicly called for an election boycott, in protest of continued American presence and influence. Many voters were intimidated by the continued insurgency, concentrated predominantly in Sunni regions, which prevented them from going to the polls.

An overall turnout of approximately 58 percent of eligible voters was predicted for these elections. The leading political forces in the January 2005 election were the Iraqiya List led by interim Prime Minister Iyad Allawi; Abdul Aziz al-Hakim's United Iraqi Alliance; and the Democratic Patriotic Alliance of Kurdistan, which posted candidates both for the national election and for the Kurdish regional elections that took place the same day. Consistent with the "de-Ba'athification" regulations, army officials, militia members and former representatives of Saddam's Ba'ath Party were prohibited from running for election. More than 8.5 million voters turned out within Iraq and an additional 93,000 Iraqis cast ballots overseas. Final official voter turnout was reported at 53.3 percent of registered voters.[112] Turnout may have been reduced by the Sunni boycott, threats of attacks on polling stations, and the fighting still ongoing in some regions of Iraq. On Election Day, 16 attacks on polling centers were reported, in which at least 37 people died.[113] As expected, active participation in voting occurred primarily in Shi'a and Kurdish regions.[114]

Final results gave 140 seats to the United Iraqi Alliance to secure a majority in the transitional Parliament. The Democratic Patriotic Alliance of Kurdistan (DPAK) was second with 75 seats, followed by the Iraqiya List with 40. A total of 87 women were elected for a total greater than the minimum 25 percent requirement posed by the quota—31.5 percent female representation.[115]

December 2005:—First Elections Under the New Constitution

January 30, 2005 saw the first elections for the National Assembly of Iraq under the new constitution. This National Assembly, consisting of 275 members, was a Parliament created during the American occupation of Iraq under the Transitional Aministrational Law. As many as 6,655 candidates, 228 parties and 21 coalitions registered to stand for these elections.[116] Voters were asked to choose between these coalitions, and attempts were made to compensate for disproportionate voter turnout between the different regions and ethnic groups. Seats were allocated based on a formula that considered the number of voters in each governorate and their respective voter turnouts to provide compensatory seats to lists where the number of seats won did not reflect the total share of the national vote.[117] This proportional representation system gave more weight to Sunni voters who constituted the majority in several provinces and who had largely boycotted the transitional elections.[118]

The United Iraqi Alliance (a coalition of six Shi'a Islamic parties), supported by Grand Ayatollah Ali al-Sistani, led the field with approximately 48 percent of the vote. The DPAK was in second place with 26 percent. Tawafuq (the Iraqi Accord Front), the Hewar (Dialogue) National Iraqi Front representing the Sunnis and the DPAK won 128, 55 and 53 parliamentary seats, respectively. Prime Minister Ayad Allawi's party, the Iraqi List, came third with 14 percent winning 25 seats.[119] Overall, 12 parties received sufficient votes required to win a seat in the assembly.

Voter turnout was high: more than 12 million ballots were cast representing 79.63 percent of some 15.6 million registered voters, including nearly 300,000 votes received from Iraqis living outside the country. Despite continued insurgency and protest during the campaign, the actual voting day was predominantly free from large-scale attacks, with only a few minor bombings and mortar attacks plaguing voters.[120]

Article 30(c) of the Transitional Administration Law (interim constitution) adopted in March 2004 stated that "the electoral law shall aim to achieve the goal of having women constitute no less than one-quarter of the members of the National Assembly." Furthermore, Article 4(3), which the CPA adopted in July 2004, also stated that "at least one woman must be among the first three nominees on the list and at least two women must be among the first six nominees on the list and so on until the end of the list." Included in Article 11 of the Iraqi Elections Law (relating to parliamentary elections), which the National Assembly adopted in September 2005, is a gender quota identical to that found in Article 4(3) of the CPA Order 96 mentioned above. Following the establishment of a permanent constitution in October 2005, Article 49 (fourth) was adopted in the constitution to incorporate the same objectives regarding female political representation as was included in the interim constitution: that at least 25 percent of the Council of Representatives (CoR; the name of the new legislative body) be women. In December 2005, this CoR was elected under the new legal framework, replacing the transitional National Assembly while still operating under the same gender quota system.[121]

The Hare quota (simple quota) was used to select the female members of the National Assembly from 196 candidate lists to ensure proportional representation. This quota is essentially a formula utilized in some Single Transferable Vote (STV) systems, and it is the largest remaining method of party-list proportional representation. In such systems, the quota describes the minimum number of votes required for a candidate or party to win a seat in Parliament. A total of 70 women (see Table 4.1) were elected in 2005 for a total parliamentary representation of 25.45 percent. The proportional list system for implementing the gender quota resulted in a relatively equal split among the female parliamentarians as represented by party divisions. A total of 43

Table 4.1 Numbers of women elected to Iraqi Parliament by governorate, December 2005 elections

Name of Governorate	Number of Seats	Number of Women
Al-Anbar	9	2
Babil	11	3
Baghdad	59	7
Basra	16	4
Dohuk	7	2
Diyala	10	1
Irbil	13	4
Karbala	6	1
Kirkuk	9	1
Missan	7	2
Al-Muthanna	5	2
Al-Najaf	8	2
Ninawa	19	3
Al-Qadisiyah	8	2
Salah El-Din	8	1
Sulaimaniya	15	4
Thi Qar	12	3
Wasit	8	2
Compensatory Seats	45	14
Total	**275**	**70**

(61.4 percent) of the female MPs elected were members of the United Iraqi Alliance (Shi'a Muslim); 13 (18.6 percent) were members of Tawafuq or Hewar (Sunni Muslim) and 10 (14.3 percent) were members of DPAK (Kurdish). Three women were members of the Iraqi National List, and the final seat under the quota went to a female independent.[122]

By adopting a new constitution in October 2005, Iraq joined a growing list of nations that placed high value on ensuring that women were adequately represented in political office by mandating that at least 25 percent of legislative seats must be held by women. Valuing women leaders as important players in shaping the new Iraq was clearly a significant step taken at a critical time, with important consequences regarding the public policy agenda, the voicing of women's interests, good governance and the maintenance of democratic legitimacy. Mechanisms for ensuring that females are adequately represented in governing bodies are embedded within Iraq's parliamentary and provincial election laws, as well as within its current electoral system.

2010 Elections

The parliamentary election scheduled for March 7, 2010 was an important milestone in the progress of Iraq's political system. In 2009, the Presidential Council called for an increase of the number of members to 325. The 2010 elections were originally set for January but postponed while revisions to the electoral law were debated. The revised electoral law maintained the 25 percent quota for women. However, the provision was amended from a proportional to an open list system, meaning that for each winning list the candidates with the highest number of votes would be elected rather than the candidates listed first. Ensuring that each third candidate on a list was female did not necessarily ensure that one-third of those elected would be women; a corrective mechanism would be applied only if fewer than 25 percent of elected candidates were female.[123] The complex mathematical formula for assigning seats to women under the quota was difficult to understand even for the political parties and their candidates. Table 4.2 presents the 2010 election results for women.

More than 6,500 candidates representing 86 parties vied for parliamentary seats in 2010. It was reported that the Iraqi Independent High Electoral Commission (IHEC) rejected nearly 500 candidates due to ostensible ties to the dissolved Ba'ath Party.[124] Security issues formed the platform for most candidates as violent insurgencies continued to escalate. Early voting held the Thursday before Election Day was afflicted by a string of rocket attacks and suicide bombings that killed at least 17 people.[125] To help ensure voter security, all vehicles except those piloted by security forces were banned on Election Day.[126] Further security measures included the IHEC setting up 50,000 polling stations each of which served just 420 voters, to ensure that voters could find a station near their homes and so polling stations would not be overwhelmed by large numbers of voters. Extremist groups including al-Qaeda issued numerous threats to disrupt elections. Nonetheless, 62.4 percent of the 18.9 million eligible registered voters turned out; despite enhanced security measures, multiple blasts killed approximately 40 people as they attempted to vote.[127]

Female candidates representing one party, the militant Islamist Sadrist Movement (part of al-Hakim's Iraqi National Alliance) headed by Shi'a Muslim cleric Muqtada al-Sadr, fared much better at the polls than did women on other party lists. Five of the female candidates affiliated with the Sadrist Movement succeeded in winning their seats outside of the quota, an accomplishment that was not achieved by any competing party in 2010. The Sadrists were quite successful in promoting female candidates on Internet message boards and via

Table 4.2 Numbers of women elected to Iraqi Parliament by governorate, 2010 elections

Name of Governorate	Number of Seats	Number of Women
Al-Anbar	29	7
Babil	30	8
Baghdad	57	16
Basra	35	7
Dohuk		
Diyala	29	8
Erbil		
Karbala	27	8
Kirkuk		
Missan	27	7
Al-Muthanna	26	4
Al-Najaf	28	7
Ninawa	37	11
Al-Qadisiyah	28	6
Salah El-Din		
Sulaimaniya		
Thi Qar	31	8
Wasit	28	9
Compensatory Seats		
Total	**392**	**98**

instructions allegedly passed along to voters from Sadr himself.[128] The 2010 election results gave 91 seats to former interim prime minister Ayad Allawi's Iraqi National Movement (INM), just two more than the 89 won by Maliki's State of Law Coalition. The Iraqi National Alliance won 70 and the Kurdish Alliance 43. Just 82 women (25.23 percent) were elected in 2010, the minimum number required by the quota.[129] Fairly consistent with the Iraqi population, 92.6 percent of the female MPs elected in 2010 were Muslim and 49.5 percent were Shi'a Muslim.[130] Most of the women elected were educated with a bachelor's degree or higher and many held MDs or PhDs.[131]

The 2010 parliamentary elections were held on the eve of March 8, International Women's Day, whose theme in that year was "Equal Rights, Equal Opportunities." The closeness of these two events made it a valuable opportunity to harbor discussions regarding gender issues. Despite the continuous violence in Iraq, in January 2010 the American National Democratic Institute (NDI) orientated intensive skills-building workshops for female MPs designed to maximize their impact in the CoR by enhancing their skills in public communication, identifying the main issues of concern for Iraqi women and brainstorming potential policy recommendations. In addition, the institute collaborated with existing female branches of political parties to better connect them with party leadership, provincial party branches and party blocs within the CoR.[132]

2014 Elections

The Iraqi local and regional elections held on April 30, 2014 were the first since withdrawal of US troops from Iraq in 2011, and the first since the 2003 invasion to be run entirely by Iraqis themselves without international intervention. Overall, 100 political groups and 9,200 candidates competed for the 328 CoR seats. Eight seats were reserved for Iraq's minority groups. The presence of the female quota resulted in 82 female representatives (25 percent) elected into Parliament. In these elections, 2,500 female candidates were officially listed to compete for parliamentary seats by IHEC, successfully meeting the 25 percent quota. In the case where the 25 percent quota was not met, a specific compensatory mechanism would have been enacted. Each government was tasked to decide the number of women to be included in the final list of elected candidates, including those who gained majority votes but still fell short of winning a seat.[133] For example, Iraq's Kurdistan region mandates that no less 30 percent of its total members be women, and so the candidates' lists must be arranged accordingly to meet this requirement.[134]

The 2014 elections were fraught with even more turbulence and violence than experienced in prior election years. In response to threats or violence against Iraqi female candidates, some women refused to allow their pictures to be displayed publicly, instead electing to use a picture of a husband, father or brother on their electoral posters.[135] Assigning a new Speaker was perceived to be a first step in forming—according to lawmakers—a government able to defeat the militant uprising. Delegates elected Salim al-Jabouri, a moderate Sunni, as Speaker. A Shi'a and a Kurd were selected to fill the two Deputy Speaker positions in attempts to establish ethnosectarian leadership balance.[136] Al-Jabouri gained 198 votes of 328 members, Shrouq al-Abaaji, a female MP, gained 19 votes, and 60 members abstained.[137] The development came as Iraq's army launched a fresh offensive to retake the town of Dhuluiya, about 43 miles north of Baghdad, two days after Sunni Islamist insurgents, who had carved off large segments of the country, seized it.[138]

The security crisis was also exacerbated by a deadlock over forming a new government. The negotiations snagged over Shi'a Prime Minister Nouri al-Maliki's bid to stay in power despite pressure to step aside from political leaders in Iraq—even some from within his own Shi'a sect—as well as foreign diplomats and religious leaders.[139] Maliki's government had come under substantial fire during the 18 months prior to the elections due to its widespread repression, marginalization and even executions of Sunnis and Kurds, which fuelled the burgeoning sectarian strife.[140] The perceived failures of political leadership in Iraq led the World Bank to list the country as having one of the worst governance qualities in the world,[141] and Transparency International to list it in the top sixteenth percentile of most corrupt countries globally.[142] According to the United Nations, insurgents in 2013 killed more than 8,800 Iraqis (including 7,800 civilians), the highest number of casualties in five years.[143] While opposition parties blamed Maliki for the insecurity, the prime minister blamed external factors such as the conflict in Syria.[144]

Approximately 50 percent of the Iraqi population voted in April 2014, and 40 percent of voters were women. The electoral law had been amended again slightly in 2013 to abolish the national compensatory seats and move to a modified Saint-Lagüe method (highest quotient method for allocating seats in party-list proportional representation, used in many voting systems). This change was expected to increase the chances of smaller political parties winning representation. However, election results did little to assuage the widespread lack of faith in the existing government. Maliki's State of Law Coalition took 95 of the 328 parliamentary seats at stake (increased from 325 available in 2010) and two other large Shi'a blocs (the Sadrist Movement and Hakim's Citizens' Coalition) won a total of 65; in total Shi'a parties took 170 seats in the Assembly.[145] Kurdish parties achieved 62 seats while Sunnis took 38. Charges of corruption and kleptocracy were leveled at the government and the electoral process from several quarters, both within Iraq and around the world.[146]

During the campaign leading up to the 2014 elections, UN Women and the Iraq Foundation collaborated in an effort to train potential women candidates in various aspects of the campaign process.[147] More than 300 women from five governorates were trained in such skills as putting together a campaign, talking with the press, public speaking, parliamentary process and self-management.[148] UN Women—whose Iraq representative at the time was Frances Guy, former member of the British Diplomatic Service—maintained a presence in Iraq to mentor and coach the elected female parliamentarians as needed in effective governance, policy-making and public presence. A total of 83 women were elected to Parliament in 2014, for 25.3 percent representation.

Analysis of Descriptive Representation

Since the mid-1990s, across the world, quota legislation has fostered a breakthrough pattern in women's representation. Upon adopting quotas for women in national Parliaments, more than 20 countries have made a historic leap. These countries have seen exceptional spikes in women's representation with an average increase of 16 percent in women's presence in Parliaments from one or two elections to the next.[149] The Iraqi CoR in 2016 was composed of 25.5 percent females, compared to 16.8 percent women in the US House of Representatives. Statistics gathered by the Inter-Parliamentary Union highlight that Iraqi levels of female representation exceed the world average of 19.1 percent, and exceed those found in any of its neighboring countries.

The dramatic change in women's parliamentary representation in Iraq happened over one election cycle—from 2000 to 2005. According to Isobel Coleman, "in the run-up to the January 2005 elections, political parties were required to field electoral slates on which every third candidate was a woman."[150] As a result, 87 women won seats in the interim national assembly, making up 31 percent of the total.[151] Through the transition phase from the Transitional National Assembly (January 2005) to the CoR (December 2005), the percentage of women parliamentarians dropped slightly to 25 percent.[152] Thus, over one election cycle women made a gain of 18 percent in Iraq's Parliament. Based on this sudden gain, Paxton and Hughes classify Iraq as falling into the "big jump pattern" of representation.[153]

Iraq's changes in development, religiosity, democratization and conflict have affected beliefs in women's ability to govern. The level of societal development in Iraq is strongly linked to gender equality values, including support for women's political leadership.[154] Norris and Inglehart conclude, "Egalitarian attitudes toward women in office are more widespread in post-industrial societies, reflecting broad patterns of socioeconomic development and cultural modernization."[155] Societal modernization, particularly forms that improve equality of opportunity in human capabilities, erodes conditions and traditional authority structures that perpetuate women's public exclusion.[156] As a major consequence, there is growth in public support for women's political involvement and leadership. Thus, in less developed democracies, with agrarian and industrial economies, the level of societal development creates a cultural barrier to the development of gender egalitarian orientations and the practice of gender equality. The belief in women's ability to govern and gender equality in women's recruitment and presence in national Parliaments are among these views and practices.[157]

Alexander and Welzel argue that increases in the level of a country's development bring about these positive changes in attitudes toward gender equality by improving individuals' cognitive and material resources.[158] This improves individuals' autonomy and increases support for equality and diversity.[159] Hence, resources and values are key individual-level mechanisms through which gains in societal levels of development improve support for female leaders.[160]

Another issue in Iraq is religion and sectarianism, which are primary agents of gender role socialization.[161] Religious organizations from all faiths support traditional and subordinate roles for women.[162] Cross-national studies link religious beliefs to fewer women in Parliaments.[163] Unlike societal development, religious belief is not a country-level measure because it is assessed at an individual, rather than a collective, level.[164] The effects of religiosity are relevant to descriptive representation inasmuch as religion is politicized in a country and religious sects and organizations gain political roles and influence. Iraq did indeed institutionalize Islam into its political structure in the 2005 Constitution, and some effects of religiosity can be seen in the election results since then. The Shi'a Islamist parties initially sought to guarantee their own dominance in the emerging polity and thereby reverse their historic marginalization in Iraq's nation-building.[165] This motivation inspired the De-Ba'athification Laws and led to the drafting of a constitution designed to reshape the identity of the new Iraq to reflect the Shi'i majority status by promoting Islamic ideology through the legislative process.[166] Shi'i religious parties strongly opposed the quota, ostensibly due to concern that they would be unable to nominate a sufficient number of female candidates.[167] Although Islam does not necessarily contradict political rights for women,[168] various interpretations of Islam are invoked to justify domestic violence and to prevent women from travelling without a male escort, for example.[169] In Iraq's 2010 elections, religiosity played an important role as the Accountability and Justice Commission decided to disqualify 500 candidates—most of whom were Sunni or secular—on grounds that they had ties to the Ba'ath Party.[170] This action enraged Sunnis who viewed the act as further effort to exclude them from Iraqi politics.[171] These illustrations underscore the fact that the United States, in pursuit of its own strategic interests, accommodated and augmented the power of Iraqi religio-political actors whose ideologies construct gender relations in ways that reinforce their own authority.[172] The consequence at least, if not the objective, of the invasion thus was not to reform gender relations in Iraq but rather "to construct a war story that ... camouflaged the realities of war for women."[173]

The effects of war have been particularly striking. There is some evidence in general that civil conflict politicizes women and mobilizes them to support more women in positions of political leadership.[174] Specific research investigating Iraq from 2004 to 2006 noted that conflict played a significant role in mobilizing women's groups in support of the quota policy that led to the change in Iraq.[175] This research focused on the role of women's organizations in mobilizing the policy adoption; however, it falls short of analyzing whether this was directly related to increased support of women's ability to govern in the general population. Scholars such as Inglehart, Moaddel and Tessler assert that markedly high levels of xenophobia and discriminatory attitudes are associated with extraordinarily high levels of existential insecurity.[176] Working with Iraqi public opinion data from the World Values Surveys, Inglehart et al. note that Iraq has the highest level of xenophobia found in any of the 85 societies for which data were available. These data are used to confirm a consequent strong tendency to reject out-groups including women.[177] These perspectives on the conflict in Iraq and how it has influenced support for women's ability to govern, therefore, are plausible and supported by convincing evidence. However, other evidence suggests that Iraq is unique due to multiple cultural and societal factors. Hughes's theoretical framework applies to the case of Iraq: she sees conflict as leading to positive outcomes for female leadership when (1) conflict is transformative of the political structure and exposes individuals to alternative, less traditional models of leadership; (2) conflict increases individuals' links to supportive international organizations; and (3) conflict confronts traditional gender roles in a way that is broadly transformative of female inclusion across various public roles.[178]

However, women's descriptive representation in Iraqi politics, comparatively analyzed across time since they gained suffrage in 1980, affirms the view that any national gains made during wartime rarely extend post-conflict. The United Nation Development's Gender Inequality and Human Development Program indicates that Iraq has a significantly higher level of gender inequality and lower level of human development than other countries. Furthermore, it could be argued that Iraq as a modern nation-state has made few political, economic, cultural or societal gains—and has in fact sustained significant losses—since the 1980 invasion of Iran. Although in places like Europe and North America, war and the shortage of manpower it engenders often serve to empower women and improve their life stations, the Iraq situation has been mixed. While labor participation increased in the short-term, widows and abandoned women have, in the long-term, been thrown further into poverty, become displaced and found it difficult to return to their former homes in the absence of men to support them and fight for their lands. Formal peace negotiations between conflicting powers define basic power relations in emerging reconstructed states and set priorities for political activity. Yet there has been little or no peace in Iraq since the Iran-Iraq war as the sanctions era following Iraqi's invasion of Kuwait in 1990 was marked by similar deprivations and security challenges to those encountered during wartime, and there has been no real cessation of internal warfare since the 2003 US occupation. The fact that only a relatively small number of Iraqi women have found the ability to express their political wishes and dissent since 2003 may be less a result of Iraq's lack of democratization than it is due to the persistent threats to personal security. Decades of war and sanctions have ripped apart the fabric of Iraqi society, bolstering traditional structures that shelter women from widespread crime and corruption and reinforce the prejudicial norms that prevent them from freely and actively participating in public life.

The symbolic effects created by the presence of female MPs as role models in Parliament represent, nevertheless, a key mode of gender socialization. According to Bussey and Bandura, "A great deal of gender-linked behavior is exemplified by models in one's immediate environment such as parents and peers, and significant persons in social, educational and occupational contexts."[179] Male and female role models send powerful signals on what is possible given one's gender. Depending on the gender equality or inequality in modeled behaviors, individuals develop weaker or stronger sex-typed expectations that govern their perceptions of their ability to perform those behaviors. The sheer lack of role models perpetuates a vicious, supportive exchange between sexist beliefs and inequality that maintains or even strengthens the discouragement of one of the genders from participation.[180]

Summary

An authoritative behavior that has operated to the exclusion of women in Iraq is governing. For this reason, women and politics scholars focus their attention on the importance of increasing female role models in political leadership.[181]

An increase in the sheer number of female representatives—descriptive representation—can create "a social meaning of 'ability to rule' for members of a group in historical contexts where that ability has been seriously questioned."[182] This sort of inclusion is necessary for reversing previous histories of exclusion and assumptions that certain people are less suited to govern than others—a notion supported here.[183] Indeed, the literature agrees that women's historical exclusion from positions of political representation and their continuing underrepresentation make them and their male counterparts, in all parts of the world, susceptible to the belief in women's inferiority in governing.[184]

The level of descriptive representation women have gained in Iraq does suggest an important first step. Even the impartial institutionalization of political liberties and civil rights establishes norms that support human autonomy and tolerance of social diversity. This, in turn, is likely to create a political climate conducive to egalitarian gender attitudes and women's formal representation. This first step is consistent with many cross-national studies in the literature highlighting the linkage between women's representation and the level of democracy.[185]

Indeed, global theoretical discourses on women in politics in recent years have come to emphasize the need for women's full participation in development and democratization processes.[186] Underrepresentation of women in a country's polity is viewed as a product of those mechanisms that exclude women from political institutions and prevent them from obtaining an equal share of political positions.[187] The theory of the "politics of presence"[188] suggests a link between descriptive and substantive representation.[189] Analysis and discussion should investigate the extent to which the descriptive representation gained via the gender quota has helped or hindered the ability of Iraqi women to achieve a real political voice. Further analysis is needed to illuminate the successes and failures of the female political agents elected post-2003 as they have striven to become influential policy-makers. Has the quota enhanced women's advancement in Iraqi politics? Or has it hindered them by creating a perception that they are mere figureheads, rather than viable politicians and agents of change? That discussion is undertaken in Chapter 6, where substantive representation for women since the implementation of the quota is analyzed. But, first, Chapter 5 presents the case studies compiled for this research, delineating the demographic characteristics, political contributions and experiences of 12 Iraqi female parliamentarians.

5

Case Studies: Twelve Iraqi Female Members of Parliament since 2005

Characterizing the level of female representation achieved in the Iraqi Parliament post-2003 requires an analysis of the lives of these female parliamentarians prior to being elected, their educational, religious and ethnic backgrounds, family life, how they came to enter politics, the reasons behind their intention to stand for office and any affiliations they have with male political counterparts. This chapter, which presents details regarding the selected MPs, representing a variety of blocs and ethnic backgrounds, provides an insight into the past lives, experiences and outlooks of these female politicians, and how they have developed their political voices. This chapter documents the histories of a selected, but varied, number of women elected to the Iraqi Parliament post-2003.

Sources documenting the histories and experiences of Iraqi women in politics are limited. However, this chapter compiles some of the available interviews and media statements regarding the following 12 Iraqi female politicians (listed alphabetically): Noura al-Bajari, Etab al-Douri, Hanan al-Fatlawi, Ashwaq al-Jaf, Karima al-Jawari, Huda Sajjad Mahmoud, Jinan Mubarak, Suhad al-Obaidi, Mariam al-Rayyis, Safia al-Suhail, Alaa' al-Talabani and Majida al-Tamimi.

Sources of Evidence

During the month-long religious observance of Ramadan in 2012 and 2013, the Iraqi television channels *al-Baghdadia* and *al-Iraqiya* aired interviews with ten female members of the Iraqi Parliament. These interviews were extracted from among a larger group of broadcasts featuring ministers, MPs, tribal leaders and other prominent figures in Iraqi politics. The interviews appeared on regularly scheduled news television programs, were conducted live and were aired both within Iraq and internationally.[1]

To illustrate the position of these media outlets in Iraqi society post-2003, a brief description of their history is merited. Under Saddam's regime, like all of civil society, the Iraqi media were heavily censored and controlled.[2] Immediately following the March 2003 invasion, the state-run Iraqi television stations abruptly went off the air and both the Iraqi Security Services and the Ministry of Information were abolished.[3] Soon thereafter, the US Coalitional Provisional Authority (CPA) leveraged the infrastructure of Saddam's existing media network and allocated $108.2 million paid to US contractors to establish the Iraqi Media Network (IMN). The IMN comprised the 24-hour *al-Iraqiya* news television channel, *al-Sabah* newspaper and the *Radio Sawa* radio station.[4] Loosely modeled after the United Kingdom's British Broadcasting Corporation (BBC) and the United States' Public Broadcasting Service (PBS), the IMN was said to have promised Iraqis "comprehensive, accurate, fair, and balanced news," and to instill a "code of ethics" among Iraqi journalists.[5] In July 2004, an oversight body was put in place and charged with establishing rules and editorial standards for television and radio program content in post-Saddam Iraq—the Iraqi National Communications and Media Commission (INCMC). However, US backing meant *al-Iraqiya* TV, regarded as the voice of the occupying forces, struggled at first to gain credibility.[6] To exacerbate this perceived lack of credibility, the IMN came under scrutiny in late 2005 when reports surfaced that the Pentagon was secretly feeding pro-US news stories to the network for publication.[7] Over time, the IMN has generally come to be considered a mouthpiece for the government, and therefore its primary audience is likely to be Shi'a Muslims.[8] Today *al-Iraqiya* TV is accessible to 93 percent of the Iraqi populace and watched by about 40 percent.[9]

Al-Baghdadia TV is a satellite news TV channel founded in 2005, based in Cairo but privately owned by Iraqi businessman and engineer Dr. Awn Hussain al-Kashlok. *Al-Baghdadia* is often considered a secular/moderate Sunni channel and indeed was established for the purpose of representing a secular voice in opposition to the al-Maliki government.[10] The channel gained an early reputation for opposing the occupying forces, and it was a correspondent from *al-Baghdadia* TV who famously threw his shoes at then-US President George W. Bush during a 2009 Baghdad press conference.[11] Controversial programs on *al-Baghdadia* TV that aired complaints from Iraqis interviewed on the streets led the INCMC to revoke the channel's license and order its Iraq-based offices to be closed in 2010, an action believed by many to have been spearheaded by Maliki.[12] Although the channel touts itself as "a professional independent channel that adheres to the national identity of Iraq as an inclusive and common component of the diversity of Iraq,"[13] the actual independence of *al-Baghdadia* TV may be debatable due to its private ownership by an educated urban businessman, and the fact that despite al-Kashlok's vision to make *al-Baghdadia* TV a model of the free media, there remains a strong likelihood that it is a primarily educated urban audience to which the channel appeals.[14]

One group of televised interviews included in this book—those representing MP Safia al-Suhail—was drawn from the television station *al-Fayhaa*. *Al-Fayhaa* TV, an independent Arabic satellite station owned by Mohammed al-Tay is based in Sulaymaniyah in Kurdistan province; it was founded in 2004 and is known for broadcasting news and cultural programming appealing to a Shi'a Muslim audience.[15] Further, in addition to the televised programs, a presentation published online via the video sharing website YouTube was gathered and transcribed representing one further female political figure who has achieved prominence in Iraq's government since 2003. Dr. Hanan al-Fatlawi, former advisor to Prime Minister al-Maliki, former chairwoman of the parliamentary Development Committee and current MP, presented at a conference held on April 19, 2013 at Boston University titled "Iraq +10: Looking Forward," centering on the future of Iraqi politics; the conference was sponsored by the Institute for Iraqi Studies on the occasion of the tenth anniversary of the invasion.[16] Fatlawi's presentation focused on the workings of the Iraqi Parliament since the 2005 Constitution, and related information also was gathered from the question-and-answer session held directly after the talk.

Selection of the Case Studies

The interviews collected from these television and online channels form one piece of developing a comprehensive picture to characterize the experience of Iraq's female politicians since 2003. The 12 women highlighted as case studies were selected because they represent different political affiliations, religious backgrounds and demographics to allow for comparative analysis regarding their parliamentary experiences. The televised interviews provide partial information describing first-hand the experience of Iraqi MPs with Iraq's evolving parliamentary system in their attempt to become politically mobile and influential. In addition to the recorded interviews, substantial secondary research was conducted to gather print and digital news articles mentioning and/or quoting the MPs of interest. To address the concept of descriptive representation, information was collected and analyzed regarding how the female MPs chose their political paths and their ties (if any) to influential male politicians, tribal and religious leaders. To examine substantive representation, attention was given to specific policies the MPs have promoted and how many of those have passed into law; the level at which these women have felt liberated and empowered by their political roles, contrasted with the extent of marginalization they experience in Parliament; and challenges the female MPs face in Parliament and how those compare to the challenges encountered by their male counterparts. To characterize levels of symbolic representation, information was collected regarding support for and barriers to their campaigns and election as well as the influence of religious ideologies, cultural norms and the media on how the women are perceived, identified and approached as political forces.

Potential Limitations of Secondary Data

The case studies and analyses presented here are founded upon data collected from secondary sources, rather than obtained via direct interviews with the female MPs. It is acknowledged that this approach may have potential limitations. The women who gave televised interviews during the data collection period do not represent every region of Iraq or every sociopolitical and demographic background found therein. Therefore, the results are not necessarily representative of all women present in Iraq, nor can they be generalized to all female politicians in the country. Further, it is possible that the women interviewed by the television stations were not entirely open in sharing their thoughts and perspectives for a variety of reasons. These reasons may have included male domination, security risks, religious/sectarian allegiance or ideological persuasions. At the time of data collection and writing, gaining access to the Baghdad Green Zone was virtually impossible for an ordinary Iraqi citizen, and attempts to gain consent and willingness to undergo direct interviews with the target MPs were unsuccessful. It is the author's belief that lack of security and the tenuous position of women in Iraqi politics was the primary reason for the inability to conduct primary data collection.

The following sections summarize the case studies that emerged out of data analysis from the televised and online interviews, print and digital news media sources, and in-person interviews. Table 5.1 provides a comparative look at their key features.

Table 5.1 Key features and characteristics of the case study MPs

Case Study	Born	Marital Status	Education	Religious Affiliation	Occupation	Children	Party Affiliation	Parliamentary Committee(s)
Bajari, Noura al-	1966 Mosul	Married	High school	Sunni Muslim	Clothing factory manager	6 (1 deceased)	al-Hal Bloc, al-Iraqiya Alliance	Economy and Investment
Douri, Etab al-	1969 Baghdad	Married	PhD	Sunni Muslim	Professor	3	al-Hal Bloc, al-Iraqiya Alliance	Health and Environment
Fatlawi, Hanan al-	1968 Babil	Divorced	MD	Shia Muslim	Dermatologist	None	State of Law Coalition	Members Affairs and Development
Jaf, Ashwaq al-	1973 Sulaymaniyyah	Married	PhD	Sufi Muslim	Pharmacist	1	Kurdish Democratic Party	Human Rights
Jawari, Karima al-	Balad, Salah al-Din	Married	Bachelor's	Sunni Muslim	Lawyer	2	al-Hurra Bloc, al-Iraqiya Alliance	Committee for the Displaced
Mahmoud, Huda Sajjad	1978 Diywaniyyah	Married	Bachelor's	Shia Muslim	Chemistry Teacher	3	Da'wa Party, State of Law Coalition	Women, Families and Children
Mubarak, Jinan	1961 Baghdad	Married	Bachelor's	Secular	NGO Director	1	Jinan Mubarak Party	None
Obaidi, Suhad al-	1974 Balad, Salah al-Din	Married	Bachelor's	Sunni Muslim	Municipal Engineer	5	Al-Hal Bloc, al-Iraqiya Alliance	Public Services & Reconstruction; Federations
Rayyis, Mariam al-	1972	Married	Bachelor's	Shia Muslim	Lawyer	None	State of Law Coalition	Media Relations
Suhail, Safia al-	1965 Basra	Married	Bachelor's	Secular	Ambassador	1	Iraqi National List	Foreign Relations
Talabani, Alaa' al-	1966 Baghdad	Married	Master's	Sufi Muslim	Trainer/Lecturer	2	Kurdish National Alliance	International Affairs

Case Studies

Noura al-Bajari

Noura al-Bajari was born in 1966 in Mosul, also the city in which she grew up. She graduated from high school in 1988. At age 22, she became engaged to her cousin, Abu Akram, born in 1963. Akram reports that he, rather than his family, chose Bajari as his wife and that they had loved each other for five years prior to becoming engaged. The couple was married in 1991 after a two-year engagement. In her 2012 interview with *al-Baghdadia* TV, Bajari described her husband as coming from a well-known Mosul family that owns oil tanks and automobiles. Bajari's father was a political prisoner under Saddam's regime, a fact she and her family are proud of. Akram was a US prisoner of war for six months during the occupation.

Bajari has borne six children (four boys and two girls), five of whom are living: Karam born 1992, Asalah born 1994, Abd al-Rahman born 1998, Mustafa born 2000 and Zayn al-Abidin born 2002. She has had several years of work experience in the manufacturing sector. She began as a secretary to the production manager in a clothing factory and progressed to being the head of the ironing department. Bajari went on to gain more than 11 years of experience as a store manager. She also worked as a member of the Mosul governing City Council, which helped pave the way for her entry into the political sphere.

A friend of Bajari's husband, a lieutenant colonel in the Iraqi army, first suggested that she consider standing for election to the Provincial Councils due to her social connections and eloquence. Bajari was the first woman to stand for Parliament as a member of the Iraqiya List in December 2005. She reports receiving 3,156 votes in that election and being the number one female MP elected that year. She credits her mother for providing inspiration to enter politics; Bajari describes her mother as having a large social base, and claims that her mother taught her the value of hard work and the importance of supporting her husband. Bajari also adds that she continues to prepare her family's meals at her own kitchen, often staying up until 1:00 a.m. to complete her MP duties. Bajari has a close relationship with Osama al-Nujaifi, former parliamentary Speaker of the House who, like her, was raised in Mosul and also with Ahmad al-Karbouli, the Minister of Manufacturing. The rent for the house she occupies in Baghdad is paid by Parliament (three million Iraqi dinars [ID] per year). She owns between 250 to 300 grams of gold, which she claims to buy solely to help secure her children's future.

Bajari was first selected to the Iraqi Parliament in the March 2010 elections as a representative of al-Hal ("The Solution") Bloc, a mostly Sunni-based party representing one component of the al-Iraqiya (Iraq National Movement) Alliance. Al-Iraqiya emerged in 2009 as a coalition of parties conjointly led by Iyad al-Allawi, a long-time anti-Saddam activist who served as Iraq's prime minister during the transitional government of 2004–5; Osama al-Najaifi, Speaker of the House from 2006 to 2014; and Deputy Prime Minister Saleh al-Mutlaq (Allawi and Najaifi were both vice presidents in the government formed in September 2014, while Mutlaq retained his deputy minister position). Although cross-sectarian and secular in philosophy (Allawi himself is Shi'a Muslim), al-Iraqiya had strong appeal to Sunni Arabs and many of the bloc's supporters were former Ba'athists.[17] The al-Iraqiya Alliance was formed primarily to unseat Premier Nouri al-Maliki in the March 2010 elections.[18] Although the alliance failed in this goal, al-Iraqiya did succeed in winning the majority of parliamentary seats (91) in that election, of which 12 were accomplished in Shi'a-dominated governorates. These results were notable since Maliki's State of Law Party failed to win any seats in Sunni-majority areas. Thus al-Iraqiya showed promise as a secular alternative to the ethnosectarian politics so deeply entrenched in Iraq.[19] However, al-Iraqiya may have overreached when Allawi insisted on obtaining the prime minister seat as leader of the winning list. In concern that former Ba'athists would return to power, Shi'a parties that had previously fallen out with Maliki once more gathered around him to form the largest parliamentary bloc. On November 10, 2010, the so-called Erbil Agreement was reached in which both Prime Minister Maliki and President Talabani would serve a second term, although the agreement also stipulated that al-Iraqiya would be heavily represented in government by taking three posts including parliamentary Speaker, Minister of Defence and chair of the National Council for Strategic Policy.[20] Thus Allawi lost his chance to form a new government; subsequently al-Iraqiya became fragmented and lost its leverage.[21] The al-Hal Bloc was one such fragment, which emerged under Najaifi's leadership and to which Bajari adhered.

Throughout her political career, Bajari has drawn upon her Mosul grassroots base to underpin her political campaigning and represent her constituency. In her interview with *al-Baghdadia* TV, she described the positive and mutually supportive relationships she developed with the women who worked in her ironing department at the clothing manufacturing factory as an important factor behind her political success. She claims that most of her employees—primarily women—stood by her when she ran for Parliament and played an invaluable role in her campaign. Her management style and methods for establishing work relationships also illustrate her strategies for relating to and addressing the needs of her political constituents. For example, she would work alongside her employees in the factory: "I never made them feel that I was their boss. I used to iron and fold the clothes with them in the store. I was like a sister, not a boss to them." This nonhierarchical philosophy has carried over into Bajari's relationships with her constituency. She describes her style of presentation as one of humility and simplicity. "Honestly, Iraqis are not used to this style; the person with authority is always tyrannical. I am known when I visit a place not to sit at the desks used by people with authority." Bajari claims it was her ability to relate to her constituents—rather than her scholastic background or management experience—that allowed her to achieve a parliamentary position. "It was the support of the people. I remained a humble and simple person and my house is open to anyone." Despite the difficult security situation in Mosul, Bajari's home city and political base, she continues to receive frequent visits from members of her electorate. "I never turn anyone away. I welcome my visitors; I show them hospitality and cook for them. One time a [female] visitor was very surprised that I was an MP yet so humble in my conduct." Like many Iraqi politicians, Bajari has made attempts to find employment for her constituents in need. However, she says her efforts—unlike those of other MPs—have particularly benefited people outside her personal social network. "I have found employment from outside of my parliamentary bloc for orphans and single-parent families," she stated to *al-Baghdadia* TV. "Most MPs who receive positions in government give them to their own family and friends and not to strangers."

Bajari also mentions that her extensive work experience eased her transition into the legislative role. "Most MPs do not have such experience," she told *al-Baghdadia* TV. "We need training and courses, however, to learn from the experiences of our predecessors so we can enact our role in Parliament."

As an MP, Bajari serves on the parliamentary Economy and Investment Committee, directing significant energy toward rooting out and combating administrative corruption in Iraq. She expresses the belief that Iraq's investment sector has not met sustainable levels due to this corruption, which she describes as "rampant." The efforts toward eliminating corruption have enjoyed limited success and faced administrative resistance. In November 2012, Bajari was quoted in the *Iraqi Parliament Guide*: "Investors face many obstacles, especially with regards to administrative corruption. Our committee formed a subcommittee to address the investment law and amend some important articles related to the investment, but the National Investment Commission did not regularly attend the committee's meetings."²² In April 2013, Bajari maintained that some political figures within Iraq were the impetus behind a delay in countries endorsing the Iraq Customs Tariff law. "The Customs Tariff law has a political impact more than the economic impact, as there are countries behind delaying the legalization of this law so they can continue to use Iraq as the only port to import their goods," she stated. "The political figures, who are accused of delaying the legalization of this law, have companies, and so their profits are jeopardized by the legalization of this law. The constructing of the Iraqi state and the local products are damaging as long as this law is not endorsed."²³

Bajari has been vocal in advocating for minimizing this administrative corruption and red tape to keep Iraqi investment capital within the country, rather than allowing investors to migrate their funds to other countries. In January 2014, she stressed: "The tedious routine in reviewing state departments, bureaucracy and financial and administrative corruption all have discouraged investors from investing Iraqi capital in the country. [The government] must provide financial and security guarantees as well as incentives that bring specialized companies to invest in the country. The country needs investment projects to revive and develop its infrastructure."²⁴

Bajari has professed support for the strategies outlined by Iraqi economic expert Abdul Majid al-Khalidi, who has suggested the following potential solutions for restricting the migration of domestic investment capital outside of Iraq: enacting laws to govern investment and development, creating financial and banking apparatuses, lifting restrictions on investment, enhancing privatization programs, eliminating bureaucracy for investment procedures, maintaining clarity and transparency around investment, and development of economic information technology.²⁵ To date, these strategies have yet to be fully implemented, delayed by ongoing bloody strife between Iraq's political, social and religious factions. Bajari has opined that the motivations underlying these conflicts are political. When in early 2013 large groups of Sunni demonstrators took to the streets to protest Maliki's Shi'a-based leadership,²⁶ Bajari told *AIN*, "Some political sides are playing a hidden role in destabilizing the security situation. The political disputes and the current crisis among the political sides are affecting the situation negatively … [but] the sides are not revealed yet by the security forces."²⁷ In March 2013, Bajari warned the government that these demonstrations, if allowed to continue, would result in unwanted foreign interference. Speaking for her parliamentary committee, Bajari said, "We advised the government to respond to the legitimate demonstrators' demands and request the Parliament and the judiciary to respond to the demands that belong to them. When the demonstrations take a long time, there will be foreign interferences in Iraqi affairs and the citizens will feel that no one considers their opinions. The government has to settle the crisis and prove its adherence to settle it to the satisfaction of the citizens and the politicians." Bajari further stated the need for action, rather than just nominal support: "We want practical procedures to settle the crisis and unity among the political sides to neglect the sectarianism and not only through the statements."[28] In April 2013, Bajari called for all political factions to meet "to achieve real resolutions that could stop shedding Iraqi blood."[29] It is worth noting that Sunni and Shi'a groups did try to initiate such a meeting at Um al-Qura mosque in May of that year. However, the escalation of insurgencies and civil conflicts across Iraq and neighboring Syria throughout 2015 and 2016 illustrated the failure to achieve any long-term resolution to the crisis.

In accord with her status as a member of the Economy and Investment Committee, Bajari's political focus has been particularly on economic development and improvement. She notes that political divisions in the country tend to impede economic progress. During election campaigning in January 2014, she stated that the electoral campaigns were distracting the Iraqi government from making plans to upgrade the economy. "Iraq lacks long-term strategic plans to create variable resources for the country while the set plans are not implemented in the actual scene," she commented, adding, "The private sector in Iraq is not supported to participate with the general sector in developing the economic situation. The government is concerned with political disputes, ignoring the process of setting plans to enhance the economy."[30] Bajari is a particular champion of promoting construction of housing units to address Iraq's housing crisis in the wake of bombings and family displacement.

While Bajari has been quite visible and at times has been the spokesperson for her parliamentary committee, that committee's achievements have been slow due to the insurgent and sectarian politics that continue to dominate the Iraq scene. Still, Bajari's voice has enjoyed some prominence in Parliament and in the press, perhaps a contributing factor to her 2014 reelection.

Etab al-Douri

Etab al-Douri was born on May 27, 1969 in Baghdad, grew up in the Palestine Street area, and then moved to the al-Adel Quarter; however she has spent the majority of her life in al-Taji, a Sunni Arab district north of Baghdad in Salah al-Din, where she also held the position of an MP. A Sunni Muslim, Douri was married at age 26 to Kareem Khalaf Muhammad Abu Hatem, a friend and military college colleague of her martyred brother Rabie. They have three sons: Hatem, Mustafa and Amir. Abu Hatem is now the first deputy governor representing Taji in Baghdad. Douri holds bachelor's, master's and PhD degrees in philosophy and was a professor in that field at Baghdad University prior to entering the political arena. She owns one house, which she inherited from her father, in the al-Adel area and another in al-Yarmuk, which she built in 1999 while a university professor; she also owns ploughing machines and harvesters. Abu Hatem is a farmer by trade and holds farming lands in Salah al-Din. As to her decision to stand for Parliament, her students and local dignitaries pressed into entering politics, as she was the only one to have a doctorate degree in the al-Taji area. She credits her husband for making her the person she is, citing his good relations, morals and quiet nature. Douri completed her higher education while married to Abu Hatem.

Douri is a member of al-Hal Bloc under the al-Iraqiya Slate. "My life, residence, and position are in al-Taji," she told *al-Baghdadia* TV in 2012. Douri has served two parliamentary terms from 2005 to 2014. She believes her rural roots to have been supportive to both her campaign and her MP successes. She considers herself a servant to her constituents and strives to help them solve all their problems, not just those political in nature: "My supporters know the details of what I have given them in all respects. When I was living with them I was there for all their small matters of daily life; even a woman who argues with her husband, I try to bring them back together," she said. She told *al-Baghdadia* TV that although she was done having children she had always wished for a girl, a sympathy that lies behind her interest in advocating for Iraq's widows and orphans. "I consider girls to be bereft and wronged constantly from education ... we need to take greater care of women in the countryside."

Addressing poverty in Iraq has been an important plank in Douri's political platform while campaigning and a priority during her parliamentary service. As an example, she strongly advocated for the availability and quality of state-sponsored food rations, stating: "Where are the allocated rations? It is a big failure in our [rural] areas. By the time [the rations] reach the average person it consists of only one or two items." As she told *al-Baghdadia* TV, she dresses austerely to express sympathy with the poor, widowed and orphaned. "I am too ashamed to wear any colors other than black or to put on makeup. I feel ashamed from my people that since 2003 and until now these events we are going through, the suffering and poverty, when we are the richest people in the world with the oil and the two great rivers. Why? Look at other countries. They have nothing, but their financial situation is better than Iraqis'. If you went and saw Istanbul, how beautiful it is." "When will you change your dress?" inquired the interviewer. "When Iraq returns to its natural place," Douri replied. "When I see the developments and improvement in the living conditions and the people are happy again. And if I am satisfied with myself and if my public is satisfied with me, I will still be simple together with my husband Abu Hatem."

Douri has put in a good deal of effort as an MP in order to help her constituents obtain employment, duty transfers and services. She described bringing local dignitaries to petition for their cases to be heard by various ministries, including the Ministers of Electricity, Water Resources, Agriculture and Education. "I take teachers of schools; sometimes the number of cars reaches 150 for 200 people. The ministries are surprised by that number and take it as an invasion." But Douri continues to share her financial gains as an MP with the people of her district. "Everything I earn I share with my people, such as the widows, orphans, the needy and the handicapped. I share with their special occasions such as weddings, and if they become sick. Undergoing operations, circumcision, even the woman who has left her house, I bring them back together and give them a gift." Douri's untiring service to her constituents has taken a toll on her own health, as she was diagnosed with diabetes and hypertension during her parliamentary tenure.

Douri's commitment to helping those in need of health and medical services led to her involvement on the parliamentary Health and Environment Committee. In 2012, when statistics were published indicating a rise in cancer cases in Iraq since 2003 (due at least in part to the effects of war on environmental pollution), Douri advocated for the construction of a cancer hospital in Baghdad, telling *AIN* that "the Health Parliamentary Committee is united to support persons suffering from cancer. The work [to build the hospital] needs the spirit of one team and all are asked to participate in supporting the Health and Environment Committee and health departments." In the same interview she called upon Prime Minister Nouri al-Maliki to increase fiscal support to the Ministry of Health: "I wish that a huge financial amount would be allocated for this ministry because Iraq witnesses the spread of cancer disease due to lack of support during previous years."[31]

Douri also works toward more equitable distribution of resources. In July 2012, she backed laws that would prohibit merchants from drastically raising prices during religious holidays. "[Given] the increase of prices coinciding with Ramadan and the exploitation of merchants to the citizens, [we] request the officials to impose tight punishments [on] those merchants who aim to gain exorbitant wealth," she stated to *AIN*. "The government can stop the increases of the prices and ruin the benefits of the merchants by increasing the items of the Ration Card to help the citizens avoid buying expensive foodstuff from the public markets."[32] Later that month, she also called upon the parliamentary Finance Committee to "allocate funds from the supplementary budget ... to be distributed as grants for the poor citizens and the widows ... Baghdad suffers from deteriorated services like the shortage of electric power and potable water, in addition to the crisis of the housing units, and all these aspects should be considered when the supplementary budget is distributed."[33] On occasion, Douri has addressed concerns over water scarcity. For example, in August 2012 when Iran blocked water flowing into the Alwand river (a river in eastern Iraq and western Iran, which rises in the Iranian Zagros Mountains), she called for both the Iraqi government and the United Nations to "take a role to settle this issue with the neighbouring countries and to solve the disputes [in order to protect] Iraq's share of water."[34] Douri has continued to work toward budget laws that would ensure equitable treatment of all Iraqi citizens, saying al-Iraqiya Slate would "vote on the budget law to achieve the interest of the Iraqis who suffered from disturbed security, service and economic situations ... it is time to change these situations."[35]

Douri has spoken to the press frequently about Iraq's security issues, and how they have affected both her and the people in her home district. In March 2011, she reported escaping an assassination attempt as she travelled to Parliament in her armored car. According to Douri, three gunmen fired four bullets at the car as it passed. The attackers fled before they were captured; Douri and her bodyguards were not injured.[36] In August 2012, she commended Baghdad Commander of Operations Ahmed Hashim Ouda for settling the crisis arising over random sectarian-based arrests in al-Taji (Douri's district), Tarmiya and Abu Ghraib. "Ouda visited al-Taji district…and held a conference presented by many tribal figures and some security leaders where he ordered ... the blocked roads [to be opened] and to make the curfew from 1 a.m. to 6 a.m. and ordered ... the random arrest operations [to be stopped]," she told *AIN*, calling the move "a great achievement that saved the families of those districts who felt targeted and discriminated."[37] Douri has been unequivocal in her rejection of Iraqi involvement in foreign crises such as the Syrian civil conflict. She has vocalized support for a movement toward greater nationalism and unity between sects. In a January 2013 interview she stated, "We call Parliament to strictly punish those who instigate sectarianism, in order to achieve intimacy and brotherhood among Iraqis."[38] Douri believes the sectarian crisis is motivated by political aims: "The lack of services and security was caused by the political disputes and the tense statements of some politicians, which negatively affected the citizens," she said in 2013, urging "all sides to adhere to the dialogue and make the enemies of Iraq lose the chance of creating instability in Iraq in order to serve the citizens and achieve the national interest.[39] Toward this end, she suggested prohibiting sectarian agitators from taking political posts, calling for "voting by majority on a law draft that prohibits granting the politicians who agitate [for] sectarianism any post and to be nominated for the next Parliament membership and even the retirement salary," adding, "It is unacceptable to allow such politicians to get a post after creating sectarian sedition among Iraqis."[40] During Maliki's tenure as premier, Douri posited that lack of an active intelligence system lay behind terrorist attacks against civilians: "The occurrence of terrorist operations at the same time in several provinces demonstrates the lack of intelligence coordination among the security forces…and absence of competence of the security leaders."[41]

Douri has clearly stated her opinion that women are marginalized within Parliament and kept from achieving a vital role in policy-making, going so far as to say that "there is a conspiracy in Parliament against female MPs to marginalize them politically."[42] She called for the Independent High Electoral Commission (IHEC) to adhere to the open slate electoral system during the 2014 parliamentary elections to help avoid corruption and increase women's representation.[43] Yet she remains adamant that women are as capable politically as men, if not more so. As she told *al-Baghdadia* TV during Ramadan 2012, "I have a message to all politicians who think they are big and women small, weak and frail…we women are here and if you can't be Ministers of Defence then we are ready to be in your place." This conviction in the ability of women is demonstrated by her response to the question, "do you have ambitions to become Prime Minister?," posed by the *al-Baghdadia* TV interviewer. "Why not?" replied al-Douri. "I am ready and qualified for any position no matter how big it is…Not for the sake of the position, but to serve my people."

Hanan al-Fatlawi

Hanan al-Fatlawi was born in 1968 in Babil and represents Babil Governorate in Parliament. She is a dermatologist who received her MD from the highly competitive Medical School at Baghdad University and formerly practiced dermatology at a hospital in Babil Province. She was married to a medical doctor who worked in the same hospital, but divorced her husband (by some reports) to enter politics. For several years she served as Maliki's press/public relations advisor and media spokesperson for provincial affairs. Fatlawi is a Shiʻa Muslim and member of the State of Law Coalition. She was first elected to Parliament in 2010 with 9,200 votes and accomplished reelection in 2014 without aid of the quota, seventh out of 328 candidates. She sits on the Members Affairs Committee and the parliamentary Development Committee, the latter of which she previously chaired. Interestingly, Fatlawi briefly stood as candidate for the Iraqi presidency in 2014. During the first round of voting in those elections, Fatlawi received 37 out of 275 votes for the post.[44] Although she was the strongest competitor in the field, she withdrew her nomination under pressure from the State of Law bloc, and Fouad Massoum was elected president with 211 votes.[45]

Fatlawi has been extremely outspoken both in Iraq and internationally. The causes she has espoused include medical provisions, such as healthcare law, immunization, the prevention and eradication of infectious disease, increasing the Iraqi life expectancy age and reducing infant mortality rates. She has championed investigation into the corruption of the Election Commission, gathering more than 100 MPs' signatures on a 2011 petition to lobby for such an inquiry.[46] "The questioning is part of Parliament's duty—to assess the work of government institutions that have been accused of failing in their duties or accused of corruption," Fatlawi said on April 21, 2011.[47] Investigation into these charges resulted in the arrest of Faraj al-Haidari, head of the IHEC, along with IHEC member Karim al-Tamimi, in April 2012.[48]

From April to June of 2013, Fatlawi was a member of the Drafting Committee for the Charter of Cooperation between Public Authorities and NGOs for the Development of Iraqi Society, a policy outlining a system of cooperation between nongovernmental organizations (NGOs), Parliament and the government. The charter was meant to serve as a gateway for sustainable collaboration between public authorities and Iraqi civil society in the interests of societal development.[49] The policy included the following provisions:

- proposing mutual respect and equal partnership as values and principles to govern relations between civil society and public authority;
- increasing mechanisms for citizen action and participation by citizens and non-governmental organizations in public life and policy-making;
- protecting the political independence of civic initiatives;
- improving transparency and accountability of public authorities and non-governmental organizations; and
- establishing channels for sustainable funding for civic initiatives.

During a presentation at Boston University in April 2013, Fatlawi spoke out strongly against the Saddam regime, calling that era "the darkest period for Iraq, the darkest period for our history,"[50] and expressing the gratitude of many Iraqi citizens for the 2003 multinational intervention that unseated Saddam. However, she was quick to add that not all Iraqis were grateful for the mistakes made post-occupation. "Probably we are now facing a lot of troubles as a consequence of the mistakes done during that time," she stated.[51] During the question-and-answer segment following the presentation, Fatlawi reacted stridently to a suggestion from a woman in the audience that the violence and sectarianism had worsened post-Saddam rather than improved. "You are far away from Iraq in reality," she told the questioner vehemently. "You said there was no sectarianism during Saddam regime, where you daily lost one of your brothers or relatives or friends in a war with Iran… we spent many years of our lives in unfair war, we don't know why!…or Kuwait, one of our brothers…invading them, and for what? Destroying our economy, destroying our oil resources?…You can't imagine that time of UN sanctions when your kids are diseased, and you can't find medicine…You can't eat; five or six members of one family have to share one bread."[52] Fatlawi went on to express her opinion regarding the balance of power in Iraq through present times: "We have to…be grateful for the positive things and at the same time mention the negative things. Leaving the border open for terrorism to enter, resolution [disbanding] of the army and all these bad decisions, of course we are paying right now for them. So we have to mention the positive and the negative at the same time."[53]

The theme of Fatlawi's presentation at the Iraq + 10 Conference was to highlight the positive and negative aspects of Iraq's parliamentary system under the 2005 Constitution. On the positive side, she mentioned fair elections and peaceful transference of power, with elections held at the federal, provincial and local levels. She emphasized government decentralization in contrast to the strong centrality of Saddam's rule. Decentralization, said Fatlawi, has resulted in a sharing of power and opportunity indicated by "the budget…job opportunity …and scholarships [all] divided between different provinces according to the number of population. The judicial system is supposed to be independent and work separately. There [are] a lot of safeguards for preventing us from going through a dictatorship."[54] The reconstruction of a civil society and emergence of many NGOs also represent positive aspects of Iraq's progress toward democracy, according to Fatlawi.

As negative aspects of Iraq's parliamentary system, Fatlawi first cited weak (sometimes absent) oversight and the lack of a real opposition. "Weak such alliance between all caucuses [referring to the political disagreements between parties and blocs], such participation produces weak government. At the same time there is no real opposition. This is one of the reasons...the government is not productive, and the Parliament is not productive."[55] Political conflicts were another negative upon which Fatlawi touched. "Every time you hear we have...an entire religious, ethnic, or sectarian caucus withdrawn from the Parliament because they have a political issue or political objection...this prevents the Parliament from working and from legislating law."[56] Closed electoral lists tend to weaken legislative function, Fatlawi posited. Further, she believes a misunderstanding of the extent of executive authority has had negative impact on Iraq's political system. "We have a provision in our constitution that there is a complete distinction, complete separation between three authorities: the judicial and the legislative and the executive," she stated. "But in reality in Iraq there is no clear distinction. Each authority tries to extend on the other."[57]

Fatlawi made several recommendations for parliamentary reform. First, she suggested that many outsiders had the opinion that Iraq should move toward a presidential system where the president was elected by the people rather than by parliamentary consensus. Achieving a majority government rather than allocating equal power to each separate bloc would strengthen both the government and Parliament, she said. Such majority government would require the creation of a national party or national list. Building the high federal court set forth by the constitution, to deal with political and regional conflicts, would be another positive step. Fatlawi opined that constitutional amendments were needed to move the government closer to democracy. "We have to work hard in order to reach a prosperous and safe and peaceful Iraq...I am not very optimistic that it will be very soon...But with the cooperation of all political parties, with the cooperation of all participating groups in politics we could reach it," she concluded.[58]

As a strong member of the State of Law Coalition and former Maliki advisor, it is not surprising that Hanan al-Fatlawi has been vocal in offering support to Maliki's policies and practices and criticizing opposition to his government, particularly from the Kurds and Sadrists. This position has earned her a good deal of censure from such oppositional groups. In March 2015, she reportedly survived an assassination attempt upon her return from the liberated areas of Albu-Ajil and Dour in Salah al-Din Province where she had visited the Army and Volunteer Fighters.[59]

Ashwaq al-Jaf

Ashwaq Najm al-Din al-Jaf was born in Sulaymaniyyah in 1973 into a family with a background in political activism. She was married in 2006 to Mohammad Abu Awly, a retired general director and former member of the Kurdish Peshmerga (militia). They have one son, Awly, born in 2009, whom she leaves with her sister in Sulaymaniyyah while Parliament is in session in Baghdad. Jaf reports that her husband was an activist against Saddam and threatened with the death penalty, but released in 2003. Both Jaf and her husband belong to the Kurdistan Democratic Party (KDP) that she formally represents and of which Abu Awly is still a leader and Peshmerga activist. Jaf received her PhD and later became an assistant professor in Clinical Pharmacology at Baghdad University. In 1996, she went to work as a pharmacist. As an MP, Jaf says, her income is much less than as a professor or pharmacist. She has no other income now that her husband is retired. Her MP salary is greatly reduced by expenses for food (35,000 ID per week), renting office space and hosting luncheons for constituents at her home.

Jaf explains that she always pursued leadership roles even as a child. Her love of leadership continued as an MP, although she also views her position as an opportunity to serve and help others. Prior to becoming elected as MP in 2010, Jaf conducted trainings with Provincial Councils on behalf of the American Rental Association, a US-based NGO. She serves on the parliamentary Committee for Human Rights. "As a pharmacist I treated individuals with medications," she told *al-Iraqiya* TV, "and now as an MP I heal people with legislations and solving problems. True as it may be that the two fields are apart from each other, they meet on one goal which is helping people."

Jaf's interest in human rights stems from her experience with motherhood, and from her involvement with NGOs prior to becoming a politician. "I learnt from the reality of living in Iraq...what violations of human rights take place," she explained in her *al-Iraqiya* TV televised interview translated for this research. "I supported that with reading the international laws and declarations, as well as the exchange of experience with international organizations...here I would like to say for the record that the British Human Rights Commission, which parallels our commission in Iraq, has supported us and this gives [Iraq] a push forward." When asked whether the Iraqi citizen most needed a medicinal formula or political concord, Jaf responded, "Iraq needs national alliance. I have always said to my colleagues in politics: have mercy on the citizens; leave out the tension-laden statements, give politics to the politicians and give life to the people. Unfortunately, politics has entered into every aspect of life so that the citizen is not given a chance to live even for a moment. This is wrong, and we need national concord in order to ease the pains of people and ameliorate the status of Iraqis."

Jaf has expressed support for improved human rights across societal sectors. While she states she herself has faced no discrimination from her male Kurdish political colleagues, in September 2012, she spoke out against abuses suffered by women and girls in Iraq. In an interview with *Deutsche Welle* she said, "We've wasted an awful lot of time trying to ban those laws that go against us [women], but in vain. We've been moving backwards since 2003 regarding human rights. The crux of the matter here is that we have two penal codes: there's the Iraqi Constitution, but also the *shari'a*—the Islamic law. Accordingly, contradictions between both often lead to ambiguous vacuums that make us even more vulnerable."[60] The same article reported that, as of that date, Iraqi Kurdistan was the only province in Iraq where female circumcision (genital mutilation) was still practiced in some rural areas, and that the Iraqi government had registered 3,766 cases of abuse against women in Kurdistan in 2011. Jaf held a press conference near International Women's Day in March 2013 to further publicize the abuses of Iraqi women, quoted in *AIN*, "The situation of Iraqi women is dramatic, frustrating and fails to meet the ambition where women enjoy their rights guaranteed by the Iraqi Constitution." She added, "The Iraqi women celebrate World Women's Day in light of serious circumstances [in which] they live and great violations that cannot be ignored... [they] suffer systematic policy of political and social marginalization and exclusion, despite the Constitution guaranteeing their humanitarian and political rights."[61] In August 2014, Jaf spoke in favor of greater inclusion of women in politics: "There is ambiguity over the situation of the Iraqi woman where she does not get her complete rights compared with man," and calling on Parliament to "include women in the decision-making process due to their political role, in spite of the few chances given to them."[62]

Jaf also has spoken out for *AIN* in September 2012 when she called upon the Iraqi government to activate the principles of incentives and punishments to deal with cases of torture of prison detainees, "This phenomenon has been displayed on TV repeatedly but the justification comes to describe these acts as personal violations...Those who commit these violations should be punished because they defame the reputation of Iraq towards the world and give a negative image about the situation in Iraqi prisons."[63] When in February 2013 then-president Jalal Talabani's office handed Parliament a draft of a Victims of Justice law that would compensate individuals detained in prison under false charges, Jaf supported the reading and vote on the law on behalf of her committee: "Our committee calls all sides to vote on this law to compensate those who were detained due to false notifications," she told *AIN*. "This law is among the demands that the citizens call for at the current stage because of the misuse of the secret informer law."[64] Other human rights efforts by Jaf include speaking out against government cancellation of the Rations Card, which she blamed on ministerial corruption;[65] and calling for the allocation of funds to aid families displaced by damage caused in the 2013 floods.[66]

Jaf has leveraged her parliamentary post to vocalize support for the Peshmerga. In August 2012 she issued a press statement against politicians and the media describing the Peshmerga as a nonofficial and "unorganized" body. "Everyone who describes the Peshmerga as being unorganized has to reconsider his opinion," she said. "The Peshmerga elements are part of the national defence system as stated in the Constitution. Approving the [budget] allocations to the Peshmerga elements [will] refute those accusations."[67] When Maliki formed the Dijla Operations Command (OC) as a force to eradicate terrorism in the Diyala, Kirkuk and Salah al-Din governorates,[68] Jaf criticized the move as unconstitutional and contradictory to Peshmerga efforts. "There is a deal signed by the cooperating committee in Kurdistan Region and the central government [which] states that there should not be any military force in the disputed areas without coordination between the two sides," she said in a press statement. "The leader of Dijla OC…was one of the leaders who participated in the Anfal military operation against the Kurdish people in the former regime. Tensions that might happen between these two forces due to the accusation [against the] Kurdistan Regional Government by the central government…will result in killing many citizens."[69]

To summarize Jaf's views on Iraqi women in politics, one may turn to her response to the *al-Iraqiya* TV interviewer's questions regarding whether she feels successful as a politician: "Before God I am satisfied with what I am doing but this work is not bearing fruit in reality…It is not my fault, but the political reality in which we are living… political struggles are really affecting the performance of the Parliament and…have weakened its role. This is why our work is not fruitful."

Karima al-Jawari

Karima al-Jawari, was born in 1959 in Baghdad and was elected to Parliament as a member of the Iraqiya List. She is married and has two adult sons—one a military officer and the other a public servant. Jawari reportedly receives a monthly salary of 5.7 million ID[70] as MP, although at times the salary is less. MPs also receive a housing supplement of 36 million per year, which amounts to 30 million after deductions. She pays $35,000 per month to rent a house in the Yarmuk Quarter and also rents a flat in the Green Zone for her two sons. She must pay salary and food for her bodyguards and hospitality expenses. Jawari takes out loans to make up the difference when her salary is not enough. At the time of the interview she claimed having three outstanding loans, one of which was one hundred times her salary. Prior to the 2003 invasion, Jawari owned a building containing residential flats and shops from which she earned rental income. However, her sons were kidnapped by insurgents in 2005 and she sold the building to pay their ransom. She also owned a metal tin and paint factory prior to the US occupation that was subsequently looted during sectarian conflict. Jawari currently owns no gold, as she has had to sell off her gold jewelry to cover expenses.

Jawari is a lawyer and her personal dream is to attain a PhD in law. She has been member of a humanitarian NGO since 2003 dealing with Iraqis displaced from their homes. Representing the al-Hurra Bloc of the al-Iraqiya Coalition, she served just one term in the Iraqi Parliament, from 2010 to 2014. Her decision to enter the political arena was driven by her wish to help the people of Iraq. In a 2012 interview with *al-Iraqiya* TV, Jawari told the interviewer, "[I ran for Parliament] because our hearts burn for our country and to stand up for our people; I am a lawyer and our financial situation was very good and when we entered into the political arena we wanted to give something to this country and benefit its people." Jawari also spoke of her dreams for a more secure future for Iraqi citizens: "I just wanted the Iraqis to live in security whereby a person walks around without the concrete slabs and no personal guards—as it was the case in the past when MPs would commute by taxi."

Jawari herself has been particularly affected by the lack of security in the country. In addition to her sons' kidnapping, in January 2013, she, along with two members of her family, narrowly avoided being killed in an assassination attempt in her governorate, the Balad district of Salah al-Din Province. According to a statement from the parliamentary media office, Jawari, her mother and her son were travelling through empty streets in Balad when their vehicle passed a car bomb parked at the roadside, which detonated just after their passage.[71] None of the three was injured. It is unknown whether the parked car bomb was meant specifically for Jawari; however, it is suspected that she was indeed the target; the incident underscores the violence and lack of security MPs face in Iraq, for which even bodyguards offer no protection.

According to Jawari, the motive behind the attempt on her life may have been her resistance to signing the motion of "no confidence" against Prime Minister Maliki. The Maliki government had begun falling apart shortly after the final withdrawal of US troops from Iraq in December 2011. The governmental arrest warrant, *in absentia* trial, and death sentence of prominent Sunni al-Iraqiya figure and Vice President Tariq al-Hashimi led a group of Iraqiya MPs to boycott the parliamentary session, until US officials intervened and obtained Maliki's agreement to release some Ba'athist prisoners and grant more autonomy to the Provincial Councils.[72] In the wake of this agreement, the boycotting MPs resumed their posts in February 2012. Although the various sects agreed to attend a National Conference led by President (and Kurd) Talabani, Kurdistan Regional Government (KRG) President Masoud Barzani later accused Maliki of attempting a power play and the conference was never held. Maliki's opponents then proceeded to collect signatures from MPs to request a "no-confidence" vote against Maliki (20 percent, or 65, signatures would be required to initiate the request for vote). Although 176 signatures were gathered, President Talabani declared the number of valid signatures insufficient, and the no-confidence effort failed.[73] Jawari, despite her allegiance to the largely Sunni and anti-Maliki al-Iraqiya Coalition, did not support the no-confidence vote, which earned her much criticism from her party. In her *al-Iraqiya* TV interview she explained, "These things are often misunderstood. They asked me why I did not vote on the withdrawal of confidence. I asked them to let me explain my point of view because I had sworn an oath that I would only do what is right for my country because it is our responsibility. My position was: did you make plans for after that withdrawal of confidence, and what will happen then?"

Jawari further clarified in the *al-Iraqiya* TV interview and in other press statements that she did not object to the withdrawal of confidence per se; she merely could not support the process by which the signatures were gathered. "On principle I did not object to the vote, but I objected to the mechanism by which it was done," she told *al-Iraqiya* TV. "I told [my party] that 90 MPs [the number of seats gained by Maliki's party in the 2010 elections] is a large number as each one of them represents 100,000 people from their constituency—and you are trivializing this number!" Jawari had posed several questions about the "no-confidence" procedure, which she went on to list: "Firstly, who is the alternative [to Maliki]? Secondly, what do you have to offer the Kurds, knowing that we have red lines that we can't cross into Kirkuk and the disputed areas? I told them that Iraqiya has already made a few blunders since the Erbil agreement; who signed the agreement in Erbil, and what were the terms?" She added, "I told them there are legislations waiting to be voted on, why do you want to nullify those legislations? Why don't we join together with the Dawlat al-Qanun [Maliki's State of Law] list to be a strong force in Parliament? ...It was better to remain in opposition to save our faces but they continued with their fight over the positions and the negotiators made many mistakes. We need to have a covenant before we can sign the withdrawal of trust." In a May 2012 interview Jawari was quoted: "Unfortunately, some politicians neglect objectivity and neutrality in dealing with the issue of withdrawing confidence from the Premier...by following ways that are not suitable with political performance. The political leaders should avoid personal and partisan interests [and]...avoid adopting illegitimate ways to topple Maliki."[74]

Jawari claimed her statements regarding the no-confidence vote made her the target for assassination by al-Qaeda militants. "They [her party members] told me, 'You are going in the wrong direction,'" she explained to *al-Iraqiya* TV. "They said, 'You are now on the assassination list.' One MP told me that my name is on the list and I told him, 'If I die at the hands of my own people I die as a martyr. When I embarked on a political career I put my coffin on my shoulder for Iraq.' Then we learnt that our names had been put on the Internet on a website that belongs to the Ba'ath Party." Jawari then related that a male MP from her party, Talal al-Zawba'i, had telephoned to inform her that he had signed the withdrawal of trust resolution on her behalf. "I told him, 'I did not authorize you to do so!' He said [jokingly], 'I will do it whether you like it or not!'" This incident illuminates the struggles in authority between male and female MPs in the Iraqi Parliament.

Since 2003, Karima al-Jawari has been a member of a humanitarian NGO that works with the United Nations High Commission for Refugees to provide health care, social services and housing for citizens and families that have been displaced from their homes due to conflict. As an MP, she continued this work as a member of the parliamentary Committee for the Displaced. Jawari has worked tirelessly to offer aid to emigrants to help them return from refugee camps in Palestine, Syria and Iran. In April 2012, members of the Committee for the Displaced visited the al-Waleed camp situated on the Iraq-Syria border. In June of that year, Jawari told *NSNBC International* that Palestinian camp residents were subject to deplorable conditions and earlier had suffered many violations of the Geneva Convention in Baghdad before being displaced to the camp.[75] She reported that the Humanitarian Committee was in constant contact with the Iraqi Ministry of Migration and the UN High Commissioner to facilitate the migration of al-Waleed residents to the United States and Europe.[76]

In the 2012 *al-Iraqiya* TV interview Jawari stated, "My relations are constant with the forced emigrants...I attend all the meetings of the committees except in extreme emergencies when I had to undergo surgery. As you know I am the only legal expert on the committee and they need me." And Jawari's humanitarian undertakings are not restricted to Iraqis alone: "I am in touch with the forced emigrants everywhere in the world like the US, Sweden and Denmark. They call me at 2:00 a.m. to discuss some issues. Also inside Iraq I visit them in Kurdistan and I also visited Sweden with the envoy which attempted to repatriate the Iraqis from there." Early in 2013, Jawari expressed frustration with the arguing between political blocs that delayed vote on the General Amnesty law that could lead to the release of innocent detainees held in Iraqi prisons and camps. She called on Parliament to "form specialized committees to speed up the legal procedures to release the innocent detainees and to submit the criminals to the courts."[77] She noted, "The General Amnesty law includes many exceptions and some political blocs intend to cancel these exceptions. Some of the prisoners are involved in killing Iraqis so they could not be released if we have a State that adopts laws and democracy."[78]

Jawari is also outspoken against unemployment, service shortages, cuts to government food rations and other governmental failures that lay behind the demonstrations in Hamza (February 2011) and Ashraf (July 2011). Regarding the Hamza uprisings, she spoke to *The National*, warning that the unrest could rapidly spread nationwide. "Iraq is boiling and it could blow up at any moment," she said. "The people are sending their message to the Prime Minister, to [al-Iraqiya leader] Iyad Allawi and all of the politicians that we must pay immediate attention to their needs."[79] Regarding the anti-Maliki demonstrations in Ashraf, Jawari publicly condemned the interference of Iranian authorities in Iraqi affairs and called upon the United States to protect the region. She told *Azzaman Daily*, "This case is related to them [the United States] and from the beginning of the occupation they insisted on their responsibility on the issue of protection, yet unfortunately they have refused to live up to their responsibilities," adding, "[The Ashraf protestors] have committed no sin other than opposing the regime ruling their country. The Iranian regime's interferences in Iraq and especially in Ashraf have reached a very dangerous stage."[80]

Despite her allegiance to al-Iraqiya Coalition, public perception may have existed among her constituency that Jawari supported the Maliki government—ostensibly illustrated by her unwillingness to sign the no-confidence resolution. This image may have resulted in her failure to achieve reelection in 2014. Also, as mentioned previously, al-Iraqiya became fragmented and lost power during the

2010–14 parliamentary term. Jawari protested the results of the 2014 election, requesting a vote recount by the IHEC due to professed election rigging in her Salah al-Din electorate: "The ballot process in Salah al-Din saw many forgeries and manipulation where many polling centres did not make the sorting and counting of votes and ballot boxes were transported to an unknown destination," she told Alfarat News Agency.[81] However, even the requested recount did not result in Jawari's reelection.

This portrait of Jawari's efforts as MP highlights her sense of commitment toward as well as faith in parliamentary law and process. She continues to believe that women in the Iraqi Parliament still lack full capacity to manage their parliamentary affairs; the influence of their male counterparts remains heavy. "The problem is in the political blocs which we belong to, which do not give [women] the right to vote [in party meetings]," she told *al-Iraqiya* TV. "I even said in one TV interview, 'Men of Iraq! Give us one year to rule Iraq and you will see what we will do!' And as you know, women make up 60 per cent of society."

Huda Sajjad Mahmoud

Huda Sajjad Mahmoud was born in Diywaniyyah in 1978, the second eldest in a family of six children. Her father was executed when she was in grade six due to his affiliation with the al-Da'wa Party, illegal during the Saddam regime. Mahmoud herself still represents the Da'wa Party under Maliki's State of Law Bloc. She was married in 2001 and has three children: Aya, Sajjad and Ja'far. When she ran for elections in 2010, she was expecting her son Ja'far, who was born two months after the 2010 election. Mahmoud graduated from the University of Kufa with a bachelor's degree in chemistry education. She is proud to come from a highly educated family: her older sister has a bachelor's in Arabic language; her younger brother (Abu Muhammad) has a master's degree in engineering and is teaching at the University of Kufa; her other brother (Abu Maryam) holds a law degree; her sister (Um Fatima) has a bachelor's degree in education (Physics); and her youngest brother is studying at the College of Digital Technologies. Mahmoud cites her status as the daughter of a martyr as her primary impetus to stand for parliamentary election. Both Mahmoud and her husband are long-term activists in the Da'wa Party, and he supported her both morally and financially during her campaign. Mahmoud's husband also is the brother of a martyr.

Mahmoud was first elected to the Iraqi Parliament in 2010 representing Diywaniyyah Governorate and was reelected in 2014. As she explained in her 2012 interview with *al-Iraqiya* TV, her husband was an important support for her campaign and election. "He supported me morally and financially." She feels her father's martyrdom lent credibility to her campaign. "Getting into Parliament is an impetus [to stand for election]," she stated to *al-Iraqiya* TV. "We have the right because we gave martyrs—I am a daughter of a martyr and this qualifies us to elect ourselves. [My husband] also is a member of the same party and is a brother of a martyr who was executed in 1981." She added, "My work is hard and is divided between Baghdad and Diywaniyyah, and also my husband supports me with it."

When asked by the *al-Iraqiya* TV reporter to elaborate on her opinion of the reality experienced by Iraqi women since 2003, Mahmoud discussed how Iraqi women's status has evolved in the years since the invasion. "Women are like a pyramid," she said. "Its base consists of women who suffer from domestic violence, and the top of the pyramid consists of women suffering from political violence. Also women in the past reached the prisons and even the gallows. When the change that we wanted occurred in the previous regime, it was obvious that the Iraqi woman was creative in her role inside the house, on the street, and in office, and that the woman is trustworthy and prudent and far from manipulating with public wealth." Mahmoud has exhibited these qualities during her experience as an MP, focusing on advocating for laws protecting the disabled. "Article 32 obliges the government to establish a commission for the protection of disabled people and to be responsible for all their needs until a commission is established," she observed. As of 2012, Mahmoud had held four meetings in Diywaniyyah to which the city's disabled persons were invited to discuss how to best address their needs.

Mahmoud sits on the parliamentary Committee for Women, Families and Children, and women's issues sit at the top of her priority list. In March 2012, she made a press statement for her committee recommending that budget funds be diverted away from the purchase of armored cars for MPs, and allocated toward support for widows, orphans and elders. "The committee suggested to transfer some of the funds, even if a small rate, located to purchase armored cars to the MPs to support the widows, orphans and female elders because these sections of the society are in need of care and attention to improve their hard living conditions," she told *AIN*. In the same statement Mahmoud described some of the committee's scheduled activities: "The committee is determined to change some women's and children's laws such as amending penalties law number 111 in 1969 in addition to five other laws relating to domestic violence," she stated. "The committee discussed with the Speaker to assign a legal consultant for the committee to consult in legislating laws concerned with the Iraqi families."[82]

Although outspoken against violence toward Iraqi women, in November 2012 Mahmoud interestingly criticized a report issued by the parliamentary Human Rights Committee claiming instances of torture against female detainees in Iraqi prisons. "The Parliament chairmanship requested the HR Committee to submit its reports over the transgressions against the female prisoners," she stated. "There is some inside work to change the facts and disturb the situation," she added, calling the facts of the report into doubt.[83] Her criticism apparently rested mainly upon the HR Committee's lack of consultation with other relevant governmental and parliamentary bodies. In December 2012 she said, "The Human Rights Committee drafted a report pertaining to the violations taking place in a number of detention centres without discussing the situation with the Committee on Women and Children and the Commission on Security and Defence, in order to find the real truth behind these allegations. We were not invited to any of their meetings. The first time we read the report was during the Parliament session, which proves that there are certain forces instigating these allegations."[84] She further refuted the report's claims of prisoner abuse: "We have visited the female prisons and did not find any of the transgressions mentioned in the report...we have seen the opposite and the prison administrations behave with the female prisoners in a humanitarian way."[85]

Nonetheless, Mahmoud vocalized support for legislation and strategies to counter violence against women in Iraq. "We have to determine a specific strategy to confront violence against women and to implement it through all the Ministries," she said in December 2012. "Women need a genuine stance on [both] legislative and executive levels to overcome crises."[86] She further voiced support for designating the first of Safar (the second month of the Hijri calendar) as an official Day of Confronting Violence against Women. As the internal sectarian conflict and political disputes have resulted in ongoing threats to women's security, Mahmoud says, "Women need huge financial allocations that consider the social diversity in the society to eliminate the crises that women suffer from."[87] Toward resolving security issues, in 2013, she called for Parliament to support the Honour Document proposed by Vice President Khudhir al-Khuzaiye, saying, "Khuzaiye's initiative and all the discussed initiatives in Iraq are to settle the political crisis and set a new mechanism for the performance of the leaders of the political blocs. Iraq witnesses big crises such as the unstable security situation and the Iraqiya Slate has to support Khuzaiye's initiative to settle the crises in Iraq in a serious way."

Mahmoud has been invited to speak for women's rights and political representation at several international conferences. In November 2014, she presented at the Spring Forward for Women Conference hosted in Brussels by the European Parliament Committee on Women's Rights and Gender Equality, speaking at a conference session titled, "Challenges and opportunities to women's political participation."[88] Mahmoud has continued to speak out against terrorism and violence. In February 2015, she urged residents of areas infiltrated by the Islamic State to join liberating security forces. "The people living in the areas under occupation of the terrorists affiliated to what is so called the Islamic State of Iraq and Levant are also responsible for liberating their areas," she said. "The endorsement of the national guard law will guarantee the rights of volunteers of all components."[89] Thus from 2010 to the present, Huda Sajjad Mahmoud has done what she considers her best to represent the constituents of Diywaniyyah and particularly the women and disabled of that city. As she told *al-Iraqiya* TV in 2012, "My presence in Parliament is a binding responsibility on me and I do my best to serve the people of my city. I trust that I am doing well as I have worked on the centers for the disabled and for women."

Jinan Mubarak

Jinan Mubarak was born on April 16, 1961 in Baghdad. She is married to a chief civil engineer. They have one adult son, currently in the Faculty of Dentistry at Baghdad University, and one grandson. Mubarak received a bachelor's degree from Baghdad University's Faculty of Science in 1982. She also has a creative and cultural side. As a fashion designer, she has had several exhibitions in Beirut; she also writes free verse and short story fiction. Since 2004, she has sponsored five art exhibitions for Iraqi youth.

The case study of Mubarak differs from that of the others in that to date she has not become an elected Member of Parliament. Her case is included here because she has made powerful contributions to the inclusion of women in Iraq's political agenda. She became the first Iraqi woman to establish an official political body; the party was registered in the Electoral Commission in 2010 under her own name as the Jinan Mubarak Party—one of the combined entities under the Iraqi Union Coalition—and Mubarak ran for parliamentary election under the auspices of her own party that year. At that time Mubarak issued the following press release to the media:

> I am writing these words not because I want to talk about myself but because I believe that we are like that, always seeking our close groups. We want to spread the values of peace and love—from here, the land of peace. My beloved

Iraq, fate has made you alien to your true identity. I speak to people and tell them that life can start in graveyards and the Jinan Mubarak Party is borne out of civil society organizations and share with their worries, issues and struggles for Iraq during the periods of violence, pain and weeping. I extend my hand to support women and I swore an oath to live for Iraq. For Iraq to take its part and rightful place and to tell the world we live despite death and the future is ours—a light unto people. Again I am from here speaking to women everywhere in the world to show them that women support each other anywhere and she is her sister. I also speak to my brother the man to give him a trust unmatched by any other trust—it is the Iraqi woman. The suffering of the Iraqi people, which included all aspects of human life and on various economic, cultural, social, security dimensions that I lived through as head of a mass organization which is the Iraqi Centre for the Rehabilitation and Employment of Women.

The organization sought the good of people and the community; lived with the concerns of the country and adopted its struggles, particularly women's issues and peace-building. I worked through my campaigns to stop bloodshed and to establish an Iraqi peace network which endeavoured towards peace-building in various provinces during the period of sectarian violence and until now.

In addition to women's issues in terms of rehabilitation the ordeals of widows and divorced and single women, as well as orphans—through to the constitutional amendments to ensure a fixed women's quota in the Iraqi constitution. Based on all of these achievements and as a result of the clear deficiency in the role of women in Parliament, I aimed at establishing the first Iraqi political entity for individual women running for elections in the history of Iraq.

This will be a political body for all Iraqis, women and men. It is an independent entity which seeks to build our country and to say the word of truth out loud. As I lay the terms of my political program, I'd like to show you that the Jinan Mubarak Party is one of the political entities working under the coalition of Iraqi Unity Alliance.[90]

In 2004, Mubarak founded the Iraqi Centre for Women's Rehabilitation and Employment (ICWRE). This nongovernmental, nonprofit body was licensed and registered that year by the Council of Ministries NGO Directorate. Now the ICWRE claims membership exceeds 5,000, with members representing each of the Iraqi governorates. Headquartered in Baghdad, the organization has branch offices in Kirkuk, Erbil and Diyala, with coordinators situated in five other Iraq locations. The stated mission of the ICWRE is to "empower women economically and culturally by increasing their knowledge horizons in a way that can serve their cases and guarantee their rights, develop their abilities, and enable them to build a democratic society that achieves equal opportunity for the two genders and protects women from any kind of violence."[91] These goals are pursued by seeking to address culturally contextual influences on women's situation: politics, society, education, health, economics and employment. The ICWRE works to provide economic stability and employment opportunities for single and divorced women, as well as for widows.

During the early years post-2003 as the constitution was being drafted, the ICWRE was extremely influential in lobbying to ensure that the existing Personal Status Law originally legislated in 1959 was not replaced with the much more conservative Decree 137 proposed by some members of the transitional government. The ICWRE's Personal Status Law Campaign included publication and distribution of a booklet (titled "Why Personal Status Law is Important"); hosting a regional conference to mobilize lobbying forces; a radio program; and establishment of an outreach network.[92] The ICWRE also founded the Iraqi Peace Net, a coalition of more than 40 NGOs active in peace-building processes, and the Civil Alliance of Free Elections, which has conducted more than 50 civil awareness workshops to train and encourage citizens to participate in elections. The center offers psychological, legal and economic counsel to Iraqi women; a young women's leadership training program (claiming more than 500 graduates) and a businesswomen's training program (claiming more than 600 graduates). Providing education to support female candidates who seek public office is an important stated objective for the organization.

Mubarak herself was quite active and vocal toward ending the US occupation in Iraq. In 2005, she spoke to the press about the erosion of women's freedoms brought about by the invasion. The *Los Angeles Times* interviewed Mubarak in August of that year, when she showed the reporters a photograph of her mother in the 1960s wearing a knee-length sleeveless dress and no head covering: "I can't wear what my mother was wearing at that time," said Mubarak. "It's really sad. Women had better conditions then. Now, they are challenged every day."[93] In an interview with *Associated Free Press* later in 2005, Mubarak expanded: "We cover and change the way we dress unwillingly due to pressure," she stated. She expressed the concerns of some women that American influence in post-Saddam Iraq played a major role in protecting women's rights, and that the departure of US troops might lead to further deterioration of their status. "This might regrettably be the case," admitted Mubarak, "as much as we would like to see the Americans out of Iraq."[94]

In 2006, Mubarak spoke about the tendency of the Iraqi government to give women's rights a back seat in the issues of the day, evidenced by the lack of funding and support tendered to the Ministry of Women's Affairs. An allocation of just $2,000 per month was afforded to that ministry at the time, in contrast to the hundreds of millions set aside for other ministry budgets. Despite this shortage of funding, the Ministry of Women's Affairs had managed to conduct some projects such as supporting women's groups and offering microfinance grants to help women start up small businesses. The ICWRE was at work behind these scenes, as the NGO relied upon international donors as opposed to governmental budgets for its funding. Mubarak told the *Middle East Times* that coordination with the ministry was often difficult due to its lack of resources, and called for greater attention to the ministry's funding: "We need an active governmental institution, support, and open-mindedness," she said.[95]

In her work with the ICWRE, Mubarak has put in a good deal of effort into helping educated young women gain employment within government and cabinet ministries. In a 2008 article by the Institute for War and Peace Reporting (IWPR), she discussed the pessimism and depression among young female university graduates placed on lengthy waiting lists during the application process for governmental positions. "They don't know what will happen to them tomorrow," Mubarak mentioned. "They have no hope in the future because they don't have work or job openings, and they've missed the opportunity to get married."[96] Many of these young women spoke of fleeing Iraq in hope of better opportunities in other countries. Mubarak placed the issue at the feet of both civil society and the government: "The cultural, social and economic progress made by women is slipping away because of the security situation and fear," she opined, stating that the government "needs to do a better job of looking out for its youth."[97]

When Mubarak first ran for Parliament in 2010, opposition to the parliamentary gender quota and its collateral consequences formed one plank in her platform, stating that political parties had exploited the quota in the December 2005 elections to pack Parliament with women they could control. "They used the quota against women, not for women," she asserted. "These kinds of parties, they prefer that they have a very weak woman, just to say yes."[98] Mubarak's position was that the quota served as a nominal pacifier for the women's rights movement. "I want much more than a women's quota," she told the Institute for War and Peace Reporting. "I want to tell women, 'You can do a lot.' I want them to know they have choices; that they can be whatever they want. 'Your achievements are who you are.' That's my message for women." She continued, "Only a few women have been active in decision-making during the former legislatures because they are members of political parties run by others and they can't express their own opinion. We need a strong woman's voice that has the ability to convince others in Parliament."⁹⁹

Mubarak's 2010 campaign sought to further the ICWRE agenda; she stated that if elected she would push for legislation to create employment opportunities for divorced, widowed and unmarried women. She planned to continue lobbying against further erosion of the Personal Status Law. Although Mubarak's 2010 parliamentary bid was unsuccessful, she continued to make her mark on Iraqi society as an advocate for women as leaders, businesspeople and economic forces. In 2012, she was interviewed about a local project to empower businesswomen in Basra, emphasizing the need to "first start with the launch of an awareness campaign to educate Iraqi society about the nature of a businesswoman's activity in order to address the concerns of husbands, fathers and brothers regarding women entering the labor market, thus creating a situation where qualified businesswomen can be successful."¹⁰⁰ In September of that year, Mubarak responded positively to the drafting of Iraq's first policy on civil society, which would offer more opportunity for the Iraqi citizenry to contribute to the public debate: "This initiative will give high support for the future of Iraqi NGOs to be real partners on the ground with government and Parliament," she told the Office for the Coordination of Humanitarian Affairs (OCHA): "The policy will provide a concrete base to address the needs of the Iraqi people. It is great for NGOs and great for the Iraqi public."¹⁰¹

While Mubarak has not yet sat in Parliament, the significance of her contributions to furthering women's rights and situation cannot be disputed. Her ongoing work to empower women to undertake equal roles with men in Iraq's political, business, economic and cultural sectors has been both practical and successful. Although much work remains to be done, there is no doubt that Mubarak has made a difference toward advancing women's achievements in the political sphere.

Suhad al-Obaidi

Suhad al-Obaidi was born on June 11, 1974 in Balad, Salah al-Din Province. She is married and has five children (four girls and one boy), ranging in age from two years to high school. She and her husband call one of their daughters the "little parliamentarian" because she was born during the elections. Obaidi completed her primary education at Doha School in Balad in 1986 and graduated from Balad Girls High School in 1992. The central acceptance system and her demographic profile helped her become accepted at Tikirit University College of

Engineering, from which she graduated in 1997. She went to work as a municipal engineer in Balad on August 15, 1998. Obaidi worked for the municipality for 12 years, earning leadership positions including that of a technical department manager and director of project determents, prior to being elected MP in 2010.

Obaidi, who was raised in and serves Salah al-Din Province, began her political career in 2004 when she stood for election to the Balad Municipal Council; later she served on the Salah al-Din Provincial Council. According to Obaidi in a 2012 interview with *al-Baghdadia* TV, one of her male colleagues, who was once legal advisor to and is now director of Balad Municipality, was a primary influence behind her decision to become involved in the political scene. "He has political interests and stood in the governor of Balad elections more than once, and never stopped supporting me until I reached the position I'm in now," she told *al-Baghdadia* TV. "As the saying behind every great man there is a woman goes, I say behind every great woman there is a man." Obaidi cites providing a service to the citizens of her province as her main motivation for becoming an MP, as opposed to seeking material gains (although she reports her financial situation has improved approximately eightfold since being elected to Parliament). "My beginnings were in a public service department and it [Parliament] is a public service position for citizens. We look at the Iraqi citizen as being victimized along various stages and for decades and he deserves to be given a service. Also, I had an ambition to be part of the political process in Iraq."

This ambition has been at least descriptively realized, as Obaidi landed her parliamentary seat in 2010 and was reelected in 2014 by means of the party quota. She represents al-Hal Bloc within al-Iraqiya Slate and was elected initially in that party's open-list system by gaining 4,000 votes from the city of Salah al-Din, the largest number of votes garnered by a woman from that list in 2010. Obaidi stated in her television interview that some of her party leaders had otherwise suggested recommending her for a ministry post. "There was a suggestion that I take a ministerial post such as Ministry of Municipalities or Ministry of Women. My ambition is not to be a minister but to have my voice heard, because the ministry will restrict me in making statements. If it is offered to me, I say it depends on the situation. But right now I do not have this ambition."

Obaidi describes her role as an MP as both challenging and time-consuming, requiring her to be farther away from her family and household duties than was required as a local politician. "Political work is not as easy as some people think; it is very difficult and there needs to be a harmony of thoughts and visions," she explained to *al-Baghdadia* TV. In keeping with the thoughts of many of Iraq's female MPs, in the 2012 interview, Obaidi cited sectarianism, lack of security and violence as important barriers to parliamentary progress, placing blame on the United States for its ongoing involvement in Iraqi affairs:

> The Iraqi political process was made under the pressure of the US and caused these sectarian alignments. A current politician remarked how Paul Bremer asked him whether he was Sunni or Shi'a—and on that basis the Interim Governing Council was established and then the party lists and so on…they were chosen on a sectarian basis and this sets a dangerous precedent…this makes for a non-institutional state, though everyone is calling for an institution-based state utilizing relevant expertise and technocracy. But as it is now we cannot establish a state except along sectarian lines (political and religious).

Suhad al-Obaidi's education, expertise and experience in civil engineering initially placed her on the parliamentary Committee of Public Services and Reconstruction, a committee that she frequently represented to the press. According to Obaidi, this committee supervises several ministries including the Ministry of Reconstruction, Municipalities and Transport in addition to the Municipality of Baghdad. "I have extensive experience in public service departments and have supervised a number of projects," she told *al-Baghdadia* TV. "All of this enabled me to perform my duties on the Reconstruction Committee." However, in 2012 she transitioned her efforts to the Federations Committee partly due to her desire to have an impact on corruption being reported at the level of the Provincial Councils. As a former Provincial Council member, Obaidi explained, "The work of the Provincial Councils is supposed to be a monitoring one, in support of the executive authority in the province. But unfortunately through being on the Provincial Council and meetings with people and being with Iraqis on the street…we noticed that many complaints come through against the members of the Provincial Councils; they extend beyond their monitoring duties and most Provincial Councils are accused of corruption." Obaidi also changed parliamentary committees to help address issues with election laws related to the gender quota: "I moved to the Federations Committee out of national concern because there are amendments to the Provincial Council laws in addition to the law of the Kirkuk Provincial Council, and there was a deficiency in the quota of the al-Iraqiya List. I moved to this committee to fix this problem."

In 2012, Obaidi represented al-Hal Bloc in its stance against withdrawing confidence from the Maliki government. In June of that year, al-Hal Bloc had retracted its MPs' signatures from the no-confidence resolution due to the bloc's opinion that the request was motivated by influences outside Iraq. At that time

Obaidi told *AIN*, "Hal Bloc decided to suspend its MPs' signatures from this project because it is a regional one set by Saudi Arabia, Qatar and Turkey…it is not an Iraqi project. In addition to that the Iraqiya Slate did not reply to the demands of the bloc."[102] She warned against sectarianism which she opined would lead to the dissolution of the Iraqi state: "This project [the no-confidence resolution] will be followed by the project of dividing Iraq called for by the President of Kurdistan Region, Masoud Barzani, and some sides within the Iraqiya Slate."[103] During this crisis Obaidi reported feeling her own security at risk. "There are threats by some of the heads of the blocs to the members of the Hal Bloc," she stated. "Personally, I did not receive any threat until this time."[104] Obaidi criticized al-Iraqiya Slate leaders, claiming they were assuming a position of dictatorship within the party: "I emphasize with great regret that we as MPs in the Iraqiya Slate suffer from marginalization, exclusion and dictatorship of the Iraqiya Slate leaders as they work for favour of their personal and partisan interests."[105]

Shortly thereafter Obaidi played a role in encouraging resolution to the sectarian political crisis. On July 21, 2012 she stated, "The conflicting parties held individual meetings and this is a good sign for possibility of reaching a solution for the crisis…I think that a compromise will be reached to dissolve the political disputes."[106] Later that month, meetings indeed were arranged between Ibrahim al-Jafari (head of the Iraq National Alliance), Iyad Allawi (leader of the al-Iraqiya Slate) and Minister of Telecommunications Mohamed Allawi. However, the meetings did not result in finding a resolution to the crisis and, as described above related to Bajari, a group of MPs formed a new alliance within the Iraqiya Slate, fragmenting the party's influence. "There is no suspension within the Iraqiya Slate," she stated to *AIN*. "But the new alliance will correct the performance of the Iraqiya Slate and make it adhere to its national project."[107]

Despite her substantive efforts to promote the agenda of her political bloc, Obaidi still maintained ties to her former parliamentary committee. She told *al-Baghdadia* TV, "I am not a defeatist by nature, and I always wish to return to my previous committee and we maintain contact with each other." In 2013, Obaidi returned to the Public Services and Reconstruction Committee. In June of that year she spoke with *Iraqi News* about potential corruption discovered among contractors associated with the office of Prime Minister Nouri al-Maliki: "The commissions of the projects start from the Premier's office, however when we investigated [the] Baghdad Mayorship over its flounder[ing] in implementing some projects which were supposed to be accomplished a year ago, we found that some contractors are associated … [with] the Premier's office." She concluded, "Moreover, many projects are implemented with poor technical specifications where the contractor's goal is to gain large profits rather than to ensure high technical specifications."[108] Clearly, Obaidi's engineering expertise assisted her committee to conduct these investigations of corruption related to municipal improvements.[109]

Obaidi has continued to focus her energies toward issues of greatest importance to her and her constituency including: women's and children's rights, maintaining fairness in electoral laws and battling the extremist insurgency. In 2012, the wife of al-Qaeda leader Ayman al-Zawahiri issued a statement calling on all Muslims to raise their children "in the cult of jihad and martyrdom."[110] Obaidi was one of many female Iraqi leaders to counter this statement by calling for efforts to fight extremism and religious prejudice and confront those who promote terror. In an interview with *Mawtani al-Shorfa* she said, "It is necessary to reject any call to raise children on or embrace teachings that incite violence and shedding innocent blood. The essence of Islamic belief stands counter to such calls because Islam urges to raise children on the values of compassion, goodwill, virtue and good deeds." In statements reflecting her position as a mother and human rights advocate, Obaidi added, "Children are the future generation, the pillars of nations and societies. It is essential to raise them in a healthy way based on compassion, acceptance of others and peaceful coexistence, whatever their affiliations and tendencies."[111]

Early in 2013, Obaidi expressed the opinion that the ongoing violence, terrorism and threats to Iraqi security were motivated by political agendas and international influences. On January 19, she told *AIN*, "The security file is correlated with the political situation where any retreat in the political posture would lead to destabilize[ing] the security situation or vice versa. The confused political situation could be easily exploited by regional countries or terrorist organizations to create tense political and security situations." Instead, she called for shared responsibility for security measures involving all the political blocs according to the electoral procedures set forth in the constitution.[112] In May 2013, Obaidi called upon Maliki to reveal names of political officials involved in bombings, telling *Iraqi News*, "Some politicians are leading terrorist groups and carry out bombings to create sectarianism and get more votes in the elections. It is difficult to eliminate terrorism in Iraq because the terrorists are protected by the government."[113] Obaidi has continued to advocate against terrorism and in favor of achieving accord among Iraq's political blocs. As recently as June 2014, amid the crisis with extremist groups surfacing in Iraq and Syria, she told *Alforat News* that Iraq's political forces needed to unite their position against providing aid to terrorist groups: "Iraq needs regional and international support to deter the pro-terrorism countries. Hence, the country is in serious need of political stability and harmony."[114]

Election promotion and reform also are important to Obaidi's political agenda. When Prime Minister Maliki, House Speaker Osama al-Najaifi and Kurdistan President Masoud Barzani attempted to postpone parliamentary elections in October 2013, Obaidi voiced her disapproval and exposed the political agenda behind the plan. As quoted in *Dinarvets*, she said, "There is an agreement behind postponing the elections between Osama al-Maliki and Massoud Barzani, to postpone the elections for six months or a year, so as to restore some of the [political] blocs' structure."[115] In 2014, Obaidi supported an initiative cosponsored by the IHEC and the Ministry of Transportation to display posters with messages promoting voter participation in that year's elections, such as urging citizens to pick up their voter registration cards, delineating the identification documents required to register, encouraging all citizens to go to the polls and educating them about the voting process. As Obaidi said, public bus promotion for the elections "could help in achieving good results as far as increasing awareness of Iraqi voters of the importance of the electoral process, and how to partake in it." She went on to encourage civil organizations and public opinion leaders to support the IHEC's efforts to urge all Iraqi citizens to cast their votes.[116]

Even among Iraq's ongoing struggles to maintain security and accord, Suhad al-Obaidi continues to believe that women in Parliament have a strong and influential voice. In her 2012 interview with *al-Baghdadia* TV, she explained her belief that the Iraqi woman is political by nature and that the parliamentary gender quota finally offered women a chance at democracy. "I can say that 75 per cent of the successful parliamentarians are women, and the ones who give most to the Iraqi citizens are women because they are more disciplined and faithful—with all my respects to my male colleagues. Most political bloc leaders speak highly of the role of women and [transitional government prime minister] Dr. Ibrahim al-Jafari testified to this in 2005 saying that [women were] 'more practical and honest in fulfilling the duties of the ministerial posts.'" Apparently Suhad al-Obaidi, despite the many opposing views of her sister MPs, maintains a firm belief in the power of women to influence policy.

Mariam al-Rayyis

Mariam Taleb Majeed al-Rayyis was born the seventh child in a family of children in 1972. Her father died two months before her election to Parliament and her mother is a housewife. When Rayyis became an MP, she reports that her mother expressed deep concern for her safety due to the security situation. Rayyis was married in 2012 to fellow parliamentarian Hasan al-Mousawai; they have no children. She holds a Bachelor of Law degree from Baghdad University and ran her own law practice for seven years prior to entering Iraqi politics in 2003.

In collaboration with a group of professionals including doctors, engineers and fellow lawyers, Rayyis helped to form the Assembly of the Coalition Movement, with which she continued to work until 2005. The movement included Ahmad al-Chalabi, leader of Iraq's National Congress during the interim government; Ibrahim al-Jaafari, the interim prime minister; and Nouri al-Maliki. In a 2012 interview with *al-Iraqiya* TV, Rayyis explained, "When you work as a lawyer there is a close bond between law and politics because the lawyer defends the vulnerable and wealthy citizens alike; in politics too." Rayyis has a long history of serving as liaison between government and the press. She was spokesperson for the 2005 Constitution Drafting Committee. As a prominent representative of the Shiʻite Iraqi National Coalition, Rayyis eventually became Maliki's senior media advisor, a position she left briefly in 2008 (due to a misunderstanding over a media release) but returned to in 2009 and retained until 2014.

A Shiʻa Muslim herself, Rayyis spoke to the media in 2005 regarding changes to the composition of the Constitution Drafting Committee resulting from protests arising from Sunni Arab groups that the committee lacked adequate Sunni representation. As committee spokesperson, Rayyis noted that Sunni Arabs comprised "an excellent percentage" of committee membership after several Sunnis were invited to join the Constitution Drafting Committee. In the same interview she stated that practical effort had begun toward drafting the constitution and that "it is now the most active element among other work teams in the National Assembly," holding daily meetings to achieve its mission. At that time, Rayyis described the emergent topics of interest being discussed by the Drafting Committee as the shape of Iraq's federalism; the relationship between church and state; and the official state language.[117]

In 2006, Rayyis personally attended the execution of Saddam and two of his key allies (half-brother Barzan al-Tikriti and former chief judge Awad Hamed al-Bandar). After the execution, Rayyis told state television network *al-Iraqiya* that the hanging occurred "between 5:30 and 6:30 am; Saddam was hanged first, then Barzan, then Bandar," and that "the whole thing was filmed."[118] This video of the execution, reportedly filmed using a cell phone by at least two of the officials in attendance (of whom Rayyis may have been one), was released on the Internet and was met with public outcry from international human rights groups.[119]

In a February 2007 interview published by the International Relations and Security Network, Rayyis spoke in favor of Maliki's plan to launch a security crackdown in Baghdad to stabilize sectarian conflicts and adequately distribute security resources. The plan involved the deployment of tens of thousands of US and Iraqi troops to the city and its division into nine districts, each of which would be placed under the authority of an independent Iraqi commander. Although some Sunni MPs criticized the plan as biased against certain sects, Rayyis claimed the plan was likely to succeed as both Americans and Iraqis backed it. A further reason for optimism, she stated, lay in the fact that the plan involved cooperation between the Ministries of Defence and the Interior, whose collaboration had been lacking in previous security efforts.[120] As this security plan had troops advancing in March 2007 into the volatile neighborhood of Sadr City, headquarters of the Mahdi army loyal to Moqtada al-Sadr, Maliki affirmed that the security crackdown would extend to every inch of Iraq, saying also that progress toward stabilizing the country would require a reorganization of his cabinet. Rayyis was reached by the press later that day to comment on the cabinet overhaul, stating that the reshuffle would involve new leadership for at least ten ministries and that a new independent Ministry of Health candidate would be appointed to replace the Sadrist loyalist who filled the post.[121]

In April 2007, Moqtada al-Sadr withdrew six ministers loyal to his movement from the government to protest Maliki's failure to set a timeline for US troops to leave Iraq. Rayyis was quoted on Maliki's behalf as saying that the Sadr Bloc was "exercising its democratic rights" by boycotting the government. "Despite the difference in our views, our national vision is the same," she stated. "Only the methods of achieving it are different. The Sadr Movement believes there should be a real timetable for the multinational forces to withdraw, but the government thinks such a thing at this time would be like putting a spoke in its wheel." She commented that Sadr could in fact provide an opposition that would prove effective to the existing (Maliki) government. "We need to have real opposition from outside the government," she posited. "This is a great beginning. The Prime Minister needs real opposition that can act as a watchdog inside the Parliament."[122] Some political analysts at the time opined that Maliki could use Sadr's defection to strengthen his own position, while he might use the threat of radical opposition to extract more US aid.[123]

Mariam al-Rayyis left her position as press advisor briefly in 2008, reportedly due to a misunderstanding about a press statement she had made regarding breaches to the constitution made by the Office of the Presidency (related to

Tariq al-Hashimi, Iraq's vice president from 2005 to 2009). "I was speaking about the Constitution Article 38,[124] Chapter 4," she explained to *al-Iraqiya* TV. "I spoke about the powers of the Presidency, especially Tariq al-Hashimi…I gave the Speaker of the House a list of breaches of the constitution and after that al-Maliki asked me to return and I am happy to work with him." Rayyis remained advisor to Maliki until his demotion in 2014.

Rayyis was noted to be in favor of greater cooperation between Maliki's central government and the Provincial Councils. Questioned in February 2012 regarding holding the Council of Ministers' session in Basra rather than in Baghdad, she described the decision as a positive step toward enhancing trust between the central government and provinces. "This is the first step yet is not the last, for the other provinces will be dealt with in the same way. The next stage will witness holding other sessions for the council in all other provinces to develop the cooperation between the central government and the local governments."[125] The purpose of the Basra session was to handle problems raised by the provincial governments and to work toward solutions. For example, "The central government will consider the problems with the local governments to set the solutions for them, like the calls of some of the Provincial Councils to be granted more authorit[y]," Rayyis stated.[126] Later in the year, the central government made good on its promise, as Ministry Council meetings were held in Kirkuk and Nineveh. "The CoM will hold its meeting on Tuesday [May 29, 2012] in Nineveh to discuss the means of cooperation between the central government and the local government there to perform the projects. This meeting will be the same as those held in Kirkuk and Basra provinces."[127]

Rayyis has continued to offer support to the State of Law Coalition. In December 2013, the prominent MP Ezzat al-Shahbander resigned as member, claiming Maliki had turned the coalition from a nationalist into a sectarian body. Rayyis was quoted: "We got used to some politicians or who claim being politicians who always change their political stances and release contradicted statements. Shahbander was close to the head of the [previously segmented] Iraqiya Slate, Iyad Allawi, and then he accused [Allawi] of being a dictator."[128] In January 2014, Rayyis spoke about the wide bloc alliances that would be required to form the new cabinet and set forth the nominees for the position of the prime minister: "The current political efforts among the political blocs are a normal issue especially those that have many political principals in common," she said. "We will have the wide alliances because we need the largest bloc to form the new cabinet and to nominate the new PM."[129]

Safia al-Suhail

Safia al-Suhail was born in 1965 in Basra and was the youngest of seven sisters. She considers herself to be a secular liberal. Her father, Talib al-Suhail al-Tamimi, was a sheikh and leader of the Banu Tamim tribe; her mother was Lebanese and Suhail has dual citizenship. Her family moved into exile in Beirut after the Ba'ath Party coup of 1968 led by Ahmed Hassan al-Bakr. They moved to Jordan in the early 1970s, then back to Beirut, where Suhail's father was assassinated in 1994 after taking part in a failed coup to overthrow Saddam. As Suhail explained in a 2012 interview with *al-Fayhaa* TV, she assumed her father's role after his assassination when she was 29. She became editor of the oppositional newspaper *al-Manar al-Arabi* and Advocacy Director for the human rights organization International Alliance for Justice. Suhail married the Kurdish/French dual citizen Bakhtiar Amin in 2000 and they have one son. The family returned to Iraq in 2003 and Amin was appointed Minister of Human Rights for the Iraqi Interim Government (IIG).

Suhail received her bachelor's degree in economy and management science at the University of South Lebanon. In her interview with *al-Fayhaa* TV, Suhail stated that both her father and husband influenced her decision to enter politics. Prior to the 2003 invasion, Suhail was one of only a handful of women invited to the opposition meetings in London and New York and was appointed to the Follow-up and Arrangement Committee of the National Campaign to Free Iraq from Dictatorship. There Suhail met both US President George W. Bush and British Prime Minister Tony Blair. In 2005, she sat in the balcony next to First Lady Laura Bush during President Bush's State of the Union Address, during which he publicly recognized her as a US ally and head of the Iraqi Women's Political Council.[130] Suhail was appointed Iraqi Ambassador to Egypt, a position she declined because, she claimed in her *al-Fayhaa* interview, many Ba'athists served in Egypt's Ministry of Foreign Affairs. Suhail stated her suspicion that the Iraqi Consul in Egypt at the time was one of those responsible for her father's assassination.

Suhail was elected MP in December 2005 under the secular Iraqi National List. She left the Iraqi National List in 2007, citing her opinion that party leadership made decisions without considering the opinions and participation of members. She further felt the party's stated pluralism in nationalities and political ideas of Islamic democracy, liberalism and equitable distribution of positions was not implemented in practice. Running as an independent, Suhail was reelected to Parliament in both 2010 and 2014 without aid of the quota.

Suhail has particularly backed causes related to women's and human rights. She was a strong advocate for the gender quota, for empowering women in Parliament, and for ending violence against women. In February 2012, she gathered signatures from 50 female MPs on a petition to Speaker Osama al-Najaifi for Parliament to host the Minister of Women's Affairs, Ibtihal al-Zaidi, for purposes of discussing gender inequalities in Iraq.[131] She also urges strongly for Iraq to form a truly IHEC wherein women are fairly represented, although she has stated that building such an independent body is "impossible."[132] In September 2013, Suhail called for 50 percent of seats on the Social Peace Committee to be granted to women, "…in appreciation for their sacrifices for Iraq."[133]

Suhail has spoken out against sectarianism and in favor of a constitutional amendment to criminalize sectarian agitation. In January 2012 she stated, "The Iraqi Constitution needs many amendments," noting that "the most important amendment is to include in the constitution an article over incriminating sectarianism, especially by politicians."[134] In the wake of tensions between Baghdad and Erbil in late 2012, she noted, "After 2003, we witnessed great disappointments where we did not succeed in building the political and security stability and still there is nothing that reassures us of the possibility of addressing the current political scene, which is infested with tensions and disputes."[135] In early 2013, Suhail called for Parliament to summon the security leaders to its next legislative session and for unrestricted investigations into the failure of security forces to combat terrorism in Iraq.[136]

Suhail is an active member of the parliamentary Foreign Relations Committee, paying close attention to events across the Middle Eastern regions and their potential impact on Iraqis. She has called for the Iraqi government to exhibit diplomacy in dealing with the crises in Turkey,[137] Syria[138] and Egypt,[139] and for efforts to protect the constitutionally established voting rights of Iraqi citizens abroad.[140]

Alaa' al-Talabani

The name of Alaa' al-Talabani is one that has long been recognized in the arena of human and women's rights advocacy in Iraq and across the Middle East. Born in 1966 in Baghdad, Talabani is Kurdish by heritage and grew up in Kirkuk. She is married and has children. Talabani is a Sufi Muslim of the Qadiriyyah *tariqa* (spiritual order) in Kirkuk, the daughter of a sheikh who placed very high importance on the traditions of Ramadan, especially *tarawih* prayer said in that month. The Talabani family has its own *takyah* (Sufi meeting place) in Kirkuk.

Talabani completed her early education in Kirkuk. She was accepted to university in Basra, but her family did not allow her to attend there; she studied at the Technical Institute in Kirkuk. She joined the Patriotic Union of Kurdistan in 1986 and served as the vice president of the Kurdistan Women's Union. Following the 1991 Gulf War, Talabani was fired from her teaching position at the Technical Institute, and was detained and interrogated for not being a member of the Ba'ath Party. She then fled Iraq with her children; they moved to Iran, back to Iraq, to Syria and finally to the United Kingdom where she studied language and human rights defence. She holds a master's degree in English literature. Since returning to Iraq after the 2003 invasion, Talabani has completed several international courses in politics, conflict resolution, women's affairs and peace promotion. Talabani received two certificates in public policy from the Harvard Kennedy School of Government.

Talabani continued to speak out for Kurdish and Iraqi women's rights while living in the diaspora. Back in Iraq in 2003, she cofounded Women for a Free Iraq with Zainab al-Suwaij after the two women had met earlier that year. Talabani also cofounded the Iraqi Women's High Council, which in collaboration with Women for a Free Iraq helped to draft policies on the role of women in the country's post-conflict reconstruction; unfortunately, there is no evidence that these drafts have been finalized or enacted. In 2003, Talabani was quoted by the Centre for Media and Democracy's SourceWatch.org project to have stated thus, "We, the women of Iraq, are uniting. We are the most organised sector of the civil society in our country. We won't be ignored anymore."[141] At present, she provides leadership training at the Women's Centre for Capacity Building and has organized and/or chaired several conferences on women's political participation in Iraq.

Talabani has represented the Kirkuk Governorate in the Iraqi Parliament for all three successive terms since 2005. Jalal al-Talabani, who served as president of Iraq from 2005 to 2014 and secretary general of the Patriotic Union of Kurdistan, is Alaa' al-Talabani's uncle (her mother's brother). In her 2012 television interview for *al-Baghdadia* TV, she claimed it was not her uncle's support that won her a parliamentary seat. She said:

> Thanks to God, I did it with my own personal effort. From the beginning I loved political activism and started from zero. I did not become an MP overnight and I did not become a person of authority because my uncle Jalal Talabani helped

me. I worked in the branches of the party from the smallest department and with the most junior members until I achieved a leadership position in the Kurdish National Alliance and then stood for parliamentary elections. And thank God, in a recent report about our performance in the Parliament in the previous round of sessions they described our performance as one of the best among the Kurdish women MPs in Baghdad. And they nominated me for re-election due to my quality performance. Although, of course the President has added a lot of credibility to me and I consider him my role model in his faith towards work and sacrifice.

According to Talabani, her academic achievements in the United Kingdom greatly assisted her to achieve success in her parliamentary role as an active member of the Committee on International Affairs. A sizeable portion of her *al-Baghdadia* TV interview focused on her philosophies surrounding relationships between Baghdad and Kurdistan. At one point the interviewer brought up some public criticism Talabani incurred in the Iraqi media when she sided with her uncle in a statement he made that Kirkuk is the al-Quds (Jerusalem) of Kurdistan. "Is Kirkuk occupied like al-Quds?" the interviewer posed. "I wouldn't put it this way," Talabani responded. "This slogan existed also during the previous [Saddam] regime, and President Talabani, being also the president of the Kurdish National Union, made this statement during his years of struggles with the previous regime. He meant that Kirkuk is dear to us in the same way that al-Quds is dear to the Palestinians; Kirkuk is our Kurdistan's Quds. When he was asked on one occasion he said Kirkuk has the sanctity of al-Quds for the Kurds; and at the time we saw it as occupied by the old regime." When questioned as to why this was repeated after the old regime was long gone, she replied "again, for the special place that Kirkuk is to the Kurds," replied Talabani. "All our demands during the liberation movement had Kirkuk as its priority. It is still our first priority and cause, if not even more. All the negotiations that we underwent with subsequent Iraqi governments from [President of Kurdistan] Mulla Mustafa Barzani to his highness Jalal Talabani were unsuccessful due to the issue of Kirkuk. It is as sacred to us as al-Quds is to Palestine. But now we want to pursue our goals using the constitutional and legal methods and tools and the consent of the people of Kirkuk."

This exchange referred to the ongoing political battle over Kirkuk. This oil-rich city is situated approximately 180 miles north of Baghdad and marks the border between northern Kurdistan and southern Iraq. Kirkuk historically was home to three separate ethnic groups: Kurds, Turkmen and Christians. During the 1970s and 1980s, Saddam—to solidify his hold over the city—banished tens of thousands of Kurds and Turkmen from Kirkuk and replaced them with Arabs loyal to his regime.[142] Shortly after the US-led invasion, the deportees began returning to Kirkuk, primarily Kurds who wanted Kirkuk to become a part of the semiautonomous Kurdistan region. Article 58 of the Transitional Constitution (changed to Article 140 in the 2005 version) stipulated that a referendum to decide Kirkuk's fate would be collected by the end of 2007.[143] The referendum was subsequently postponed until summer 2008 and continued to result in a standoff that delayed provincial elections.[144] At the time of her 2012 interview, the Article 140 mandate had still not been carried out and the struggles—at the root of which lies the control of Kirkuk's substantial oil resources—continued.[145] "Article 140 of the Constitution says there was a demographic transformation due to the policies of the old regime," Talabani said in her *al-Baghdadia* TV interview. "We need to do a census and then the referendum which means all the people of Kirkuk will take part including Arabs, Turkmen and Christians. Then we can decide whether it should be part of Kurdistan." Talabani indeed stood for parliamentary election with the Kirkuk mandate as the first and second planks in her campaigning platform, stated as follows in the Iraqi Parliament Guide:[146]

> First: Demanding the land, in implementation of Article 140 of the Iraqi Constitution, which provides for the following: • Complete elimination of the effects of Arabisation, displacement and ousting. • The peaceful return of Kurdish areas including the city of Kirkuk to the Kurdistan Province. Second: Demanding the wealth ownership [sic], in implementation of Articles 111, 112 and 141, which provides for the following: • Kurdistan people to benefit from the natural resources and wealth including the oil. • Revival of the economic infrastructure of Kurdistan in order to achieve citizens' prosperity in the present and in the future.

Talabani continued to vocalize support for implementation of the referendum mandated by Article 140. In May 2012, she criticized Maliki's visit to Kirkuk and his statements at the Council of Ministers meeting there, telling *AIN*: "We expected Maliki to talk about Kirkuk suffering from the former regime which displaced its original people, the Kurds and the Turkmen. We hoped Maliki would discuss the means of applying Article 140 and the agreements concluded between [Maliki's] State of Law Coalition and the Kurdistani Alliance, but he ignored the Kurds and the Turkmen's lost rights." She added, "This visit complicated the disputes between the Central Government and Kurdistan Regional Government while Iraq is facing a political crisis."[147] It is notable that the collapse of the Iraqi Security Forces in the battle against ISIS militants—primarily fought by the

Kurdish Peshmerga—resulted in the Kurds seizing control of Kirkuk in June 2014.[148] Talk of a referendum to declare full independence of Kurdistan from Iraq continued, although movements to enact such a referendum were suspended by the threat of ISIS against Kurdish territories.[149]

In 2013, Talabani spoke out against demonstrators demanding the release of political prisoners Sultan Hashim Ahmad al-Ta'i (who was Saddam's Minister of Defence) and Watban al-Tikriti (Saddam's half-brother), invoking their crimes against the Kurdish people. She said, "Unfortunately, some of the demands of the demonstrators in the western provinces are not related to the services or bringing justice to the innocent people, but related to cancelling the law of the Criminal Committee related to the crimes against Kurdistan Region and releasing Hashim and Tikriti who committed anti-humanitarian crimes against the Iraqi people during the former regime."[150] She further called for increased representation for the Kurdistan Alliance "in the ministerial committee headed by the Deputy Premier, Saddam al-Shihristani, tasked with discussing the demonstrators' demands in attempts to achieve the balance in bringing back the dismissed employees from the governmental institutions, especially those of the North Oil Company."[151] The cases against these two war criminals, particularly Sultan Hashim, embody the complex ethnic and sectarian divisions that Iraq continues to face. While many Iraqi nationalists venerated Hashim for his role in the Iran-Iraq war, the Kurds know him as a major perpetrator of the Anfal genocide from 1986 to 1989 in which 180,000 Kurdish rebels and civilians were murdered.[152] As Talabani stated, "Releasing Hashim and Tikriti is an underestimation of the Iraqi blood and the victims of the Shaaban revolution and Anfal."[153]

In addition to her interest in the status of Kurdistan, Talabani has been a major champion for Iraqi women. As an active member of the Kurdistan Women's Union she successfully lobbied to change articles of Iraqi law to reflect greater gender sensitivity.[154] In the early years of the post-2003 government, she provided leadership training at the Women's Centre for Capacity Building. She has organized and chaired several conferences on women's political participation.

Talabani was instrumental in building a Multi-Party Women's Caucus in Parliament. In an interview with *iKNOW Politics* at the International Conference on Effective and Sustainable Participation by Women, Algeria, in December 2013, Talabani described the initiative as one for which women from different parties and backgrounds came together for the first time. "After…months of discussions and letting everybody be aware of the importance of having a women's caucus, we have spoken to the leader of the bloc and parties inside our Parliament and trying to make them just agree and understand as well why this caucus is not something against men, it's not something against political parties, it's just to collect the womanpower and women's capabilities towards more rights," she explained.[155] The Women's Caucus was responsible for creating and publishing the National Platform for Women just prior to the 2010 parliamentary elections. In collaboration with the US National Democratic Institute (NDI), the caucus began work toward the National Platform for Women in October 2009 by staging a three-day conference to identify policy priorities.[156] When the National Platform was released in February 2010, NDI quoted Talabani as saying, "I consider economic empowerment for women as the most important issue. If a woman is well-situated economically, she will be able to participate and have a greater role in all areas of life."[157] Since the 2010 elections, the Women's Caucus has debated and amended several pieces of important legislation affecting women. According to Talabani, the caucus has been able so far to "work with the Minister of Women's Affairs and with...civil society and women activists, journalists as well, to try to put recommendations for drafting new laws for women and family, and also on so many other issues that reflect the whole society, not only women, and especially the security issue."[158]

Despite her significant and substantive efforts, Talabani still characterizes the participation of women in Iraq's governance as minimal and their contributions as marginalized. As she told *al-Baghdadia* TV in 2012, "Women are still far from having an impact on political decision-making." She expressed profound concern that candidates with an extremist religious agenda could prevail and usher in an era of suppression of women's rights like what has happened in neighboring Iran. "In the elections, the candidates will be elected based upon religious orientation," Talabani said. "This will be a party-based election, not based upon their points of view on issues or projects."

Majida al-Tamimi

Majida al-Tamimi was born on September 9, 1961 in Baghdad. She is married to a physician and academic at the University of Mustansiriyah, Ismail al-Saffar. The couple has one son, Mohammad. Tamimi was elected to Parliament as a member of the al-Ahrar (Sadrist) bloc. She is a Shi'a Muslim. Tamimi earned a PhD in business management from the University of Mustansiriyah after receiving her bachelor's degree in 1981 and her master's degree in 1988. She reports being at the top of her class in all her years of university study. She was appointed as a teacher in the College of Management and Economics at the University of Mustansiriyah and continued to teach until she received her master's degree.

Tamimi also holds an advanced certificate in English language and certificates in ICDL, E-Learning and computer applications specific to her profession. She has authored several works. At the University of Mustansiriyah, she supervised and taught both graduate and postgraduate students and was head of university quality monitoring. She has attended several conferences, guest taught at various Arab universities and been a member of the Higher Council of Quality at the Ministry of Higher Education.

Tamimi's business expertise along with her other qualifications landed her a leadership position on the parliamentary Finance Committee when first elected as MP in 2010. She continued to lead and represent this committee upon reelection in 2014. Tamimi belongs to the al-Ahrar (Liberal) Bloc, which is a Shi'a Islamist political coalition formed by previous followers of religious and political leader Muqtada al-Sadr. The Sadrist Movement had been part of the United Iraqi Alliance (UIA) during the December 2005 elections—the UIA subsuming at that time most of Iraq's Shi'a Islamist parties. The Sadrists detached from the UIA prior to the 2009 provincial elections due to disputes with Maliki and the Supreme Council. For the 2010 parliamentary elections, the UIA re-formed—excluding Maliki's Dawa Party—as the National Iraqi Alliance. Strong opposition to what appeared to be Maliki's third term as PM led Muqtada al-Sadr to officially withdraw from the political scene in 2014 and his movement to re-form as al-Ahrar Bloc under the political leadership of Basra Governorate representative Dia al-Asadi (although Sadr retains the bloc's spiritual and ideological leadership). Al-Ahrar Bloc runs on a platform of fiscal reform and the elimination of corruption, which the bloc believes ran rampant during Maliki's government. Al-Ahrar Bloc won 34 seats in the 2014 Parliament, making it the second largest grouping in the central governing body.

Tamimi refers to Muqtada al-Sadr as *Sayyid* (a title of respect given by Shi'a Muslims to people believed to be directly descended from the Prophet Mohammed through his daughter Fatimah's marriage with Ali). In her 2012 interview with *al-Iraqiya* TV, she told the reporter: "When we returned from Jordan [in 2009], the Sayyid and his al-Ahrar Bloc said that the independent candidates are welcome to serve Iraq, especially those with higher degrees...My colleagues and students at the college encouraged me a lot and on that basis I [acquiesced] and al-Ahrar bloc had initial elections...it was a very good experience...there was a quartet consisting of all the specialties and they asked me specific questions in the field of management and economics and in politics and culture. The bloc's slogan was 'the people's choice is our choice' and so the people chose and I was one of the elected ones for the Rasafa side of Baghdad."

She added, "Al-Ahrar bloc has an admirable history; the Sadr family gave a lot of martyrs; no one could overestimate what they gave, which was their lives...especially when I remember the Second Martyr [Muhammad Sadiq al-Sadr] and his two sons were martyred because they said truth to a tyrant. Who would dare speak under Saddam? ...the Second Sadr Martyr dared, and from his Friday sermon pit [pulpit]—that's why I am honored to work under their support."

Tamimi firmly backs al-Ahrar Bloc's ideological stance against governmental fiscal corruption. She serves on a Branch Committee of the main parliamentary Finance Committee that provides oversight to the performance of the Iraq Central Bank and other powerful banks in the country. In 2012 she told *al-Iraqiya* TV, "Myself and Mr Ali Abd al-Husain al-Yasiri, we received reports from more than one source and now we are investigating...The governor of the Central Bank and his deputy and team have been invited for questions more than once...it is a fact confirmed 100 percent that the Central Bank's performance has been deteriorating since 2011." In September 2012, Tamimi reported that the Ministry of Finance had run out of funds due to Minister Rafi al-Issawi's payments of salary advances to staff and installments toward loans taken by the minister's predecessor, Baqr Jabr al-Zubeidi. "The payment of instalments on these advances and loans needed to solve this situation in the long-term is preventing us from stopping advances and additional loans until the funds have been recovered into the State Treasury," she stated.[159] However, when in October 2012 arrest warrants were issued against the Central Bank Governor and 36 Central Bank employees accused of corruption, Tamimi called the action hasty, unprofessional and politically motivated. "I officially asked all stakeholders about some files suspected of corruption, although I am not convinced that their answer or failure to respond should be disclosed to the public," she told *Iraqi Dinar News*. Tamimi further explained that the statement of objection to the Central Bank was not aimed at a specific person, but at certain procedures; and should have been handled professionally and confidentially "because the Central Bank is an institution concerned with the country's monetary policy, and its reference in this format is a hasty action that affects the Iraq economy and our reputation in international forums."[160]

As the Central Bank Governor was replaced after these investigations and arrests, Tamimi told *Voice of Iraq* late in 2012 that the way was paved toward removing three zeroes from the ID. Administrative currency reform was identified as needed to reduce costs of cash transactions, in addition to providing coins for small denominations to be used in daily circulation. While proponents of removing the zeroes claimed it would be a step toward improving ID purchasing power, some economists considered that the cost would outweigh the benefits. "The process of lifting the zeroes from the currency in 2013 depends on the nature of the policy of the new Central Bank Governor," Tamimi stated to *Voice of Iraq*. "The ground is prepared for the process...especially if there is fear that counterfeit currency will enter and replace the original currency. If this happens the inflation rate will reduce [international] trading."[161] Central Bank concern over spread of counterfeit currency did delay the elimination of the zeroes from the ID in 2013, despite the fact that "the [oversight] committee did not receive a letter from the CBI [Central Bank of Iraq] about this proposal or postponing it," Tamimi said.[162]

Tamimi has carried her high standards of financial integrity into the realm of political campaigning. In her *al-Iraqiya* TV interview she asked, "When a person votes for an MP, do they know who they are, their history?" adding, "Some MPs—not all—reached a point of bribing voters with mobile phones, blankets, or $100 to buy their votes. [Citizens should ask] If he is giving me this money, how else is he going to compensate for his losses except by stealing from Iraq?" She herself claims never to turn down a financial request from a constituent, instead giving what little she has. "I try not to reject them because, as [Fourth Islamic Caliph] Ali ibn Abi Talib said, do not be shy from giving little because pure deprivation is surely less than what you give."

As a loyal representative of her Bloc, Tamimi strongly criticized the Maliki government for its failure to attract international investments, although she told *al-Iraqiya* TV that her statements were professionally, rather than politically, inspired. "My statements are professional...investment capital is cowardly and it needs a secure environment politically and otherwise. We are not preparing this environment [to appeal to] outside investors with all the bombings and assassinations," she said. Tamimi tied the necessity to attract investors to the fundamental needs of Iraqi citizens, saying, "When we interview people the thing they ask for most is employment. This person who finished his or her study and graduated wants to secure his future and to have an income and this is his right. We must put all the blame on the government because we must activate the private sector and the Investment Commission has the responsibility to attract investment." In April 2013, Tamimi announced the Finance Committee's resolution to calculate surplus oil revenues in the State Budget and redistribute those funds to the people. "The surplus from oil revenues will be distributed to poor families, not all segments of society," she told the *Iraqi Gazette*, "so it will be fair and in accordance with legal procedures."[163]

Since her reelection and Maliki's resignation as prime minister in 2014, Majida al-Tamimi has continued her efforts on the Finance, Economic and Investment Committees in Parliament. Late in 2014, she was heavily involved in a workshop to discuss Parliament's role in preparation and oversight of the National Budget. She was one of 23 MPs to participate in the conference, which highlighted the importance of enhancing Parliament's capacity to substantively contribute to budget revisions and provide necessary oversight to ensure that the National Budget is spent in line with governmental programs and according to the needs of Iraqi people. Discussion also focused on the engagement of MPs with civil society to encourage a "bottom-up" approach to ensure inclusiveness of all Iraqi citizens in the National Budget process. Results of the workshop included a recommendation to establish a parliamentary Budget Directorate to provide the necessary analysis and research to ensure budget transparency and to perform parliamentary oversight with maximum professionalism. At the end of the workshop, Tamimi awarded the host organization, Arab Region Parliamentarians against Corruption (ARPAC), with a trophy to commemorate their contributions to the program.[164]

Tamimi continued to strive toward eliminating corruption by leveraging the National Budget. In December 2014, she informed *al-Baghdadia News* that the Finance Committee would recommend to Parliament substantial cuts to four ministries (Interior, Defence, Education and Health) in the 2015 budget to reduce the rampant corruption in those state institutions. "If the money is very limited there will certainly be a reduced level of corruption," she stated, "And when funds are available in abundance in this case it is likely to corrupt them [the ministries]." Tamimi further stressed the need to "balance internal and external loans to bridge the existing deficit, which is likely to reach 37 trillion dinars...the adoption of the budget must include all the necessary things...[such as] salaries, allowances and the defence and interior ministries and displaced persons, and social welfare...As for the rest, such as the allocation of funds for investments, we did not seek anything up to this moment, so for investments and other recreational things we do not need [to budget] at the moment."[165] In January 2015, Tamimi criticized a fellow Finance Committee member for using phantom numbers to estimate oil revenues. The continued decline in oil prices in the Middle Eastern region at that time brought to Iraq financial hardship, lack of liquidity and a fiscal deficit of as much as 60 trillion dinars given that the country's federal budget is based 85 percent on oil revenues. "According to [the committee member's] ratios the deficit is 60 trillion rather than 25 trillion Iraqi dinars because when the allocation is based on phantom numbers the results surely will be fake as well," Tamimi stated to *AIN*, also calling upon Kirkuk to deliver the agreed-upon levels of oil exports. "The Kurdistan region does not deliver the amount of oil agreed upon under the recent federal agreement...we receive 193,000 barrels out of 550,000 barrels...where is the remainder of these quantities?"[166]

Tamimi clearly has had impact on Iraq's future in her parliamentary role and is frequently consulted for her expertise in economic and fiscal responsibility. In her 2012 *al-Iraqiya* TV interview, she iterated her faith in due diligence and proper parliamentary process to accomplish goals in the public interest: "On the legislative front, the projects originate with the government and as for the Financial Committee...when we get a project we study it immediately and give it a first and a second reading, then vote on it, but we wait for the government to take action. We say there are problems with ownerships legally, administratively and technically—then isn't this a problem we need to discuss and find solutions to? It is not enough to say it is a problem but do nothing about it," she told the reporter. "If our compass is not pointing towards the best for Iraq, no project will be successful. Our starting point must be the question, 'is this project going to benefit Iraq or not?'" Tamimi's approach to legislative action has earned her notable respect and influence.

Summary

This chapter summarized the case studies developed from the extensive data gathered via televised interviews and secondary research, illuminating the backgrounds and demographics of the MPs of interest, influences on their election, and the special causes and legislative efforts they have championed.

Many Iraqi female MPs perceive that the gender quota has had minimal value in assisting them to attain their parliamentary seats. Rather, these women have tended to rely upon encouragement from their constituencies, connections with influential leaders (generally males), and support from colleagues, husbands and other family members to campaign for and achieve election. Only Hanan al-Fatlawi and Suhad al-Obaidi believed the gender quota was working well for women in Parliament. In several instances, the MPs have gained election and/or reelection without assistance from the quota.

The case studies derive from diverse backgrounds and religious and political affiliations. Four represent the al-Iraqiya Coalition (secular opposition to Maliki's State of Law Coalition); three of those are in al-Hal Bloc while the fourth is in al-Hurra. Three represent the State of Law Coalition. Two represent Kurdistan (one each with the Patriotic Union of Kurdistan and the KDP). One represents the al-Ahrar (Sadrist) Bloc, one is politically Independent, and Jinan Mubarak sponsored her own eponymous party under the Iraqi Union Coalition in 2010. Of the 11 case studies who have served as MPs, 3 have served a single parliamentary term; 6 have been reelected once; and 2 have been reelected twice. Six of the women are Shi'a Muslims; two are Sunni Muslims; one identifies as Sufi Muslim; and three are secular.

Yet despite the diversity of their ethnicities, experiences and affiliations, the case studies have many common challenges. For example, they struggle to balance the demands of political office with family obligations. Many of them report that participating in Parliament places them under financial constraints. As they strive to uphold the principles and platforms of their respective political parties, some of them have encountered difficulties when their opinions or ideologies differ from those held forth by party leadership. Probably the most ubiquitous issue shared among the case studies is Iraq's prevailing insecurity. Female MPs live under constant apprehension of potential violence; they face death threats and are forced to hire bodyguards to protect them, even while inside the Green Zone. Three of the case studies have survived assassination attempts specifically targeting their own persons.

Most of the case studies report having been active in civic organizations prior to standing for office, and this grassroots activism has offered them some degree of training and preparation to function in their parliamentary roles. Further, these women are quite highly educated. All but one (Noura al-Bajari) of the case studies are educated at the bachelor's level or higher. Two (Karima al-Jawari and Alaa' al-Talabani) have master's degrees and three (Etab al-Douri, Hanan al-Fatlawi and Majida al-Tamimi) have PhD- or MD-level education. Yet several mentioned that women in Iraq's Parliament are relatively unversed in parliamentary procedures and unprepared for full political participation.

These MPs have tended to sit on the parliamentary committees most relevant to their educational backgrounds and expertise. They have worked toward and championed policies consistent with their passions and knowledge bases. These efforts begin to speak to their ability to attain parliamentary representation of a substantive nature. Chapter 6 delves more deeply into the qualitative analysis of the substantive representation Iraqi female MPs have achieved since introduction of the gender quota, including legislation introduced and policy outcomes achieved—both real and perceived—within the evolving infrastructure of Iraq's political system.

6

Substantive Representation: How Have Women Affected Public Policy?

This book has discussed how, immediately after the 2003 occupation, the role of women in the Iraqi political arena became a central topic of debate among the United States, the emerging Iraqi government, Iraqi women and women's groups. The Bush administration used rhetoric on Iraqi women's rights to justify and validate the ill-advised war and subsequent occupation and to serve as a barometer for the success of democratization in the country.[1] Within Iraq, the status of women was symbolically framed to represent competing ideologies: conservative religious groups sought to restrict women's political empowerment in order to limit the infiltration of Western influence,[2] while Iraq's history of tribalism and patriarchy dictated women's participation in politics as unacceptable under traditionalist interpretations of gender and family roles.[3] The establishment of governmental and electoral systems by the Western interventionists, formed along sectarian divides with little input or support from Iraqis, exacerbated sectarianism and contributed to ongoing violence and insecurity rather than building the infrastructure that would allow durable democratic systems to evolve.[4] It is from within this contradictory and volatile environment that women in Iraq's Parliament have sought to gain a political voice. On one hand, women's political participation has been supported by the electoral gender quota, financial incentives and educational programs. On the other, their ability to achieve political empowerment is stifled by threats of violence, lack of confidence and self-efficacy, and continuing patriarchal traditions in parliamentary procedures.

This chapter presents a qualitative analysis of the political gains, supportive and oppositional factors that have affected women's substantive representation in the Iraqi Parliament since adoption of the 2005 Constitution and electoral gender quota. Collected data consisted of 19 transcribed televised interviews, 10 reports and 280 news articles/press releases. These data contained specific reports of the performance of Iraqi women in legislative roles and/or specific mentions or quotations related to political action by the 12 women who formed the case studies. All data were entered and analyzed using nVivo Pro v. 11 qualitative analysis software.[5]

The qualitative analysis focused on exploring the values, meanings, beliefs, thoughts and feelings characterizing the experiences of Iraqi women MPs as they achieved and undertook their political roles.[6] The analyses revealed that the Iraqi female MPs elected since 2005 have encountered far more challenges than supports during their journey toward political empowerment.

Major Achievements in Women's Substantive Representation since 2005

The data were explored through the lens of democratization and feminist theory, and the sociopolitical concept of gender quota, which posited the term "substantive representation" to describe the degree to which women elected to legislative office become able to exert active influence on public policy. Democratization theory suggests that female legislators must achieve a significant level of substantive representation for a polity to successfully transition to a democratic state, and that the degree to which democratic systems have been established and integrated into society also influences the political efficacy women may gain. Feminist scholars conjecture that positive changes toward gender equality can be achieved only by the creation of political structures within which women's interests can be autonomously represented, and women's political agency is a defining characteristic of a democratic state. Therefore, these analyses sought to illuminate whether and how women's increased involvement in public roles mandated by the quota has facilitated Iraq's progress toward democratization, and how the nation-state's failure to achieve full-fledged democracy has impeded women's progress toward becoming mobilized as political agents. First and foremost, the analysis involved assessing the degree to which women in the Iraqi Parliament have become able to actively and effectively shape policy debates that have resulted in the enactment of constitutional provisions and/or law.

The 2005 Constitution and Parliamentary Gender Quota

The Transitional National Assembly (TNA) elected in January 2005 was the body charged with drafting the permanent constitution for Iraq's emerging nation-state. This constitution was drafted hastily in the aftermath of the invasion, according to a strict timetable imposed by the interventionists, and under conditions of continuing occupation and insurgency during which the Iraqi government was not fully in control of or responsible for its own military forces or national security.[7] The TNA paid at least superficial attention to ensuring the legitimacy and widespread acceptance of the resulting constitutional document by installing some guarantees of public participation. The constitution was to be drafted by an elected assembly, presented for discussion and then for ratification; if not ratified, the process was to be reinitiated from the beginning. Majority support from at least 16 of Iraq's 18 provinces was mandated for ratification.[8]

Three contentious issues infused the drafting of Iraq's permanent constitution: the appropriate constitutional role for Islamic laws and values; the level at which to incorporate guarantees for basic human rights, including freedoms of religion, thought and expression; and the equality of rights and freedoms for marginalized groups, particularly women.[9] Democratic and feminist advocates suggest that fair legislative environments provide a base of human security from which the advancement of women's rights can be promoted.[10] The 2005 drafting of Iraq's permanent constitution presented multiple opportunities to achieve justice, fairness, protection and representation for women; and indeed the ratified document and pursuant laws adopted many fundamental rights for women including the right to education, health, political participation, labor, choice of spouse, divorce in case of fault and alimony. The constitution confirmed that Iraqis are equal before the law regardless of gender or ethnic variables, setting the stage for equal opportunity, litigation rights, labor, property, protection of motherhood and childhood, health care, education, social security and other rights for women.[11] Yet in practice, actual implementation of such constitutional provisions, especially in a traditionally conservative and patriarchal society such as Iraq's, depends upon a number of diverse factors such as level of state control, the stability of the governmental system, checks and balances, judiciary independence and executive oversight.[12] Although gender equality may be set forth on paper, the reality on the ground is that many gaps and inconsistencies remain in the legal and legislative systems that have potential to adversely affect the implementation of political and human rights for women.[13]

Despite lackluster support from the US-led Coalition Provisional Authority (CPA), the gender quota was adopted and implemented in the January 2005 elections for the TNA, and women filled more than the mandated 25 percent of parliamentary seats in the transitional body (87 of 275 members, 31.6 percent). Just 8 women served on the 55-member Constitution Drafting Committee;

consistent with transitional election results in the composition of the overall committee, 5 of the women were Shi'a Muslims who represented the United Iraqi Alliance (UIA), 2 were Kurds and just 1 (Radha al-Kuzai'i) was a secular independent.¹⁴ Among the female committee members was Mariam al-Rayyis, one of the case studies. Foreshadowing her later role as media advisor to Maliki, Rayyis was named media spokesperson for the Constitution Drafting Committee. As such she undertook some responsibility to smooth over the controversy that erupted due to the inclusion of only one Sunni Muslim on the initial Drafting Committee rolls. Two months later, the TNA attempted to rectify this situation by nominating an additional 14 Sunni members to the committee, drawn from various Sunni political parties and other entities. Sunni members then comprised "an excellent percentage" of the Drafting Committee, according to Rayyis's report to Baghdad's *al-Mada News* in June 2005.¹⁵ Regarding the status of women in the emerging constitutional draft, Rayyis expressed her view that the constitution should focus on widespread human rights, rather than narrowing on the rights of women: "When people talk about women and their role in the future constitution I usually say, we should not be talking about women's rights, but about the rights of the Iraqi citizen, be it man or woman. Whenever the citizen gets any rights women will automatically benefit from this. Talking about women's rights all the time is not very constructive. You might produce an image of oppression of women in Iraq, which I cannot share."¹⁶ Rayyis further opined that there was "no conflict" between the adaptation of *shari'a* in the constitution and the principles of secularism, stating, "We have a country with a Muslim majority. Thus we have to respect this character without compromising the other beliefs and confessions. There will be no problem, if these guarantees will be fixed by the constitution."¹⁷

The strict timetable for drafting the constitution, the poor and deteriorating security situation and the dearth of women's representation on the Drafting Committee contributed toward thwarting any efforts by the TNA to make the constitutional drafting process transparent and accountable.¹⁸ In particular, women's organizations campaigning for the inclusion of gender rights in the document were excluded from exerting any significant influence over the process.¹⁹ Further, traditionalist leaders dominated the committee, and half of the women on the committee were in favor of drafting a constitution in which Islamic law would take precedence over secular codes.²⁰ Therefore in the final draft some significant ambiguity and openness to interpretation remains.²¹ Article 14, Chapter 1 states that Iraqis are equal before the law without discrimination because of gender, race, nationality, origin, color, religion, sect, beliefs, opinion, economic or social status. At the same time, Article 41 states that no laws may be passed that contradict the "established rulings" of Islam and that Iraqi citizens are "free in their *personal status* according to their religions, sects, beliefs, or choices" (emphasis mine).[22] As a result, certain interpretations of the Article could fundamentally compromise women's access to divorce and rights to inherit property;[23] according to the Iraq Legal Development Project, "Article 41 of the Constitution essentially calls for the withdrawal of the 1959 [Personal Status] Code and the establishment of a new regime in its place. Although the existing code and its amendments contain provisions which discriminate against women, a new regime opens the door to a wider range of uncertainties for women in terms of the rules that will apply and the individuals or institutions that will apply them."[24]

Other provisions stipulate equality between women and men in the right to work (Article 22/1), access education (Article 34) and health services (Articles 31.32.33); and the right of women to give their nationality to their children (Article 18/1).[25] Despite endeavors by conservatives to remove it, the 25 percent electoral quota and women's right to the same political rights enjoyed by men (Chapter I—Article 20) were maintained in the permanent constitution.[26] However, the interpretive ambiguity between Articles 14 and 41 set a precedent that equality before the law does not have to mean equality in all rights, as reflected in implementation or nonpractice in applying the quota.[27] The 2005 Iraqi Constitution did not enhance women's rights, and in fact may not even have protected the (nominal) rights that were in place under Saddam's regime.[28]

During her presentation at Boston University in 2013, Hanan al-Fatlawi discussed the inadvisability of producing a permanent constitution within such a short time frame. "Writing a constitution in a very short time put us in front of a lot of challenges," she said. "This is one of the messages that daily we say to our brothers in other countries: don't go very fast. You need to stop, you need to think, you need to go through things that are in the favour of your country, rather than just to make someone else happy about you."[29] Fatlawi also advocated for constitutional reform in this talk, saying, "Our constitution needs some amendments so that the system could work properly." She added, "Of course, to be in a country with a real constitution written by an Iraqi is better than to be without a constitution." Regarding the quota, Fatlawi said, "Previously we don't have women in politics unless they [are] a member of the Ba'ath Party. Now women [are] present in politics, present in Parliament, present in the Provincial Council, of course below our ambition, below our expectation, but still it's a fair system for women to prove themselves and to work."[30] Clearly at least some female political figures perceive the 2005 Constitution as, at best, a compromise for women's advancement. Among the constitutional provisions that Fatlawi suggests are needed for the parliamentary system to work properly are those articles addressing the fundamental issues of personal status.

Personal Status Law

The centrality of Iraq's Personal Status Law in the debate about democratization, women's rights and political mobilization has been discussed previously. Relevant to the analysis of substantive representation, however, are the labors women spent on upholding the relatively progressive Personal Status Law No. 188 that had been in place since 1959 and the degree to which those efforts met with success. Attempts to insert language in the Iraqi Constitution that would effectively repeal Law No. 188 and replace it with the much more conservative *shari'a*-based Resolution 137 began less than six months after the Iraqi Governing Council (IGC) put the interim constitution into effect in July 2003. Within weeks, when the news reached the ears of women's activist groups, large-scale protests were staged both inside and outside of Iraq urging for the resolution to be withdrawn.[31] The fact that Resolution 137 was introduced behind closed doors without so much as a nod to democratic debate spurred the most vocal outcry among prominent Iraqi women. Nasreen Barwari, who was the Minister of Public Affairs at the time, was quoted, "It was the secret way this was done that is such a shock. Iraq is a multiethnic society with many different religious schools. Such a sweeping decision should be made over time, with an opportunity for public dialogue."[32] Two months later, the resolution was repealed. However, the repeal did not curtail further moves to undermine the Personal Status Law that continued during the constitutional drafting process.[33] Fierce debate ensued in the Constitution Drafting Committee between Kurds, liberal politicians and women activists on the side of preserving the 1959 code; pitted against the Shi'a clerics and religious politicians (notably, both men and women) seeking its abolition.[34] Elimination of the 1959 code posed threats not only to those advancements in personal rights that women had achieved, but also to the very channels through which progress toward such advancements were possible.[35] Perhaps more importantly, the battle required women's activists to divert their attentions to preserving a law that was nearly 50 years old and had been inconsistently enacted at best,[36] at the expense of missing a prime opportunity to lobby for improved personal status legislation.[37]

The interpretive contradiction between Articles 14 and 41 was the final result of the constitutional debate over Iraq's Personal Status Code, an outcome dreaded and decried by activists who feared that removing jurisdiction over family affairs from the state and placing it in the hands of clerics would have dire ramifications.[38] Activist and retired judge Zakiyya Isma'il Haqqi summarized the sentiment of many women's protests at the time: "This new law will send Iraqi families back to the Middle Ages. It will allow men to have four or five or six wives. It will take children away from their mothers. It will allow anyone who calls himself a cleric to open an Islamic court in his house and decide who can marry and divorce and have rights."[39] Even Mariam al-Rayyis, who had campaigned for inclusion of Islamic interpretations of personal status in the constitution prior to the introduction of Resolution 137, a year later expressed concern about the potential effect of Article 41 on the Personal Status Code, stating that the 1959 code was "the pride of the Iraqi woman."[40] Upholding tenets of the Personal Status Code formed planks in the campaign platforms of two case studies. Safia al-Suhail, interviewed by *al-Fayhaa* TV in 2010, was asked her position on the law. "It is still one of the disputed issues," she told the interviewer. "We continue to call for review of the next phase after the establishment of the Constitutional Review Committee. The personal status act is in effect and in Iraqi courts but now we are wary of the amendment of Article 41. I've got a feeling we will be able to keep this law if part of its articles are modified to stay on. Iraqi family rights are interrelated," Suhail added. And in the online biography posted for her 2010 parliamentary campaign, Jinan Mubarak noted the following as a priority for her stance on domestic politics: "Working to install the rights of women which are stated in the constitution and to work on the amendment of Article 41 of the Iraqi Constitution to ensure no cancellation of the Amended Personal Status Law No. 188 of 1958 [sic]."

Al-Ali and Pratt have argued that the failure of the United States, the IGC and the Constitution Drafting Committee to designate personal status law as an area to be decided by the central government has allowed leaders from among the Kurdish, Shi'a and Sunni sects effectively to have separate laws, thus becoming a prime contributor to the sectarianism and strife that persists.[41] The end result for women has been not just the marginalization of their interests, but indeed the sacrifice of their well-being and rights as in some areas they have been pulled back to pre-1959 conditions.[42] As an illustration, in February 2014, Minister of Justice Hassan al-Shimari of the Islamic al-Fadila (Virtue) Bloc introduced new legislation for parliamentary consideration that would permit marriage of girls as young as nine years (recognized by law as the age of puberty), as well as legalizing marital rape, granting men who divorced their wives automatic custody of children over two years of age and making the practice of polygamy less difficult.⁴³ The proposed law, which came to be known, after the main Shi'i school of law, as the Jaafari Personal Status Law, would have applied only to Iraq's majority Shi'a population. On International Women's Day (March 8), thousands of women took to Tahrir Square to protest the bill, calling it a "Day of Mourning."⁴⁴ These protests along with general outcry against the measure delayed the vote until the April 30 elections made its consideration moot, and the Jaafari legislation has not been reconsidered to date.

Policy Legislation Promoted by the Case Studies

Since the electoral gender quota came into effect for Iraq's Parliament in 2005, elected women MPs have attempted to introduce policy change by serving in parliamentary committee roles and seeking to influence the legislative agenda, social and political attitudes and constituent opinions. The case studies (with the exception of Jinan Mubarak) represent women who held parliamentary seats in 2012, and therefore had won those seats in the 2010 election. In 2010, the Iraq Foundation and the Middle East Program at the Woodrow Wilson International Centre for Scholars collaborated to deliver an educational program designed to help incoming women parliamentarians to build skill sets that would prepare them to succeed as legislators. The trainings included three regional meetings between July 2010 and June 2013, held in Beirut, Lebanon and Amman, and covering such key topics as policy analysis; conflict resolution, consensus building and negotiation; committee operation; public speaking and leadership; parliamentary and party alliances; creating women's caucuses; and constituent relations.⁴⁵ To evaluate the outcomes of these training programs, the perceived accomplishments of the female MPs in their legislative functions and perceived obstacles to success, the Iraq Foundation administered questionnaire surveys to the women in July 2010 (baseline), spring 2011, summer 2011 and spring 2013. Survey results were cross-analyzed both quantitatively and qualitatively to determine trends, and the ensuing report highlights the ways in which women MPs have made impact on the Iraqi Parliament and overcome barriers to political mobilization.

The Iraq Foundation analysis reported that the vast majority of women in Iraq's Parliament said their primary goals and most significant accomplishments had been drafting, voting on and ratifying laws.⁴⁶ Specific laws championed by the women MPs mentioned in the survey data included legislation on "health services, education, literacy, welfare, smoking ban, retirement, justice and accountability, amnesty, property seizure, journalists' rights, compensation, and specific laws for ministries."[47] These legislative priorities also are well represented among the case studies for this book. Safia al-Suhail is quoted in the report as citing the following as the most important strides gained by women in Iraq's Parliament since quota implementation: "Drafting and amending priority laws serving Iraqis and meeting their basic needs, such as the Social Security and Health Insurance law, the retirement law, and the fundamental rights related to public and private freedoms, women being the main beneficiary...Monitoring the work of all public institutions and ensuring women's participation with a reasonable percentage, compared to women's proportion in the community, their efficiency and their maturity...The law of political parties and women's share in that law at the level of leadership not less than 25% [i.e., the quota]; [and] the law to establish the Independent Women['s] Commission."[48] In addition to the priorities of social services, human rights and women's political representation mentioned by Suhail, the case studies also reported working on legislation related to infrastructure, budget issues, amnesty, justice, discouraging sectarianism, governmental corruption and the enablement of civil society.

The case study MPs appear well placed on legislative committees, choosing or being assigned to parliamentary committees in close alignment with their respective educational and professional backgrounds. The policies promoted and advocated by the women also reflect the charges and goals of the legislative committees upon which they sit, as well as frequently falling in line with the platforms of their political parties.

Infrastructure and social services. Iraqi citizens suffered greatly across the decades of wars and sanctions, facing ongoing struggles to obtain sustenance and basic services including food, water, health care and electricity. Ashwaq al-Jaf, Etab al-Douri, Huda Sajjad Mahmoud, Hanan al-Fatlawi and Suhad al-Obaidi all publicly vocalized opinions regarding the need for legislation to rebuild and improve the Iraqi infrastructure. Such infrastructural improvements would have impact on such establishments as housing, health services and education.

Upon imposition of the international sanctions on Iraq in the early 1990s, a social welfare food assistance program was introduced by the Saddam regime whereby Iraqis received ration cards that allowed them to claim government-distributed household staples. Beginning in 1997, these humanitarian goods were obtained through the UN Security Council's "Oil-for-Food Program" which allowed the Iraqi government to export limited amounts of oil in order to purchase the food.[49] When war intervened in 2003, the Oil-for-Food Program was cancelled and thereafter the ration card system drastically deteriorated under conditions of insecurity, ineffective management and widespread administrative corruption.[50] The system was modified twice in 2010, first to cancel ration cards for those with incomes above a certain level and then to reduce the foodstuffs available to just five categories: flour, sugar, rice, cooking oil and baby formula.[51]

At the urging of economic analysts, in early November 2012 the Iraqi Cabinet announced its intention to completely abolish the ration card system, a move that met with substantial outcry from the populace and sparked controversy among political leaders.[52] Ashwaq al-Jaf and Etab al-Douri were among the MPs who spoke out against cancelling the system. As spokesperson for the parliamentary Agriculture Committee, Douri made public statements in July 2012 linking corruption in the food distribution program with merchant exploitation in the form of artificially inflated food prices, calling on Parliament to "Endorse tight law drafts against the merchants who exploit the national and religious occasions to exorbitantly increase the prices of the food materials." The following month, Douri also expressed support for the Agriculture Committee's draft of legislation to support the Modern Agricultural Villages, saying in a press statement that the law would "participate in reducing the unemployment of the agricultural engineers and the veterinarians in addition to its role in sustaining the food security." On November 9, Jaf stated that cancelling the ration card would be "a violation of the rights of the Iraqi citizens...poor families depend entirely on the ration card." Jaf used the Iraqi Constitution to back up her statements, noting, "The constitution obliged the government to ensure the prosperous life for Iraqis." Jaf's opinion at the time was that the ration program should be expanded and improved, that program corruption should be rooted out and dealt with rather than "correcting the mistake by making another mistake." And on November 11, Jaf called upon "all MPs to stand against the corruption accompanying the distribution of ration card foodstuffs." Just five days after announcing plans to cancel the rations program, the Iraq Cabinet rescinded its statement and the ration card system remained in place.[53]

Several case studies have worked toward policies related to governmental aid to the disadvantaged, including social security, the national retirement law, care for the disabled and support for widows and orphans. Data collected by the Free Iraq Foundation indicated that need for social services was the third most important issue facing Iraq (behind security and economic concerns) according to the female MPs surveyed.[54] In her televised *al-Iraqiya* TV interview, Huda Sajjad Mahmoud said laws to care for the disabled and establishment of a commission to protect the disabled were legislative efforts for which she had particularly pushed in Parliament. Safia al-Suhail was interviewed by *al-Fayhaa* TV specifically about her involvement in an event supporting the disability rights movement in Iraq. "We stress that we need many organizations which work in collaboration with many members of society and Parliament, both men and women, which represent the Iraqi population in all its diversity to support these movements," Suhail said. "We also strive to monitor and fight for laws and agreements that specifically cater for our needs and meet our aims… we believe that we need more in terms of legislation, government support and also support from international organizations." Jinan Mubarak's 2010 platform incorporated a plank calling for aid to widows and divorced women; Huda Sajjad Mahmoud advocated in 2012 that funds earmarked for armored cars be diverted to support widows, orphans and elders. Jinan Mubarak, Huda Sajjad Mahmoud and Majida al-Tamimi all worked on legislation to distribute Iraq's oil resources equally among Iraqis. This latter refers to a set of laws aimed at establishing a modern legal framework for the oil sector and a mechanism to divide oil revenues equitably within the nation. To date, these social services initiatives remain under negotiation and controversial, and are likely to require structural reforms and reduced administrative corruption to enact and implement.[55]

Human rights. According to the Free Iraq Foundation report, female MPs perceived their advocacy for the unveiling and management of human rights violations in Iraq as one of their greatest achievements in their parliamentary roles.[56] Among the case studies, human rights issues the women have championed include amnesty, treatment of prisoners, the death penalty, violence against women and freedom of opinion and expression.

Some MPs were vocal against the wrongful detainment, mistreatment and torture of prisoners in Iraq, particularly female prisoners, and the related question of legislation granting amnesty to innocent prison detainees. Amnesty remains an important issue for Iraq due to the way sociopolitical fractionalization was fostered by the interventionists after the Saddam regime fell. One of the first acts undertaken by Paul Bremer and the CPA post-invasion was to disband the Iraqi army (which was entirely led by Ba'athist officers) and to institute a widespread proscription of Ba'athism across Iraq,[57] officially recognized in the 2003 De-Ba'athification Law that barred Ba'athists from serving in any role in the emerging Iraqi government. The measure, which aimed to penalize Ba'athists who had engaged in terrorist acts under Saddam, effectively led to the exclusion of Sunnis from governmental participation, compromised the perceived legitimacy of the 2005 national elections among Sunnis and caused persistent insurgency and endemic violence throughout the ensuing decade.

Misapplication of the De-Ba'athification Law by Maliki's government led to the imprisonment of thousands of Sunnis—many of whom were not members of the Ba'ath Party, and others of whom had become Ba'athists merely as a condition of employment—who were innocent of any terrorist crimes.[58] Parliament passed an Amnesty Law in February 2008 that was ratified by the Presidential Council on March 27, leading to the release of 109,087 prisoners by July of that year.[59] The Amnesty Law sought to allow the release of those who had not been charged or tried, while excluding those being detained for violent crimes; however, the law has not been fully or consistently applied, and more than 100,000 Sunnis remained imprisoned as of 2016.[60]

Etab al-Douri worked toward full implementation of the Amnesty Law, stating in September 2012 that "the vote on the General Amnesty law… is an urgent need especially that many innocent people are still inside prisons unfairly and without committing offenses but they are the victims of the secret informant," inviting "the political sides which call for conducting reforms to prove their good will through endorsing the Amnesty law." At the same time, she stressed the "necessity to exclude whoever committed crimes against the Iraqi people from this law." Karima al-Jawari has also spoken for amnesty, calling on Parliament in January 2013 to "form specialized committees to speed up the legal procedures to release the innocent detainees and to submit the criminals to the courts." Both women were addressing the issue at a time when widespread Sunni protests were being carried out (beginning in December 2012 and ensuing throughout 2013) which centered on the repeal of the De-Ba'athification Law and the full implementation of the Amnesty Law. Unfortunately, as of 2016, the Amnesty Law has yet to be fully applied.

An interrelated issue was the push to introduce punitive justice for those who engage in sectarian violence. Both Etab al-Douri and Safia al-Suhail called for legislation that would incriminate those who agitate sectarianism. Suhail has taken the notion a step further to call for the punishment of politicians who allow sectarian language to be constitutionalized, stating in January 2012, "The Iraqi Constitution needs many amendments. The most important amendment is to include in the constitution an article over incriminating sectarianism, especially by the politicians." This effort coincided with the withdrawal of US troops at a time when the Iraqiya Slate suspended attendance of its MPs to parliamentary sessions in protest of what it called "marginalization and monopolization policies" adopted by the Maliki government.[61]

Budget, economy, and the Oil and Gas Law. Virtually all the case studies expressed opinions regarding the allocation of governmental budget funds during their political careers. The most volatile, and perhaps most important, economic issue considered by the Iraqi Parliament is the creation of an Oil and Gas Framework Law that would mandate—among other issues—the allocation of oil revenues among various sectors of Iraqi society. In particular contention is settlement of the stipulations set forth in Article 140 of the constitution, relating to disputed territories in the Diyala, Kirkuk and Nineveh provinces of Kurdistan claimed by both the Iraqi central government and the Kurdistan Regional Government (KRG).[62] Due to controversy surrounding control of these territories, settling the Oil and Gas Law questions has been highly advocated by the case study MPs who represent the Kurdistan Alliance, Ashwaq al-Jaf and Alaa' al-Talabani; however, others of the case studies have also spoken for its resolution. Fair and equitable distribution of oil revenues has been a major issue facing Parliament since 2003. To take meaningful action toward negotiating these much-needed policies, reduced corruption and infrastructural reforms are required.[63]

Because hydrocarbons form the mainstay of the Iraqi economy, viable oil and gas legislation has lain at the center of sectarian political debate. The multifaceted discussion closely relates to issues of federalism versus central governance and encompasses not only the federal Oil and Gas Framework Law but also development agreements, production-sharing agreements between Iraq and Kurdistan, oil and gas revenue sharing structures, the nature and responsibilities of the cabinet Ministry of Oil, and the reconstitution of the Iraq National Oil Company.[64] While international investment and knowledge may be required to enhance Iraqi oil and natural gas production, a fair and equitable legal environment surrounding oil and gas revenues must be in place to attract such outside investors.[65] The UN sanctions imposed in the 1990s severely curtailed Iraq's oil exports, a situation that improved marginally with the introduction of the Oil-for-Food Program.[66] Iraq has the fifth largest proven oil reserves in the world, the bulk of which are situated in the Shi'a-dominated southern regions of the country; however, substantial fields also lie in Kurdistan.[67] Both the first Gulf War and the 2003 invasion inflicted serious damage on the oil fields, and sectarian turmoil has compounded those damages. In the early post-occupation years, neither the UN nor the CPA appeared eager to alter the legal status of the Iraqi oil reserves.[68] But redevelopment of the reserves and renegotiation of field production targets after the Saddam regime have been high priority for the Iraqi government.[69] Despite crude oil production estimated at a growth rate of 950,000 barrels per day (bbl/d) over the past five years, production actually has grown much more slowly than the ambitious output targets set by the Iraqi government; a rapid general decline in oil prices after late 2015 adversely affected targets in Iraq as elsewhere.[70] Key challenges to meeting these targets include the failure to pass an Oil and Gas Law that would establish the export infrastructure, streamline the administrative process and improve contract terms to attract new international investors.[71]

Nearly all the hydrocarbon-related political disputes since adoption of the 2005 Constitution have pitted the central government in Baghdad against the KRG.[72] Controversies have erupted over the constitutional authority of subcentral governmental units to enter into hydrocarbon development agreements, dating from 2006 when the KRG attempted to negotiate previously drafted drilling and production-sharing agreements with companies from Norway and Turkey.[73] By 2007, the KRG had struck deals with more than 20 international oil companies (IOCs), arrangements which the KRG asserted were consistent with 2005 constitutional provisions yet to which the Maliki government strongly objected, indicating at the end of that year that the central government was considering excluding foreign oil firms that had entered into such contracts from doing business in Iraq.[74] As of 2016, these issues have yet to be completely settled and although an Oil and Gas Law was proposed in 2007, such legislation has neither been agreed upon nor enacted. Because Iraq's oil reserves are not evenly distributed across sectarian-demographic lines, the question of how oil revenues are to be equitably allocated also remains under debate. These uncertainties and disputes were compounded by the infiltration of the so-called Islamic State terrorist group, which staged attacks upon and, in some cases, seized oil fields and sold contraband oil on the black market.[75]

In February 2014, Ashwaq al-Jaf (whose husband is a former member of the Kurdish Peshmerga militia) warned Parliament against approving the 2014 budget law on grounds that it failed to provide adequate support for the Peshmerga forces fighting against the Islamic State. "Most of the disputed articles in the Budget Law are related to Article 140 of the constitution, the Peshmerga forces, the sanctions imposed on Kurdistan Region and the oil and gas file," she said in a press statement to *AIN*. A week later she asked for the government to redraft the budget and send it to Parliament immediately for approval: "Some political blocs started to use this issue for electoral propaganda and to topple others where the government has to redraft it and send it to Parliament as soon as possible," she said. Hanan al-Fatlawi also spoke out on several occasions to call for the Oil and Gas Law to be enacted. "After ten years of parliamentary system, we still don't have an oil and gas law right now," she decried in her 2013 presentation.[76] As the Oil and Gas Law issues remain unsettled, the efforts of the case studies to resolve them have been no more or less effective than those of their male counterparts in Parliament.

Electoral reform. Case study MPs have called for electoral reform to increase women's representation in government, to cement the authority and responsibility of the Independent High Electoral Commission (IHEC) and to restrict the development of dictatorial tendencies within the central Iraqi government by establishing term limits for the Premier. Safia al-Suhail called for Parliament and the IHEC to adopt mechanisms that would grant voting rights to Iraqi citizens living abroad. In 2012, Karima al-Jawari voiced disapproval of Parliament's endorsement of the commissioners named to the IHEC Board, stating that the vote was "done by political deals," and saying, "The endorsement of this law overrides the wills of the Iraqi provinces and minorities as it was based on political agreements rather than constitutional and legal bases." Unfortunately, to date these calls for electoral reform have yet to be answered, and the complicated and largely government-directed electoral process remains.

Women's issues. The advocacy action in which women and women's NGOs engaged to enact the parliamentary gender quota was described previously. In more recent years, Etab al-Douri, Hanan al-Fatlawi and Jinan Mubarak called for modifications to the gender quota system, both to increase the proportion of parliamentary representation for women and to extend the quota to other areas of government. Female MPs who participated in the May–June 2013 training conference conducted in Amman by the Free Iraq Foundation expressed that, although quotas alone are not enough, they initially were necessary to grant women a chance to pursue political roles in the first place. Participants suggested that quotas should be adopted across the board—that is in ministries, government, the private sector and education—in addition to Parliament.[77]

At the inception of her eponymously named political party in 2010, Jinan Mubarak advocated in her platform the enactment of a law that would allocate 10 percent of all jobs in Iraq's public and private sectors to be granted to qualified widows, divorced women and their relatives. Since 2003, Mubarak has worked through the Iraqi Centre for Women's Rehabilitation and the Iraqi Network for Peace to help women achieve employment and handle their legal affairs.

According to the Free Iraq Foundation report—although many female MPs do place focus on issues that particularly affect women—in 2011, 88 percent said they believed their colleagues did not pay enough attention to women's issues. Nearly all the MPs completing the 2011 survey reported believing that females in public office have neither advanced nor hindered women's issues. In 2013, again the majority (93 percent) indicated that their fellow parliamentarians (both male and female) do not pay enough attention to women's issues, and many (57 percent) said women's issues are marginalized in Parliament. By 2013, more than half of respondents said their colleagues had advanced women's issues, although others still reported that they have neither advanced nor hindered those causes.

The case studies provide a suitable illustration of the ways in which female parliamentarians have striven toward drafting, advocating for, debating and enacting public policy related to the important issues involved with the rebuilding of the Iraqi nation-state post-2003. Women in public office have been important contributors to these processes, and there is little evidence to indicate whether their contributions have been more or less effective than those exerted by their male counterparts in Parliament. As expressed by Hanan al-Fatlawi in 2013, all parliamentarians face significant obstacles: "We have many negative aspects especially in the Parliament right now. First of all, weak oversight rule [,] and sometimes it is absent. Because all caucuses participated in the government, all of them have ministers in the cabinet. So there is no real opposition…This is one of the reasons that the government is not productive and the Parliament is not productive at the same time."[78] Clarifying how these obstacles particularly affect the public contributions of women, and illuminating the levels of substantive representation these women have achieved, requires deeper analysis of the supports and barriers to political participation the female MPs have experienced from all societal segments.

Supports for Women's Substantive Representation in Iraq Parliament

Data were analyzed in terms of whether their sources contained references expressing supports for, versus barriers to, the achievement of significant policy-making contributions by female MPs in Iraq, especially the case studies. Among the coded data sources, by far more oppositional factors were discovered in comparison to factors in support: 520 references (62 percent) were coded as "oppositional," versus 316 (38 percent) coded as "supportive."

It was expected that supports to women's substantive representation might include such factors as having been involved in grassroots activism and/or belonging to or receiving endorsement from NGOs; international influences; connections with influential figures; education level and education in political processes; self-confidence and sense of political efficacy; availability of key

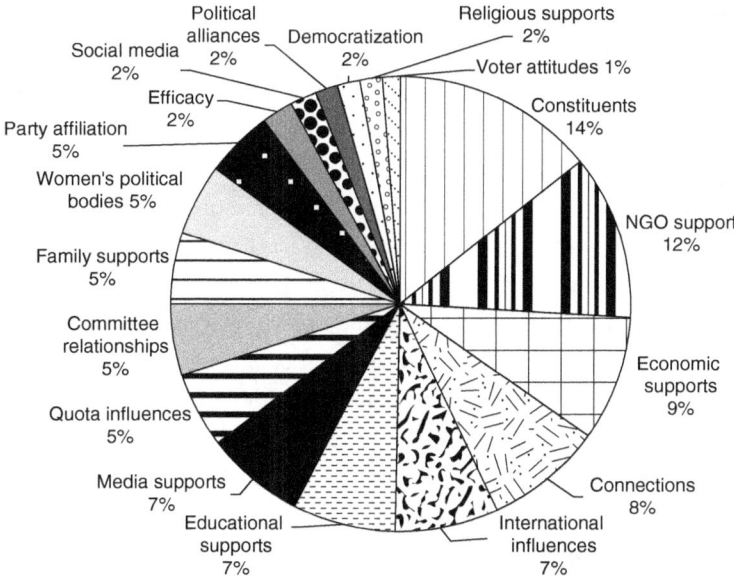

Figure 6.1 Factors in support of women's political empowerment in Iraqi Parliament

resources such as campaign financing; and party and religious affiliation. Figure 6.1 itemizes the supportive factors coded from the research data. Three of these categories, "Media supports," "Social media" and "Voter attitudes," are appropriately related to symbolic, rather than substantive, representation; those categories are discussed in Chapter 7.

Constituents. The supportive factor appearing most frequently in the coded data was constituent support. Six of the case study MPs discussed relationships with their constituents and the ways in which they received support from the people they represented, both during their campaigns and while in office. This opinion was echoed in the questionnaire data collected by the Free Iraq Foundation: according to the respondents, "serving their constituencies" was an accomplishment that was ranked first in order of importance in 2011, and the fourth in order of importance in 2013.[79] The MPs interact with their constituents primarily through public meetings and in-person visits. They also reach the people they serve by making media appearances and through web pages and social media platforms (see Chapter 7).

The majority of women responding to the Free Iraq Foundation surveys reported that serving their constituencies was the most important way in which they made impact on social and political attitudes.[80] Influence by women in Iraqi politics on public attitudes has been accomplished by such interactions as sharing opinions, assisting constituents to solve problems, making decisions according to constituent priorities, striving to narrow gaps between divergent opinions, being active and present in the community and following up on responsibilities and promises. The Free Iraq Foundation report confirms that the female MPs are aware and up-to-date regarding their constituents' priorities; 88 percent said they met with their constituents at least once per month, while the remaining 12 percent said they met with constituents at least once per quarter; and more than half said they had met 1,000 or more of the people they represented.[81] As of 2013, all the female MPs who completed the survey reported having offices in their constituencies.[82] Women MPs also form coalitions to address constituent issues, seeking to engage with constituents to foster trust and serve as mediators between constituents and political officials. Many MPs have established follow-up systems to address constituent concerns. Women MPs make sincere attempts to place focus on those issues that matter most to their communities, to prove their efficacy to make a difference in constituents' lives.[83]

The high priority on constituent relationships and the supports such relationships provide to women in public roles are also strongly reflected among the case studies. In her television interview with *al-Iraqiya* TV in 2012, Ashwaq al-Jaf explained that, although she does have an office in Parliament, her preference is for citizens to visit her Sulaymaniyyah office. The interviewer asked Jaf, "Is it easy to get into your office or is it blocked by concrete slabs and checkpoints?" She responded, "Never. It is just an office and has one guard. It is open, and the average citizen can drop by any time." Jaf says she has two phone lines, one for parliamentary business and one personal, but "both numbers are accessible to the average citizen." "Even prisoners call," she added. Jaf claims that she pays many visits to families of the sick and of martyrs, stating, "I do them on an individual basis, not as a group."

According to Etab al-Douri, her students at university and the dignitaries from her farming village of al-Taji encouraged and supported her campaign for parliamentary election. Douri gives back to her constituents by serving as a liaison between citizens and cabinet ministries to address their needs, such as employment or transference of duties. She shares her parliamentary salary with her constituency: "Everything I earn I share it with my people such as the widows, orphans, the needy and handicapped. I share with their special occasions such as weddings and if they become sick—undergoing operations, circumcision, even the woman who's left her house, I bring them back together and give them a gift," she told the *al-Baghdadia* TV interviewer in 2012. Huda Sajjad Mahmoud's experience is similar; she attributes her political accomplishments to interactions with her community's citizens. "The secret to my success is my office in the city and meeting people. I opened four offices in the city to facilitate for people and I pay for the rent and expenses," she stated on *al-Iraqiya* TV. Mahmoud expressed preference for granting priority to female constituents: "I am prejudiced towards women. Even in getting into the office, women first, then men, because women have more house responsibilities than men." Mahmoud claimed she also helps solve problems within provincial governmental departments by taking managers to the relevant ministries and facilitating cooperation between them. In July 2013, Mahmoud claimed to have reviewed and officially confirmed 400 applications for retirement salaries from members of the Diwaniyah Provincial Councils, with 800 applications still pending completion.

Majida al-Tamimi explained that her colleagues and students at the college were a prime source of encouragement in her parliamentary bid. Noura al-Bajari similarly credits employees in the clothing factory department she managed as important campaign supports. Bajari professed on *al-Baghdadia* TV that her electorate often accesses her at home, where she entertains and cooks for them. Suhad al-Obaidi explained in her televised interview that the Iraqi citizenry does not necessarily understand the role of an MP: "Some people come to the MP if they need to see a doctor or to follow up on an application." Yet Obaidi notes that being well known personally among voters is an important factor that helped her win her parliamentary seat.

NGO support. The place of civil society in democratization is critical, but variable. It can be an important element in facilitating transition from authoritarianism to more participatory governance. This is less likely to occur, however, when the regime is internally strong and willing to use repression, as was the case in the Ba'athist period when all NGOs were made illegal if they did not pledge allegiance to the Ba'ath Party. But civil society has a better chance of encouraging democratization when the regime is weak and divided and when NGOs receive crucial external support. The revival of former NGOs and the emergence of new ones in Iraq post-2003 represent a significant contribution toward political openings, including empowerment for women. This contribution is demonstrated among the case studies, as assistance from NGOs was indicated as the second most prevalent supportive factor in the data.

NGOs formed since 2003 worked closely with the UN to support national and local strategies for women's empowerment and civil society capacity-building, such as the implementation of programs to improve women's socioeconomic participation through literacy and educational interventions and vocational training.[84] One prominent example of how NGOs support women in Iraqi politics can be witnessed in the formation of the State Ministry for Women's Affairs, which is developing a national strategy for promoting the status of Iraqi women that will seek to mainstream the discourse surrounding gender and human rights in all cabinet planning and programming.[85] Further, NGOs such as the Organization of Women's Freedom in Iraq (OWFI) and the Women's Empowerment Organization (WEO) are working to reduce violence against women and providing shelter for women and girls escaping from honor killings and sexual slavery.[86] Increasing security for women would substantially facilitate their ability to contribute meaningfully to public policy. It is notable that the WEO efforts are being staged in cooperation with religious leaders and the Ministry of Religious Affairs, because women's ability to mobilize for progressive change within the constitutionally established framework of Islamic law is fundamental to their achievement of sociopolitical agency.[87]

The Free Iraq Foundation report discusses the alliances women MPs have formed outside Parliament. Respondents to their surveys reported recognizing that civil society organizations represent necessary partners outside Parliament to assist in promoting women's issues. Collaborative relationships with NGOs have helped female MPs gain support, run campaigns and organize protests. Women MPs also work with progressive judges and religious scholars to improve women's status through jurisprudence and the interpretation of *shari'a* as related to legislation.[88] Hanan al-Fatlawi expressed the belief that Iraq since 2003 has the largest number of NGOs in the Middle Eastern region; to illustrate the contributions of civil society, Fatlawi points to an NGO coalition that, when Iraq experienced a nine-month delay between elections and establishment of a government in 2010, took the case to federal court and won it.[89]

Alaa' al-Talabani's experience exemplifies the resurgence of civil society and women's NGOs post-2003. Talabani cofounded both Women for a Free Iraq and the Iraqi Women's High Council in October 2003, has provided leadership training at the Women's Centre for Capacity Building and has organized and spoken at several conferences on women's political participation. She remains an active member of the Kurdistan Women's Union. Ashwaq al-Jaf reports working with NGOs prior to becoming an elected MP, including the US-based American Rental Association and the British Human Rights Commission. Huda Sajjad Mahmoud was appointed to represent the Iraq Parliament at a regional conference for female Arab MPs, and Majida al-Tamimi represented the parliamentary Budget Committee at a 2012 workshop in Lebanon. Jinan Mubarak founded the Iraqi Centre for Women's Rehabilitation and Employment, and she continues to work with the center. Mubarak also formed the coalition of

NGOs known as the Iraqi Network for Peace, and has worked with the UN and other international organizations to aid Iraq's internal refugees. Prior to entering political life Maryam al-Rayyis belonged to the Assembly of the Coalition Movement.

In a 2012 interview with *al-Fayhaa* TV, Safia al-Suhail summed up the importance of NGOs and a civil society that represents collaboration between genders and among all segments of society, both to democratization and to the political empowerment of women:

> I believe that collaboration is the most important thing. Everyone supports these initiatives and supports them in their own ways, be it within political structures, strategic national organizations, the media, intellectual youth groups, and also key religious figures which play a vital role in addressing the incorrect understandings of the place of women in religion and society, condemning transgressions on women's rights and empowering women as active, valuable members of society. Therefore, I consider that collaboration is really important, and I believe that it is achievable… We see this as a really positive step towards establishing the role of female leaders as strong, independent figures of society worthy of contribution, and we thank the media for helping us spread this message and allowing the wider society to remain engaged in pressing issues surrounding the rights of women.

Economic supports. Approximately 9 percent of supportive references coded from the data were related to economic supports, such as constituents offering campaign donations and other campaign resources as well as MP salaries. Supportive factors related to the national economy also were referenced; for example, Iraq has worked with the International Monetary Fund and the World Bank to strengthen its economic institutions. Proposed legislations to restructure the banking system and stimulate development in the private sector have included reforms aimed at creating greater opportunity for women. The Iraqi government since 2005 has encouraged increased women's participation in the labor force by offering small business loans to women, educating women about employee rights and ensuring that employers in all sectors comply with the rules of employment.

Further economic supports were offered through US assistance given between 2003 and 2005 for Iraqi elections, election administration and training. The United States allocated $130 million in funds to support the 2005 elections, with $41 million obligated to assist with elections administration with tasks such as identifying Iraq's electoral needs, establishing an electoral institution and legal framework, delivering voter education, providing for election security and testing the reliability of the Public Distribution Information System database for use in voter registration.[90] The United States devoted nearly $6 million in grants to Iraqi NGOs to encourage women's mobilization in the electoral process. Grant recipients provided leadership training to women candidates in Baghdad, Basra, Erbil and Sulaymaniyyah, and conducted follow-up consultations with women elected to national and provincial legislative bodies. Grant funds were used to establish women's centers to organize trainings, provide resources, build a women's advocacy network and deliver voter education to increase awareness and public support for women's involvement in politics.[91]

Four of the case study MPs (Etab al-Douri, Noura al-Bajari, Majida al-Tamimi and Suhad al-Obaidi) reported having significant levels of personal wealth prior to their political campaigns, which they attributed to individual earnings, family inheritance and/or their husbands' occupations or holdings. Two other case studies reported that their finances had improved since becoming MPs.

Connections to high-profile male figures. The extent to which Iraqi female parliamentarians reach their political seats as a result of their socially accepted connections with influential males is important because the avenue through which women's political agency becomes legitimized affects the level and nature of political influence they achieve.[92] It is notable, therefore, that 9 of the 12 case study MPs have ties to male politicians or to other men with significant societal influence. Alaa' al-Talabani is niece to Jalal al-Talabani, who was Iraq's president from 2005 to 2014 and secretary general of the Patriotic Union of Kurdistan. Ashwaq al-Jaf's husband is a leader in the Kurdistan Democratic Party in Sulaymaniyyah and a Peshmerga activist. Etab al-Douri is married to Kareem Khalaf Muhammad Abu Hatem, once deputy governor of Baghdad. Huda Sajjad Mahmoud's spouse is a leader in the Da'wa Party. Mariam al-Rayyis has a strong connection with former prime minister Maliki, for whom she once served as public relations advisor. Noura al-Bajari has a close relationship with former Speaker of the House Osama al-Nujayfi, a friend of Bajari's husband and a denizen of Mosul, Bajari's home city; Bajari also is close with Minister of Manufacturing Ahmad al-Karbouli. Majida al-Tamimi is married to an influential physician and university lecturer. Safia al-Suhail has a strong tie to Hoshyar Zebari, who served as Iraq's Minister of Foreign Affairs. Suhad al-Obaidi has received much support from a former male colleague who is director of Balad Municipality.

These findings suggest that Iraqi women with close ties to socially and politically influential men thus increase their likelihood of becoming elected to Parliament. It is interesting, however, that female MPs with such connections often seek to downplay the contribution of those ties to their own electoral successes. For example, Alaa' al-Talabani told *al-Baghdadia* TV that "Honestly, Jalal Talabani did not support me...Thank God I did it with my own personal effort... From the beginning I loved political activism and started from zero. I did not become MP overnight and did not become a person with authority because my uncle Jalal Talabani helped me." Noura al-Bajari, when asked by an *al-Baghdadia* TV interviewer whether she used her close relationship with Osama al-Nujayfi and Ahmad al-Karbouli for her own personal interests, replied, "Not true. Mr. Osama al-Nujayfi will always be the Speaker of the House and he is the son of our city [Mosul] and I have a right to be proud of him and to seek his help. As for the Minister of Manufacturing, I have a normal relationship with him, like my relation with other MPs, and he has not helped me with anything, even the government positions we got."

Further evidence suggests that women campaigning for public office recognize the importance of enlisting influential male support in addition to the endorsement of women and women's groups. When Jinan Mubarak launched her political party in 2010, she sought out high-profile male dignitaries to help fill party rolls. And despite the power exerted by religion and tribalism on Iraqi politics, some men—even Islamist conservatives—openly support women's right to enter and participate in the political sphere. One such supporter is Ala'a Makki, Islamist chair of the parliamentary Education Committee. Makki was quoted in a CBS News article in March 2010 as stating that the Prophet Muhammad "...was taking advice and consulting with women around him, and the consultation was real consultation. I mean, he built decisions on that consultation." "I'm not liberal. I'm Islamist. But I understand that women should have a real role," he added.[93]

International influences. The influence of international interventionists and organizations in Iraq since 2003 may be interpreted as both a support and an obstacle to Iraqi women's political agency, and this analysis supports both interpretations. Supportive aspects of international influence overlap in some cases with NGO supports, because much aid to encourage and facilitate women's political mobilization was delivered through international NGOs. For example, the UN collaborated with local groups to promote gender equality and support national strategies for women's empowerment and civil society capacity-building. The UN also implemented several projects to address barriers to women's socioeconomic development, including literacy education and vocational training.[94] UN Women supported legislation to combat domestic violence. As of 2013, the UN Development Program had provided 1,000 women with microbusiness loans through Iraq's Private Sector Development

Program and enhanced access to justice for women and children by supporting the development of a regional anti-domestic violence bill. UNESCO strives to mainstream gender equality across programs encompassing education, science, culture, and communication and information, helping to link women with the peace and security agenda in Iraq. The International Organization for Migration (IOM) provided socioeconomic assistance for women including support for female-headed households, vocational training in business management and the formation of women's empowerment groups.[95] The Free Iraq Foundation capacity-building program for female parliamentarians was a collaborative partnership between the UN and the Middle East Program at the Woodrow Wilson International Center for Scholars. This foundation conducted a conference titled "Women Leaders in an Era of Change" to explore how Iraqi and other women parliamentarians in the Middle East and North Africa may take advantage of opportunities that have arisen following the regional changes resulting from the 2011 Arab Awakening or Arab Spring. This conference was the second to pair Iraqi women parliamentarians with female MPs from other countries across the Middle Eastern region, following the "Women's Political Participation" conference in June 2012.[96]

The 2005 Iraq Constitution, at least nominally, responded to internationally established conventions demanding gender equality, in particular Convention to End All Forms of Discrimination against Women (CEDAW), which stipulates that states embody the principle of gender equality in their national constitutions and other legislations. CEDAW emphasizes the principles contained in the Universal Declaration of Human Rights, the Convention on Political Rights of Women (1954), the Convention on the Nationality of Women (1957), the Convention on Consent to Marriage, Minimum Age for Marriage (1962) and the Declaration on the Elimination of Discrimination against Women (1967).[97]

As mentioned, the United States provided support through State Department grants to train female parliamentary candidates in political process. The US Institute of Peace also provided funding to conduct conferences to train Iraqi women on candidacy and political participation, and United States Agency for International Development (USAID) supported women's participation by developing a strategy to incorporate gender considerations into its grant opportunities. The US Department of Defence provided security and logistics advice in support of the 2005 and 2010 elections.[98]

Among the case studies, several worked with international figures and organizations post-2003. Alaa' al-Talabani led the constitution and democracy symposia at the "Voices of Women in Iraq" conference sponsored by the United

States in Baghdad in 2003. Prior to and shortly after the 2003 war, Talabani met several times with US President George Bush and UK Prime Minister Tony Blair. She contributed to a number of British and Arab regional newspaper and magazine articles on the status of Iraq and its Kurdish population in particular. Safia al-Suhail was an invited member of the preinvasion International Planning Committee and had working relationships with former US president George W. Bush and members of the US Congress; as mentioned in Chapter 5, she was once publicly recognized by Bush at a State of the Union address as one of Iraq's "leading democracy and human rights advocates"; Bush also mentioned Suhail's father, who was assassinated by Saddam's agents in 1994.[99] Ashwaq al-Jaf collaborated with the British Human Rights Commission as part of her work on the parliamentary Human Rights Committee.

During her 2013 Boston University presentation, Hanan al-Fatlawi expressed her belief that the majority of Iraqis were grateful for the multinational intervention that deposed Saddam. It was interesting, however, that this opinion was strongly challenged by a female audience member who introduced herself as Iraqi: "Frankly speaking, the majority of Iraqis do not feel grateful for this," the woman admonished Fatlawi:

> Even though Saddam was a dictator, if we are not brave enough to overthrow him, then we do not deserve freedom, so we are not grateful. The other thing, with my respect of course, you keep talking about dictatorship and Saddam and sectarianism as well. Well, yes, Saddam was a dictator, but after these ten years we discover that he was a mild dictator. Because what we are seeing ... now in Iraq is worse thousands of times what we had in his time. Explosions, cars, I thought we never have apartheid, we never had militias. Yes, he was a dictator, yes, he was hard, but he wasn't a murderer in the same way we have now. It is now that we have sectarianism in Iraq. It's now, not before that.

Fatlawi responded strongly: "Believe me, without such interference maybe Saddam [would rule] till now and maybe more than one hundred years ruling Iraq through himself and through his son and maybe grandson! We are of course grateful for the interference, but I am not going to say all of us are grateful for what happened later on. A lot of mistakes [were] done. Probably we are now facing a lot of troubles as a consequence of the mistakes done during that time. So this is what Iraqis right now believe."[100] This impassioned interchange only underscores the multiple viewpoints from which the results of the 2003 intervention are perceived.

Educational supports. A public education system that ensures that citizens from all societal segments are well prepared to participate in a country's polity is prerequisite for democratization. The 1991 Gulf War and years of UN sanctions eroded the Iraqi educational system, particularly in ways that affected women's educational achievement and ability to secure employment and an understanding of political process.[101] After 2003, even with a gender quota in place, female aspirants to public office needed to be identified, available and trained by their political parties or other interested bodies to be effective legislative contributors.[102] Educational programs such as the ones sponsored by the Free Iraq Foundation, the Wilson Center and UN Women proved invaluable for capacity-building and essential leadership training among female parliamentarians. A total of 63 female politicians received training through the three Iraq Foundation workshops held in Lebanon and Jordan between 2010 and 2012.

Closely related to economic privileges, the educational supports of the case study MPs likely contributed greatly to their election and their subsequent efficacy as political entities. Of the 12 case studies, 10 have advanced university degrees. Their educational backgrounds have influenced the parliamentary committees on which they served and undoubtedly have facilitated their sense of political efficacy.

Supportive influence of the parliamentary gender quota. Similar to international influences, the gender quota has been perceived as both supportive of and detractive to the agency of women in Iraqi politics. References to the quota as a supportive factor in the research data were found at a much lower level than expected. As stated in the 2013 Free Iraq Foundation report,

> Parliamentary quotas can help women MPs overcome some obstacles related to male dominance in Parliament. However, women's quotas are often seen as "window dressing," designed solely to present a positive image but without parallel political allowance for women to use their reserved seats to enact change. Some perceive the quota for Iraqi women as imposed by Western ideas. Most IWPs [Incoming Women Parliamentarians] are in Parliament because of the parliamentary quota, and although the quota system has shortcomings, IWPs respect the system. Quota systems must be well designed, well implemented, and temporary to be effective.[103]

The paucity of reference to quota support offers further evidence that, although the parliamentary quota has allowed women to gain a foothold in Iraqi politics, their full-fledged contribution to legislative reforms, nation-state reconstruction and democratization has yet to be realized. Safia al-Suhail commented in an interview with *al-Fayhaa* TV regarding the 2010 elections: "Really, all parties raised slogans that promoted the rights of women within political programs and stressed the partnership between women and men in state administration and in the country's future. But then it became all about the struggle for power and interests and quotas among men from within the same party, not seeing the fact that women are part of the building process and an essential part of building democracy in Iraq ... All political blocs used women and did not give women any real appreciation in the level of representation of the community." Within this frame of reference, it is noteworthy that Suhail won her parliamentary seat as an independent candidate in 2010 without the quota.

Other supportive factors. The remaining references in the data coded as supportive of Iraqi women's substantive representation included parliamentary committee relationships, supports from family, the existence of women's political bodies, the influence of political party affiliation and other political alliances, a sense of efficacy as political agents, supports from religious communities and efforts toward democratization. The case study MPs emphasize the importance of positive relationships and teamwork—whether those relations be with fellow committee members, family, one's political bloc or one's religious leaders— for accomplishing the duties of an MP and creating alliances that lead to the enactment of legislation. All the case study MPs sit on parliamentary committees and three of them have served as committee chairs. Five of the case studies mention supports they have received from their husbands and/or families while pursuing their political careers. Three case study women express a sense of the efficacy exhibited by both themselves and other women in legislative roles. For example, Huda Sajjad Mahmoud told *al-Iraqiya* TV, "When the change that we wanted occurred in the previous regime, it was obvious that the Iraqi woman was creative in her role inside the house, on the street, and in office and that the woman is trustworthy and prudent and far from manipulating with public wealth." And when asked by *al-Baghdadia* TV whether she felt powerful, Suhad al-Obaidi stated, "I can say that 75 percent of the successful parliamentarians are women and the ones who give most to the Iraqi citizen are women because they are more disciplined and faithful—with all my respects to my male colleagues."

The first step toward democratization that can be taken post-intervention is simply to engage in the processes requisite for democracy, such as holding credible elections that establish a government according to popular mandate. Iraq has achieved this first step and now can be said to have formed a "procedural or minimalist" democracy according to Saikal and Schnabel's definition.[104] As expressed by Hanan al-Fatlawi, Iraq now has "fair elections and real elections, unlike in the past many of you heard about the result of election for Saddam—99 percent of vote in each election—that is not a real election. So many people are happy that we are in the first processes ever of democracy, and this will lead us to real democracy probably later on."

Barriers to Women's Substantive Representation in Iraq Parliament

Previous research indicates that Iraqi women face obstacles to achieving complete political participation that are rarely shared by their male counterparts.[105] A number of Middle Eastern scholars have posited that many of these challenges stem from the lingering influences of patriarchy in Arab societies.[106] Patriarchal systems impose intrinsic gender-based hierarchies on social relations wherein women's identities become dependent upon their relationships with men, such as husbands or fathers.[107] In patriarchal society, interactions reflect the gender divisions of labor experienced in the household; women and men have unequal access to both socioeconomic opportunity and political power.[108] In the public arena, women may be expected to defer to male affiliates of their political parties, and parliamentary life may lack supportive structures wherein women can balance dual burdens of responsibility to work and family.[109] Other obstacles impeding women's full political roles might include lack of political self-efficacy and the interpretation of attempts toward women's political empowerment as serving a "Western agenda."[110]

The qualitative analysis conducted for this research revealed that the challenges Iraqi women face with respect to political agency are much more numerous than supportive factors, and often are interconnected. Figure 6.2 itemizes the breakdown of references coded in the research data as opposing factors to women's substantive representation. Two categories—"Media barriers" and "Voter attitudes"—relate more appropriately to symbolic than to substantive representation, and are deferred to Chapter 7.

Security. It is not surprising that the largest number of data coded to any analytic node referred to the lack of national security in Iraq. The violent insurgencies accompanying the 2003 invasion and continual during the occupation gave way in more recent years to an even more marked deterioration of human rights as armed conflict intensified between government forces and Islamic State fighters.[111] This situation affects all Iraqis, but gender-based violence is one of the particularly salient factors severely curtailing women's full political, social and economic participation.[112] Women and girls remain threatened by domestic

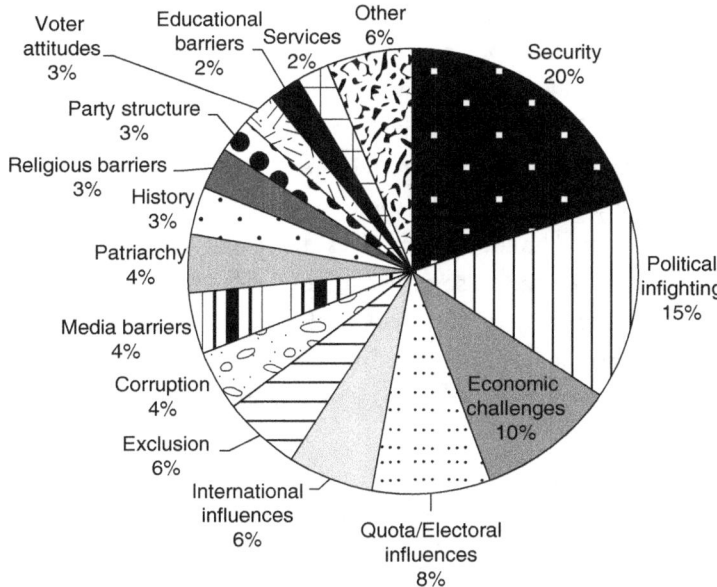

Figure 6.2 Barriers to women's political empowerment in Iraq Parliament

violence, honor killings, genital mutilation and sex trafficking for a variety of reasons underpinned by the intercomplexity of Iraq's cultural, societal, tribal and religious traditions.[113]

Changing cultural and societal beliefs to alleviate gender violence will require a sensitization of men at every societal level: parliamentary, judicial and legal, as well as among the policing forces, civil society, community and religious leaders. Yet as Deniz Kandiyoti has postulated, the dynamics of violent acts against women in post-conflict societies are far more complex than can simply be written off as expression of "patriarchy-as-usual."[114] It becomes important to analyze whether and how assaults on women represent profoundly political acts perpetrated (or at least overlooked and unpunished) by agents of the state.[115] Although no country is likely to have written statutes sanctioning gender-violent behavior by the forces of law and order, there may be contradictions between legal and constitutional provisions that foster ambiguity in interpreting culpability when female activists and politicians are subject to violent attack.

Such a contradiction indeed was formalized into the 2005 Iraq Constitution in the form of Articles 14 and 41 addressing Personal Status Law. According to Ashwaq al-Jaf, the resulting ambiguity lies at the center of human rights violations after 2003. In 2012, Jaf was quoted: "Since 2003 we have taken a step backwards regarding human rights issues."[116] In its 2011 country report on Iraq,

Human Rights Watch describes the rise in violence against women as politically motivated and legally supported: "Militias promoting misogynist ideologies have targeted women and girls for assassination, and intimidated them to stay out of public life...If they seek official protection from violence in the home, women risk harassment and abuse from Iraq's virtually all-male police and other security forces. Iraqi law protects perpetrators of violence against women: Iraq's penal code considers "honourable motives" to be a mitigating factor in crimes including murder. The code also gives husbands a legal right to discipline their wives."[117] As Jaf commented, "The crux of the matter here is that we have two penal codes: there's the Iraqi Constitution, but also the *shari'a* law. Accordingly, contradictions between both often lead to ambiguous vacuums that make us even more vulnerable."[118]

In the 2013 Free Iraq Foundation report, Iraq's female parliamentarians ranked security concerns as the most important obstacle standing in the way of their ability to make real political progress. Women across the Middle East and North Africa face greater political, economic and physical insecurity as a result of regional upheaval. "There are now fewer women in Parliament in several countries and fewer women in leadership and government positions...Many women MPs are working to overcome these and other obstacles to advance the current status of women and the progression of women's rights."[119] Terrorism and insecurity threaten the ability of female legislators to adequately perform their political functions, creating tensions between societal segments and placing Iraq's current and future status as a nation at major risk.

All the case study MPs were highly outspoken regarding Iraq's deteriorating security situation since 2003. While lack of security threatens all Iraqi citizens, women pursuing or serving in public roles face even greater risk than the general population of women. "Women are like a pyramid," said Huda Sajjad Mahmoud in her televised interview with *al-Iraqiya* TV. "Its base consists of women who suffer from domestic violence and the top of the pyramid consists of women suffering from political violence." Female candidates for Parliament have been assassinated and sexually harassed, received death threats and suffered psychological abuse both during their campaigns and after becoming elected. Three of the case study women (Etab al-Douri, Karima al-Jawari and Hanan al-Fatlawi) have survived assassination attempts, and all of them fear for their safety. Iraqi insecurity has escalated further since the Arab Spring, and was profoundly affected by the complex and bloody Syrian civil conflict. Former prime minister Maliki—as part of his 2012 power grab—granted Ministers of Security posts in exchange for bribery and ignored constitutional security and power-sharing provisions.[120] In the wake of 2012–13 violent demonstrations by Iraq's Sunni minority populations calling for the release of Sunni prisoners held on false charges, several case study MPs reintroduced the call for policy reforms including ratification of the Amnesty Law, closing Iraq's borders to Syrian refugees, and statutes to punish terrorism and sectarianism. These women appear well informed and aware that Iraq's insecurity is politically charged and motivated. In September 2012, Etab al-Douri declared on behalf of the parliamentary Human Rights Committee: "The political blocs are responsible for the deteriorated security situation due to the political disputes among them which enabled the terrorists to implement their plots, which are supported by a foreign agenda. The escalation of the Syrian crisis has its consequences on the region and especially on Iraq." Douri urged the government to "deploy the security forces all over the Iraqi provinces and to equip them with arms from the best international sources, in addition to installing observatory cameras to monitor the main roads."

Iraq's horrific security conditions and the human rights violations exacted upon its most vulnerable citizens, notably women, girls and prison detainees, emphasize the nation's failure to transition to a functioning, sustainable democracy founded upon rule of law. As suggested by other conflict cases, such as Bosnia, establishing rule of law is prerequisite to democratizing developments such as transparency of governance, consistency of judicial process for all citizens, respect for civil and political liberties and subordination of government to the legal system.[121] The 2003 intervention fell far short of establishing a governmental and constitutional infrastructure to support democratic systems founded on rule of law, and tens of thousands of Iraqis have lost their lives in consequence. As stated eloquently by Human Rights Watch, "Iraq's future as a society based on respect for fundamental human rights depends in large part on whether Iraqi authorities will adequately defend those rights and establish a credible national criminal justice system embodying international standards with respect to torture, free expression, and violence against women and other vulnerable sectors of society."[122] Iraq's female MPs recognize the need for reforms that would lead the nation closer to democratic functionality, and they are personally and politically threatened by the chaotic and violent situation. Etab al-Douri made this call in 2012: "The Iraqi people need services, construction, and the elimination of unemployment" rather than political infighting, she said. "The culture of tolerance, harmony and love should float on the surface of the new Iraq."

Political infighting. Inextricably connected with Iraq's failed security over the past 13 years is the issue of infighting between political blocs. The political situation remains linked to implications of previous armed and internal conflicts, going back as far as Saddam's war with Kuwait. The access and wielding of political power in Iraq has rarely been a peaceful, and often has been a bloody, endeavor across the country's entire modern history. "It is not possible to deny the impact of the political and social violence that reached most regions and social groups, the security instability that followed the fall of the regime, the control of the US forces and their implications," claims a 2012 UN report.[123] These conditions continued five years after US troops withdrew. As Suhad al-Obaidi stated in 2013, "The security file is correlated with the political situation where any retreat in the political posture would lead to destabilize the security situation or vice versa...The confused political situation could be easily exploited by regional countries or terrorist organizations to create [tense] political and security situations." The case study MPs as a whole perceive the weakness of parliamentary performance since 2003 as not due to any failure on their own parts, but mainly attributable to struggles between political factions. Disputes engendered by sectarian politics threaten and severely impede Iraq's progress toward democratization, and ergo toward complete political mobilization for women.

While their voices have decried the continuous political infighting and its consequences, the female MPs also have contributed to these disputes. In statements made publicly and to the press these women have criticized the actions of parties and blocs other than their own and several expressed their lack of confidence with the Maliki government prior to Maliki's resignation. During the 2011 and 2012 surveys of female MPs by the Free Iraq Foundation, 100% of respondents indicated that political gridlock has made getting things done in Parliament either "very challenging" (79 percent) or "somewhat challenging" (29 percent).[124] Party conflicts also challenge female parliamentarians' capability to work together and to find opportunities for achieving progress toward women's rights. "Women MPs...have difficulty working as peace-makers when their political parties are also parties to conflict. It is problematic for women MPs to extract themselves from their parties to participate in peaceful projects or movements."[125]

Economic challenges. Iraq has faced nationwide economic challenges for decades, internationally noted but not beginning with the 1991 UN sanctions. The insurgencies and insecurity post-2003 Iraq had their origins at least in part in earlier class struggles inspired by agitation against the British monarchy;[126] and Iraq's complex sectarian divisions have caused transition into the global industrial market to erode rather than to strengthen many Iraqi economic structures.[127] More economic issues that threatened democratization and thus impeded women's political empowerment began nearly immediately following the 2003 invasion. Neither the Bush nor the Obama administration in the United States gave Iraq the necessary economic and social incentives to rebuild its business, education, health and agricultural structures. Although the United States ostensibly invested three trillion dollars toward Iraq's reconstruction, those funds failed to support achievement of a functional democracy because the monies were distributed primarily to a group of US-based private contractors. The government remained unstable because these economic benefits were not equally distributed and because such a small proportion of the funds were allocated to Iraqi individuals, businesses or institutions.[128]

Years of war and political and economic instability have posed barriers to women's economic status as huge gender differences persist in the Iraqi labor market. As of 2013, only 14 percent of Iraqi women were employed or seeking work as compared to 73 percent of men.[129] These barriers were stronger in the private than in the public sector—only 2 percent of employees in private industry were female.[130] Women with higher education levels faced greater difficulty locating employment, and 95 percent of women with a high school diploma or higher worked in the government or public sector.[131] Indeed, in the first five years after the 2003 invasion, many highly educated female university lecturers fled Iraq to seek opportunity abroad.[132] Women's contributions to the Iraqi economy primarily are achieved through agricultural employment, voluntary (uncompensated) work and in the informal sector (e.g., cottage sewing and weaving industries).[133] Casualties of war and internal conflicts have meant that, as of 2011, 10 percent of Iraqi households were headed by women who are widowed, divorced, separated or caring for ill husbands, and only 2 percent of these female heads of households were employed with a regular salary.[134] A 2012 UN report observes the "feminization of poverty" in Iraq since the 1991 sanctions as more women than men have fallen below the poverty line, citing "the policies of neglect, the spread of sectarian violence and the growing incidences of widowhood" as the causes.[135] The number of widows increased according to some accounts by a factor of 25 percent since the escalation of conflict with the Islamic State in 2013.[136]

According to the Free Iraq Foundation surveys, women parliamentarians since 2003 have faced substantial obstacles while campaigning for election and the largest such obstacle was lack of funding (48 percent of those surveyed in 2011 indicated economic challenges to their campaigns).[137] The case study MPs made no mention of funding issues during their campaigns in their televised interviews or elsewhere in the data. However, many of them do refer to economic challenges encountered as elected parliamentarians. Those who were employed in professional positions prior to their political careers reported drastically reduced incomes as a result of entering the political sphere. Case study MPs encountered many expenses related to their parliamentary roles including entertaining their constituents, renting offices and paying for salaries, weapons and other support for bodyguards to help ensure their security. Some were forced to sell jewelry and/or take out loans to cover these additional expenses.

Electoral influences. These research findings support the conclusion that the gender quota established in the 2005 Iraq Constitution had mixed results for women's political mobilization. Upon completion of the constitution, the quota system represented a rank-ordered candidate listing wherein each bloc submitted a candidate list upon which every third nominee was required to be a woman. However, in 2009 the relevant constitutional article was amended to instill a voting results-based "best loser" system whereby, among the female candidates, the women who receive the most votes (up until the 25 percent quota is fulfilled) are elected, even if male candidates garner more votes. Quota research has determined that this latter system is less effective at increasing women's representation in a legislative body and has potential to engender greater controversy than the former system.[138] It is not difficult to envision the controversies that become likely when voters perceive that their candidate preferences are preempted by the quota. Further, the amended law did not require a gender quota for candidate lists, which is necessary to ensure that there are sufficient female candidates to fulfill the seat quota. The electoral quota as revised is open to interpretation and potentially inconsistent application by the electoral management body.

The lingeringly patriarchal Iraqi society with its thousand-year history of tribalism remains skeptical about the capabilities of women to contribute robustly in the traditionally male-dominated legislative arena.[139] One effect of the quota has been to portray women in Parliament as mere "window dressing," superficially presenting a positive image but lacking a parallel political allowance for women to use their parliamentary seats to enact real change.[140] Some Iraqis view the quota purely as an imposition of Western ideals. During her 2010 campaign, Jinan Mubarak opined to the Associated Press that political parties exploited the quota in the 2005 elections in order to pack the Parliament with women they could control. "They used the quota against women, not for women," Mubarak stated. "These kinds of parties, they prefer that they have very weak woman, just to say yes."[141] The quota alone was insufficient to offer women opportunities to pursue meaningful political participation and induce legislative reform. Some female MPs argue that quotas imposed across societal segments—that is, beyond Parliament and into cabinet ministries, private employment and educational institutions—are needed before women can achieve a true voice in Iraq's future.[142]

The case studies report other obstacles to women's political mobilization posed by Iraq's current electoral laws and management. Ashwaq al-Jaf called for collapsing electoral units (currently distributed by province) into a single national electorate, to "consolidate the national unity and make any MP a representative to all Iraqis, not a certain province."[143] Hanan al-Fatlawi, Karima al-Jawari and Safia al-Suhail advocated for rooting out corruption in Iraq's IHEC; Jawari expressed suspicion that the IHEC had rigged elections in Salah-al-Din that year.[144] In September 2012, Etab al-Douri claimed female MPs would boycott parliamentary sessions unless women were granted the ninth seat on the IHEC: "We will have a front against the political figures who stand against gaining the electoral rights of women. Women have to vote for figures who support their rights rather than these figures who deprive them from their rights," adding, "Democracy does not exist when women, who represent 65 percent of the society, are not represented in the government."[145]

International influences. For Iraqi women, Iraq's tentative endeavors toward establishing democracy after 2003 balanced the advancement of women's political, societal and cultural liberation on one hand and conservative backlash against Western influence on the other; in the face of this complex interplay, women's status became a bargaining chip.[146] The data demonstrate that women MPs have expressed both support for and dismay at the consequences of US interference in Iraqi affairs, which inspired not only the 2005 Constitution, gender quota and positive legal reforms but also insurgencies, sectarianism, conflict and violence. In addition, the 2003 intervention had a domino effect that contributed to spilling terrorism and rebellion into neighboring countries including Turkey, Egypt, Libya and—most germane to the Iraq situation—Syria. It has been argued previously that United States' tactics to impose interventionist democracy on Iraq exacerbated the very sectarian divides that would stand in the way of establishing functional democratic systems. The data indicate that all case study MPs voiced strong support for strategies to eradicate sectarian conflict and unify Iraq as a nation. Some, including Alaa' al-Talabani, Etab al-Douri and Noura al-Bajari, warned against foreign influences seeking to bring the Syrian crisis across Iraqi borders and negatively affect Iraq's role in the Arab world. Until these internal and regional questions are settled, Iraqi women will be unable to realize their potential as participants in the Iraq polity and the process of democratization will be severely hampered.

Exclusion. The electoral gender quota ensures that a certain proportion of Iraq's parliamentary seats are filled by women. Nonetheless, women remain excluded from party leadership and from the political bodies and processes wherein real decisions are made. Since equality for women in the political arena requires their full participation in processes of reconstruction, development and democratization, the 2003 intervention represents more of a step back than a stride forward toward mobilizing women's leadership.[147] In 2009, the Ministry of Human Rights conducted a survey to assess Iraqi women's awareness of their rights to vote and to stand for elections. This evaluation uncovered discouraging evidence of the weakness of women's political empowerment, reporting converging results between educated and illiterate women.[148] The same year, the annual committee report on the reality experienced by Iraqi women indicated that the performance of parliamentary women was low in comparison to the performance of their male counterparts.[149] Customary exclusion of women from the legislative process, given that male parliamentarians frequently make decisions in secret behind closed doors, is a primary contributor.

Corruption. The global NGO Transparency International ranks Iraq among the top 16 percent of nations for corruption, and in the lowest second percentile for having achieved rule of law.[150] The corruption which has been rampant across sectors of the Iraqi government as it has been tenuously rebuilt post-2003 is strongly interconnected with the sectarian schisms in Iraq's political and societal institutions, divisions supported and encouraged by the coalition interventionist forces. Case study Hanan al-Fatlawi opined in her 2013 Boston University presentation that governmental corruption stems from weak (even absent) governmental oversight and the fact that, in the past two elections, no political actor or body in Iraq has been willing to act as a valid democratic opposition.[151]

Closely tied to the lack of opposition is the dynamic by which the Maliki government attained and held power. The Iraqi government under Maliki was called a "kleptocracy" or "rentier political marketplace"—that is, a political-economic system structured around the dynamics of bargaining for shares of power and resources.[152] The term "kleptocracy" was coined by sociologist Stanislav Andreski to refer to governments in which economic mechanisms, rather than rule of law, determine the functions and institutions of the state; thus moral laxity—that is, corruption—becomes the prevailing governmental system.[153] Such a corrupt system of patronage wherein public positions are essentially up for sale severely limits the potential of electoral process to have transformative democratizing effects.

The case study MPs actively attempted to identify and publicize corruption in the Iraq government at many junctures during their parliamentary tenure. A good deal of these efforts have focused on corruption within the IHEC, which has been accused of such dishonest and partisan behavior as rigged elections, poor organization, subsidy payments and unauthorized overseas travel for commission members and employees, and inexplicable high-security clearance access to the Baghdad Green Zone.[154] In 2011, Hanan al-Fatlawi petitioned Parliament and collected more than 100 signatures lobbying for an enquiry into allegations of IHEC corruption. Although Parliament voted against withdrawing confidence from the IHEC, the investigation eventually led to the arrest of commission head Faraj al-Haidari and his second-in-command, Karim al-Tamimi, in April 2012.

Many other charges of governmental corruption were mentioned and pursued by the case study MPs including purchases of Canadian aircraft, awarding false service and infrastructure contracts, hospital fraud, mishandling of flood damage repair, mismanagement of the government food subsidy program, and smuggling and embezzlement of funds from the Central Bank. Majida al-Tamimi likens governmental corruption to organized crime: "There are mafias led by powerful governmental politicians who are not made accountable to the public," she told *AIN* in April 2013, in a statement wherein she accused key government officials of manipulating general funds.[155] Noura al-Bajari believed the widespread administrative corruption stood in the way of foreign investments in Iraq markets: "The tedious routine in reviewing state departments, bureaucracy and financial and administrative corruption all have discouraged investors from investing Iraqi capital in the country," she said in 2014, adding, "[The government] must provide financial and security guarantees as well as incentives that bring specialized companies to invest in the country. The country needs investment projects to revive and develop its infrastructure."[156]

Patriarchy. Male dominance and other traditionally patriarchal cultural traditions contribute to obstacles impeding women's progress toward parliamentary legislation. Some male MPs believe that the increased presence of women in Parliament reduces their own power and domination. Ideologies such as Islamic fundamentalism and the incorporation of *shari'a* law into the Iraqi Constitution potentially lead to greater marginalization for women and make it more difficult for females to reach leadership positions. According to the Free Iraq Foundation, 69 percent of female MPs surveyed in 2011–13 reported that they were not given the same opportunities to advance or lead in Parliament as their male counterparts, and most attributed this differential treatment to the fact that men are more respected in Parliament.[157] The case studies report being ignored on the parliamentary floor, cut off while speaking and relegated to only those discussions dealing with women's issues. An example of this disrespect came during a 2008 parliamentary session during which the Speaker of Parliament Mahmoud al-Mashhadan joked that women made poor leaders because they would be distracted by the worry that their husbands would take second wives. To protest this insult, nearly all of the 74 female parliamentarians boycotted the following day's session, which could not continue in the absence of a quorum. When the women reentered the parliamentary chamber, their male colleagues applauded, and the Speaker apologized. Alaa' al-Talabani—one of the MPs who boycotted—was quoted as saying, "We decided to show them that without women, you cannot pass laws. We gained so much from what happened that day."[158]

Other oppositional factors. Several additional barriers to women's substantive representation in Iraq's Parliament received minimal attention in the data and merit brief mention here. These factors include historical impacts, religious influences, the country's political party structure, barriers to women's education, lack of social services, family factors, tribalism, health-related influences and lack of perceived political self-efficacy among women. Decades of wars, internal strife and economic sanctions resulted in persistent hardships that forced women out of the labor force and kept young girls from receiving an education.[159] Many Iraqi women after 2003 lacked the education or skills they needed to acquire adequate employment, much less participate in electoral processes or stand for election.[160] The case studies reported frustration with their inability to provide deliverables and necessary social services to their constituents, among which lack of services is a primary concern.[161] Public spending in the health sector decreased dramatically beginning in the 1990s, resulting in a decline in all health indicators nationwide.[162] Two of the case studies reported that serving in Parliament was detrimental to their own health.

Summary

From out of the political vacuum left by the collapse of the Saddam regime, post-intervention Iraq was faced with renegotiating the terms of its polity in the absence of a shared vision between societal and political groups.[163] Establishing the foundations for democratization depended upon transcending class and gender differences in public policy processes.[164] While the void of power created by the demise of an autocracy can encourage dynamic and innovative change, the resulting transitory state also has potential to inspire chaos and disorder.[165] The laws of governance established by the CPA post-invasion and carried over into the 2005 Constitution focused primarily on establishing freedoms from authoritarianism, failing to foster inclusive roles for all segments of society toward democratizing politics, culture and the media.[166] Thus Iraq's strides toward democracy have been viewed as both a support and an obstacle to achieving substantive representation from all societal sectors, including women.

Iraqi women filling parliamentary seats have been important contributors to some political processes and enacted policies, and the data analyzed here offer little evidence to indicate whether their contributions have been more or less effective than those of male MPs. All parliamentarians—male or female—face significant obstacles to establishing and exercising true efficacy in Iraq's growing political systems. However, quantitatively it appears clear that men in Iraq's Parliament have contributed to many more public policies at the broader national level than have women, whose contributions tend to be marginalized and relegated to those issues related to women, children and family institutions.

Indeed, the data analyzed here suggest that Iraq's female parliamentarians have encountered significant challenges, along with some supports, to becoming fully mobilized political entities in the emerging Iraqi polity. The efficacy of a foreign intervention at promoting democratization without taking into consideration the country's historical, religious and/or cultural rifts or its level of economic development remains deeply questionable when viewed from the Iraq perspective. The weakness of the political domain and the religious-cultural values that have become institutionalized have created obstacles to women's political experience, which will require major shifts in thinking and process to remove. Women's status and political empowerment may be viewed as the proving ground for democratic transition. Although the regime change and the constitutional gender quota provided space for female participation in public life, Iraqi women still face the challenge of translating this political provision into meaningful interaction within the government and legislative action that supports women's rights. Difficult work lies ahead to support and initiate these changes.

7

Symbolic Representation: Legitimacy and Media Treatment of Women as Political Agents

The final dimension to be explored in this book is the level of *symbolic representation* achieved by female MPs in Iraq since adoption of the gender quota in the 2005 Constitution and its implementation in subsequent elections. Symbolic representation, as defined by Dahlerup and Friedenvall, refers to "the impact that quotas may have on the legitimacy of the polity and of voters' conceptions of and contacts with their elected representatives."[1] This concept is underpinned by the strong connection between the inclusion of women in politics and the legitimization of democracy: voters' perceptions of being represented, the legitimacy of political institutions and the influential presence of female voices all are crucial aspects of a representative democracy and are requisite in order for democratic processes to function adequately. Analyzing the effects of gender quotas on women's symbolic representation in post-conflict societies requires investigating public opinions regarding gender quotas and their effects—including examination of media debates and discourses—comparing shifting views over time and across groups.[2]

Symbolic representation implies that a representative symbolizes his or her constituency and is designated to act on their behalf. Therefore, this construct is concerned not with personal characteristics or actions of the representatives, but rather how they are perceived and how their constituents evaluate their political agency.[3] Symbolic representation fulfils a number of politically significant processes such as constructing social identity, creating or fostering legitimacy of the agent and building avenues for political control.[4] Women may be interpreted to have achieved symbolic political representation to the extent that discursive constructions legitimize them as principal players in the political sphere.[5] An important question to be analyzed, then, is how women in politics become represented by symbols: how are they represented, by what symbols and what meanings do female politicians evoke in the minds of the citizens they represent?[6]

Qualitative analyses of the supportive and oppositional factors surrounding women's substantive representation in the Iraqi Parliament since adoption of the gender quota uncovered some aspects related to symbolic representation. The sections that follow outline the theoretical framework behind symbolic representation as related to gender quota effects; offer a brief examination of the evolution of the Iraqi media post-2003 as relevant to the depiction of female politicians; and present content analysis of the data to reveal oppositional and supportive factors relevant to the symbolic meanings attached to women in political roles by their constituents and by the Iraqi public as a whole.

Symbolic Representation in Theoretical Context

Symbolization is central to political mobilization as there are close links between symbolic representation and power relations.[7] According to sociopolitical and anthropological theory, modern politics has become an increasingly autonomous field (meaning the field largely follows its own logic and places relatively high barriers before new entrants). Consequently, entry into the political arena requires new actors to know, accept and follow accepted "rules of the game" in order to gain access to positions of power.[8] Symbolic representation not only refers to the simple concept of a politician standing for his or her constituency, but also can be understood as the practices of constructing social groups and gaining legitimacy as a representative of their collective identities and interests.[9] Successful political representation requires specific knowledge about political programs, traditions and arguments and practical skills of oration and debate to gain popularity and handle relationships with parliamentary colleagues and constituents.[10] Thus "political representation is both a product and a producer of discursively constructed identities and interests."[11]

Entry points to achieving political power involve possession of forms of capital, including economic capital (material assets such as money and property), social capital (durable social networks) and cultural capital (embodied cultural competence, objectified cultural assets and educational credentials).[12] These assets can become converted into *symbolic capital*, meaning that possession of other forms of capital makes one recognizable as a legitimate authority in a specific field. Symbolic power may be attributed erroneously by public opinion when the unequal distribution of capital becomes misrecognized as natural, granting legitimacy to domination—for example, by one gender over another.[13]

While symbolic representation has a visual dimension expressed through imagery and publicly recognizable symbols (i.e., a national flag becomes the symbol of a nation-state), the notion also has a discursive aspect that can be found in metaphors, stereotypes, frames and cultural norms and values.[14] Policy actors shape the meaning of concepts by embedding them in frameworks for political debate that become institutionalized in such authoritative texts as constitutions, laws and judicial decisions.[15] Laws—particularly fundamental infrastructural laws such as constitutional provisions—and the interpretation of those laws constitute one type of discursive symbolic representation.[16] The use of language and discourse to construct symbolic representation is very important to consider, particularly when seeking to understand gendered symbols. Such discourses can have an unintentional dimension: they may reflect deeply rooted, internalized cultural and institutional meanings that can inadvertently reproduce biases such as sexism, racism or homophobia.[17] The symbolic representation of nations, states and their central institutions is gendered, and attributes differential roles to men and women. For example, in many Arab societies women are conceptualized as the "guardians of tradition" and are attributed responsibility for transmitting traditional culture and values to the next generations.[18]

The meaning attached to a principal representative by constituents is not fixed and static, but rather continuously constructed in political debates, and it can be stretched to assume new meanings depending upon the historical moment and context.[19] An example can be found in Iraqi politics under the Ba'athist regime, which was monotonously expressed in rhetoric exclusively dominated by Saddam's articulation of national identity and unity.[20] There was wide variation in that discourse over time, as Saddam would adeptly alter his own persona and adapt his rhetorical representation of the Iraqi nation to suit his political agenda.[21] Smiles charts the evolution of the symbolic value Saddam ascribed to the Iraqi woman, objectifying the female body as a symbol of national boundaries and manipulating gender constructs in nationalist discourses to maintain authoritarian power within an atmosphere of internal and international conflict.[22]

After 2003, reactionary responses to decades of dictatorship caused the authors of the Transitional Coalition and Constitution to place primary emphasis on establishing freedoms from autocracy, failing to promote active individual and societal roles toward democratizing Iraq's political system, culture and media. Any discussion of symbolism in relation to Iraqi politics cannot overlook the extent to which women's participation in the public sphere has come to symbolize "Western" ideology—that is, capitalism and individualism, which religious fundamentalists believe deviate from societal morality and stand directly at odds with the tenets of Islam.[23] For many Iraqis, and Sunni Muslims in particular, the invasion represented yet another stage of foreign occupation and imperialist intervention, whereas to the United States, its allies and Shi'a leaders returning from exile, the invasion heralded liberation from Saddam's brutal autocracy and the beginnings of progress toward democratization. From a symbolic standpoint, the legitimization of political formulae reflected the struggle to strike a balance between the need to present a unified nationalist front on the one hand, and the desire of each ethnopolitical sect to assert its identity as the sole voice of the Iraqi people—thereby marginalizing all other claimants—on the other.[24] The lengthy foreign occupancy placed increased focus on debates regarding women's societal role, leading Islamic fundamentalists to situate women as symbols of stability and Islamic honor during a time of upheaval and uncertainty.[25]

Symbolic representation is determined by relationships not only between representatives and the represented, but also between competing representatives.[26] Atkeson indicates that the competitiveness of an intergender political contest builds a context within which the symbolic framing of women in the political sphere may be manipulated.[27] The perceived viability of women candidates may lead female voters to feel more connected to and part of the political system.[28] The presence of viable female candidates can indicate a degree of policy responsiveness, system openness and fairness not found when there are few women involved in the political realm.[29] Having women in political roles is expected to change political methods, for example by reducing levels of corruption.[30] Women are more likely to include traditional women's and family issues (such as education, the environment, health care, children's and senior issues, social welfare and women's rights) as planks in their campaign platforms.[31] Moreover, there is evidence on the global stage that male candidates revise their campaign strategies to reflect more emphasis on issues of women's interest when competing against a woman for public office.[32] The presence of female candidates provides both a symbolic and a substantive context for the greater engagement of female voters in the political process. Conversely, the symbolic cues provided when there is minimal female representation in politics and campaigning are that women are not full citizens and that they are unwelcome in the political world.[33] Full political mobilization for women will occur only within a diverse contextual environment that sends viable cues that politics is an acceptable and appropriate arena for women to enter. Therefore, the presence of a gender quota system, whereby women will be elected notwithstanding the proportion of votes they garner, may detract from the perceived viability of women candidates and thus fail to encourage and foster engagement by female citizens in the political process. "Viable symbolic representation enhances political engagement and may increase substantive representation, but token symbolic representation does not."[34]

The realization of democracy in a post-conflict interventionist state requires fulfillment of a standard checklist of steps, a very important one of which is the development of "independent media." Diverse, robust political parties and thriving media outlets outside of state control are requisite to advance the evolution of both civil and political society. The gendered nature of symbolic representation is carried out through the media: symbolic frames are conditioned by how women are represented in the media, the extent to which representations are stereotypical, usage of sex-specific narratives and how these factors contribute to the marginalization of women politicians, specific groups of women, or women in general.[35] Gendered mediation deployed by the media when representing female politicians in historically male-dominated higher offices, especially using gender frames in which the male is treated as normative, has crucial potential to depress the symbolic effects of women's political presence.[36] Representation of men and women in the media tends to reproduce gender stereotypes, depicting men in professional and public roles while women are shown in the private sphere in traditional roles as wives, mothers or victims of violence.[37] These media representations perpetuate hierarchical gender divisions where men are associated with more highly valued spheres while women are associated with the less-valued areas of society. In addition, journalists treat male and female politicians differently; they pay closer attention to the physical appearance of women, ask questions about their private lives that would not be posed to their male colleagues and cast public doubt on female politicians' political leadership ability and competency.[38]

The complex processes of nation-building in a post-conflict state can stretch across decades, particularly (as in Iraq) when fundamental issues remain unresolved; and opportunities for democratization are in large part shaped by media approaches before, during and after the conflict.[39] Because the symbolic representation of women in Iraqi politics is so closely tied to democratic transition, a brief analysis of Iraq's post-2003 news media is warranted. The following section briefly discusses the evolution of this media environment.

The Iraqi Media Post-2003: A Brief Analysis

Under the Saddam regime, Iraq had five daily newspapers, four radio stations and two television channels, all completely controlled and monitored by the state; satellite dishes, Internet access and consumption of outside media were illegal except for members of the Ba'athist political elite.[40] This media landscape was typical across the Middle Eastern region, wherein most governments have traditionally operated their own print and broadcast services to legitimize and stabilize their authority.[41] In the hands of the ruling elite, the Iraqi media were employed almost entirely to suppress opposition and to glorify the dictator and his clan[42]—indeed, William Rugh called pre-2003 Iraq the quintessential case of "mobilization media."[43] Journalists were treated brutally by the Ba'athists and the media subjected to severe scrutiny, restriction and censorship.[44] After Saddam's eldest son Uday took over the Iraqi Journalists' Union in 1992, the media became solely a dissemination tool for governmental propaganda; many journalists fled the country in the face of Uday's crackdown on perceived subversion.[45]

All these state-controlled media outlets abruptly collapsed and went off the air, and the state-run Iraqi Information Ministry was abolished, when coalition forces took over Baghdad in March 2003. Almost overnight the country witnessed a rapid proliferation of media outlets. By the middle of 2003, Iraq suddenly was home to more than 20 radio stations, at least 15 television channels and more than 200 Iraqi-owned and -run newspapers.[46] Iraqis flocked to retailers to purchase satellite dishes imported from abroad, thus gaining access to more than 300 regional channels and the growing number of indigenous stations.[47] These rapid and dramatic changes to the media landscape, standing in such stark contrast to the Ba'athist era, were unsurprising given the degree to which independent speech had been stifled and persecuted.[48]

In May 2003, the Coalition Provisional Authority (CPA) established the Iraqi Media Network (IMN) to replace the now-defunct Information Ministry. The IMN comprised a television channel (*al-Iraqiya* TV), two radio stations (Republic of Iraq Radio and Voice of Free Iraq) and a daily newspaper printed in both Arabic and English (*al-Sabaah*).[49] The IMN faced several challenges. At first, Iraqis viewed the state-run networks as outlets for American propaganda; subsequently the IMN, particularly *al-Iraqiya* TV, came to reflect the Shi'a sectarian ideologies of the Maliki government, promoting a pro-government line that stressed "optimism" about progress being made in "reconstruction" and "security."[50] Much of the populace viewed *al-Iraqiya* TV as "Maliki TV" rather than fulfilling its ostensible role as a public service broadcasting outlet projecting the interest of all Iraqis.[51] During the 2010 parliamentary campaign, according to Amos, "Iraq's state-run system failed to offer a neutral media space to all of the candidates and parties running in the election, despite a $500 million US effort to make Iraqiya a national public service system."[52] Simultaneously across the last decade, the emergent privately owned media channels have gradually grown in professionalism and sophistication to create an increasingly complex media environment where state-run media have lost audience share to competitors within and outside Iraq.[53]

The CPA attempted regulation by issuing Order No. 14 on June 10, 2003 prohibiting media organizations from publishing or broadcasting material that "incites violence against any individual or group, including racial, ethnic or religious groups and women; incites civil disorder, rioting or damage to property; incites violence against Coalition Forces or CPA personnel." In practice, however, this regulation was applied solely in the latter context: to safeguard CPA personnel.[54] The development of the IMN and implementation of the CPA media regulations reflected post-war political processes in Iraq, including important missteps by the United States: the CPA overstepped its boundaries in applying the regulations by closing down a number of independent media outlets for infractions perceived as anti-US, while failing to react toward other channels that incited violence and hatred against fellow Iraqi sects, groups and religions.[55] Little attention was given to relationships between media licensing applicants and power distribution within the society, with licenses essentially awarded on a first-come, first-served basis.[56] Thus the newly found freedom of the media sector post-Saddam yielded a highly partisan set of broadcast and print media outlets, geared toward expressing divergent political and ethnoreligious agendas. In other words, the divisive ethnic and sectarian discourses that have fragmented Iraqi politics since 2003 have also been strongly reflected in the country's rapidly expanding media outlets.[57]

Indeed, almost every political party has had different media channels including terrestrial or satellite television channels, radio stations, newspapers, magazines, websites, forums or blogs; journalists too have become polarized toward, variously, their sect, race or region as they seek protection or favor from their party or community leaders.[58] This polarization extends also to female journalists, who are highly pressured or even blackmailed to support one side or another and face numerous risks, challenges, harassment and security threats.[59] At times of high insecurity, the various ethnosectarian factions have used their media networks to legitimize intercommunal violence and portray their respective groups as victims.⁶⁰ Currently, "violence in Iraq is not simply fought on the streets, but is represented in the tele-visual and thus [the] socio-cultural sphere."⁶¹

Due to illiteracy rates and other factors, fewer than half of Iraqis read newspapers on a regular basis. Television is by far the dominant medium by which citizens receive political communication and information, including political campaigning and election coverage.⁶² Most Iraqis (93 percent) consume news via television; however, there remains a high level of distrust for all news outlets among the citizenry.⁶³ The most popular television network in Iraq, *al-Sharqiya*, has won a large audience share with entertainment programs and drama despite the noticeable slant toward a Sunni agenda in its news broadcasts.⁶⁴ The four satellite television channels currently receiving the largest Iraqi audience shares are *al-Sharqiya* (Sunni), *al-Iraqiya* (state-run), *al-Furat* (Shiʻa) and *al-Hurria* (Kurdish). A 2013 study by al-Rawi and Gunter analyzing candidate coverage by these top channels during the 2010 elections revealed that all four were one-sided and biased toward candidates representing their respective ideologies, despite claiming to follow the principles of good journalism such as fairness, balance and objectivity.⁶⁵ However, Price et al. (2009) have pointed out that pluralism in media development has also allowed for an Iraqi media with no political affiliation or agenda to emerge, such as *al-Baghdadia* TV which attempts to provide an alternative to Islamist media by trying to ensure that guests on its news programs are inclusive of Arab Shiʻa and Sunni, Kurds and Christians.⁶⁶ Another example is *al-Sumariyya*, which claims not to be affiliated with any sect and strives to maintain neutrality by refusing to air live statements or press conferences with any Iraqi politician.⁶⁷

Another facet of the communications environment that bears heavily on the current research is the portrayal of Iraqi women in the media. Media images of women in the Arab region have attracted increasing attention in recent years, although research on how depiction of women in the media influences political participation is largely lacking. Historically Arab women have been portrayed across all types of media according to the dichotomous symbolism of "angels or whores"⁶⁸—that is, the more positively framed and likeable characters are the quiet, meek, obedient mothers and housewives, whereas strong female characters such as those who would enter politics are depicted as domineering, sly and untrustworthy.⁶⁹ Across the Middle East, the visual media rarely reflect positively on women and women's rights; rather, women are objectified and their bodies used as tools for advertisement.⁷⁰ Television projects stereotypes of women as possessors of little to no mental capacity, further detracting from society's ability to perceive them as able legislators or leaders.[71] Only recently have women been featured on political programs where guests are interviewed regarding topics of interest and, even then, women appear as "expert" guests far less often than men do.[72] In news coverage about accidents, violence or natural disasters, women are much more likely to be featured as victims than as professionals commenting on the events.[73] Entertainment programming continues to emphasize women's roles as homemakers and nurturers appropriately relegated to the domestic sphere.[74]

Media gender inequalities, however, are not unique to Iraq or even the Middle East but seem to be a global phenomenon. The Global Media Monitoring Project (GMMP) is a research and advocacy initiative that pursues gender inequality in and through the news. The initiative gathers longitudinal data twice each decade to evaluate select indicators of gender representation in the news media, studying women's presence in relation to men, gender bias and stereotyping in news content. Preliminary results from GMMP 2015 revealed almost no improvement over 2010 figures in the percentage of females heard or read about in print, radio or television news worldwide, showing an increase of just 1 percent from the 24 percent recorded in 2010.[75]

Nevertheless, Arab women are embracing the new information technologies that have swept the communications landscape in recent years, and they are beginning to turn to the media as an avenue for their own empowerment, as an educational tool that transcends temporal and spatial barriers, and as a means to advance progress and community development.[76] Several media-related conferences have been held across the Middle Eastern region since 2008 with the goals of providing media training, production support, collaborative opportunities and social media message conceptualization and strategies for female activists, journalists and politicians.[77] There is little question that the rapid growth of media technologies and the emergence of new platforms such as the social media have enhanced the presence of women in the Arab media and provided them with greater opportunities to publicly discuss, investigate and present various issues.[78] The question to be examined, therefore, is the extent to which this increased media presence has contributed to qualitative changes in women's political and social standing.

Amid the evolving media environment, web logging or "blogging" has become a practicable means for ordinary women to express themselves publicly while maintaining anonymity and relative safety from persecution. In Iraq specifically, several bloggers emerged post-2003 to chronicle the lives and experiences of women during the US occupation and ensuing fragmentation of Iraqi society.[79] Reading an accounting of the everyday experiences of a real woman as expressed through her weblog offers a closer understanding of those experiences from the feminine point of view. One prominent and compelling Iraqi blogger wrote under the pseudonym Riverbend; her blog, titled "Baghdad Burning," became published in two volumes by The Feminist Press of CUNY in 2005 and 2006.[80] Campbell (2007) analyzed Riverbend's unique voice, her responses to and criticism of the role of (1) religious politicians in Iraq and how their influence affects the role of women in political processes; (2) the possible implications for women's rights due to the incorporation of *shari'a* into the 2005 Iraqi Constitution and (3) the impact of fundamentalist violence upon women in Baghdad.[81] According to Campbell, "Religion is brought into the picture when it is used by insurgents, fundamentalists and terrorists as moral justification for their actions…There needs to be a clearer understanding of the history and role of Muslim women through the actual lives of women, rather than commentaries on, and interpretation of, their lives."[82] Female voices such as Riverbend's remain at the center of social movements for gender equality in Iraq's civil society, representing democratic processes in real life as communicated through cyberspace.[83] Blogging offers women not only an additional communication space outside traditional political and media environments, but also an instant audience and recognition that transcend national boundaries.

Unfortunately, the voices of Iraqi women and indeed the free expression of all Iraqi citizens were effectively stifled once again due to a set of governmental restrictions instituted by the Maliki government in June 2014. Ostensibly a reaction to the uprising of the Islamic State, these guidelines demanded that the media avoid publicizing information about insurgent organizations and required them to report on governmental forces only in favorable terms.[84] Human Rights Watch called these regulations unjustifiable and stated further that the rules were being applied arbitrarily, targeting privately owned outlets that had reported critically about the government while taking no action against those that support the government or the pro-government Shi'a militias.[85] The implications of these and other guidelines for the symbolic representation of Iraqi female MPs are discussed later.

Supports for Women's Symbolic Representation in Iraq Parliament

Data were analyzed in terms of whether they contained references expressing supports versus barriers to the symbolic representation experienced by female

MPs in Iraq, particularly the case studies. Of special interest was the extent to which the Iraqi media have played a role in supporting or obstructing a woman's election to public office and the imagery used by the media to depict Iraqi women in political roles. The media strategies female MPs have embraced, including Internet and social media communications, were analyzed as well as the methods they employ to communicate with their constituencies. In addition to media influences, prevailing voter attitudes are relevant to symbolic representation. Further supports and barriers to symbolic representation can be found in female MPs' collaborative relationships with NGOs, or lack thereof.

Media Supports

A small proportion (7 percent) of the factors coded as supportive to women's representation in the Iraq Parliament were related to media supports. A political environment that offers relative freedom of the press is important for women MPs because it provides platforms for promoting their political agendas and communicating with constituents. The more access female parliamentarians have to independent media sources, the more opportunities exist to publicize and reinforce messages aimed at combating stereotypes and working toward greater gender balance in the political sphere. By engaging with the media in collaboration with civil society organizations, women MPs can increase their effectiveness at exposing relevant issues to the public. For example, at the 2013 Amman conference, "Women Leaders in an Era of Change," sponsored by the Free Iraq Foundation and the Woodrow Wilson International Center for Scholars, one MP reported using the media to expose the inaccuracy of recent studies in Iraq that significantly underestimated illiteracy levels.[86] Employing media channels to effectively promote one's agenda and influence public opinion was cited as an important way to maximize the impact of women MPs, increasing their influence on government decision-making and policy. Radio and television are important targets for garnering such media attention due to the high rates of illiteracy and relatively low readerships of Iraqi newspapers, magazines and other written media, particularly in certain areas.[87]

The media are of primary importance to a woman's campaign for public office, as access to public media and campaign resources influence women's success in presenting themselves as candidates.[88] According to the Free Iraq Foundation report, in spring 2011, 84 percent of MPs surveyed said they used print advertisements to promote their campaigns; 52 percent used radio and 44 percent used television.[89] Campaign posters and billboards are widespread across the country near election times, with women candidates' posters competing for space with those of men. Close to the 2010 elections, CBS News reported about such posters: "Some are conservative religious women like [MP Maha] al-Douri, clothed from head to toe in black cloaks known as *abayas*, sometimes even with gloves to hide their hands, pictured staring solemnly or in a moment of action in Parliament…But there are just as many posters of women with their hair uncovered, sporting business suits and makeup. In the northern city of Kirkuk, police have reported traffic jams in an area where one particularly attractive candidate has posters hanging."[90]

Upon election to Parliament, female MPs choose the media networks and communication strategies they believe most effective to promote their agendas and connect with their constituents. In the autumn of 2011, Free Iraq Foundation reported that the majority of women MPs surveyed (88 percent) had a website to interact with constituents, more than half (59 percent) had a database or other tracking system to record communication with constituents and 65 percent had a follow-up system for such communications.[91] Still, at that time MPs said personal visits and public meetings were the most effective way in which they reached the voters they represent; followed by social media, television appearances and newsletters.[92] In a 2016 interview, Frances Guy, who was Iraqi representative for UN Women during 2010–2014, confirmed this information. When asked what methods the female MPs used to connect with voters, Guy commented, "They did many of the traditional things; newsletters and such like."[93]

In general, the research case study MPs have been successful at developing messages and gaining media presence. Most have discovered that maintaining contact with the media is essential, and some have established media or communications offices and/or employed staff to help them strategize and work with media outlets. In a 2015 personal interview, Jacqueline Sutton who was a scholar of the Iraqi media mentioned that, in many cases, these women have been named media spokespeople for their parliamentary committees.[94] They regularly hold press conferences and issue press statements to announce committee decisions and/or comment on parliamentary achievements in areas of most interest to them or their constituencies. For example, they have used the media to bring attention to priority issues such as education, corruption, human rights, budget laws, oil and gas revenue distribution, electoral reform and women's rights. It is worth noting that at the "Women Leaders" conference referenced above, some participants said they were conflicted about whether to address women's issues to the press or not to do so to avoid being branded as an MP who addresses only women's issues.[95] Conference participants and several case study MPs agreed that it may be best to begin with a focus on issues of interest to women and then transition to other issues later in their political careers.[96]

Conferences and training programs attended by female parliamentarians have made several recommendations for Iraqi women MPs as related to the media. First, they must strongly identify their political positions as politicians and then seize opportunities to appear publicly to discuss relevant issues and share stories of their policy-making successes. When female MPs adopt strong positions, issue bold policy statements and defend the issues of import to them, they will attract media attention. Although MPs cannot control the media, they can express their opinions and take stances on issues that are of interest to a media outlet's audience. Both the Iraq Foundation and the Global Justice Project have recommended that the women MPs determine what attracts media attention and tailor their messages accordingly. Messages must be clear and focused with a defined goal in mind; understanding the needs of the medium and its audience is vital. MPs should avoid becoming frustrated about what the media choose to cover, and they should keep sending messages they believe to be important, and be ambitious while conducting media outreach.[97]

Social media. Social media platforms form a subcategory of media outlets with compelling potential to provide impetus for the mobilization of women in politics. In fact, there is evidence that usage of social media has contributed to greater women's empowerment across the Arab world since 2010 and that the number of Arab women using these new media has been steadily on the rise.[98] Women may be quicker to embrace these new technologies and realize their potential for campaign strategy, constituent communication and spreading the word about important issues.[99] Guy stated the following regarding the MPs with whom she worked during her tenure for UN Women in Iraq: "Some of them were very active on Facebook and used social media a lot to communicate with constituents ... Superficially they might do this a bit more than the men."[100] Social media offers unprecedented opportunities to build public images and make statements to a wide audience without need to court the interest of journalists and press outlets. For the purposes of this analysis, then, the extent to which the case studies employ social media strategies in their parliamentary work bears examination.

As of November 2015, 10 of the 12 case study MPs had Facebook pages; 8 of those are publicly accessible and can be used by constituents to connect with the MP, while the others are restricted to access only by the MP's identified friends or followers on the site. One case study MP, Ashwaq al-Jaf, has an extremely active, searchable and visible presence online on Facebook, email, Google Plus, the professional online network LinkedIn and the video sharing platform

YouTube. In her 2012 television interview, Jaf explained to *al-Iraqiya* TV: "[My constituents] can send me a request via Facebook and I study it and if I need to discuss it by phone I ask for it. If I don't need the phone, I forward the email to the committee—in my opinion the email and Facebook are more convenient for both MP and the citizen." Two other case studies—Hanan al-Fatlawi and Huda Sajjad Mahmoud—are extremely active and up-to-date on their Facebook pages. Four case study MPs had Twitter (microblog) accounts in November 2015 and four others (in addition to Jaf) had multiple videos posted on YouTube wherein they were interviewed about their stances on various political issues.

Voter Attitudes

A small number of references related to Iraqi voter attitudes were coded as supportive of women's symbolic representation. In the Free Iraq Foundation report published in 2013, the female MPs surveyed were cited as saying that, along with impacting the legislative agenda, they also have influenced social and political attitudes in the public.[101] They achieve this influence by means of "voting, providing their opinions, seeking solutions to problems, making decisions according to priorities, ensuring rights without discrimination, narrowing the gap between divergent opinions, embracing plurality and community, and following up on responsibilities."[102] Approximately one-third of MPs surveyed reported believing that the public perceives them as role models. Responses from the remaining two-thirds were split between saying the public thought women MPs serve a needed purpose, women MPs should hold more traditional jobs and it is the citizen's decision how they perceive women MPs.[103]

The same report discusses changes in public perceptions of female MPs since advent of the parliamentary quota, suggesting that the citizenry holds some positive stereotypes regarding women leaders.[104] Some people believe that female MPs inherently provide different and valuable counterpoints to the views of male politicians, and that women are less corrupt than men. There is evidence that women's voices have become more widely accepted in the political arena, leading to some improvements in public perception. As women become able to express themselves and share their views, some of them for the first time, their confidence, legislative performance and leadership skills also have increased. Some of these gains are attributed to greater freedom of and access to the media. Increased media access may translate into an ability to combat stereotypes among the population and build more positive public images; greater access offers more opportunities to air and reinforce a target message and disseminate it to a wider audience.

NGO Supports

A thriving civil society populated with a variety of legitimate and active NGOs provides support for the legitimacy with which female political actors are perceived. Azza Karam states, "Networking between women's interest groups and women politicians is crucial in the successful institutionalization of gender equality policies."[105] Chapter 6 established the essential role of NGOs in promoting women's issues for consideration on the political stage and in encouraging women's substantive representation in Parliament. Forming collaborative alliances with NGOs can also aid in building a female parliamentarian's symbolic capital.[106] NGOs can help women garner support and recognition, interact with the press, fund and run campaigns for office, and organize demonstrations around issues of import.[107] Iraqi women's rights NGOs and international agencies have conducted tremendous efforts in support of women's political participation, such as candidate training and parliamentary capacity-building, efforts that also aid to build a more positive image of their legislative capabilities in the public view. In addition, in more recent years, women have begun to organize more actively inside Parliament around such issues as UN Security Council Resolution 1325 in order to have a more unified voice across party lines.[108] (Security Council Resolution 1325 is a set of standards recognizing the relevance of women's experiences of conflict to the UN peace and security mandate, and engages the Security Council in advancing women's rights in conflict resolution and peace-building processes.)[109] As Guy commented, "Other women ought to be a support. So, women in government, women in top positions in the civil service, other women MPs could be supporting each other ... examples from elsewhere, especially Jordan are helpful."[110] The case study MPs have interacted and collaborated with civil society organizations to a high degree during their prepolitical and political careers. Unfortunately, many of Iraq's female MPs may tend to overlook or avoid opportunities to establish collaborative relationships with NGOs that might enhance their symbolic representation.

Barriers to Women's Symbolic Representation in Iraq Parliament

Symbolic representation is closely related to balances of power and some levels of economic, social and cultural capital must be accumulated for the political agent to achieve entry into the legislative sphere. In post-2003 Iraq, most elected female MPs have been selected from among relatives of high-level members of the prominent political parties. Being granted this selective favor affects their conduct in parliamentary affairs, leading the public at times to dismiss them as not being true politicians.[111] In a report on women's political representation in the Middle East and North Africa, Zeina Zaatari observes that, while only a few female MPs appear motivated by significant issues facing their countries, "a good number are invested in issues of culture and cuisine."[112] In addition, women MPs face discrimination within Parliament itself and frequently are excluded from important meetings and committees.[113] Other barriers to women's symbolic representation in Iraq include difficulties meeting the double burden of parliamentary obligations and family, which damages their political reputation; threats to security that discourage women from appearing in public; citizen perceptions of politics as a "dirty game" best handled by males and the proliferation of negative stereotypical discourses on women in the media.[114] This section presents qualitative analysis of the factors coded as oppositional to women's symbolic representation.

Media Barriers

As noted above, new technologies—particularly media technologies—can support and promote women's symbolic political representation as well as perpetuate inequalities, suppress diversity and foster exclusivity.[115] Iraqi female MPs must struggle to bolster their image as viable politicians within a media environment that continues to portray women in negative stereotypes. The media tend to depict women in traditional contexts that marginalize their societal roles and impede their advancement.[116] Women's progress is framed by the media in terms of the female body, either focusing on the woman's level of "beauty" or placing her in traditional roles referring to her physical characteristics when they use terms such as "pregnant, childbirth, breast-feeding, and care."[117] More specifically to the political arena, the media often attack female MPs for their lack of experience and present them as ineffective leaders.[118] Poor relationships are struck between women MPs and the media, and the media blame Parliament for problems in the government. In the Free Iraq Foundation study, several survey respondents suggested that female MPs would fare even worse if they tried to defend themselves from media attack, and that those who appeared in the media frequently were likely to be considered liars.[119]

Further media obstacles to women's symbolic representation have been put in place by the Iraqi government. Communication managers in the administrations since 2003 have shown little interest in women's issues, and thus there is limited awareness of such issues among those—both men and women—who work as media professionals.[120] Further, women remain underrepresented in media professions and female journalists have little decision-making capability.[121] Many female politicians express a reluctance to discuss political issues they want to promote with the media because some media channels portray them as partisan, which negatively affects their reputations with constituencies.[122] Moreover, funding sources influence the ways in which news is reported by media outlets, most of which serve the interests of specific political parties. Because of their political and ethnosectarian allegiances, the Iraqi media are subjective and tend to focus on a small percentage of available information, typically those aspects which are most controversial and that support the political stances of the sect.[123] The press focuses on sensational topics such as political conflict and division, and looks for parliamentary deficiencies to exploit.[124]

Lack of access to public media and campaign coverage greatly detracts from women's success at presenting themselves as viable political candidates.[125] In her 2016 interview, Guy confirmed that women receive little press coverage during parliamentary election campaigns:

> Women were generally not covered very much on the media. Pictures in the newspaper were very few. Women in Parliament occasionally got coverage but disproportionately much less than the men. They did get some airtime on the radio. The woman who got elected with the most votes to the Parliament in 2014 [Maysoun al-Damlouji] got quite favourable coverage but then she was on the Prime Minister's list and so that helped. There were some all-female debates. But in general MPs didn't get that much coverage and as the system works on a lot of patronage, those wielding the patronage system got the most political coverage.
>
> …women don't get much coverage and there was a tendency to mock them. In the run up to World Press Freedom Day in 2014 UNESCO and UN Women did an informal scan of the printed press for a couple of weeks. There were very few images of women at all in the press. A very occasional MP and a number of Lebanese singers…and that was all. Similarly limited TV coverage, and I think it is safe to say that women are largely absent…this is slightly different in Kurdistan partly because up until 2014 there were some very vocal women and perhaps the TV stations are a bit more "western."[126]

Many Iraqi women entering politics for the first time are unaware how to use media to their advantage. Among the case study MPs, despite the fact that the primary data source was televised interviews, many noted negative exposure received through media channels. In the data analyzed, seven MPs made mention of rumors or attacks on themselves perpetuated by the press. Alaa' al-Talabani told *al-Baghdadia* TV in 2012 that she was heavily criticized in the media for siding with her uncle, then-president Jalal Talabani, when he characterized Kirkuk as the "al-Quds of Kurdistan." Ashwaq al-Jaf was questioned in her televised interview about a journalist who had publicly claimed she was connected to the Mujahidin-i Khalq organization, which the journalist called terrorist. "Unfortunately, if he was genuinely wanting democracy he would not deny a person his or her rights," Jaf responded. "I request him through this TV channel that he presents a document proving my relation with the organization." At her 2013 presentation to Boston University, Hanan al-Fatlawi was questioned about media reports that her brother had been a Ba'ath Party member. She retorted: "When you heard about that, you heard about that a few weeks ago when I [had] a lot of interrogation, a lot of discussion ... it's negative things from other groups; of course they have to find something against me and put it in [the] media. It's not only that my brother was from al-Ba'ath [that they were commenting on]. They said my father died in 1991 with cancer, not related to al-Ba'ath Party. They said I... was a prisoner and on and on. If you ... watch, media would say, probably you would be one of the, I don't know, CIA agents."[127]

Majida al-Tamimi commented to *al-Iraqiya* TV that many Iraqi politicians misspeak on the media, saying, "Frankly, I don't like to appear on the media or be part of political argumentations and debates. My experience in the Parliament is that MPs make statements or comment without permission—even between members of the same bloc. This means these statements are not based on facts and it causes tension and problems; I get contacted in order to attend debates or discussions but I don't. If there is something that I want to talk about, I verify the facts and collect all the documents which prove my point; then I talk to the media because I must respect my people and give them the right information and don't want to be a cause for political crises like other irresponsible politicians." In her televised interview, Mariam al-Rayyis explained that she left her position as media advisor to Nouri al-Maliki briefly in 2008: "In one of the media releases I was misunderstood by the presidency as I was speaking about the constitution, article 38[128], chapter 4. I spoke about the powers of the presidency, especially with [then vice president] Tareq al-Hashimi. After three months I wanted to resign but Maliki refused and after that I submitted it to his office manager and it was accepted and I gave to Mahmoud al-Mash'hadani, the Speaker of the House, a list of breaches of the constitutions. And after that al-Maliki asked me to return and I am happy to work with him."

Noura al-Bajari attributed rumors about her personal wealth and success to the media in her 2012 television interview. "Unfortunately, those weak souls from my city and fellow MPs (male and female) believed the rumors that I am successful and my name is known to men of power and the political blocs because I do not make statements to the media. They took it from the Internet and spread the rumor in the Parliament," she told *al-Baghdadia* TV. And finally, Safia al-Suhail reported being accused by the media of falsifying her preparatory certification for the Agricultural Institute in Abu Ghraib region. "This was a rumor," she stated.

In addition to being portrayed negatively in the press, two further case studies expressed reticence to appear in the media for other reasons. Huda Sajjad Mahmoud claimed she did not appear much in the press citing, "The most important reason is that I have no time." "And there are MPs from the State of Law responsible towards the media,"[129] she explained. Karima al-Jawari, questioned on television as to whether she places her interest in politics over humanitarian social services, repudiated that allegation saying, "No, on the contrary. I care about the humanitarian side a lot. But I work quietly and as you may have noted I do not appear on media a lot to talk about my work."

Social media. The Internet and social media have been introduced very recently in Iraq relative to other countries. As of 2015, the UN's International Telecommunications Union reports that 40.3 percent of populations in Arab states have Internet access, and Africa and the Arab states stand out as the regions with the fewest fixed-broadband subscriptions in the world per 100 inhabitants, at 1 and 3.7, respectively.[130] Iraq lacks infrastructure for the diffusion of Internet access, and the entire Arab region lacks independent regulation to keep the Internet free of governmental control.[131] Yet despite the low Internet penetration in Iraq, 2.3 million Iraqis were Facebook users in 2012.[132]

Until very recently the Internet and social media platforms were largely unregulated in Iraq, making Iraq's Internet sector "one of the freest in the world."[133] In 2012, the Parliament considered legislation titled the "Informatics Crimes Law," which would have placed substantial limitations on online expression and imposed severe punishments for violating those restrictions.[134] This legislation ostensibly was proposed in reaction to the advances of terrorist groups and rumors of their sophisticated use of social media to recruit new fighters.[135]

In June 2014, in reaction to intelligence regarding the Islamic State's use of social media for recruitment, the Iraqi government blocked some social media websites including Facebook, Twitter, Skype and YouTube, and in some regions of Iraq tried to block Internet access altogether. Although international news agencies reported that the block was lifted as of June 30, some residents (particularly those in Tikrit and Mosul, areas held by the Islamic State at that time) still may have no or limited access to the Internet. In December 2014, incoming Prime Minister Haider al-Abadi withdrew all governmental legal cases against media outlets and journalists, yet the new media restrictions remained on the books. These restrictions place obstacles in the path of female MPs who depend at least to some extent on social networks to reach and communicate with constituents. As several of the case study MPs are active on social media, they are likely to have found these regulations inhibiting to relations with the citizens they represent.

Voter Attitudes and Perceptions

There is an important connection between women's political attitudes and behaviors and the presence (or absence) of viable, competitive female candidates for public office.[136] Along with challenges within Parliament from male colleagues and male-led political parties, Iraq's female MPs must also face obstacles stemming from public attitudes toward women in leadership positions.[137] Negative attitudes toward women leaders are fostered by the media, which often promote the stereotypical notion that women are less politically capable than men. The prevailing cultural attitude in Iraq is still that women lack decision-making ability. In a 2009 survey on youth and youthfulness, 35 percent of men aged 10 to 30 reported believing that women were unable to take important decisions for themselves or their families; and only 66 percent believed women were suited for leadership roles.[138] This reality, when viewed from the perspective of young voters, becomes an indicator of a society where these attitudes are translated into institutional practices that squelch women's ambitions to enter the political sphere. Oppressive and conservative cultures that perceive women as less capable propagate low numbers of women in leadership positions and detract from symbolic representation when women do attain public office. These public perceptions are worsened by voter apathy and the distractions on ordinary citizens posed by lack of basic and social services, unresolved domestic problems and continued political instability.

There is evidence that even many women eligible to vote in Iraq remain unengaged in the political process. According to a 2013 survey conducted by UN Women, only 67.7 percent of female Iraqi citizens believe that women should participate in political elections as candidates and 84.8 percent believe that women should vote. For the 41.5 percent of women who do not wish to participate in political affairs, the prevailing belief is that politics is a "man's business."[139] The Free Iraq Foundation surveys highlight these negative voter attitudes: in spring of 2011, 35 percent of incoming female MPs surveyed said the most challenging aspect of the parliamentary process was lack of interest from constituents.[140]

The parliamentary gender quota may contribute to disparities in voter attitudes between female and male candidates. During the 2010 elections, parliamentarian Maha al-Douri told the Associated Press that the quota should be removed. "The quota was very important in the previous elections because we live in a male-dominated society and the quota was necessary to give women a chance to have a political role," al-Douri said, "But in the future this quota should be removed and women should compete equally with men, because women politicians have proven their competence and reliability in politics." However, in the same article Maysoun al-Damlouji, the woman who received the highest number of votes among female candidates in the 2010 election, was quoted as acknowledging the drawbacks of the quota system: "Women have been brought to Parliament who do not necessarily believe in women's rights or even the quota that brought them into it. Now, people have the impression that women were brought in to fill a vacant space, and that they were not very effective."[141] The dominant attitude that women MPs are less capable or accomplished than their male colleagues both supports and stems from women's restricted access to the knowledge and information they need to make educated legislative decisions. Because women often are excluded from bloc or committee discussions that occur behind closed doors, they find it difficult to learn the important details of legislation.[142]

In addition to these common notions about female politicians' lesser capabilities, the challenges of balancing the dual burden of a political career and family obligations also detracts from voter perceptions of women in the political arena. Women's roles and responsibilities as caretakers are highly visible and assumed; when they succeed to become politically active, that activity is perceived as an exception to the societal narrative rather than the rule.[143] The proportion of women outside Iraq's entire labor force remains high, underscoring cultural emphasis on the importance of women's work at home over priority to engage in the labor market; and this attitude extends into the political realm. It also indicates the nature of the social division of labor between men and women and the structure of gender; women's role is nearly always confined to looking after home affairs and child-rearing. When women do work, their productive role goes unrecognized and thus they cannot access the support they need to ease the burden of playing multiple roles.[144] Guy commented thus in her 2016 interview:

> Politics takes time, and women have many tasks in looking after children etc. which mean they have less time [than men]. Single women have to be very tough, and married women need tough husbands to go into politics, so none of that is easy. In a predominantly patriarchal society dominated even by levels of misogyny it is difficult for women to be included in key decision-making meetings which may be held by men at night. Traditional tribal norms also prohibit women's engagement with men. Basically, security followed by societal and cultural pressures stop women from becoming politically active.[145]

Two case study MPs commented publicly about voter attitudes. In her 2012 interview with *al-Baghdadia* TV, Noura al-Bajari discussed efforts to damage her reputation made by a group to which she formerly belonged. "95 percent [of them have] jealousy, envy, and feelings of inferiority. I believe those who did that [targeted her] have a psychological sickness or suffer from an inferiority complex," Bajari said. "This move to sabotage my reputation is not by people but started by the group I used to belong to. Some other MPs (male and female) have feelings of inferiority." And Majida al-Tamimi commented to *al-Iraqiya* TV regarding the average citizen's lack of knowledge regarding parliamentary candidates' backgrounds, which leaves them open to coercive campaign strategies. "I do not mean everyone, but where did the MPs come from? They came as a result of being voted in," she stated. "When a person votes for an MP do they know who they are, their history? Some MPs—not all—reached a point of bribing voters with mobile phones, blankets or $100 to buy their votes. If he is giving me this money, how else is he going to compensate for his losses except by stealing Iraq?"

NGO Barriers

A further challenge to the symbolic representation of women in Iraq's Parliament is posed by the lack of cooperation between female parliamentarians and women's civil society organizations. Although NGOs exerted important influence toward adoption of the gender quota and overturning Decree 137, which would have amended Personal Status Law, there remains little collaboration between the government and political parties on the one hand, and women's organizations on the other, excepting those groups institutionalized or sanctioned by the state. Soon after 2003, there was divisiveness between organizations spearheaded by women returning from the diaspora—many of whom had strong ties to male political leaders and were perceived as urban bourgeois—and grassroots NGOs springing up from within Iraq[146] The United States during occupation did little toward resolving those schisms as the bulk of NGO development grants and donations went to US or internationally based organizations.[147] Occupational development agencies focused on cultural and religious challenges to women's rights, avoiding more important structural, economic and political obstacles given that they—as promoters of capitalist and neoliberal economic policies— were complicit in those obstacles.[148]

There also have been marked disagreements between organizations with religious ties and those formed by secular-oriented women.[149] The large numbers of "Islamic" women elected to Parliament in 2005 even led some secular women to question the benefits of having a gender quota.[150] Perceptions that female MPs become elected due to their affiliations with male political or religious leaders have at times caused relationships between women's NGOs and female parliamentarians to become antagonistic.[151] Some activists claim that women who are elected or appointed on grounds of familial associations with influential men have their voices co-opted by the state so the ruling elite does not have to engage in direct, honest debate with those working toward long-term change in women's status.[152] And since these women often lack political and organizing experience, their presence in Parliament erodes women's symbolic representation.

Summary

Learning how female parliamentarians are represented, by what symbols and the meanings attributed to them by their constituents helps illuminate the levels of symbolic capital women have attained toward establishing their legitimacy as policy actors. In keeping with Bourdieu's notion of symbolic power through language and while measuring symbolic capital as a concrete construct can be difficult, its presence is recognizable through media imagery and popular perceptions.[153] The inextricable links between symbolic representation and democratization are reflected in media practices, voter attitudes and citizen engagement in civil society.

The vast number of media networks emerging after 2003 did little either to facilitate dialogue between government and its opposition or to smooth progress toward peace-building and national unity. Rather, the media have greatly contributed to the ethnosectarian fragmentation of Iraqi society and its politics. Regulatory efforts, first instituted by the CPA and later amended by the floundering Maliki government, failed to restrain the media from encouraging and exacerbating violence among sects. Sectarian tensions particularly affect women who fulfill political, civil service and journalistic roles, as they face heavy pressures to support one side or another combined with harassment and great risk to personal security. Creation of a relatively independent media environment is important to symbolic representation because it builds avenues whereby women can promote political agendas and communicate with constituents. Yet conditions in Iraq post-occupation have not contributed to freedom of the press. While it could be argued that the media are rarely independent anywhere in the world, the extent to which Iraqi media reflect the politics of identity and sectarian schisms is unusually pronounced.

Iraqi female MPs have encountered some support for symbolic representation as politicians. The post-Ba'athist media offered women greater access to the press for political campaigns, during which they have employed print advertisements, billboards, posters and television and radio spots to promote their candidacies. Upon election to Parliament, they have used websites, social media, television appearances and newsletters to conduct constituent outreach and communication. Many have established positive relationships with certain media outlets, regularly release press statements on behalf of their parliamentary committees and use the media to bring attention to their prioritized issues. Social media may be evolving into a significant outlet through which Iraqi female politicians may increase their empowerment. Some female MPs also believe that voter attitudes toward women leaders have improved, that some citizens view them as role models and that a certain segment of the population values the female counterpoint to male political views.

However, Iraqi female politicians encounter more obstacles than supports to gaining symbolic capital. The public symbols and imagery used to depict Iraqi women—both female politicians and women in general—remain predominantly stereotypical and negative, framed in ways consistent with traditionalist patriarchal culture. Female MPs rarely appear in the television news, and when they do they are likely to be portrayed in a context wherein their contributions to politics are marginalized, their leadership and legislative capabilities placed in question. The gender quota is frequently invoked by male politicians and the press as the culprit for lifting inexperienced, incapable women into public office where they are pictured as focusing only on those issues commonly viewed as of import to women, such as childrearing and cuisine. Further, voters across all population segments are minimally engaged in the political process as they struggle to handle more immediate problems and feel disconnected from their legislative representatives. Women in public office must juggle dual responsibilities of politics and family, a burden placed disproportionately upon them than upon their male counterparts. Although popular perceptions of male MPs in Iraq may also be negative, these factors contribute further to the specific marginalization and exclusion of female MPs from legislative knowledge and participation.

The manner and extent to which public discourse legitimizes Iraqi female MPs as political actors remain marginal. The majority of Iraqis evaluate women neither as representatives of the nation's social identity nor as legitimate players in the political sphere. The symbolic representation achieved thus far by women in Iraqi politics has fallen short of creating avenues for gaining political power and control.

8

The Iraqi Political Situation and Women's Representation Post-2014: An Update on Case Study MP Activities since 2014

Major Political Developments

The bulk of the data analyzed for this research were collected in late 2012 and early 2013. Since then, major developments in Iraqi politics have transpired. First, there was an escalation of hostilities in the ongoing battle to retake key regions of the country from the Sunni insurgent force calling itself the Islamic State of Iraq and Syria, or ISIS (also called Daesh). A second important development, interrelated with the first, was the Kurdish referendum to declare independence from the Iraqi nation, for which a vote was held on September 25, 2017. These events, in keeping with political developments across Iraq's modern history, had significant impact on the representation and efficacy of Iraqi women in the public sphere. Tracking and updating the progresses of the case study MPs examined for this research again offer examples that aid in illuminating the condition of women in Iraqi politics in more recent years.

The Battle for Iraq

A comprehensive history of the rise of ISIS is not undertaken here; however, there is general agreement among scholars, military experts and the press that the roots of the militant group's formation lie largely in the 2003 US invasion and the improvident solidification of ethnosectarian divisions into Iraqi politics via the 2005 Constitution.[1] After segmenting from the al-Qaeda terrorist group, ISIS set up its presence in the Syrian civil war that erupted in 2011 on the wave of the Arab Spring, and became the first rebel group in that war to capture control of major Syrian cities (Raqqa and Deir ez-Zor). In 2014, insurgencies in Iraq escalated into what amounted to civil war when ISIS militants—emboldened by successes achieved on Syrian soil—seized control of most of Anbar Province, including the cities of Fallujah, Al-Qaim and Ramadi; took Mosul, Iraq's second largest city; and moved south to infiltrate regions bordering on Baghdad itself. ISIS then proclaimed itself a caliphate with the ambitious Iraqi militant whose nom de guerre is Abu Bakr al-Baghdadi as its caliph, and it launched a campaign of massacre, targeted genocide, terrorism and destruction of mosques and shrines across Iraq. News of ISIS activity spread widely across both traditional and social media.

The counterinsurgency mounted in response was undertaken by multiple opposition groups: the Iraqi Security Forces (ISF) led by the state government, in alignment with the Popular Mobilization Forces (PMF; an organization of more than 40 militias, primarily Shi'a); the Kurdish Peshmerga and the military forces of the Kurdish Regional Government (KRG); and armed forces sponsored by regional actors such as Syria, Turkey and Iran.[2] In addition, the conflict drew intervention by a host of international agents including the United States, the United Kingdom, France, Australia and Russia.

The struggle against ISIS in Iraq represents yet another iteration in the cycle of armed conflict and ethnosectarian violence that has devastated the country for more than three decades. In face of the ongoing conflict and his failure to maintain conditions of the power-sharing bargain set forth in the Erbil accord, Prime Minister Nouri al-Maliki stepped down at the end of his second term in 2014, under mounting pressure from international leaders and his own political party. The appointment of his successor Haider al-Abadi (also a Shi'a Muslim with ties to the Dawa Party) was met with widespread approval both within and outside Iraq, as Abadi vowed to close the divides between the primary ethnosectarian factions: the Shi'as, Sunnis and Kurds.[3] However, any strides made toward bridging sectarian schisms were largely eclipsed by the more pressing issue of managing the battle against ISIS. Under Abadi's leadership, the combined armed forces succeeded to retake most of the cities under ISIS siege, including Tal Afar, Hawija and most of Mosul; in October 2017 Abadi claimed in a Twitter post that the "end of the fake Daesh state" was at hand.[4] On October 26, 2017, Abadi announced the commencement of state-led military operations to retake the districts of Al-Qaim and Rawa in western Anbar, the last remaining ISIS strongholds in Iraq.

This civil war created a complex emergency of casualties, population displacement and humanitarian need. Although the media's focus was trained primarily on ISIS atrocities, both the ISF and the PMF have reputations for abuses against local populations as well.⁵ By the end of 2017, although much of the Islamic State's influence had been overthrown, the conflict was not over; and as many as 50,000 people remained besieged in the two sections of western Anbar ISIS still held. The war had resulted in 3.2 million internally displaced persons, nearly 265,000 Iraqi refugees in neighboring countries, and 11 million Iraqis in need of humanitarian assistance.⁶

The Kurdish Independence Referendum

In a development closely intertwined with the ISIS conflict, on September 25, 2017 the Kurdish leader Masoud Barzani held a referendum on the independence of Iraqi Kurdistan. Upon Saddam's fall in 2003, Kurdistan was recognized as a federal region within the state of Iraq, although the city of Kirkuk (where much of Iraq's oil deposits lie) was indicated as disputed. Article 140 of the 2005 Iraq Constitution called for normalization of Kurdistan to be implemented via census by the end of 2007, with "a referendum in Kirkuk and other disputed territories to determine the will of their citizens."⁷ The stipulations set forth in this ambitious article were never carried out. The Kurds have enjoyed semiautonomy from Iraq since 2003, establishing some of the foundations of self-governance. Yet competition between the two primary political parties—the Kurdistan Democratic Party (KDP) and the Patriotic Union of Kurdistan (PUK)—built an essential Kurdish duopoly. The regional turmoil fostered by the rise of ISIS only exacerbated this dichotomy.⁸ Simultaneously, the price of oil fell dramatically,⁹ with drastic effects on oil-rich Kurdistan's economy. The referendum (which is not legally binding) represented an effort of the declining leadership to cling to power while silencing domestic dissent.¹⁰ More than 92 percent of voters endorsed the split from Iraq, and the Kurdish flag was hoisted next to the Iraqi flag in Kirkuk.¹¹

In quick response to the referendum, Abadi redeployed state military units to Kirkuk and other parts of northern Iraq. Hostilities erupted between ISF and Peshmerga forces, resulting in further casualties and population displacement. In an opinion editorial published in *The New York Times* on October 18, 2017, Abadi stated that the referendum "emboldens the remnants of Daesh…Just as Iraq united to defeat Daesh over the past three years, we now need to apply that same unity to our next challenges: reconstruction and building a democratic country where each citizen enjoys full access to the protection of the state."¹² In November 2017, the Iraqi Supreme Federal Court ruled the vote unconstitutional and the results void, strengthening Baghdad's hand.¹³

Ongoing military movements and political tensions between the Iraqi government and the KRG continued to engender insecurity and population displacement through 2017. The situation further complicated and impeded combined efforts to eradicate the remaining ISIS cells operating within Iraq.

Case Study Updates

Characterizing the movements of the 12 case study MPs since 2014 offers an illuminating lens through which to evaluate the status of women in Iraqi politics as the current situation has evolved. As we approach the 2018 parliamentary elections, it is interesting to review the progress these women have made toward political efficacy. Clearly their contributions as public officials have been affected by recent major political events, and they continue to wrestle with many of the same issues they faced in earlier years.

Noura al-Bajari

Noura al-Bajari, a member of the parliamentary Economic and Investment Committee, is a representative of al-Hal (The Solution) Bloc that is part of the al-Iraqiya Alliance. First elected to the Iraqi Parliament in 2010, Bajari was reelected in 2014. Much of her political activity has been directed toward fighting corruption, with an ultimate goal of achieving economic improvement and development. As of 2017, she aims to shed light on the problems Iraq faces today and suggest solutions to the government for improving the country. The problems that Bajari currently focuses on are Iraq's foreign policy, the concerns facing evacuees in al-Mosul, and Iraq's budget and growing national debt.

In a 2017 interview, Bajari stated her opinion that Iraqi foreign policy has changed completely since the end of Saddam's dictatorship in 2003, expressing that the malicious American policy during the occupation affected Iraq's status with other countries and built increasing tension in foreign relations. These troubles, according to Bajari, contributed to Iraq's current vulnerabilities, isolating the country both regionally and internationally. One solution she suggested is that the Iraqi government should improve relations with its neighbors and other countries gradually. She pointed to a recent visit by the Saudi Arabian Foreign Minister as a promising step, recommending that the government build bilateral relations with Saudi Arabia to enhance their common interests.

Given her strong Mosul roots, the struggle against ISIS in Iraq drew Bajari's attention. She announced that the living conditions in the Al-Mosul evacuee camps—in places beleaguered under ISIS authority and even in liberated areas—were drastic. In a 2017 visit to those camps, she noticed lack of coordination and absence of governmental efforts to support the evacuees, especially calling out the Ministries of Health and Immigration. As for the liberated regions, Bajari said, the security forces exerted significant effort toward citizen aid; however, local governments had yet to solve the multiple problems citizens face. Bajari called for cooperation between government and the ministries to solve the main issues encountered by citizens in the liberated areas and to provide evacuees with the essential services they lack. She also suggested that the Ministry of Education make concerted efforts to build schools in the evacuee camps, and called upon the Ministry of Health to construct hospitals as soon as possible, noting that people were dying daily from shortage of medical services.

Bajari remained concerned about Iraq's growing national debt, now estimated at $69 billion. She cited the difficulty of repaying the high debt load if Iraq continues to depend upon oil as its main revenue source, and has played an important role in attempting to solve this problem. Her parliamentary Economic Committee submitted a report to the Finance Committee concerning the national budget, mentioning the importance of activating the private sector—especially in the governorates—to conduct projects that will generate new financial sources to supplement oil revenues. This suggestion may offer partial solution to the financial crisis Iraq has faced following the drop in oil prices. Further, the report offered solutions to decrease governmental expenses without detracting from essential services. One such idea Bajari posed is reducing pension payments to martyrs' families. In a 2017 statement to Al-Ghad Press, she advocated for changes to the Law of Rafha granting pensions to Gulf War refugees and their families: "The Rafha prisoners are about 20,000, but it is not fair to give a whole family a pension, especially since there is a major financial crisis."[14]

Bajari noted that the relatively new Law of Investment required modification. Lack of security and corruption are the main problems facing investors in Iraq, she said, as most investors suffer from the so-called whales of investing who controlled the bulk of Iraqi investment projects, leading smaller investors to lose their capital. She continued to press for the investigation of governmental corruption, which she posited is likely to affect Iraq's ability to obtain loans for rebuilding the regions damaged by ISIS.[15]

Etab al-Douri

Etab al-Douri, a member of al-Hal Bloc and al-Iraqiya Slate, has remained focused on improving the plight of the oppressed in Iraqi prisons, widows and orphans. She served on the Agricultural Committee in Parliament, and since 2014 she played an important role in addressing the lack of water and electricity in al-Taji city, with the help of the Ministry of Water Resources. She collected 180 MP signatures on a petition to support farmers living in misery due to the high rates of migration from the countryside to Iraqi cities. She helped Iraqi farmers by giving them loans to build greenhouses, paying off their debts and attempting to amend the Irrigation Act. She spearheaded efforts to improve living conditions for Iraqi peasants by providing them with compost and pesticides to increase poultry production and bolster populations of local livestock (fish, cattle, goats and poultry), which are essential to the Iraqi economy.

Douri asked for effective governmental action to impose a tax on imports, to protect both industrial and agricultural products produced within Iraq as products from neighboring countries flooded the Iraqi market. She encouraged national and local production to support the peasants. In an attempt to increase the national palms fortune, she petitioned the government for helicopters to help eradicate the endemic disease plaguing Iraq's palm trees. She played a role in agreements between Iraq, Turkey and Iran to solve problems of water scarcity.

As of 2017, although Etab al-Douri no longer served in Parliament, she continued to participate in political issues. She asked all political parties to open serious and comprehensive dialogue to face Iraq's critical problems, especially those in Kurdistan, to achieve Iraqi unity and maintain security and stability. In an interview in 2017, Douri stated that the raising of the flag of Kurdistan in Kirkuk was opposed by most Iraqis, adding that the political parties rejected this action and called for the resignation of the governor of Kirkuk and the dissolution of the Provisional Council, referring to the expiration of constitutional Article 140. In fact, she has criticized the constitution itself, saying in October 2017 that it "must be burned because it is failed and built on the basis of sectarian quotas."[16]

Hanan al-Fatlawi

Hanan al-Fatlawi remained a prominent and highly visible parliamentarian in 2017. She was a member of the parliamentary Committee of International Affairs, head of the Iraqi-British Friendship Committee and vice president of the Iraqi-Japanese, Chinese and Korean Friendship Committee. Her *erada* (will) movement was the first Iraqi political movement initiated by a woman.

In 2017, Fatlawi discussed Iraq's pressing issues and searched for solutions to help build the new Iraq. In an interview she opined strongly about Saudi Arabia, stating that no one denies Saudi Arabian support to Iraq during the Iran-Iraq war, from which the Iraqi people still suffer; yet those who defended Iraq in that war have been convicted as militias and terrorists. Due to this unfairness, Fatlawi claimed the relationship between Baghdad and El-Riyadh was strained, suggesting that the Iraqi people did not need anything from Saudi Arabia and only ask it to curtail its expiatory legal declarations (fatwa). Thanks to Iraqi citizens, army and police forces, Iraq was successful in overcoming American colonization and ISIS, whereas—according to Fatlawi—the Arabs only raised mottos against America and had no role in defending Iraq in the war against ISIS. In June 2016, Fatlawi called for the expulsion of the Saudi ambassador to Baghdad, Tamer al-Sabhan, if he failed to abstain from violating diplomatic norms.[17]

Fatlawi also expressed strident rejection of the Kurdish referendum, stating that the Iraqi government declined the referendum on constitutional grounds and that it threatens Iraq's unity. Along with other members of the State of Law Coalition, Fatlawi led a campaign against the referendum, declaring that officials would be dismissed if they participated in the referendum and that the Iraqi Federal Court would cancel it. In September 2017, PM Haider al-Abadi declined Fatlawi's request to participate in the referendum when he attended a parliamentary session to make a decision concerning Kurdish independence.[18] After the referendum vote, Baghdad issued several arrest warrants for Kurdish leaders on multiple charges, including one for Kurd and former Iraqi army chief of staff Babaker Zebari for misappropriation of public funds; and one for Kurdish Vice President Kosrat Rasul for provocation against the ISF.[19] In apparent retaliation, in October, the Office of Presidency in Kurdistan named Fatlawi and ten other Iraqi politicians in a lawsuit and called for their arrests.[20]

A strong Shi'a Muslim, the outspoken Fatlawi held a secret meeting in 2017 with Jan Kubis, the UN envoy to Iraq. In this meeting Fatlawi allegedly asked Kubis to petition the UN to impose sanctions on the KRG and thereby stop the Kurdish referendum. Subsequently, Fatlawi was accused of treason and collusion with Iran. She refused these convictions and denied any responsibility for Iranian involvement in Iraqi affairs, pointing out that the Iraqi government did not agree with these allegations and had condemned Iran officially. Kubis's disputed actions reportedly led at least some Iraqi politicians to consider then-UN general secretary António Guterres wholly responsible for the crimes and violations of human rights against many ethnic and minority groups in Iraq—most notably Sunnis—committed by Iranian Militias in Iraq and Syria (IMIS).[21]

Ashwaq al-Jaf

As of 2017, Ashwaq al-Jaf had become leader of the KDP. As such, Jaf gave the push for Kurdish independence high priority on her political agenda. She also was active on issues surrounding human rights, including persecution of the Yazidi minority group, Iraqi child labor violations and harassment of Iraqi bloggers.

In 2016, Jaf spoke out against the ostensible support given by Western authorities to the Iranian terrorist organization known as the People's Mohajedin Organization of Iran (abbreviated as PMOI, MKO or MEK). In a July 29 interview, Jaf explained to *Ashraf News* that the Kurdish people were the first victims of these militants during the killings waged against the Kurds by the Saddam Hussein regime. When Western leaders removed the organization from their terrorism lists, Jaf asked, "Why has American and Western outlook changed towards the MEK terrorist organization of Iran, which was several years ago a terrorist group? Did the behaviour of this organization change?"[22]

Al-Jaf represented the KDP across the months leading up to, during and after the Kurdish independence referendum. The Kurdish Minister of Finance in Iraq, Hoshyar Zebari, was dismissed from his post amid charges of graft in September 2016, a move that many believed was spearheaded by Shiʿa lawmakers (led by former premier Nouri al-Maliki) in an attempt to marginalize Kurdish influence. Zebari's removal was "political targeting, 100 percent," Jaf was quoted in the *Middle East Monitor*. When Kurdistan President Masoud Barzani was accused of allowing Turkish forces onto Iraqi soil for purposes of eliminating rival party PUK, Jaf called the accusation an aim by "failed political figures" to cripple Barzani's efforts toward Kurdish independence.[23] In August 2017, Jaf asserted publicly that the Kurdish referendum would be held on schedule, with no possibility of postponement.

As representative of the parliamentary Human Rights Committee, human rights remained an important focus to Jaf. She vocalized her opposition to the prevalence of child labor in Iraq, which deprives Iraqi children of their minimal rights to education and health care. As ongoing insecurity and political fluctuations in Iraq inhibited economic growth and disrupted essential social services, many businesses took to employing children to reduce costs, while families felt compelled to send children into the work force when fathers were disabled or killed. "Families and children have been the main victims of acute economic and security deterioration that plagued the country in the past six years," Jaf told *The Arab Weekly* in July 2016. "We have tried many times to push for a law to grant widows soft loans, but we were cut short by political differences."[24] Jaf also proposed legislation in 2017 to provide aid to Yazidi girls and women subsequent to that minority population's release from ISIS besiegement. In a press statement in June, she described three proposals: to recognize Yazidi girls and women as terrorist victims; to count them as martyrs or people with special needs; and to grant them a monthly salary in recompense.[25] And in November 2017, Jaf spoke about the unionization of Iraqi social media activists to protect them from growing threats of terrorist backlash. "Accessing the internet is one of our human rights in this country, after a 35-year dictatorship, so we should protect it well," Jaf stated.

Karima al-Jawari

Karima al-Jawari did not stand for reelection in 2014. However, she continued to retain a role in Iraqi policy-making. During the years since 2014, Jawari called for the unification of Iraq to reform what the ISIS corrupted in the western governorates as—in her opinion—killing, arrests and detention had led to catastrophes in those areas. In a 2015 interview, she explained that she did not oppose American aid to Iraq during her parliamentary tenure, because she confirmed that America had played an important part in Iraqi decision-making since 2003. Further, she stated, Western influences had trained many people in her al-Anbar Governorate to combat ISIS.[26] She called upon politicians, especially those in the western governorates, to abandon their political conflicts to save Iraq against international maneuvers that have aimed to destroy the country since the period of colonization when the colonialists tried to divide Iraq by arousing ethnic conflicts. Accordingly, Jawari encouraged the coordination committees for the union of Iraqi forces while they served the Iraqi people, but stated she would oppose them if they became a reason for Iraqi division.

Jawari confirmed her view that thousands of Iranians travel between Iraqi governorates every day, offering evidence that Iran still exerts control over Iraqi policy. In contrast, Iraqi people needed permission to enter some governorates. She stated in her interview that malicious politicians interfere in Iraqi politics in the western provinces, pointing out that these politicians cooperated with the enemies to divide Iraq and destroy its history and civilization. Jawari indicated

Salah al-Din, Anbar and Nineveh as examples. She added that Iraq's strength would be achieved only after its unity, claiming that Iraqi people must be aware that the occupation and subsequent terrorism did not distinguish between Shi'a and Sunni. The aim of the conference of Iraqi tribal leaders, according to Jawari, was to declare their position against terrorism and support the ISF in the war against ISIS. She confirmed that she is strongly against dividing Iraq into regions, asserting that her bloc voted against the 2005 Constitution because of its divisiveness.

Jinan Mubarak

Very little information was published regarding Jinan Mubarak's political movements since 2014, other than that she continued as head of the NGO Iraqi Centre for Women's Rehabilitation and Employment.

Suhad al-Obaidi

A civil engineer from Salah al-Din, Suhad al-Obaidi continued to serve in the Iraqi Parliament after 2014. In a 2014 televised interview, she described her political philosophy as having a primary goal of maintaining Iraq's unity, preserving its religious and national identity and building an economically and politically strong country. She expressed that internal conflicts lead to fights between political blocs and with other countries, leading to the division of Iraq and neglect of the Palestinian problem. As an MP, Obaidi commented on the weakness of Parliament due to political infighting; she declared that the chief of her parliamentary committee (Public Services and Reconstruction) was unprofessional. According to Obaidi, the 2005 Constitution was written hastily and has been breached by international influences, especially the United States. She believes relations between some Iraqi political blocs and neighboring countries had a negative impact on the constitutional process.[27]

In 2017, Obaidi shed light on the problems facing Iraq and suggested possible solutions. Commenting on the floods that wracked the country, she agreed that the government had no obvious role in solving the crisis, adding that most governorates had no paved roads or sewage treatment systems and that condition had caused the flooding after heavy rains. Because her committee was busy handling political conflicts, they developed no specific strategy for water and sewage disposal; therefore, they found no solution to this problem as the infrastructure law failed in Parliament.

Obaidi also addressed increasing poverty in Iraq, confirming that the Iraqi government since 2003 neglected many classes of citizens and brought on a state of inequality. Money was not distributed equitably according to the national budget, leading Iraqi people to suffer; this condition had persisted since the economic sanctions of the 1990s. Suhad al-Obaidi asserted that, in addition to the critical security situation, most Iraqis are afflicted by poverty, but especially orphans and widows. Although the government had stated laws to solve problems of the poverty classes, a huge number of widows and orphans still suffered under terrorist attacks. The martyrs and their families must be considered as well.

Obaidi suggested several solutions to Iraq's problems. If the Parliament applied some of the articles in the constitution, living conditions among Iraqi citizens might be improved; however, she opined, the state is biased for specific classes over others. She stressed that the government should give Iraqi citizens a share of exported oil revenues as a potential solution. She stated also that the government should build residential complexes for homeless citizens, instead of giving them lands upon which they have no capacity to build. Displaced persons lived in unsuitable conditions full of epidemics and disease. Obaidi also called upon the government to change the retirement law to calculate the years people spent fighting against American colonization, stating that many people who defended their country in Salah al-Din and other governorates were imprisoned rather than being rewarded for their service.

Mariam al-Rayyis

Mariam al-Rayyis was not reelected as MP in 2014. In her role as press liaison for Nouri al-Maliki during his terms as prime minister, her most recent available interviews were recorded in 2014, prior to that year's parliamentary elections.[28] At that time she expressed being unconcerned about having a majority government without Sunni Arab representation in the Iraqi Parliament, as Iraq has a history of brutal conflict between Shi'a and Sunni militias. She added that the political process would continue even if there was only one party, and would not deteriorate into a dictatorship; she drew parallel to the American government at times when Democrats or Republicans control all three branches. Rayyis asserted that the only alternative as of 2014 was for Iraq to form a majority government that rises above political and electoral conflicts. She believed the country needed a government that could carry out national projects with strong parliamentary support, meaning the majority in Parliament must form the government and those who oppose the government would remain outside it.

According to Rayyis, under those conditions governmental opposition would search for ways to serve the rights of Iraqi people rather than pursuing personal interests. What was happening in Parliament at the time, in contrast, was that some politicians rejected legislation due only to party interests.

Rayyis denounced what she described as people who always appeared before elections, spreading violent rhetoric of hatred and sectarianism, and called for international intervention in Iraq. She opined that these figures were afraid elections would be held in Anbar, causing them to lose their current political positions. Rayyis also believed the media had a great responsibility to reveal the facts to the people and that this was not happening in most Iraqi media. However, she was optimistic that the media would change and become aware of their responsibility to spread the truth.

Huda Sajjad Mahmoud

Huda Sajjad Mahmoud was elected to Parliament by the Dawa Party under Nouri al-Maliki's State of Law Bloc and served since 2010, representing Diywaniyyah Governorate. She was interviewed by AFAQ TV in March 2017, at which time she spoke about the Iraqi media, al-Abadi's leadership, the national budget and her role in fighting governmental corruption.[29]

Sajjad declared that the Iraqi media were underdeveloped, isolated and failed to reach all citizens. During the struggle against ISIS, she asserted, the country must improve its international media to make the international community aware of current events in Iraq. Asked about the Haider al-Abadi government, Sajjad commented that he neither differentiates between governorates nor gives advantage to some sects over others; in her opinion, this was exactly what Iraq needed to achieve unity and do away with ethnic infighting. She applauded Abadi for recognizing the efforts and role of the popular crowd in Iraq's liberation. However, she criticized Abadi's choice of ambassadors and expressed concern that they would damage Iraq's international relations. She did give Abadi credit for trying to strike a balance between the military requirements of fighting terrorism and the international meetings that must occur. According to Sajjad, living in peace is not easy; it will take time due to the ethnic differences in Iraq, which have negative effects on security and the economy.

Sajjad spoke further regarding the Iraqi economy, expressing concern over the decreasing price of oil and the resulting budget shortfall estimated at that time at $43 billion. She believed this deficit was one of the most urgent problems facing the Iraqi government. In regard to the national housing initiative, Sajjad clarified that several obstacles impeded the implementation of Resolution 254 passed by the Council of Ministers. This initiative included an agreement to address the governors of the relevant municipalities—such as the project maintenance municipality—to strengthen mechanical efforts to prepare the allocated land for the project.

In her interview, Sajjad insisted that Parliament would question Minister of Communications Hassan al-Rashed about potential corruption, pointing out that many politicians had offered large amounts of money to delay the questioning. She stressed that no offers would be accepted, even in the face of heavy political pressure. To her, the most essential instances of corruption were the waste of public money and the selling of state resources to private companies, and all corruption must be rooted out to achieve prosperity for the Iraqi people.

Safia al-Suhail

In October 2015, Safia al-Suhail—who has dual Jordanian and Iraqi citizenship—was named Iraq's first female ambassador to Jordan.[30] In that role, Suhail focused her efforts on facilitating economic interactions and reopening channels of trade between the two countries. At an Iraqi Business Council (IBC) reception held in Amman in March 2016, she commended the IBC's efforts to forge memoranda of understanding and economic cooperation with commercial and industrial unions, both in Jordan and elsewhere.[31] In May 2016, Suhail spoke at a press conference regarding the reopening of the Treibel trade route—the primary outlet between Jordan and Iraq—stating that the route was ready to open but had been planted with explosives by ISIS.[32] In August of that year, she confirmed the negotiation to remove extra fees that an Iraqi official had placed on Jordanian exports to Iraq, stating that Iraq would abide by the joint trade agreement to exchange commodities without fees.[33]

As of 2017, Suhail was interviewed by Adnkronos International regarding an issue of importance to her, the rising suicide rate among Iraqi women. "We need to quickly find a solution to the current phenomenon of Iraqi women turning to suicide to free themselves from the harshness of tradition and social customs," Suhail said, blaming this troubling trend on the "continuing pressures and psychological crises that women suffer in Iraq."[34] Calling on the state to carry out a study to unearth the causes of the phenomenon, Suhail suggested that a solution was needed to prevent physical and psychological violations against women. Both the government and the media should take responsibility "to create a cultural background that supports the rights of women" to prevent women from resorting to taking their own lives, Suhail concluded.

Alaa' al-Talabani

A high-profile Kurdish public figure, Alaa' al-Talabani has remained quite politically active since 2014, and was named head of the PUK Bloc in the Iraqi Parliament in 2015. In September 2016, she issued a press statement denying allegations of political or economic relationships between Kurdistan and Israel.[35] In early October 2017, Talabani received a personal blow when her uncle, former Iraqi president Jalal Talabani, passed away in Germany at age 83.[36]

Talabani granted an interview to the *Around the World* news program in September 2017.[37] She was questioned about the raising of the Kurdistan flag after the independence referendum, an act condemned as sedition by Haider al-Abadi. In response, she stated that the Kurds do not impose their policy upon the Iraqi people, adding that the Kurdistan government had various chances to impose its political desires on Kirkuk by force after 2003, especially when there was no Provincial Council; but Kurdistan did not act against the Iraqi Constitution or policy. According to Talabani, Arabs and Turkmen—whom some view as minorities in Kirkuk—had equal participation in the Kurdish administration. She also expressed that the National Union of Kurdistan had not seized the Kirkuk oil wells post-2003, instead only taking their legal shares; and the oil fields had been secured by the Kurdish Peshmerga forces since mid-2014, when ISF forces collapsed under ISIS attack. Talabani added that the referendum had drawn interference from neighboring countries, especially Turkey, which voiced strong opposition. She opined that Turkish interference led to the referendum, which she believed was imposed on Kurdistan by force. How did raising the flag in Kirkuk threaten Iraqi national security, she asked?

Talabani was removed from her post as PUK Bloc Chief in June 2017 by the PUK's political bureau. Some sources believed this removal was because of her association with a bloc that opposed the Kurdish independence referendum.[38] Elsewhere, however, it was noted that Talabani's opposition to the referendum was due to her belief that the push for independence was part of an agreement (KDP-affiliated Kurdish President) Masoud Barzani had struck with Baghdad for Kurdish interests, with not only Turkish but also Iranian influence at play. According to Talabani, Barzani's party controls the Kirkuk oil wells and had exported oil by force since June 2014, but the Iraqi people received no revenue from these oil sales.[39] In October 2017, she was quoted as criticizing Barzani, "We won't sacrifice for the sake of stolen oil fields, whose money went to the pockets and accounts of individuals."[40] Talabani implied Iranian involvement in this affair by mentioning the role of Qassim Sulaimani, the head of Iran's elite Quds Force, claiming he advised the Kurds to reach such an accord with Baghdad.

Majida al-Tamimi

As of 2017, Majida al-Tamimi continues to serve a prominent role on the parliamentary Finance Committee. In August 2015, she expressed concern over the increased budget deficit due to falling oil prices, saying that the real deficit would be 53 trillion Iraqi dinars, as opposed to the 23 trillion approved by the general budget law.[41] She called upon PM Abadi to reduce governmental expenditures in all sectors to offset this shortfall. Speaking to Bas News in January 2017, Tamimi claimed the Iraqi government had spent $1,000 billion USD since 2004, while the country's debts had exceeded $111 billion USD in the same period.[42] According to her investigations, these expenditures included both investment expenses and government operations costs. Calling Iraq's financial policy "futile," Tamimi pointed to many instances of corruption and waste, including three ministries in which more than 16,000 employees received more than one state salary.[43] She also referred to a rise in poverty rates among Iraqi citizens, stating the rate had risen from 22 percent in 2014 to 41 percent in 2017. Tamimi claimed she took the management of state funds to solve the poverty crisis very seriously.

A video recording posted in March 2017 shows Tamimi questioning the President of the Electoral Commission in Parliament.[44] In May of that year, she helped collect more than 50 MP signatures on a petition to withdraw confidence from the Election Commission and dismiss its members for corruption and vote manipulation. In a statement to Al-Ghad Press, she confirmed her submission of these signatures to parliamentary leaders, but expressed uncertainty whether Parliament would vote on the no-confidence measure at its next session.[45] Tamimi also had registered a complaint with the United Nations concerning the failure of the Election Commission and its members to remain impartial of the Election Commission and its members, providing evidence and documentation in an hours-long interrogation session of details suggesting falsification of election results along with financial, administrative and legal breaches of conduct.

Summary and Outlook

Updating the activities undertaken by these case studies confirms the fact that by 2017 Iraq had made little headway toward removing the obstacles that stand in the way of women's political mobilization. Conditions of violence, insecurity, political upheaval, governmental corruption, poverty and deprivation still prevailed. Ethnosectarian schisms had—if anything—been deepened rather than bridged. Progress toward democratization was stalled in a political climate where combating terrorism and handling territorial disputes demanded centerstage.

Yet even amid this turmoil some hope for women's political efficacy in Iraq still emerges. The experiences of these 12 MPs suggest that, once an Iraqi woman attains political office, she tends to remain in the public eye even after her tenure as politician has concluded. The case studies have garnered media attention both in their parliamentary roles and outside them. This media coverage has extended at times into the international arena, and has been posted and reposted across various social media platforms. The ease of finding broadcast interviews and press statements involving these women may imply that they have made at least some gains in perceived legitimacy and symbolic capital.

Further, the case studies have continued to pursue the issues of greatest import to them and which draw most closely upon their bases of knowledge and expertise. Such pursuits may represent the best avenues for women's empowerment in politics, because demonstrating depth of understanding around a problem builds legitimacy and engenders respect. For female MPs in Iraq, the degree to which their efforts can be tied to results—in reducing poverty, corruption, national debt and political infighting, for example—is the one to which they will reflect public images as political agents.

9

Conclusion

From within the context of the historical, political, sectarian and cultural influences on women's political agency, this book has undertaken to evaluate the successes and failures encountered due to institutionalizing an electoral gender quota in Iraq. The analyses drew on three bodies of scholarship: democratization theory, feminist theory and the study of political gender quotas. These approaches all recognize the importance of gender inclusiveness to the development of a functioning democracy. But the circumstances of Iraq particularly highlight what the general literature tends to understate: the difficulties of mobilizing female politicians amid instability and profound sectarian schisms resulting from deep-rooted traditions and international intervention, when conservative Islam is politicized and has a strong influence on the emerging political order.

Democratic and feminist theorists recognize the importance of elections, but even ostensibly "free" elections may produce only a "façade democracy"[1] or public officials who serve as "window dressing."[2] More is needed: a thriving civil society, the emergence of independent media and women's full participation in the political process. All these factors help to advance the cause of democracy, yet they are also themselves, in time, advanced by a mature democracy. The processes are intimately interconnected in practice: progress toward democratization builds the foundations that make free elections, civil societies and independent media possible. Therefore, the stakes for women's mobilization as formal political agents are very high. To the extent that they are the beneficiaries of formal democratic arrangements such as elections and quotas, they, in turn, facilitate democratic development by directly participating in political society; they help create the conditions that foster rule of the people, viable civil societies and an independent press. The embeddedness of such a supportive democratic political culture both encourages and sustains a consolidated democracy.[3]

The political void left by the 2003 collapse of the Saddam regime had to be renegotiated among a leadership deeply divided across ethnosectarian lines. Iraqi women (both in the country and in the diaspora) were primed and enthusiastic to play a substantive role in the reconstruction phase. However, the foundational and infrastructural preconditions needed for successful democratization were lacking. The interventionists demanded creation of a reconstructive plan and drafting of a constitution according to a strict timetable driven primarily by Western interests and objectives. The 2005 constitutional laws of governance therefore focused heavily on avoiding the possibility of future autocracies and failed to foster inclusive roles for all segments of society toward rebuilding the polity. Upon this stage, the role of women in politics became a central topic of debate between the interventionists and a host of Iraqi groups representing competing ideologies. Institutionalizing the gender quota in the 2005 Constitution was a product mainly of women's civil activism and international influences. Yet the fact that the quota remains in force has implications for the social meanings ascribed to female politicians in a country with a long tradition of excluding women from political power.

This book has examined the impact of the gender quota on women's descriptive, substantive and symbolic representation in the parliamentary elections of 2005, 2010 and 2014, and has briefly followed the political activities of 12 case studies across that time frame and up until 2017. As anticipated, the gender quota led to a significant increase in women's descriptive representation in the Iraqi Parliament; that is, the number of women parliamentarians has been on an upward trajectory. However, regarding substantive representation, this analysis suggests that the gender quota has had minimal value to support Iraqi female MPs as political agents. Women who do become elected generally rely upon sources outside the quota to support their campaigns and parliamentary functions. While the women who gain parliamentary seats come from diverse ethnic, religious, educational and experiential backgrounds, they have many common challenges in their political roles, including competing demands of work and family; financial burdens; resistance and exclusion from political party leadership and most importantly, the relentless conditions of violence and insecurity that have prevailed in Iraq since the invasion. The constant threat of violent attack is not restricted to those representing any one segment of society; all women in politics are at mortal risk.

What strides Iraq has made toward democracy serve as both supports and barriers to Iraqi women achieving substantive representation. Questions remain regarding whether Iraq was truly "ready" for democracy, and whether true democracies can emerge from military occupation and a forced constitutional process under international pressures. While female MPs have made some significant contributions to political processes and policies, the backlash against interventionist democracy promotion has led to the institutionalization of religious-cultural values that weaken the influence of women in the political domain. It must be noted that parliamentarians of both genders face significant obstacles to exercising true political efficacy. However, men in Iraq's Parliament have influenced substantially more public policies at the national and international level than have women, whose political voice tends to be marginalized and confined to those issues of concern to women, children and family institutions.

Exploring the ways in which Iraqi female MPs are framed and symbolized in the media—the focus of symbolic representation—reveals that women remain far from achieving the symbolic capital requisite to attain legitimacy as political agents. The media continue to depict Iraqi women in stereotypical traditionalist frames. Women in public office rarely appear in the press; when they do they are portrayed in a context wherein their political agency is marginalized, and their capabilities questioned. The press and male politicians accuse the gender quota of being responsible for placing inexperienced, incapable women into office. Still, Iraqi female MPs have encountered some supports to symbolic representation such as increased access to the media for political campaigning and reaching constituents; improved voter attitudes and greater value placed upon gaining a female counterpoint to male political views. Emerging social media platforms, in particular, may have contributed to increasing women's empowerment as political actors.

It is of vital importance, however, to note that the media outlets emerging since 2003 have greatly contributed to Iraq's ethnosectarian rifts, and they have exacerbated and encouraged sectarian violence. These tensions particularly affect women serving in political, civil and journalistic positions. Therefore, the symbolic representation achieved thus far by women in Iraqi politics has failed to create avenues for gaining political power and control. Until a relatively independent media environment has been created, true symbolic representation for women cannot be achieved.

Throughout this discussion, a number of broader themes have emerged. First, gender quotas, while necessary, are not sufficient for effective women's representation. As we have seen, a simple quantitative standard—the number of seats gained by women—is indicative of social change, even progress, but the quality of representation is much harder to raise. It is, in fact, subject to a number of resistances—religious, cultural, political. Since the first two, which are often interconnected, are embedded and could only change over the *longue durée*, the political is more susceptible to adaptation.

In this regard, the scope of women's ministries (such as Iraq's State Ministry of Women) could usefully be expanded to include soliciting their input on broader national issues. Political parties could also be encouraged to promote their female members to decision-making roles. Female MPs need support and encouragement to focus on the specific needs of their constituents to garner increased respect and backing. A specialized regional monitoring center might be established to analyze women's issues in Iraq. As Noura al-Bajari has said, women parliamentarians should "maintain a humble, simple image; relate to one's constituents, especially the women; strive always to receive visitors and listen to their concerns." And from Alaa' al-Talabani, female MPs must "become active and vocal around the issues most dear to one's constituents."

Second, the possibilities of improved women's representation are intimately linked to the socioeconomic position of women in general. Not unlike other societies, women's economic and social status remains inferior to that of men. But this status is reinforced by persistent patrimonial religious (whether Sunni or Shi'a), tribal and often family attitudes in Iraq, which, if not directly hostile to, are unsupportive of a culture of gender equality. Women's equal access to employment opportunities[4] would be at least one achievable step forward. Moreover, with regard to potential candidates in particular, the need for concrete incentives, such as campaign subsidies, is obvious.

Third, although individual women have had notable successes and their political reputations established, interaction and cooperation among women MPs have been distinctly limited. Different and sometimes conflicting ethnic and sectarian identities among the MPs may account for this tendency, but it may also be explained by necessarily closer links with key male politicians or by an admirable focus on constituency work rather than broader alliance-building. However, it is likely that women's coalitions built across party lines would help to minimize conflicts and magnify women's voices on critical policy issues. For example, it has been suggested that women might use their legislative roles to work toward integrating or enhancing the Convention to End All Forms of Discrimination against Women (CEDAW) and Security Council Resolution 1325 to increase women's roles in peace-building.[5] The capacity of Iraqi women to represent their constituencies, monitor executive bodies, and enact or reform laws to help eradicate state-sponsored and/or state-sanctioned gender violence is likely to be strengthened by overt collaboration with the Ministry of Women but also with women's organizations.

Fourth, the ability of women to function as effective democratic agents is severely limited when there is a fundamental absence—the lack of security. As we have seen, parliamentarians, male and female, have been hindered in their work by violent bloodshed at worst and internal fragmentation at best. A stable political order, let alone a supportive political culture, is stymied by the failure to meet the primary duty of a state—the security of its people. If stability is thus elusive, so much more so is the possibility of implanting a strong democracy. Because the movements of women parliamentarians are not generally as easy as those of men, enhanced domestic stability would enable them to move about more freely, undertake public speaking engagements and interact more widely with their constituents without fear for their personal safety.

By the end of 2017, Iraq had made little progress toward removing the obstacles impeding women's mobilization in the political sphere. Insecure conditions and political upheaval prevailed even in the wake of the proclaimed defeat of the Islamic State. Ethnosectarian schisms remained; movement toward democracy was further delayed in the face of the debate over Kurdistan. Yet still some hope for women's political efficacy can be found. A brief follow-up of the political movements by the case study women since 2014 indicates that, once they achieved election, they tended to remain prominent in the public eye even if not reelected to parliamentary seats. The continued presence of the 12 case study MPs in the press may suggest that they have gained at least some modicum of symbolic capital and political legitimacy. Continuing to pursue the causes they espouse and with which they have expertise has proven the best direction for Iraqi women to follow in order to gain political agency.

The most immediate and critical component of the Iraqi experience remaining to be addressed in order for women to achieve complete substantive and symbolic agency as politicians is ethnosectarian divisiveness and its accompanying violence. The sincere and fervent hope is that terrorist insurgence has indeed been overcome; that the territorial debates may be settled peaceably and to the satisfaction of all societal segments; and that conditions of peace and stability in Iraq can ensue. Only then will Iraqi women have the opportunity to realize full legitimacy, agency and empowerment in functioning parliamentary roles.

Notes

1 Introduction: Impetus behind the Parliamentary Gender Quota in Iraq

1. Maria Helena de Castro Santos and Ulysses Tavares Teixeira, "Is It Possible to Export Democracy by the Use of Force? Military Interventions in Iraq and Libya," paper presented at the FLACSO-ISA Joint International Conference (Global and Regional Powers in a Changing World), Buenos Aires, Argentina, 2014.
2. Usha Natarajan, "Creating and Recreating Iraq: Legacies of the Mandate System in Contemporary Understandings of Third World Sovereignty," *Leiden Journal of International Law* 24, no. 4 (2011): 799–822.
3. Nadje al-Ali, "Reconstructing Gender: Iraqi Women between Dictatorship, War, Sanctions and Occupation," *Third World Quarterly* 26, no. 4–5 (2005): 739–58; Lucy Brown and David Romano, "Women in Post-Saddam Iraq: One Step Forward or Two Steps Back?," *NWSA Journal* 18, no. 3 (2006): 51–70; Mona Lena Krook, Diana Z. O'Brien and Krista M. Swip, "Military Invasion and Women's Political Representation," *International Feminist Journal of Politics* 12, no. 1 (2010): 66–79; Nicola Pratt and Nadje al-Ali, "Women's Organizing and the Conflict in Iraq since 2003," *Feminist Review*, 2007.
4. Iraq Constitutional Committee, "Iraqi Constitution," 2005, http://www.iraqinationality.gov.iq/attach/iraqi_constitution.pdf.
5. Ibid. The constitutional quotas applied strictly to parliamentary seats. Under pressure from the United Nations Electoral Assistance Team, the Iraqi Election Commission also applied a 25 percent quota for women in the provincial council, although they were under no legal obligation to do so.
6. Provincial council elections also have taken place. Although less highly publicized, these provincial elections have significantly contributed to institutionalizing accountability at the local level.
7. Julie Ballington and Drude Dahlerup, "Gender Quotas in Post-Conflict States: East Timor, Afghanistan and Iraq," in *Women, Quotas and Politics*, ed. Drude Dahlerup (New York: Routledge, 2006), 249–58.
8. Ibid., 257.
9. Sarah Childs and Mona Lena Krook, "Critical Mass Theory and Women's Political Representation," *Political Studies* 56, no. 3 (2008): 725–36.
10. Ibid., 734.

11 Petra Meier and Emanuela Lombardo, "Towards a New Theory on the Symbolic Representation of Women" (American Political Science Association, Rochester, NY: Social Science Research Network, 2010), http://papers.ssrn.com/abstract=1643961.
12 Drude Dahlerup and Lenita Freidenvall, "Judging Gender Quotas: Predictions and Results," *Policy & Politics* 38, no. 3 (2010): 407–25.
13 Ismail Raji Al Faruqi, *Al Tawhid: Its Implications for Thought and Life*, 2nd ed. (Herndon, VA: International Institute of Islamic Thought, 1992), 10–11.
14 John L. Esposito and John Obert Voll, *Islam and Democracy* (Oxford, NY: Oxford University Press, 1996), 30; James P. Piscatori, *Islam in a World of Nation-States* (Cambridge, MA: Cambridge University Press, 1986), 11, 105.
15 Fatema Mernissi, *Islam and Democracy: Fear of the Modern World*, trans. Mary Jo Lakeland (Cambridge, MA: Perseus Publishing, 1992), 48.
16 Ibid., 50.
17 Valentine M. Moghadam, *Modernizing Women: Gender and Social Change in the Middle East*, 2nd ed. (Boulder, CO: Lynne Rienner Publishers, 2003), 2.
18 Suad Joseph, "Women and Politics in the Middle East," *Middle East Report* 16, no. 138 (February 1986).
19 Valentine M. Moghadam, *Globalization and Social Movements: Islamism, Feminism, and the Global Justice Movement*, 2nd ed., Globalization (Lanham, MD: Rowman & Littlefield, 2013), 3–4, http://site.ebrary.com/lib/ucsd/docDetail.action?docID=10587677.
20 Joseph, "Women and Politics in the Middle East"; Nikki R. Keddie, "Women in the Middle East: Progress and Backlash," *Current History* 107, no. 713 (2008): 432–38.
21 Joseph, "Women and Politics in the Middle East"; Moghadam, *Modernizing Women*, 10–11.
22 Keddie, "Women in the Middle East," 432–33.
23 Ibid., 433; Moghadam, *Globalization and Social Movements*, 104.
24 Moghadam, *Globalization and Social Movements*, 4; Sylvia Walby, "Gender, Globalisation, and Democracy," *Gender and Development* 8, no. 1 (2000): 20–28; S. Laurel Weldon, *When Protest Makes Policy: How Social Movements Represent Disadvantaged Groups* (Ann Arbor, MI: University of Michigan Press, 2011), 1–2.
25 Valentine M. Moghadam, ed., *From Patriarchy to Empowerment: Women's Participation, Movements, and Rights in the Middle East, North Africa, and South Asia* (Syracuse, NY: Syracuse University Press, 2007), 1.
26 Ibid., 2.
27 United Nations, "The United Nations Fourth World Conference on Women: Platform for Action" (Beijing, China: United Nations, September 1995), http://www.un.org/womenwatch/daw/beijing/platform/decision.htm.
28 Deniz Kandiyoti, *Women, Islam and the State* (Temple University Press, 1991), 14–18.

29 Ibid., 2.
30 Suad Joseph, "Gender and Citizenship in Middle Eastern States," *Middle East Report* 26, no. 198 (1996): 4–10.
31 Kandiyoti, *Women, Islam and the State*, 13.
32 Sarah Smiles, "On the Margins: Women, National Boundaries, and Conflict in Saddam's Iraq," *Identities* 15, no. 3 (2008): 271–96.
33 Suad Joseph, "Elite Strategies for State Building: Women, Family, Religion, and the State in Iraq and Lebanon," in *Women, Islam, and the State*, ed. Deniz Kandiyoti (Philadelphia, PA: Temple University Press, 1991), 176–200; Smiles, "On the Margins," 278.
34 Martina Kamp, "Fragmented Citizenship: Communalism, Ethnicity and Gender in Iraq," in *Women & War in the Middle East* (London: Zed Books, 2009), 193–216.
35 Nadje al-Ali and Nicola Pratt, *What Kind of Liberation? Women and the Occupation of Iraq* (Berkeley: University of California Press, 2009), http://www.ucpress.edu/book.php?isbn=9780520265813; Noga Efrati, *Women in Iraq: Past Meets Present* (New York: Columbia University Press, 2012); Joseph, "Women and Politics in the Middle East."
36 Kamp, "Fragmented Citizenship," 200–202.
37 Patrick Basham, "Can Iraq Be Democratic?," Text, Policy Analysis No. 505 (Washington, DC: Cato Institute, 2004), http://www.cato.org/publications/policy-analysis/can-iraq-be-democratic-0.
38 Isobel Coleman, "Women, Islam, and the New Iraq," *Foreign Affairs* 85, no. 1 (January 1, 2006): 24–38.
39 Kamp, "Fragmented Citizenship," 199–200; Sherifa D. Zuhur, "Iraq, Women's Empowerment, and Public Policy" (Carlisle, PA: Army War College, Strategic Studies Institute, 2006).
40 Walby, "Gender, Globalisation, and Democracy," 22.
41 Inter-Parliamentary Union, "Parline Database: Women in National Parliaments," accessed December 10, 2013, http://www.ipu.org/wmn-e/classif.htm.
42 Arab Fund for Economic and Social Development United Nations Development Program, "Arab Human Development Report 2002: Creating Opportunities for Future Generations" (New York: UNDP, 2002).
43 International Labour Organization, "ILOSTAT Database," May 22, 2014, http://www.ilo.org/ilostat/faces/home/statisticaldata;jsessionid=p5LQT2hQKBrFxkNwmJ31YwxvGv2fWNnhHzy4TgsLcxfZsDy3Jh0j!1924909119?_afrLoop=893768200015683#%40%3F_afrLoop%3D893768200015683%26_adf.ctrl-state%3D10o0l63mzc_4.
44 Walby, "Gender, Globalisation, and Democracy," 20.
45 Krook, O'Brien and Swip, "Military Invasion and Women's Political Representation," 67.

46 Mona Lee Krook, "Gender Quotas, Norms, and Politics," *Politics & Gender* 2 (2006): 110–18; Krook, O'Brien and Swip, "Military Invasion and Women's Political Representation," 68.
47 International Crisis Group, "Déjà vu All over Again: Iraq's Escalating Political Crisis," *Middle East Report* (Baghdad: International Crisis Group, July 30, 2012).
48 Amal Sabbagh, "Overview of Women's Political Representation in the Arab Region: Opportunities and Challenges," in *The Arab Quota Report: Selected Case Studies* (Stockholm: International Institute for Democracy and Electoral Assistance, 2007), 7–18.
49 Ballington and Dahlerup, "Gender Quotas in Post-Conflict States"; Drude Dahlerup, "Gender Quotas—Controversial but Trendy," *International Feminist Journal of Politics* 10, no. 3 (2008): 322–28; Dahlerup and Freidenvall, "Judging Gender Quotas,"407–25; Krook, "Gender Quotas, Norms, and Politics."
50 Eva Bellin, "The Iraqi Intervention and Democracy in Comparative Historical Perspective," *Political Science Quarterly* 119, no. 4 (May 2004) 595–608.
51 al-Ali and Pratt, *What Kind of Liberation?*; Basham, "Can Iraq Be Democratic?"; Bellin, "The Iraqi Intervention and Democracy in Comparative Historical Perspective"; Zuhur, "Iraq, Women's Empowerment, and Public Policy."
52 Mary Caprioli and Kimberly Lynn Douglass, "Nation Building and Women: The Effect of Intervention on Women's Agency," *Foreign Policy Analysis* 4, no. 1 (2008): 45–65.

2 Historical Context for Iraqi Women's Political Participation

1 Iraq Legal Development Project (ILDP), "The Status of Women in Iraq: Update to the Assessment of Iraq's de Jure and de Facto Compliance with International Legal Standards" (American Bar Association, 2006), 2.
2 Ibid., 6.
3 Marion Farouk-Sluglett and Peter Sluglett, "The Transformation of Land Tenure and Rural Social Structure in Central and Southern Iraq, C. 1870–1958," *International Journal of Middle East Studies* 15, no. 4 (1983): 492.
4 Hanna Batatu, *The Old Social Classes and the Revolutionary Movements of Iraq: A Study of Iraq's Old Landed and Commercial Classes and of Its Communists, Ba'thists, and Free Officers* (Princeton, NJ: Princeton University Press, 1978), 13.
5 Ibid., 16.
6 Efrati, *Women in Iraq*, 189.
7 Batatu, *The Old Social Classes and the Revolutionary Movements of Iraq*, 37.

8 Ebubekir Ceylan, *Ottoman Origins of Modern Iraq: Political Reform, Modernization and Development in the Nineteenth Century Middle East* (New York: I.B.Tauris, 2011), 15.
9 William L. Cleveland and Martin Bunton, *A History of the Modern Middle East*, 5th ed. (Boulder, CO: Westview Press, 2012), 57.
10 Farouk-Sluglett and Sluglett, "The Transformation of Land Tenure and Rural Social Structure in Central and Southern Iraq, C. 1870–1958," 493.
11 Ibid.
12 Phebe Marr, *The Modern History of Iraq*, 3rd ed. (Boulder, CO: Westview Press, 2012), 6.
13 Efrati, *Women in Iraq*, 1–3.
14 Batatu, *The Old Social Classes and the Revolutionary Movements of Iraq*, 18.
15 Marr, *The Modern History of Iraq*, 7.
16 Helen Chapin Metz, *Iraq: A Country Study*, Country Studies (Washington, DC: GPO for the Library of Congress, 1988).
17 Ibid.
18 Ibid.
19 Marr, *The Modern History of Iraq*, 8.
20 Batatu, *The Old Social Classes and the Revolutionary Movements of Iraq*, 211.
21 Marr, *The Modern History of Iraq*, 8.
22 Ibid.
23 Batatu, *The Old Social Classes and the Revolutionary Movements of Iraq*, 320.
24 Ibid., 321.
25 Ibid.
26 Ibid., 323.
27 Efrati, *Women in Iraq*, 37–40.
28 Marr, *The Modern History of Iraq*, 21.
29 Ibid.
30 Batatu, *The Old Social Classes and the Revolutionary Movements of Iraq*, 324.
31 Marr, *The Modern History of Iraq*, 23–24.
32 Efrati, *Women in Iraq*.
33 Saeid N. Neshat, "A Look into the Women's Movement in Iraq," *Farzaneh* 6, no. 11 (2003): 56.
34 Tareq Y. Ismael and Jacqueline S. Ismael, *Iraq in the Twenty-First Century: Regime Change and the Making of a Failed State*, 1st ed. (New York: Routledge, 2015), 175.
35 Ibid.
36 Ellen L. Fleischmann, "The Other 'Awakening': The Emergence of Women's Movements in the Modern Middle East, 1900–1940," in *A Social History of Women & Gender in the Modern Middle East*, ed. Margaret L. Meriwether and Judith E. Tucker (Boulder, CO: Westview Press, 1999), 93.

37 Ibid., 94.
38 The International Digital Library, Iraqi Books and Archive House, "Leila, No.4, January 15, 1924," https://www.wdl.org/ar/item/342/.
39 Neshat, "A Look into the Women's Movement in Iraq," 56.
40 Sahiba al-Shaikh Daud, *Awwal al-Tariq Lil Nahda al-Nisa'iyya Fi al-Iraq* (Baghdad: Matba'at al-Rabita, 1958), 35.
41 Ibid., 85.
42 Leila Ahmed, *Women and Gender in Islam: Historical Roots of a Modern Debate* (New Haven, CT: Yale University Press, 1993), 173.
43 Neshat, "A Look into the Women's Movement in Iraq," 56.
44 Efrati, *Women in Iraq*, 20.
45 Charles Tripp, *A History of Iraq*, 3rd ed. (Cambridge, UK: Cambridge University Press, 2007) 142.
46 Efrati, *Women in Iraq*, 87–88.
47 Marr, *The Modern History of Iraq*, 37–38.
48 Examples of these women are as follows: Sara Fadil al-Jamali, who founded the Women's Temperance and Social Welfare Society, was the American wife of Muhammad Fadil al-Jamali; Asiya Tawfiq Wahbi, president of women's branch of the Child Protection (or Welfare) Society during the 1940s, was the wife of Tawfiq Wahbi who was, at different times, the minister of economics, education and social affairs; Ismat Sabah al-Said, vice president of the women's branch of the Red Crescent in the mid-1940s, who was Nuri Said's daughter-in-law; Zakiyya Pachachi, chairperson of the Iraqi Women's Union in the 1940s, who came from the Pachachi family, which produced several prime ministers and ministers.
49 A.J. Thabit Abdullah, *A Short History of Iraq: From 636 to the Present*, 2nd ed. (New York: Routledge, 2013), 97.
50 Marr, *The Modern History of Iraq*, 39–40.
51 Ibid., 42.
52 Abdullah, *A Short History of Iraq*, 102.
53 Batatu, *The Old Social Classes and the Revolutionary Movements of Iraq*, 485.
54 Efrati, *Women in Iraq*, 96–99.
55 Marr, *The Modern History of Iraq*, 78.
56 Ibid., 78–79.
57 Abdullah, *A Short History of Iraq*, 106.
58 Marr, *The Modern History of Iraq*, 44.
59 Ibid., 86.
60 Batatu, *The Old Social Classes and the Revolutionary Movements of Iraq*, 710.
61 Marr, *The Modern History of Iraq*, 87.
62 Neshat, "A Look into the Women's Movement in Iraq," 56.

63 Nadje al-Ali, Mubejel Baban and Sundus Abass, "Iraq Women's Rights under Attack: Occupation, Constitution and Fundamentalisms," Occasional Paper (London: Women Living Under Muslim Laws, December 2006), 7.
64 Ibid., 8.
65 Nadje Sadig al-Ali, *Iraqi Women: Untold Stories from 1948 to the Present* (London: Zed Books, 2007), 60–62.
66 Ibid., 64.
67 The *abaya* is a black "cloak" that covers the whole body except the face, feet and hands.
68 al-Ali, *Iraqi Women*, 64.
69 Ibid.
70 Marr, *The Modern History of Iraq*, 116.
71 Batatu, *The Old Social Classes and the Revolutionary Movements of Iraq*, 1003.
72 Marr, *The Modern History of Iraq*, 119–22.
73 Ibid., 135–36.
74 Chapin Metz, Helen, *Iraq: A Country Study*. Country Studies (Washington, DC: GPO for the Library of Congress, 1988).
75 al-Ali, *Iraqi Women*, 60.
76 Ibid., 112.
77 Batatu, *The Old Social Classes and the Revolutionary Movements of Iraq*, 766.
78 Abdullah, *A Short History of Iraq*, 120.
79 Ibid., 133.
80 Marr, *The Modern History of Iraq*, 148–49.
81 UN Women, "Iraq—Women, War, and Peace," 2007.
82 al-Ali, *Iraqi Women*, 114.
83 Saddam Hussein, *Social and Foreign Affairs in Iraq*, 1st ed. (London: Routledge, 2009), 16.
84 Human Rights Watch, "Background on Women's Status in Iraq Prior to the Fall of the Saddam Hussein Government" (New York: Human Rights Watch, November 2003).
85 Ibid.
86 Brown and Romano, "Women in Post-Saddam Iraq."
87 Ibid.
88 al-Ali, *Iraqi Women*, 136.
89 Neshat, "A Look into the Women's Movement in Iraq," 56.
90 Ibid., 57.
91 Abdullah, *A Short History of Iraq*, 130.
92 Christopher M. Davidson, *The United Arab Emirates: A Study in Survival* (Boulder, CO: Lynne Rienner Publishers, 2005), 5.
93 Ibid., 131.

94 al-Ali, *Iraqi Women*, 137.
95 Iraq Legal Development Project (ILDP), "The Status of Women in Iraq," 156.
96 Human Rights Watch, "Background on Women's Status in Iraq Prior to the Fall of the Saddam Hussein Government" (New York: Human Rights Watch, November 2003).
97 Joseph, "Elite Strategies for State Building."
98 al-Ali, "Reconstructing Gender," 744–45.
99 Efrati, *Women in Iraq*, 165; UN Women, "Iraq—Women, War, and Peace."
100 UN Women, "Iraq—Women, War, and Peace."
101 Iraq Legal Development Project (ILDP), "The Status of Women in Iraq," 2.
102 Ibid.
103 Toby Dodge, *Inventing Iraq: The Failure of Nation Building and a History Denied* (New York: Columbia University Press, 2005), 163; Marr, *The Modern History of Iraq*, 179.
104 al-Ali, *Iraqi Women*, 125.
105 Ibid., 126.
106 Brown and Romano, "Women in Post-Saddam Iraq," 6–7.
107 US Department of State, "Iraqi Women under Saddam's Regime: A Population Silenced," March 20, 2003, http://2001–2009.state.gov/g/wi/rls/18877.htm.
108 Ibid.
109 Dale F. Eickelman and James Piscatori, *Muslim Politics* (Princeton, NJ: Princeton University Press, 1996), 20,61,63,140.
110 Iraq Legal Development Project (ILDP), "The Status of Women in Iraq"; Amal Rassam, "Political Ideology and Women in Iraq: Legislation and Cultural Constraints," *Journal of Developing Societies* 8 (January 1992): 82; Amal Rassam, "Revolution within the Revolution? Women and the State in Iraq," in *Iraq: The Contemporary State*, ed. Tim Niblock (London: Croom Helm, 1982), 90.
111 Annia Ciezadlo, "Iraqi Women Raise Voices—for Quotas," *Christian Science Monitor*, December 17, 2003, http://www.csmonitor.com/2003/1217/p01s02-woiq.html.
112 al-Ali, "Reconstructing Gender," 746.
113 Farhang Rajaee, *The Iran-Iraq War: The Politics of Aggression* (Gainesville, FL: University Press of Florida, 1993), 48.
114 Iraq Legal Development Project (ILDP), "The Status of Women in Iraq," 2.
115 Ibid.
116 Aaron D. Pina, "Women in Iraq: Background and Issues for US Policy," CRS Report for Congress (Washington, DC: Congressional Research Service, The Library of Congress, March 13, 2006), 2.
117 Iraq Legal Development Project (ILDP), "The Status of Women in Iraq," 2.
118 al-Ali, *Iraqi Women*, 148.

119 Ibid.
120 Ibid.
121 Noga Efrati, Negotiating Rights in Iraq: Women and the Personal Status Law," *Middle East Journal* 59, no. 4 (2005): 586.
122 Amnesty International, "Iraq: Systematic Torture of Political Prisoners" (London: Amnesty International, 2001).
123 Ibid.
124 Achim Rohde, "Opportunities for Masculinity and Love: Cultural Production in Ba'thist Iraq during the 1980s," in *Islamic Masculinities*, ed. Lahoucine Ouzgane (London: Zed Books, 2006), 185–86.
125 Ibid., 198.
126 al-Ali, *Iraqi Women*, 187.
127 UN Women, "Women in Iraq Factsheet," United Nations, 2013, http://www.jauiraq.org/documents/1864/Woman-Factsheet.pdf.
128 al-Ali, *Iraqi Women*, 155.
129 Sarah Graham-Brown, *Sanctioning Saddam: The Politics of Intervention in Iraq* (London: I.B. Tauris, 1999), 8–9.
130 William M. Arkin, Damian Durrant and Marianne Cherni, *On Impact: Modern Warfare and the Environment : A Case Study of the Gulf War* (Washington, DC: Greenpeace, 1991), 14–15.
131 Graham-Brown, *Sanctioning Saddam*, 17–20.
132 Abdullah, *A Short History of Iraq*, 146.
133 al-Ali, *Iraqi Women*, 266.
134 Ibid., 266–67.
135 Eickelman and Piscatori, *Muslim Politics*, 13–15.
136 Brown and Romano, "Women in Post-Saddam Iraq," 7.
137 Ibid.
138 Smiles, "On the Margins," 276–77.
139 Ibid., 287.
140 Marr, *The Modern History of Iraq*, 235.
141 Ibid., 244–45.
142 Cynthia Cockburn, *From Where We Stand: War, Women's Activism and Feminist Analysis* (London: Zed Books, 2007); Cynthia Cockburn, "Gender Relations as Causal in Militarization and War," *International Feminist Journal of Politics* 12, no. 2 (2010): 139–57.
143 Smiles, "On the Margins," 272.
144 Brown and Romano, "Women in Post-Saddam Iraq."
145 United Nations, "Convention on the Elimination of All Forms of Discrimination against Women," United Nations Development Fund for Women, 2003, http://www.un.org/womenwatch/daw/cedaw/.

146 Ibid.
147 Brown and Romano, "Women in Post-Saddam Iraq," 5.
148 Amnesty International, "Iraq."
149 Smiles, "On the Margins."
150 Ibid.
151 Andres Cockburn and Patrick Cockburn, *Out of the Ashes: The Resurrection of Saddam*, 2nd ed. (New York: HarperCollins, 2000).
152 Brian Bennett and Michael Weisskopf, "The Sum of Two Evils," *Time*, May 25, 2003.
153 Amnesty International, "Iraq"; Human Rights Office of the High Commissioner for Human Rights, "Report on Human Rights in Iraq: July–December 2012" (Baghdad: United Nations Assistance Mission for Iraq, 2013); UN Office for the Coordination of Human Affairs, "Women's Rights Activists Increasingly Targeted by Militants," *IRIN Humanitarian News and Analysis*, July 24, 2007.
154 US Department of State, "Iraqi Women under Saddam's Regime."
155 Smiles, "On the Margins," 273.
156 Louise Cainkar, "The Gulf War, Sanctions and the Lives of Iraqi Women," *Arab Studies Quarterly* 15, no. 2 (1993): 16–17.
157 Souad al-Azzawi, "Decline of Iraqi Women Empowerment through Education under the American Occupation of Iraq 2003–2011," Paper presented at the International Seminar on the Situation of the Iraqi Academics, Ghent University, Belgium, March 9, 2011,18.
158 Cockburn, "Gender Relations as Causal in Militarization and War," 144.
159 Brown and Romano, "Women in Post-Saddam Iraq," 8.
160 Ibid., 8–10.
161 Souad N. al-Azzawi, *Deterioration of Iraqi Women's Rights and Living Conditions under Occupation* (Brussels: Brussels Tribunal, 2007); al-Azzawi, "Decline of Iraqi Women Empowerment through Education under the American Occupation of Iraq 2003–2011."
162 Smiles, "On the Margins."
163 Moghadam, *Modernizing Women*, 22–23.
164 Efrati, *Women in Iraq*; Efrati, "Negotiating Rights in Iraq."
165 Brown and Romano, "Women in Post-Saddam Iraq," 4–5.
166 Efrati, "Negotiating Rights in Iraq," 577.
167 Ibid., 580.
168 Ibid., 580–81.
169 Abdullahi An-Na'im, "Forced Marriage," Commissioned white paper, Department of International Law, Emory University, Atlanta, GA, USA, 2000.
170 Efrati, "Negotiating Rights in Iraq," 581.
171 Ibid., 589.

172 Ibid., 590.
173 Ibid.; Efrati, *Women in Iraq*, 161.
174 al-Ali "Reconstructing Gender"; Yasmin Husein al-Jawaheri, *Women in Iraq: The Gender Impact of International Sanctions* (Boulder, CO: Lynne Rienner Publishers, 2008); Keddie, "Women in the Middle East."
175 UN News, "UN Security Council Eases Some Sanctions on Iraq over 1990 Invasion of Kuwait," *UN News Service Section*, June 27, 2013, http://www.un.org/apps/news/story.asp?NewsID=45287&Cr=iraq&Cr1=kuwait#.UtxghLTTmUl.
176 Mail Online, "What Are the UN Sanctions on Iraq?," *Mail Online*, 2013, http://www.dailymail.co.uk/news/article-180046/What-UN-sanctions-Iraq.html.
177 Inter-Agency Information and Analysis Unit, "Women in Iraq" (United Nations, March 2012), www.iauiraw.org/documents/1628/Women in Iraq Fact sheet—English.pdf.
178 al-Jawaheri, *Women in Iraq*.
179 Ibid.
180 Inter-Agency Information and Analysis Unit, "Women in Iraq."
181 Katrina Lee-Koo, "Gender-Based Violence against Civilian Women in Postinvasion Iraq: (Re)politicizing George W. Bush's Silent Legacy," *Violence Against Women* 17, no. 12 (2011): 1619–34; Brown and Romano, "Women in Post-Saddam Iraq," 7–9.
182 al-Ali, "Reconstructing Gender"; al-Jawaheri, *Women in Iraq*; Efrati, *Women in Iraq*; Keddie, "Women in the Middle East."
183 Nadje al-Ali and Nicola Pratt, "The United States, the Iraqi Women's Diaspora and Women's 'Empowerment' in Iraq," in *Women & War in the Middle East*, ed. Nadje al-Ali and Nicola Pratt (London: Zed Books, 2009), 65–98.

3 Gender Quotas and Women's Political Mobilization in Iraq and the Middle East

1 Melanie M. Hughes, "Intersectionality, Quotas, and Minority Women's Political Representation Worldwide," *American Political Science Review* 105, no. 3 (2011): 604–20.
2 Lisa Baldez, "The Pros and Cons of Gender Quota Laws: What Happens When You Kick Men out and Let Women in?," *Politics & Gender* 2 (2006): 102–9.
3 Niemat Kuku, "Women's Political Participation: Legislated Quotas and Special Measures in Sudan," in *The Arab Quota Report: Selected Case Studies* (Stockholm: International Institute for Democracy and Electoral Assistance, 2007).
4 Medha Nanivadekar, "Are Quotas a Good Idea? The Indian Experience with Reserved Seats for Women," *Politics & Gender* 2 (2006): 101–28.

5 Mernissi, *Islam and Democracy*, 48.
6 Mona Lena Krook and Diana Z. O'Brien, "The Politics of Group Representation: Quotas for Women and Minorities Worldwide," *Comparative Politics* 42, no. 3 (2010): 253–72; Nanivadekar, "Are Quotas a Good Idea?."
7 Krook and O'Brien, "The Politics of Group Representation"; quotaProject, "About Quotas | quotaProject: Global Database of Quotas for Women," accessed October 5, 2013, http://www.quotaproject.org/aboutQuotas.cfm.
8 quotaProject, "About Quotas | quotaProject: Global Database of Quotas for Women."
9 Ibid.
10 Drude Dahlerup and Lenita Freidenvall, "Quotas as a 'Fast Track' to Equal Representation for Women," *International Feminist Journal of Politics* 7, no. 1 (2006): 26–48; quotaProject, "About Quotas | quotaProject: Global Database of Quotas for Women."
11 Baldez, "The Pros and Cons of Gender Quota Laws."
12 Global Justice Project, "Women's Political Representation: Achieving the Iraqi Constitutional Objective" (Salt Lake City, UT: S.J. Quinney College of Law, University of Utah, 2009).
13 Louise K. Davidson-Schmich, "Implementation of Political Party Gender Quotas: Evidence from the German Lander 1990–2000," *Party Politics* 12, no. 2 (2006): 211–32.
14 Baldez, "The Pros and Cons of Gender Quota Laws"; Davidson-Schmich, "Implementation of Political Party Gender Quotas."
15 Lisa Baldez, "Elected Bodies: The Gender Quota Law for Legislative Candidates in Mexico," *Legislative Studies Quarterly* 29, no. 2 (2004): 231–58.
16 Ibid.
17 United Nations, "Convention on the Elimination of All Forms of Discrimination against Women."
18 Joni Lovenduski and Pippa Norris, *Gender and Party Politics* (London; Thousand Oaks, CA: Sage Publications, 1993); Katharina Inhetveen, "Can Gender Equality Be Institutionalized? The Role of Launching Values in Institutional Innovation," *International Sociology* 14, no. 4 (1999): 404.
19 Basham, "Can Iraq Be Democratic?," 1.
20 Baldez, "Elected Bodies."
21 Noga Efrati, "The Other 'Awakening' in Iraq: The Women's Movement in the First Half of the Twentieth Century," *British Journal of Middle Eastern Studies* 31, no. 2 (November 1, 2004): 153–73; Andrea Fischer-Tahir, "Competition, Cooperation and Resistance: Women in the Political Field in Iraq," *International Affairs* 86, no. 6 (2010): 1381–94; Pratt and Al-Ali, "Women's Organizing and the Conflict in Iraq since 2003."
22 quotaProject, "About Quotas | quotaProject: Global Database of Quotas for Women."

23 Ibid.
24 Ibid.
25 Dahlerup and Freidenvall, "Judging Gender Quotas."
26 Ibid.
27 Baldez, "The Pros and Cons of Gender Quota Laws"; Hughes, "Intersectionality, Quotas, and Minority Women's Political Representation Worldwide."
28 Dahlerup and Freidenvall, "Quotas as a 'Fast Track' to Equal Representation for Women."
29 Keddie, "Women in the Middle East."
30 Huda Ahmed, "Women in the Shadows of Democracy," *Middle East Report* 36, no. 239 (2006): 24–26; Al-Ali and Pratt, *What Kind of Liberation?*, 132–33.
31 Dahlerup and Freidenvall, "Quotas as a 'Fast Track' to Equal Representation for Women."
32 Basham, "Can Iraq Be Democratic?," 5; Sabbagh, "Overview of Women's Political Representation in the Arab Region," 11.
33 Krook and O'Brien, "The Politics of Group Representation."
34 Krook, O'Brien, and Swip, "Military Invasion and Women's Political Representation."
35 Dahlerup and Freidenvall, "Quotas as a 'Fast Track' to Equal Representation for Women."
36 Ibid.; TheGlobalEconomy.com, "Iraq—Women in Politics, Female Parliament Members," TheGlobalEconomy.com, 2012. http://www.theglobaleconomy.com/Iraq/indicator-SG.GEN.PARL.ZS/
37 Dahlerup and Freidenvall, "Quotas as a 'Fast Track' to Equal Representation for Women."
38 Ibid.
39 Dahlerup, "Gender Quotas—Controversial but Trendy."
40 Dahlerup and Freidenvall, "Quotas as A 'Fast Track' to Equal Representation for Women"; Dahlerup and Freidenvall, "Judging Gender Quotas."
41 International Institute for Democracy and Electoral Assistance, "The Arab Quota Report: Selected Case Studies," Quota Report Series (Stockholm: International Institute for Democracy and Electoral Assistance, 2007).
42 Ibid.
43 al-Ali and Pratt, "The United States, the Iraqi Women's Diaspora and Women's 'Empowerment' in Iraq"; Ballington and Dahlerup, "Gender Quotas in Post-Conflict States"; Brown and Romano, "Women in Post-Saddam Iraq"; Coleman, "Women, Islam, and the New Iraq."
44 Coleman, "Women, Islam, and the New Iraq."
45 quotaProject, "About Quotas | quotaProject: Global Database of Quotas for Women."

46 Dr. Salama al-Khafaji stood as an independent candidate in the 2005 elections in Iraq. She is a dentist by profession, a Shiite Muslim by religion who wears an *abaya* and is in favor of a secular government. She is also outspoken in support of women's rights. There have already been three attempts on her life and her 17-year-old son was killed during an ambush by insurgents which also killed one of her bodyguards.
47 Coleman, "Women, Islam, and the New Iraq."
48 Haider Ala Hamoudi, "Decision 88: Balance of Power under the Iraq Constitution," *Jurist*, March 18, 2011, sec. Opinion Editorials, http://jurist.org/forum/2011/03/decision-88-checks-and-balances-in-iraq.php.
49 Human Rights Watch, "Iraq: Security Forces Abusing Women in Detention," *Human Rights Watch*, February 6, 2014, http://www.hrw.org/news/2014/02/06/iraq-security-forces-abusing-women-detention.
50 Pippa Norris, "Opening the Door: Women Leaders and Constitution Building in Iraq and Afghanistan," in *Gender Quotas and Electoral Democracy II* (XX IPSA World Congress of Political Science, Fukuoka, Japan: IPSA, 2007).
51 Krook, O'Brien, and Swip, "Military Invasion and Women's Political Representation."
52 al-Ali and Pratt, *What Kind of Liberation?*, 100–101; Krook, O'Brien, and Swip, "Military Invasion and Women's Political Representation."
53 Larry Diamond, *Squandered Victory: The American Occupation and the Bungled Effort to Bring Democracy to Iraq* (New York: Henry Holt and Company, 2007), 131.
54 Ciezadlo, "Iraqi Women Raise Voices—for Quotas."
55 al-Ali and Pratt, *What Kind of Liberation?*, 95; Ballington and Dahlerup, "Gender Quotas in Post-Conflict States."
56 Ciezadlo, "Iraqi Women Raise Voices—for Quotas."
57 al-Ali and Pratt, *What Kind of Liberation?*, 130.
58 Ashraf Khalil, "Women Call for Equal Representation in Iraq," *Womens eNews*, February 6, 2004, sec. Politics & Influence, http://womensenews.org/story/the-world/040206/women-call-equal-representation-iraq#.UtwyLbTTmUk.
59 S. Hunt and C. Posa, "Where Are the Women in the New Iraq?," *Boston Globe*, June 22, 2004.
60 TheGlobalEconomy.com, "USA Women in Parliament," TheGlobalEconomy.com, 2012, http://www.theglobaleconomy.com/USA/Women_in_parliament/.
61 al-Ali and Pratt, *What Kind of Liberation?*, 131.
62 Ibid., 132.
63 Ibid., 131.
64 IHEC, Independent High Electoral Commission, http://www.ihec.iq/ar/.
65 Ballington and Dahlerup, "Gender Quotas in Post-Conflict States."
66 Pauline Lejeune, "FairVote.org | Iraq's 2010 Parliamentary Election—Part 4: Iraqi Women's Political Reality," *FairVote*, March 22, 2010, http://fairvote.org/iraq-s-2010-parliamentary-election4.

67 Krook, O'Brien, and Swip, "Military Invasion and Women's Political Representation."
68 Ibid.
69 Zaineb Naji, "Will Iraq's New Quota System Give Women More Political Power?," *Alternet*, January 24, 2009, http://www.ora.tv/homepage/2015/12/15/1.
70 Ibid.
71 Ibid.
72 Zaineb Naji, "Women Set to Take More Power Locally," *Institute for War and Peace Reporting*, January 20, 2009, https://iwpr.net/global-voices/women-set-take-more-power-locally.
73 Ibid.
74 Ibid.
75 al-Ali and Pratt, "The United States, the Iraqi Women's Diaspora and Women's 'Empowerment' in Iraq," 85–87.
76 Naji, "Women Set to Take More Power Locally."
77 Ibid.
78 Ibid.
79 Naji, "Will Iraq's New Quota System Give Women More Political Power?"
80 Ibid.
81 Krook, O'Brien, and Swip, "Military Invasion and Women's Political Representation."
82 Ibid.
83 Keddie, "Women in the Middle East."
84 International Institute for Democracy and Electoral Assistance, "The Arab Quota Report."
85 Moghadam, *Modernizing Women*, 2.
86 Rana Husseini, "Jordan," in *Women's Rights in the Middle East and North Africa: Progress amid Resistance*, ed. Sanja Kelly and Julia Breslin (New York: Freedom House, 2010), 193–221.
87 Hussein Abu Rumman, "The Women's Quota in Jordan: Crowning Three Decades of Support for Female Political Participation," in *The Arab Quota Report: Selected Case Studies* (Stockholm: International Institute for Democracy and Electoral Assistance (IDEA), 2007), 42–50.
88 TheGlobalEconomy.com, "Jordan—Women in Politics, Female Parliament Members," *TheGlobalEconomy.com*, 2012, http://www.theglobaleconomy.com/Jordan/indicator-SG.GEN.PARL.ZS/.
89 Kuku, "Women's Political Participation."
90 Ittiḥād al-Waṭanī lil-Shabāb al-Sūdānī et al., *The Comprehensive Peace Agreement between the Government of the Republic of the Sudan and the Sudan People's Liberation Movement, Sudan People's Liberation Army* (National Federation of Sudanese Youth, 2005).

91. Kuku, "Women's Political Participation."
92. Liv Tønnessen, "Beyond Numbers? Women's 25% Parliamentary Quota in Post-Conflict Sudan," *Journal of Peace, Conflict and Development* 17 (2011): 43–62.
93. quotaProject: Global Database of Quotas for Women, "Sudan," 2014, http://www.quotaproject.org/uid/countryview.cfm?CountryCode=SD.
94. TheGlobalEconomy.com, "Sudan—Women in Politics, Female Parliament Members."
95. quotaProject: Global Database of Quotas for Women, "South Sudan," 2014, http://www.quotaproject.org/uid/countryview.cfm?id=253.
96. TheGlobalEconomy.com, "Sudan—Women in Politics, Female Parliament Members."
97. Tønnessen, "Beyond Numbers?."
98. Ibid.
99. Mariz Tados, "Introduction: Quotas: Add Women and Stir?," *IDS Bulletin* 41 (2010): 1–10.
100. Clare Castillejo and Helen Tilley, "The Road to Reform: Women's Political Voice in Morocco" (London: Overseas Development Institute, April 21, 2015).
101. Development Progress, "Progress on Women's Political Empowerment in Morocco" (London: Overseas Development Institute, April 2015).
102. Castillejo and Tilley, "The Road to Reform," 7.
103. Meriem El Haitami, "Women in Morocco: Political and Religious Power," *50.50: Gender, Sexuality and Social Justice*, January 31, 2013, sec. Gender Politics Religion, https://www.opendemocracy.net/5050/meriem-el-haitami/women-in-morocco-political-and-religious-power.
104. Castillejo and Tilley, "The Road to Reform," 8.
105. Haitami, "Women in Morocco."
106. Development Progress, "Progress on Women's Political Empowerment in Morocco."
107. Castillejo and Tilley, "The Road to Reform," 16.
108. Naheran Tohidi, "Iran," in *Women's Rights in the Middle East and North Africa: Progress amid Resistance*, ed. Sanja Kelly and Julia Breslin (New York: Freedom House, 2010).
109. Ilan Pappé, *The Modern Middle East* (New York: Routledge, 2005).
110. Ibid.
111. Thomson Reuters Foundation, "Reuters Foundation Alertnet.org Iran" (UK, 2013), http://www.trust.org/country/iran/.
112. Pappé, *The Modern Middle East*.
113. Tohidi, "Iran."
114. Alvaro Serrano and Janet Jensen, "Adult Education Offers New Opportunities and Options to Iranian Women," *UNFPA News*, March 7, 2006, http://www.ungei.org/infobycountry/iran_550.html.

115 Pappé, *The Modern Middle East*.
116 Public Affairs Alliance of Iranian Americans, "Goli Ameri Sworn in as Assistant Secretary of State,"PAAIA Blog, http://www.paaia.org/CMS/goli-ameri-sworn-in-as-assistant-secretary-of-state.aspx; World Innovation Summit for Education, "WISE Community Profile: Ms. Farah Karimi," http://www.wise-qatar.org/farah-karimi.
117 Shirin Ebadi—Nobel Women's Initiative," *Meet the Laureates*, 2003. http://nobelwomensinitiative.org/meet-the-laureates/shirin-ebadi/.
118 Tohidi, "Iran."
119 Ibid.
120 TheGlobalEconomy.com, "Iran—Women in Politics, Female Parliament Members."
121 Tohidi, "Iran."
122 As many as 100,000 Iraqi citizens are estimated to have fled to Lebanon during the 2003 invasion: Serene Assir, "Invisible Lives: Iraqis in Lebanon," *Assyrian International News Agency*, April 9, 2007, http://www.aina.org/news/2007049133807.htm.
123 Paul Kingston, "Women and Political Parties in Lebanon: Reflections on the Historical Experience," in *Emerging Voices: Young Women in Lebanese Politics* (International Alert, 2011).
124 Mona Chemali Khalaf, "Lebanon," in *Women's Rights in the Middle East and North Africa: Progress amid Resistance*, ed. Sanja Kelly and Julia Breslin (New York: Freedom House, 2010), 249–81.
125 Kristen Schulze, "Communal Violence, Civil War and Foreign Occupation: Women in Lebanon," in *Women, Ethnicity and Nationalism: The Politics of Transition*, ed. Rick Wilford and Robert L. Miller (London: Routledge, 1998).
126 TheGlobalEconomy.com, "Lebanon—Women in Politics, Female Parliament Members."
127 Arend Lijphart, "Consociational Democracy," *World Politics* 21, no. 2 (January 1, 1969): 207–25.
128 Ibid.; Imad Salamey and Rhys Payne, "Parliamentary Consociationalism in Lebanon: Equal Citizenry vs. Quotated Confessionalism," *The Journal of Legislative Studies* 14, no. 4 (2008): 451–73.
129 Kingston, "Women and Political Parties in Lebanon."
130 Moghadam, *Modernizing Women*.
131 Kingston, "Women and Political Parties in Lebanon."
132 Ibid.
133 Marguerite Helou, "Lebanese Women and Political Parties: History, Issues and Options for Reform," in *Emerging Voices: Young Women in Lebanese Politics* (International Alert, 2011).

134 Lovenduski and Norris, *Gender and Party Politics*.
135 GlobalSecurity.org, "Lebanon (Civil War 1975–1991)," accessed May 23, 2014, http://www.globalsecurity.org/military/world/war/lebanon.htm.
136 Helou, "Lebanese Women and Political Parties."
137 Lina Khatib, "Gender, Citizenship and Political Agency in Lebanon," *British Journal of Middle Eastern Studies* 35, no. 3 (2008): 437–51.
138 Ibid.
139 Schulze, "Communal Violence, Civil War and Foreign Occupation."
140 Ibid.
141 Khatib, "Gender, Citizenship and Political Agency in Lebanon."
142 Ibid.
143 Kingston, "Women and Political Parties in Lebanon."
144 Khatib, "Gender, Citizenship and Political Agency in Lebanon."
145 Ibid.
146 Ibid.
147 Ibid.
148 Naila Nauphal, "Women and Other War-Affected Groups in Post-War Lebanon," in *Gender and Armed Conflicts: Challenges for Decent Work, Gender Equality and Peace Building Agendas and Programs*, Focus Program on Crisis Response and Reconstruction, Working paper 2 (Geneva: Recovery and Reconstruction Department, 2001), 57–62.
149 Ibid., 58.
150 Sofia Saadeh, "Women in Lebanese Politics: Underlying Causes of Women's Lack of Representation in Lebanese Politics," in *Emerging Voices: Young Women in Lebanese Politics* (International Alert, 2011).
151 Ibid.
152 Fatima Sbaity Kassem, "Can Women Break through? Women in Municipalities: Lebanon in Comparative Perspective," *Women's Studies International Forum* 35, no. 4 (July 2012): 233–55.
153 Ibid.
154 Ibid.
155 Nedra Cherif, "Tunisian Women in Politics: From Constitution Makers to Electoral Contenders" (FRIDE, November 2014).
156 Ibid., 2.
157 Amnesty International, "Ongoing Hunger Strikes Spotlights Rights Abuses in Tunisia" (London: Amnesty International, October 29, 2010).
158 Gabriella Borovsky and Asma Ben Yahia, "Women's Political Participation in Tunisia after the Revolution" (Washington, DC: National Democratic Institute for International Affairs, May 2012).
159 Cherif, "Tunisian Women in Politics," 2.

160 Magnus Ohman, "Political Finance and the Equal Participation of Women in Tunisia: A Situation Analysis" (The Hague, The Netherlands: Netherlands Institute for Multiparty Democracy, 2016).

4 Descriptive Representation: Quota Effects on Numbers of Women in Office

1 Norris, "Opening the Door."
2 Iraq Legal Development Project (ILDP), "The Status of Women in Iraq," 2.
3 Free Iraq Foundation, "Women in the Council of Representatives: Lessons Learned and Case Studies Report" (Washington, DC: Wilson Center, 2013), 4.
4 Dieter Nohlen, Florian Grotz and Christof Hartmann, *Elections in Asia and the Pacific: A Data Handbook*, 2nd ed., Volume I of II (Oxford, NY: Oxford University Press, 2002).
5 Efrati, *Women in Iraq*, 20–22.
6 Ibid., 86–92.
7 Nohlen, Grotz and Hartmann, *Elections in Asia and the Pacific*.
8 Efrati, *Women in Iraq*, 87–88.
9 Ibid., 87.
10 The Law Library of Congress, "Iraq: Legal History and Traditions" (Washington, DC: Global Legal Research Center, June 2004).
11 Ibid.
12 Ibid.
13 Balakrishnan Rajagopal, *International Law from below: Development, Social Movements and Third World Resistance* (Cambridge, UK: Cambridge University Press, 2003).
14 Ayad al-Qazzaz, "Power Elite in Iraq—1920–1958: A Study of the Cabinet," *The Muslim World* 61, no. 4 (1971): 267–83.
15 Ibid.
16 Efrati, *Women in Iraq*, 89.
17 Ibid., 89–90; Efrati, "The Other 'Awakening' in Iraq."
18 Joseph, "Women and Politics in the Middle East."
19 Iraqi Women's League, June 15, 2015, http://www.iraqiwomensleague.com/.
20 Neshat, "A Look into the Women's Movement in Iraq."
21 Efrati, "Negotiating Rights in Iraq."
22 Institute for Inclusive Security, "Zakia Hakki" (Washington, DC: Institute for Inclusive Security, May 2006), https://www.inclusivesecurity.org/network-bio/zakia-hakki/.
23 Ibid.

24 al-Ali, *Iraqi Women*, 53.
25 Ibid., 210.
26 Ibid., 211.
27 Ibid., 212.
28 Joseph, "Elite Strategies for State Building," 186.
29 Hanna Batatu, "Class Analysis and Iraqi Society," *Arab Studies Quarterly* 1, no. 3 (July 1, 1979): 229–44.
30 Joseph, "Elite Strategies for State Building," 179–81.
31 Batatu, "Class Analysis and Iraqi Society."
32 Joseph, "Elite Strategies for State Building," 179.
33 al-Ali, "Reconstructing Gender."
34 Sarah Graham-Brown and Chris Toensing, "Timeline of Iraq," *openDemocracy*, January 22, 2003; Joseph, "Elite Strategies for State Building."
35 Batatu, "Class Analysis and Iraqi Society."
36 Ibid.
37 Joe Wing, Iraqi Women Before and After the 2003 Invasion, Interview with Professor Nadje Al-Ali, University of London, December, 2013.
38 Marr, *The Modern History of Iraq*.
39 Ibid.
40 Joseph, "Elite Strategies for State Building," 187.
41 Joseph, "Gender and Citizenship in Middle Eastern States."
42 Joseph, "Elite Strategies for State Building," 182.
43 Joseph, "Women and Politics in the Middle East."
44 Joseph, "Elite Strategies for State Building," 182.
45 Nohlen, Grotz and Hartmann, *Elections in Asia and the Pacific*.
46 Inter-Parliamentary Union, "Iraq."
47 Marr, *The Modern History of Iraq*, 178.
48 Joseph, "Elite Strategies for State Building," 185.
49 Inter-Parliamentary Union, "Iraq."
50 Nohlen, Grotz and Hartmann, *Elections in Asia and the Pacific*.
51 Linda Layne, "Tribesmen as Citizens: 'Primordial Ties' and Democracy in Rural Jordan," in *Elections in the Middle East*, ed. Linda Layne (Boulder, CO: Westview Press, 1987), 113–51.
52 Brown and Romano, "Women in Post-Saddam Iraq."
53 Kanan Makiya, *Republic of Fear: The Politics of Modern Iraq, Updated Edition* (Berkeley: University of California Press, 1998).
54 al-Ali, *Iraqi Women*, 149.
55 Ibid., 150.
56 Inter-Parliamentary Union, "Iraq."
57 Itamar Rabinovich and Haim Shaked, eds., *Middle East Contemporary Survey, 1984–1985*, vol. 9 (Tel Aviv, Israel: The Moshe Dayan Center for Middle Eastern and African Studies, 1987).

58 *al-Thawra News*, 1984, http://www.althawranews.net/; Rabinovich and Shaked, *Middle East Contemporary Survey, 1984–1985,* 464.
59 Rabinovich and Shaked, *Middle East Contemporary Survey, 1984–1985.*
60 al-Ali, *Iraqi Women*, 152.
61 Inter-Parliamentary Union, "Iraq."
62 Ibid.
63 Zuhair al-Jaza'iri, "Ba'thist Ideology and Practice," in *Iraq since the Gulf War*, ed. Fran Hazelton (London: Zed Books, 1994), 44.
64 Ibid.
65 The 1991 *Sha'aban Intifada* (uprisings) in Iraq were a series of popular rebellions in northern and southern Iraq in March and April 1991 in a ceasefire of the Gulf War. This mostly uncoordinated insurgency, referred to as the National Uprising among Kurds, was fueled by the perception that Saddam Hussein was responsible for systemic social repression and had become vulnerable to regime change. This perception of weakness was largely the result of the outcome of two prior wars: the Iran-Iraq and the invasion of Kuwait both of which occurred within a single decade and devastated the economy and population of Iraq.
66 Sarah Graham-Brown, "Intervention, Sovereignty and Responsibility," *Middle East Report* 25, no. 193 (1995).
67 Ibid.
68 Ibid.
69 Ibid.
70 Nohlen, Grotz and Hartmann, *Elections in Asia and the Pacific*, I:97.
71 Ibid.
72 Inter-Parliamentary Union, "Iraq."
73 Cainkar, "The Gulf War, Sanctions and the Lives of Iraqi Women."
74 al-Ali, "Reconstructing Gender."
75 Ibid.
76 al-Ali and Pratt, "The United States, the Iraqi Women's Diaspora and Women's 'Empowerment' in Iraq," 66.
77 Ibid.
78 Inter-Parliamentary Union, "Iraq."
79 BBC News, "Profile: Iraq's 'Mrs Anthrax,'" *BBC*, September 22, 2004, sec. Middle East, http://news.bbc.co.uk/2/hi/middle_east/3002103.stm.
80 Ibid.
81 BBC News, "Iraq's Women Scientists," *BBC*, September 22, 2004, sec. Middle East, http://news.bbc.co.uk/2/hi/middle_east/3679040.stm.
82 Ibid.
83 Robert Windrem, "The World's Deadliest Women?," *NBC World News*, 2004.
84 BBC News, "Iraq's Women Scientists."
85 Kandiyoti, *Women, Islam and the State.*

86 Nira Yuval-Davis, "Women, Citizenship and Difference," *Feminist Review* 57 (Autumn 1997): 4–27.
87 Ibid.
88 Joseph, "Elite Strategies for State Building," 179.
89 Judith Lorber, "Strategies of Feminist Research in a Globalized World," in *Analyzing Gender, Intersectionality, and Multiple Inequalities: Global, Transnational and Local Contexts*, ed. Esther Ngan-ling Chow, Marcia Texler Segal and Lin Tan (Bingley, UK: Emerald Group Publishing, 2011).
90 al-Ali and Pratt, "The United States, the Iraqi Women's Diaspora and Women's 'Empowerment' in Iraq," 66–69.
91 Ibid., 66.
92 Ibid., 67–68.
93 Ibid., 67.
94 Ibid., 75.
95 Paul Wolfowitz, "Women in the New Iraq," *The Washington Post*, February 1, 2004, sec. Opinion, http://2001-2009.state.gov/g/wi/28686.htm.
96 al-Ali and Pratt, "The United States, the Iraqi Women's Diaspora and Women's 'Empowerment' in Iraq," 71.
97 Joshua Foust and Melinda Haring, "Who Cares How Many Women Are in Parliament?," *Democracy Lab*, June 25, 2012, http://foreignpolicy.com/2012/06/25/who-cares-how-many-women-are-in-parliament/.
98 Sarah Bush and Amaney Jamal, "Does Western Pressure for Gender Equality Help?," *The Washington Post*, July 30, 2014, https://www.washingtonpost.com/news/monkey-cage/wp/2014/07/30/does-western-pressure-for-gender-equality-help/.
99 Lila Abu-Lughod, "Do Muslim Women Need Saving?," *Time*, November 1, 2013, http://ideas.time.com/2013/11/01/do-muslim-women-need-saving/.
100 Ibid.
101 al-Ali and Pratt, *What Kind of Liberation?*, 97.
102 Ibid.
103 Ballington and Dahlerup, "Gender Quotas in Post-Conflict States."
104 The Telegraph, "Aqila al-Hashimi," *The Telegraph*, September 26, 2003, sec. Obituaries, http://www.telegraph.co.uk/news/obituaries/1442475/Aqila-al-Hashimi.html.
105 George Cross, "George Gallaway Interview," *The Independent* on Sunday, 2003, accessed September 8, 2015.
106 BBC, "Shot Iraq Council Member Dies," *BBC*, September 25, 2003, sec. Middle East, http://news.bbc.co.uk/2/hi/middle_east/3131424.stm.
107 al-Ali and Pratt, *What Kind of Liberation?*, 91.
108 Moghadam, *From Patriarchy to Empowerment*.

109 Sharon Otterman, "IRAQ: The Interim Government Leaders," *Council on Foreign Relations*, June 2, 2004, http://www.cfr.org/iraq/iraq-interim-government-leaders/p7664.
110 Ibid.
111 Dahlerup and Freidenvall, "Quotas as a 'Fast Track' to Equal Representation for Women."
112 Inter-Parliamentary Union, "Iraq."
113 AFP, "World Leaders Hail Iraq Vote," *Theage.com*, January 31, 2005, sec. Features, http://www.theage.com.au/news/Iraq/World-leaders-hail-Iraq-vote/2005/01/31/1107020303303.html.
114 Inter-Parliamentary Union, "Iraq."
115 Ballington and Dahlerup, "Gender Quotas in Post-Conflict States."
116 Inter-Parliamentary Union, "Iraq."
117 IHEC, *The Independent High Electoral Commission of Iraq*, accessed November 11, 2014, http://www.ihec.iq/ar/.
118 Robert H. Reid, "Sunni Leader Open to Coalition Government," *The Guardian*, December 19, 2005, sec. World Latest, https://web.archive.org/web/20051219104151/ http://www.guardian.co.uk/worldlatest/story/0,1280,-5485174,00.html.
119 Inter-Parliamentary Union, "Iraq."
120 Ibid.
121 Global Justice Project, "Women's Political Representation."
122 IHEC, *The Independent High Electoral Commission of Iraq*, accessed November 11, 2014, http://www.ihec.iq/ar/.
123 Lejeune, "FairVote.org | Iraq's 2010 Parliamentary Election—Part 4."
124 IHEC.
125 Rebecca Santana, "At Least 17 Killed as Iraq Voting Begins," *Huffington Post*, May 4, 2010, http://www.huffingtonpost.com/2010/03/04/at-least-17-killed-as-ira_n_485398.html.
126 Inter-Parliamentary Union, "Iraq."
127 Ibid.
128 Hannah Allam, "Complicated Quota System Helps Put Iraqi Women in Parliament," *McClatchy DC*, March 23, 2010, sec. World, http://www.mcclatchydc.com/2010/03/23/90932_complicated-quota-system-helps.html?rh=1.
129 Inter-Parliamentary Union, "Iraq."
130 IHEC.
131 Ibid.
132 National Democratic Institute, "National Platform for Women Launched in Lead up to Iraqi Elections."

133 Afrah Shawqi, "Iraq: Nearly 3,000 female candidates expected in Parliament elections," *Asharq al-Awsat*, March 8, 2014, http://english.aawsat.com/2014/03/article55329789/iraq-nearly-3000-female-candidates-expected-in-parliament-elections.

134 Unrepresented Nations and Peoples Organization (UNPO), "Election Observation Mission Report" (The Hague, The Netherlands: UNPO, July 2014).

135 Ibid.

136 Matt Bradley, "Iraqi Parliament Breaks Deadlock to Elect Speaker: Election Marks Small Step Toward Resolving Leadership Impasse," *Wall Street Journal*, July 15, 2014, sec. World, http://www.wsj.com/articles/iraqi-parliament-breaks-deadlock-to-elect-speaker-1405426884.

137 BBC Arabic, July 15, 2014.

138 Bradley, "Iraqi Parliament Breaks Deadlock to Elect Speaker."

139 Struan Stevenson, "Iraq's Revolution," *The Huffington Post*, June 16, 2014, http://www.huffingtonpost.co.uk/struan-stevenson-mep/iraqs-revolution_b_5491818.html.

140 Ibid.

141 The World Bank, "Middle East and North Africa—Middle East and North Africa."

142 Transparency International, "Corruption by Country Profiles—Iraq," 2013, http://www.transparency.org/country#IRQ.

143 United Nations Office for the Coordination of Humanitarian Affairs (UNOCHA), "Humanitarian Bulletin: Middle East and North Africa" (UNOCHA, February 2014).

144 Inter-Parliamentary Union, "Iraq."

145 Ibid.

146 Fanar Haddad, "Iraq Elections: Marred by Corruption?," *al-Jazeera*, April 26, 2014, http://www.aljazeera.com/indepth/opinion/2014/04/iraq-elections-marred-corruptio-201442116043642713.html.

147 UN Women, "Women in Power and Decision-Making: Strengthening Voices for Democracy," *headQuarters*, June 27, 2014, http://www.unwomen.org/en/news/stories/2014/6/women-in-power-and-decision-making.

148 UN Women, "With Some Electoral Gains in Iraq, Women Candidates Work towards Change," *headQuarters*, May 16, 2014, http://www.unwomen.org/en/news/stories/2013/5/with-some-electoral-gains-in-iraq-women-candidates-work-towards-change.

149 Amy C. Alexander, "Big Jumps in Women's Presence in Parliaments: Are These Sufficient for Improving Beliefs in Women's Ability to Govern?," *Advancing Women in Leadership* 35 (2015): 82–97.

150 Coleman, "Women, Islam, and the New Iraq," 4.

151 Brown and Romano, "Women in Post-Saddam Iraq," 63.

152 Inter-Parliamentary Union, "Iraq."
153 Pamela Paxton and Melanie M. Hughes, *Women, Politics and Power: A Global Perspective*, 3rd ed. (Thousand Oaks, CA: Sage Publications, 2017), 79.
154 Norris, "Opening the Door."
155 Pippa Norris and Ronald Inglehart, "Women and Democracy: Cultural Obstacles to Equal Representation," *Journal of Democracy* 12, no. 3 (2001): 137.
156 Martha C. Nussbaum, *Women and Human Development: The Capabilities Approach* (New York: Cambridge University Press, 2000), 177.
157 Norris, "Opening the Door."
158 Amy C. Alexander and Christian Welzel, "Empowering Women: The Role of Emancipative Beliefs," *European Sociological Review* 27, no. 3 (2011): 364–84.
159 Ronald Inglehart, *Modernization and Postmodernization: Cultural, Economic, and Political Change in 43 Societies* (Princeton, NJ: Princeton University Press, 1997), 191.
160 Alexander and Welzel, "Empowering Women."
161 Norris, "Opening the Door."
162 Alexander and Welzel, "Empowering Women."
163 Paxton and Hughes, *Women, Politics and Power*, 124.
164 Norris, "Opening the Door."
165 al-Ali and Pratt, "The United States, the Iraqi Women's Diaspora and Women's 'Empowerment' in Iraq," 87.
166 Ibid., 88.
167 Norris, "Opening the Door."
168 Coleman, "Women, Islam, and the New Iraq."
169 al-Ali and Pratt, "The United States, the Iraqi Women's Diaspora and Women's 'Empowerment' in Iraq," 88.
170 Nada Bakri, "Barred Politicians Mostly Secular, Iraqi Says," *The New York Times*, January 21, 2010, sec. International/Middle East, http://www.nytimes.com/2010/01/22/world/middleeast/22iraq.html.
171 Ibid.
172 al-Ali and Pratt, "The United States, the Iraqi Women's Diaspora and Women's 'Empowerment' in Iraq," 95.
173 Krista Hunt, "'Embedded Feminism' and the War on Terror," in *(En)gendering the War on Terror: War Stories and Camouflaged Politics*, ed. Krista Hunt and Kim Rygiel (Aldershot: Ashgate, 2007), 66.
174 Melanie M. Hughes, "Armed Conflict, International Linkages, and Women's Parliamentary Representation in Developing Nations," *Social Problems* 56, no. 1 (2009): 174–204.
175 Dahlerup, *Women, Quotas and Politics*.
176 Ronald Inglehart, Mansoor Moaddel and Mark Tessler, "Xenophobia and In-Group Solidarity in Iraq: A Natural Experiment on the Impact of Insecurity," *Perspectives on Politics* no. 3 (September 2006): 495–505.

177 Ibid.
178 Hughes, "Armed Conflict, International Linkages, and Women's Parliamentary Representation in Developing Nations."
179 Kay Bussey and Albert Bandura, "Social Cognitive Theory of Gender Development and Differentiation," *Psychological Review* 106 (1999): 690.
180 Ibid.
181 Jane Mansbridge, "Should Blacks Represent Blacks and Women Represent Women? A Contingent 'Yes,' " *The Journal of Politics* 61, no. 3 (1999): 628–57.
182 Ibid., 628.
183 Anne Phillips, *The Politics of Presence* (Oxford, UK: Oxford University Press, 1998).
184 Norris, "Opening the Door."
185 Pippa Norris and Mona Lena Krook, "One of Us: Multilevel Models Examining the Impact of Descriptive Representation on Civic Engagement," *SSRN Scholarly Paper* (Rochester, NY: Social Science Research Network, 2009), http://papers.ssrn.com/abstract=1451149.
186 Drude Dahlerup, "Gender Balance in Politics: Goals and Strategies in a Global Perspective," *The Arab Quota Report: Selected Case Studies* (Cairo, Egypt: International Institute for Democracy and Electoral Assistance, 2007).
187 Ibid.
188 Phillips, *The Politics of Presence*.
189 Lena Wängnerud, "Women in Parliaments: Descriptive and Substantive Representation," *Annual Review of Political Science* 12, no. 1 (2009): 51–69.

5 Case Studies: Twelve Iraqi Female Members of Parliament since 2005

1 The television programs from which the case study interviews were transcribed are referenced in the Bibliography. When referenced in the text as having been extracted from the televised interviews, quotations from these interviews are not otherwise footnoted with a source citation.
2 James R. Arnold, *Saddam's Iraq* (Minneapolis, MN: Twenty-First Century Books (CT), 2008); Marr, *The Modern History of Iraq*; Tripp, *A History of Iraq*.
3 Paul Cochrane, "The 'Lebanonization' of the Iraqi Media: An Overview of Iraq's Television Landscape," *Transnational Broadcasting Studies Journal* 16 (2006): 1–11.
4 SourceWatch, "Iraqi Media Network" (Center for Media and Democracy, February 21, 2006), http://www.sourcewatch.org/index.php/Iraqi_Media_Network.
5 Ibid.
6 Cochrane, "The 'Lebanonization' of the Iraqi Media."

7 Ibid.
8 al-Iraqiya, "Aliraqiya," *al-Iraqiya*, accessed August 23, 2014, http://www.aliraqiya.com.
9 SourceWatch, "Iraqi Media Network."
10 Cochrane, "The 'Lebanonization' of the Iraqi Media."
11 Ahmed K. al-Rawi, "The US Influence in Shaping Iraq's Sectarian Media," *International Communication Gazette* 75, no. 4 (2013): 374–91.
12 Ibid.
13 al-Baghdadia TV, "Live TV." http://wwitv.com/tv_channels/b5964.htm
14 Jacky Sutton, Personal communication, March 27, 2015.
15 al-Fayhaa, "al-Fayhaa Satellite Channel," *al-Fayhaa TV*, 2015, http://www.alfayhaa.tv/en/.
16 Hanan al-Fatlawi, "The Dynamics of Parliamentary Life in a Free Iraq," in *Iraq and Its Politics,* Iraq + 10 Conference, Boston University (Boston, MA: Institute for Iraqi Studies, 2013).
17 Kenneth Katzman, "Iraq: Politics, Governance, and Human Rights" (Washington, DC: Congressional Research Service, October 29, 2014).
18 International Crisis Group, "Iraq's Secular Opposition: The Rise and Decline of al-Iraqiya" (Brussels: International Crisis Group, July 31, 2012).
19 Katzman, "Iraq."
20 Ibid.
21 Ibid.
22 Administrator, "Widespread Corruption Paralyses Investment in Iraq, MP Forms Committee," Parliament, *Iraq Parliament Guide* (November 20, 2012), http://www.iraqiparliament.info/en/node/1516.
23 All Iraq News (AIN), "AIN Political News," April 5, 2013, accessed December 27, 2014, http://www.alliraqnews.com/en/index.php/political-news.html.
24 Iraq Directory, "Iraq Fails to Attract Domestic Capitals," *Iraq Directory*, January 1, 2014, http://www.iraqdirectory.com/en/print.aspx?sid=25947.
25 Ibid.
26 al-Jazeera, "Protests in Iraq Continue amid New Killings," *al-Jazeera*, February 22, 2013, http://www.aljazeera.com/news/middleeast/2013/02/20132221241519 82737.html.
27 All Iraq News (AIN), "AIN Political News," February 5, 2013.
28 Ibid., March 15, 2013.
29 Ibid., April 26, 2013.
30 Ibid., January 22, 2014.
31 SourceWatch, "Ala Talabani," *Center for Media and Democracy*, 2003, http://www.sourcewatch.org/index.php/Ala_Talabani.
32 Jamie Tarabay, "Political Struggle for Kirkuk Intensifies," *NPR.org* (Washington, DC: National Public Radio, June 11, 2007), http://www.npr.org/templates/story/story.php?storyId=10931833.

33 Iraq Constitutional Committee, "Iraqi Constitution."
34 Brendan O'Leary and David Bateman, "Article 140: Iraq's Constitution, Kirkuk and the Disputed Territories" (Conference at Rayburn House, Washington, DC, 2008).
35 rudaw.net, "Baghdad Sells Kirkuk's Oil as It Stalls Article 140," *Ekurd Daily*, June 3, 2012, http://ekurd.net/mismas/articles/misc2012/6/kirkuk739.htm.
36 Iraqi Parliament, "Iraqi Parliament Guide."
37 All Iraq News (AIN), "AIN Political News," May 9, 2012.
38 Jamie Tarabay, "Amid Iraq Turmoil, Kurds Seize Kirkuk, a Long Disputed Prize," *al-Jazeera America*, June 12, 2014, http://america.aljazeera.com/articles/2014/6/12/rise-of-the-kurds.html.
39 Katzman, "Iraq."
40 All Iraq News (AIN), "AIN Political News," February 23, 2013.
41 Ibid.
42 Nizar Latif, "Sultan Hashim's Death Sentence Underscores Iraq's Deep Divisions," *The National*, July 23, 2011, sec. World, http://www.thenational.ae/news/world/middle-east/sultan-hashims-death-sentence-underscores-iraqs-deep-divisions.
43 All Iraq News (AIN), "AIN Political News," February 23, 2013.
44 Institute for Inclusive Security, "Ala Talabani," *Search for Women Peace Experts*, March 2006, http://www.inclusivesecurity.org/network-bio/ala-talabani/.
45 iKNOW Politics, Ala Talabani, December 11, 2013, http://iknowpolitics.org/en/knowledge-library/interview/ala-talabani.
46 National Democratic Institute, "National Platform for Women Launched in Lead up to Iraqi Elections."
47 Ibid.
48 iKNOW Politics, Ala Talabani.
49 At time of this writing, the Iraqi Dinar (ID) was equal to 0.00090 US dollars.
50 Hawar Berwani, "MP Jawari Survives Assassination," *Iraqi News*, January 31, 2013, http://www.iraqinews.com/iraq-war/urgent-mp-jawari-survives-assassination/.
51 Katzman, "Iraq."
52 Ibid.
53 All Iraq News (AIN), "AIN Political News," May 31, 2012.
54 Laila Ahmad, "Palestinian Refugees Calling for Help," *NSNBC International*, June 9, 2012, http://nsnbc.me/2012/06/11/palestinian-refugees-calling-for-help/.
55 Ibid.
56 All Iraq News (AIN), "AIN Political News," January 9, 2013.
57 Ibid.
58 Nizar Latif, "Iraqis Step up Protest in Job and Food Crisis," *The National*, February 6, 2011, sec. World, http://www.thenational.ae/news/world/middle-east/iraqis-step-up-protest-in-job-and-food-crisis.
59 Ibid.

60 Alfarat News Agency, "MP Jawari Demands IHEC to Repeat Sorting and Counting of Salah Il-Din Polling," May 25, 2014, http://en.alforatnews.com/modules/news/article.php?storyid=7645.
61 All Iraq News (AIN), "AIN Political News," June 8, 2012.
62 Ibid.
63 Ibid.
64 Ibid., July 14, 2012.
65 Ahmed Hussein, "Meetings among Political Leaders to Settle Crisis, Says MP," *Iraqi News*, July 21, 2012, http://www.iraqinews.com/baghdad-politics/meetings-among-political-leaders-to-settle-crisis-says-mp/.
66 All Iraq News (AIN), "AIN Political News," July 22, 2012.
67 Ahmed Hussein, "MP Reveals Corrupt Contractors Associated to Maliki's Office," *Iraqi News*, June 13, 2013, http://www.iraqinews.com/baghdad-politics/mp-reveals-corrupt-contractors-associated-to-maliki-s-office/.
68 For example, in January 2014, she was interviewed regarding the implementation of new sonar devices to inspect shipments and containers coming into Iraq's Basra seaport. Obaidi told *Mawtani al-Shorfa* that she welcomed the new technology and recommended more ultrasound units to be installed not only at seaports, but at all border outlets. "This highly advanced equipment is vital in monitoring and accurately detecting all prohibited materials such as explosives, weapons or drugs, which amounts to protecting the country's security and stability." Source: Khalid al-Taie, "Iraqi Ports Introduce Modern Inspection Equipment," *Mawtani al-Shorfa.com*, January 31, 2014, sec. World, http://mawtani.al-shorfa.com/en_GB/articles/iii/features/2014/01/31/feature-01.
69 Staff Writer, "'Dark' Message from al-Zawahiri's Wife Draws Condemnation in Iraq," *Mawtani al-Shorfa.com*, June 19, 2012, sec. Terrorism, http://al-shorfa.com/en_GB/articles/meii/features/main/2012/06/19/feature-02?format=mobile.
70 Ibid.
71 All Iraq News (AIN), "AIN Political News," January 19, 2013.
72 Ahmed Hussein, "IS MP Calls Maliki to Reveal Involved Officials in Terrorist Actions," *Iraqi News*, May 24, 2013, http://www.iraqinews.com/baghdad-politics/is-mp-calls-maliki-to-reveal-involved-officials-in-terrorist-actions/.
73 Staff Writer, "Iraq Needs to Deter Pro-Terrorism Countries, Says Obaidi," *Alforat News*, June 6, 2014, http://en.alforatnews.com/modules/news/article.php?storyid=8014.
74 Staff Writer, "Suhad al-Obeidi Reveals the Agreement between Maliki and Najafi and Barzani to Postpone Parliamentary Elections," *Dinarvets.com*, October 13, 2013.
75 Khalid al-Taie, "Public Buses Promote Iraqi Election Participation," *Mawtani al-Shorfa.com*, February 28, 2014, sec. World, http://mawtani.al-shorfa.com/en_GB/articles/iii/features/2014/02/28/feature-01.

76 All Iraq News (AIN), "AIN Political News," March 12, 2012.
77 Ibid., July 22, 2012.
78 Ibid., July 25, 2012.
79 Ibid., August 9, 2012.
80 Ibid., February 23, 2014.
81 Associated Press, "Iraqis Eyeing Bahrain Protests with Anger, Caution," *Associated Press*, March 17, 2011, http://www.foxnews.com/world/2011/03/17/iraq-shiites-rally-saudi-troops-bahrain/.
82 All Iraq News (AIN), "AIN Political News," August 17, 2012.
83 Ibid., January 5, 2013.
84 Ibid., April 7, 2013.
85 Ibid., May 26, 2013.
86 Ibid., July 16, 2013.
87 Ibid., September 18, 2012.
88 Ibid., July 26, 2013.
89 Baghdadiabian, "Majida al-Tamimi: Because the Ministry of Finance to His Predecessor Percent Salary and Loans Is out of Cash in a Bank and Rafidain," *Baghdadiabian News*, September 18, 2012, http://www.dinarrecaps.com/iraqi-news-recaps/majida-al-tamimi-because-the-ministry-of-finance-to-his-predecessor-percent-salary-and-loans-is-out-of-cash-in-a-bank-and-rafidain.
90 Dinarvets, "Majda al-Tamimi Threatened to Disclose Private Financial Oversight Reports Corrupt Ministries," *Iraqi Dinar News*, October 30, 2012, http://dinarvets.com/forums/index.php?/topic/132588-majda-al-tamimi-threatened-to-disclose-private-financial-oversight-reports-corrupt-ministries/.
91 The I.Q.D. Team Connection, "Majida al-Tamimi: Ground Is Prepared for the Process of Lifting the Zeros from the Currency in 2013," *Voice of Iraq*, December 15, 2012, http://www.theiqdteamconnection.com/iraq-news/majida-al-tamimi-ground-is-prepared-for-the-process-of-lifting-the-zeros-from-the-currency-in-2013.
92 All Iraq News (AIN), "AIN Political News," December 19, 2012.
93 Staff Writer, "Majida al-Tamimi: Next June Will See the Distribution of Surplus Oil Revenues to the People," *Iraqi Gazette*, April 3, 2013, http://www.dinarspeculator.com/showthread.php?67433-Majida-al-Tamimi-next-June-will-see-the-distribution-of-surplus-oil-revenues-to-the-people.
94 Nahid Hussein, "Iraqi Parliament Set to Strengthen Its Oversight of National Budget," *United Nations Development Program*, November 16, 2014, http://www.iq.undp.org/content/iraq/en/home/presscenter/pressreleases/2014/11/16/workshop-to-support-the-iraqi-parliament-on-the-management-revision-and-the-analysis-of-the-of-the-national-budget/.
95 Administrator, "Magda Tamimi: 2015 Budget Will Reduce the Level of Corruption," *al-Baghdadia News*, December 21, 2014, http://iraqdinar.us/magda-tamimi-2015-budget-2/.

96 Administrator, "Magda Tamimi: 2015 Budget and Fake like Formulated in Another World," *All Iraq News*, January 21, 2015, http://iraqidinarchat.net/?p=32904.
97 Karlos Zurutuza, "Iraqi Women Face Widespread Abuse and Discrimination," *Deutsche Welle*, September 30, 2012, sec. World, http://www.dw.de/iraqi-women-face-widespread-abuse-and-discrimination/a-15799850.
98 All Iraq News (AIN), "AIN Political News," March 7, 2013.
99 Ibid., August 21, 2014.
100 Ibid., September 30, 2012.
101 Ibid., February 25, 2013.
102 Ibid., November 9, 2012.
103 Ibid., November 16, 2013.
104 Ibid., August 6, 2012.
105 Hamza Mustafa, "Iraq: Army Advances as al-Qaeda Militants Open New Fronts," *Asharq al-Awsat*, February 22, 2014, sec. Middle East, http://www.aawsat.net/2014/02/article55329244/iraq-army-advances-as-al-qaeda-militants-open-new-fronts.
106 All Iraq News (AIN), "AIN Political News," November 13, 2012.
107 Ibid., March 9, 2012.
108 Ibid., November 30, 2012.
109 Layth Jawad, "Iraqi Minister Dismisses Claims of Female Prisoner Abuse," *al-Monitor*, December 5, 2012, http://www.al-monitor.com/pulse/fa/politics/2012/12/iraqi-politicians-dismiss-female-prisoner-abuse-charges.html.
110 All Iraq News (AIN), "AIN Political News," November 30, 2012.
111 Ibid., December 14, 2012.
112 Ibid.
113 European Parliament Committee on Women's Rights and Gender Equality, "Spring Forward for Women Conference Program" (Brussels: European Parliament, November 5, 2014).
114 Alforat News Agency, "MP Demands Residents of Areas under Occupation of ISIL to Help in Liberating Their Areas," *Alforat News*, February 3, 2015, http://en.alforatnews.com/modules/news/article.php?storyid=15755.
115 al-Mada, "Constitution Update," *al-Mada News*, June 2, 2005, http://iraqthemodel.blogspot.com/2005/06/constitution-update.html.
116 Administrator, "Iraqi Officials Confirm Saddam's Execution," *CRI News*, December 30, 2006, http://english.cri.cn/2947/2006/12/30/189@179166.htm.
117 Staff Writer, "Rights Group Condemns Iraq Trials," *al-Jazeera English*, January 8, 2007, http://www.aljazeera.com/news/middleeast/2007/01/2008525143032353532.html.
118 Zainab Naji, "Baghdad Awaits New Security Plan," *International Relations and Security Network*, February 12, 2007, http://www.isn.ethz.ch/Digital-Library/Articles/Detail/?lng=en&id=52914.

119 Kirk Semple, "US Makes Largest Move into Shiite District since 2004," *The New York Times*, March 4, 2007, sec. International/Middle East, http://www.nytimes.com/2007/03/04/world/middleeast/04cnd-iraq.html.
120 AFP, "al-Sadr Ministers Leave Government," *Taipei Times*, April 17, 2007, http://www.taipeitimes.com/News/front/archives/2007/04/17/2003356980.
121 Ibid.
122 Iraqi Constitution, Article 38: "The State shall guarantee in a way that does not violate public order and morality: A. Freedom of expression using all means. B. Freedom of press, printing, advertisement, media and publication. C. Freedom of assembly and peaceful demonstration, and this shall be regulated by law."
123 All Iraq News (AIN), "AIN Political News," February 13, 2012.
124 Ibid.
125 Ibid., May 28, 2012.
126 Ibid., December 9, 2013.
127 Alforat News Agency, "Maliki's Advisor Expects Holding Wide Alliances after Elections," *Alforat News*, January 1, 2014, http://en.alforatnews.com/modules/news/article.php?storyid=3512.
128 Ahmed Hussein, "Fatlawi Withdraws from Presidency Race—Iraqi News," *Iraqi News*, July 24, 2014, http://www.iraqinews.com/baghdad-politics/fatlawi-withdraws-from-presidency-race/.
129 Staff Writer, "Iraqi Parliament Elects New President," *Arab News Express*, July 24, 2014, http://arabpressreleases.qa/general/19607/iraqi-parliament-elects-new-president/.
130 Haider Najm, "Electoral Commission Inquiry Not 'Political Revenge' MPs Say," *Niqash*, April 21, 2011, http://www.niqash.org/articles/?id=2824.
131 Ibid.
132 All Iraq News (AIN), "AIN Political News," April 12, 2012.
133 Mithaq, "The Charter of Cooperation between Public Authorities and NGOs for the Development of Iraqi Society," *Iraqicharter.org*, April 2013, http://iraqicharter.org/en/.
134 al-Fatlawi, "The Dynamics of Parliamentary Life in a Free Iraq."
135 Ibid.
136 Ibid.
137 Ibid.
138 Ibid.
139 Ibid.
140 Ibid.
141 Ibid.
142 Ibid.

143 Abdelhak Mamoun, "MP Hanan al-Fatlawi Survives Assassination Attempt upon Return from Salahuddin," *Iraqi News*, March 10, 2015, http://www.iraqinews.com/features/mp-hanan-al-fatlawi-survive-assassination-attempt-upon-return-salahuddin/.
144 Eleana Gordon, "Our Friend in the Gallery: Safia al-Suhail and the New Iraq," *National Review Online*, February 4, 2005, http://www.nationalreview.com/articles/213575/our-friend-gallery/eleana-gordon.
145 All Iraq News (AIN), "AIN Political News," February 2, 2012.
146 Ibid., September 13, 2012.
147 Ibid., September 20, 2013.
148 Ibid., January 18, 2012.
149 Ibid., November 21, 2012.
150 Ibid., February 17, 2013.
151 Ibid., January 27, 2012.
152 Ibid., July 21, 2012.
153 Ibid., July 6, 2013.
154 Ibid., November 11, 2013.
155 Unpublished press release, September 6, 2010. The original was written in English.
156 Jenan Mubarak, "ICWRE," *Iraqi Center for Women Rehabilitation & Employment*, 2007, http://icwre.org/default_en.aspx.
157 Ibid.
158 Alissa J. Rubin and Asmaa Waguih, "Fighting to Preserve Women's Rights in Iraq," *Los Angeles Times*, August 7, 2005, http://articles.latimes.com/2005/aug/07/world/fg-women7.
159 Associated Free Press, " 'We Can't Walk Freely,' " *News24*, September 27, 2005, http://www.news24.com/World/News/We-cant-walk-freely-20050924.
160 Administrator, "Iraq: Women's Rights in Iraq Compromised: Women Reclaiming and Redefining Cultures," *The Middle East Times*, July 13, 2006, http://www.wluml.org/node/3086.
161 Zainab Naji, "Iraq's Jobless Female Students Losing Hope," *Middle East Online*, April 25, 2008, http://www.middle-east-online.com/english/?id=25568.
162 Ibid.
163 CBS News, "Diverse Iraqi Women Seek Political Parity," *CBSNews*, March 3, 2010, http://www.cbsnews.com/news/diverse-iraqi-women-seek-political-parity/.
164 Zainab Naji, "Women's Rights Candidate Keen to Make Impact," *Institute for War and Peace Reporting (IWPR)*, March 5, 2010, http://www.ecoi.net/local_link/135064/235149_en.html.
165 M. Kareem, "International Economic Support for Women Endeavour," IraqHurr.org, August 2, 2012, sec. Iraqi File/programs, http://www.iraqhurr.org/content/article/24477362.html.

166 OCHA, "Iraq Drafts First Policy on Civil Society," Text, *ReliefWeb*, September 16, 2012, http://reliefweb.int/report/iraq/iraq-drafts-first-policy-civil-society.

6 Substantive Representation: How Have Women Affected Public Policy?

1 Jeremy Scahill, *Dirty Wars: The World Is a Battlefield* (New York: Nation Books, 2013); Laura J. Shepherd, "Veiled References: Constructions of Gender in the Bush Administration Discourse on the Attacks on Afghanistan Post-9/11," *International Feminist Journal of Politics* 8, no. 1 (2006): 19–41.
2 Kandiyoti, *Women, Islam and the State*, 3–4.
3 Sabbagh, "Overview of Women's Political Representation in the Arab Region," 12.
4 Reidar Visser, *A Responsible End?: The United States and the Iraqi Transition, 2005–2010* (Charlottesville, VA: Just World Books, 2010), 12–13.
5 *NVivo Qualitative Data Analysis Software*, version 11 (London: QSR International Pty Ltd., 2014).
6 L.P. Wong, "Data Analysis in Qualitative Research: A Brief Guide to Using NVivo," *Malaysian Family Physician* 3, no. 1 (2008): 14.
7 Nathan J. Brown, "Constitutionalism, Authoritarianism, and Imperialism in Iraq," *Drake Law Review* 53 (May 2004): 923–42.
8 Ibid.
9 Tad Stahnke and Robert C. Blitt, "The Religion-State Relationship and the Right to Freedom of Religion or Belief: A Comparative Textual Analysis of the Constitutions of Predominantly Muslim Countries," *Georgetown Journal of International Law* 36 (2005).
10 United Nations, "Strategy for the Advancement of Women in Iraq" (UNIFEM, 2012).
11 Iraq Constitutional Committee, "Iraqi Constitution."
12 Stahnke and Blitt, "The Religion-State Relationship and the Right to Freedom of Religion or Belief."
13 United Nations, "Strategy for the Advancement of Women in Iraq."
14 Coleman, "Women, Islam, and the New Iraq."
15 al-Mada, "Constitution Update."
16 Klaas Glenewinkel, "Role of women and religion in the Constitution," *Niqash*, July 18, 2005, sec. Politics, http://www.niqash.org/en/articles/society/691/.
17 Ibid.
18 Georgina Waylen, "Constitutional Engineering: What Opportunities for the Enhancement of Gender Rights?," *Third World Quarterly* 27, no. 7 (2006): 1209–21.

19 United Nations, "Strategy for the Advancement of Women in Iraq"; Waylen, "Constitutional Engineering."
20 Waylen, "Constitutional Engineering."
21 United Nations, "Strategy for the Advancement of Women in Iraq."
22 Iraq Constitutional Committee, "Iraqi Constitution."
23 Coleman, "Women, Islam, and the New Iraq."
24 Iraq Legal Development Project (ILDP), "The Status of Women in Iraq."
25 Iraq Constitutional Committee, "Iraqi Constitution."
26 Ibid.
27 United Nations, "Strategy for the Advancement of Women in Iraq."
28 Waylen, "Constitutional Engineering."
29 al-Fatlawi, "The Dynamics of Parliamentary Life in a Free Iraq."
30 Ibid.
31 Andrea Fischer-Tahir, "Competition, Cooperation and Resistance."
32 Pamela Constable, "Iraqi Women Decry Move to Cut Rights," *The Washington Post*, January 16, 2004, https://www.washingtonpost.com/archive/politics/2004/01/16/iraqi-women-decry-move-to-cut-rights/74decc2e-6724-470e-b521-8df09ec30fd2/.
33 Efrati, *Women in Iraq*.
34 Ibid.
35 Efrati, "Negotiating Rights in Iraq."
36 United Nations, "Strategy for the Advancement of Women in Iraq."
37 Efrati, "Negotiating Rights in Iraq."
38 Efrati, *Women in Iraq*.
39 Constable, "Iraqi Women Decry Move to Cut Rights."
40 al-Sharq al-Awsat Online, "Archive," *al-Sharq al-Awsat Online*, October 29, 2006, http://archive.aawsat.com/default.asp.
41 Nadje Al-Ali and Nicola Pratt, "Women in Iraq: Beyond the Rhetoric," *Middle East Report* 36, no. 239 (2006).
42 Efrati, *Women in Iraq*.
43 Jamie Tarabay, "Iraqi Law Would Legalize Marital Rape, Child Marriage for Country's Shi'a," *al-Jazeera America*, April 27, 2014, http://america.aljazeera.com/articles/2014/4/27/iraqi-shiites-protestproposedfamilylaw.html.
44 Walk Free, "Forced Child Marriage in Iraq," *Arab Human Rights Academy*, April 30, 2014, http://www.walkfree.org/iraq-child-marriage/.
45 Free Iraq Foundation, "Women in the Council of Representatives."
46 Ibid.
47 Ibid., 7.
48 Ibid.
49 United Nations Office of the Iraq Program, "Oil-for-Food: About the Program" (United Nations, November 4, 2003), http://www.un.org/Depts/oip/background/.

50 Hassan Latif al-Zubaidi, "Why Iraq's Ration Card Can't Be Scrapped," *Niqash*, November 15, 2012, http://www.niqash.org/en/articles/economy/3156/.
51 AFP, "Iraq Ration Card Reform Sparks Anger," *Breitbart*, November 12, 2012, http://www.breitbart.com/news/cng-31155d745f32809d18cd13234c1f32c4-2a1/.
52 Ibid.
53 al-Zubaidi, "Why Iraq's Ration Card Can't Be Scrapped."
54 Free Iraq Foundation, "Women in the Council of Representatives."
55 United Nations, "Strategy for the Advancement of Women in Iraq."
56 Free Iraq Foundation, "Women in the Council of Representatives."
57 David C. Hendrickson and Robert W. Tucker, *Revisions in Need of Revising: What Went Wrong in the Iraq War* (Carlisle, PA: Strategic Studies Institute, December 2005).
58 Ibid.
59 Singleton Press, "Iraq's Amnesty and De-Baathification Laws," *Dinar Recaps*, January 5, 2015, http://www.dinarrecaps.com/1/post/2015/01/iraqs-amnesty-and-de-baathification-laws-by-singleton-press.html.
60 Ibid.
61 All Iraq News (AIN), "AIN Political News," News, January 18, 2012.
62 Iraq Constitutional Committee, "Iraqi Constitution."
63 United Nations, "Strategy for the Advancement of Women in Iraq."
64 Rex J. Zedalis, *The Legal Dimensions of Oil and Gas in Iraq: Current Reality and Future Prospects* (New York: Cambridge University Press, 2009).
65 Ibid., 16.
66 United Nations Office of the Iraq Program, "Oil-for-Food."
67 US Energy Information Administration, "Country Analysis Brief: Iraq" (Washington, DC: US Energy Information Administration, January 30, 2015).
68 Zedalis, *The Legal Dimensions of Oil and Gas in Iraq*.
69 US Energy Information Administration, "Country Analysis Brief."
70 Ibid.
71 Ibid.
72 Zedalis, *The Legal Dimensions of Oil and Gas in Iraq*, 27.
73 Ibid., 28.
74 Reuters, "Baghdad to Exclude Oil Firms with KRG Deals," *TradeArabia*, November 15, 2007, http://www.tradearabia.com/news/OGN_133962.html.
75 Christopher Davidson, "ISIS and the Iraq War: Regional and International Dimensions," CNN iReport (Washington, DC: CNN, June 21, 2014); US Energy Information Administration, "Country Analysis Brief."
76 al-Fatlawi, "The Dynamics of Parliamentary Life in a Free Iraq."
77 Iraq Foundation, "Women Leaders in an Era of Change."
78 al-Fatlawi, "The Dynamics of Parliamentary Life in a Free Iraq."

79 Free Iraq Foundation, "Women in the Council of Representatives."
80 Ibid.
81 Ibid.
82 Ibid.
83 Ibid.
84 UN Women, "Women in Iraq Factsheet," United Nations (2013), http://www.jauiraq.org/documents/1864/Woman-Factsheet.pdf.
85 Ibid.
86 Ibid.
87 Coleman, "Women, Islam, and the New Iraq."
88 Free Iraq Foundation, "Women in the Council of Representatives."
89 al-Fatlawi, "The Dynamics of Parliamentary Life in a Free Iraq."
90 United States Government Accountability Office, "Report to Congressional Committees: Rebuilding Iraq: US Assistance for the January 2005 Elections" (United States Government Accountability Office, September 7, 2005).
91 Ibid.
92 Joseph, "Women and Politics in the Middle East"; Moghadam, *Modernizing Women.*
93 CBS News, "Diverse Iraqi Women Seek Political Parity."
94 UN Women, "Women in Iraq Factsheet."
95 Ibid.
96 Iraq Foundation, "Women Leaders in an Era of Change."
97 United States Government Accountability Office, "Report to Congressional Committees."
98 Ibid.
99 Gordon, "Our Friend in the Gallery."
100 al-Fatlawi, "The Dynamics of Parliamentary Life in a Free Iraq."
101 al-Azzawi, "Decline of Iraqi Women Empowerment through Education under the American Occupation of Iraq 2003–2011."
102 Global Justice Project, "Women's Political Representation."
103 Free Iraq Foundation, "Women in the Council of Representatives."
104 Amin Saikal and Albrecht Schnabel, *Democratization in the Middle East: Experiences, Struggles, Challenges* (Tokyo, Japan: United Nations University Press, 2003).
105 Sabbagh, "Overview of Women's Political Representation in the Arab Region."
106 Moghadam, *From Patriarchy to Empowerment*; Sabbagh, "Overview of Women's Political Representation in the Arab Region."
107 Hisham Sharabi, *Neopatriarchy: A Theory of Distorted Change in Arab Society* (New York: Oxford University Press, 1992).
108 Moghadam, *Modernizing Women.*

109 Nadezhda Shvedova, "Obstacles to Women's Participation in Parliament," in *Women in Parliament: Beyond Numbers. A Revised Edition* (Stockholm: International Institute for Democracy and Electoral Assistance (IDEA), 2005).
110 Sabbagh, "Overview of Women's Political Representation in the Arab Region."
111 Amnesty International, "Iraq"; Davidson, "ISIS and the Iraq War."
112 UN Women, "Women in Iraq Factsheet."
113 Ibid.
114 Deniz Kandiyoti, "Fear and Fury: Women and Post-Revolutionary Violence," *openDemocracy*, January 14, 2013, http://www.opendemocracy.net/5050/deniz-kandiyoti/fear-and-fury-women-and-post-revolutionary-violence.
115 Ibid.
116 Zurutuza, "Iraqi Women Face Widespread Abuse and Discrimination."
117 Human Rights Watch, "At a Crossroads: Human Rights in Iraq Eight Years after the US-Led Invasion" (New York: Human Rights Watch, February 21, 2011), https://www.hrw.org/report/2011/02/21/crossroads/human-rights-iraq-eight-years-after-us-led-invasion.
118 Zurutuza, "Iraqi Women Face Widespread Abuse and Discrimination."
119 Free Iraq Foundation, "Women in the Council of Representatives."
120 Aymenn Jawad al-Tamimi, "No confidence in Maliki?," *The American Spectator*, June 19, 2012, sec. At Large, http://spectator.org/articles/35299/no-confidence-maliki.
121 Thomas Carothers, *Aiding Democracy Abroad: The Learning Curve* (Washington, DC: Carnegie Endowment for International Peace, 1999), 46.
122 Human Rights Watch, "At a Crossroads."
123 United Nations, "Strategy for the Advancement of Women in Iraq."
124 Free Iraq Foundation, "Women in the Council of Representatives."
125 Ibid.
126 Batatu, *The Old Social Classes and the Revolutionary Movements of Iraq*.
127 Ibid.
128 Naomi Klein, "Baghdad Year Zero: Pillaging Iraq in Pursuit of a Neocon Utopia," *Harper's Magazine*, September 2004; Santos and Teixeira, "Is It Possible to Export Democracy by the Use of Force?"
129 UN Women, "Women in Iraq Factsheet."
130 Ibid.
131 Ibid.
132 Naji, "Iraq's Jobless Female Students Losing Hope."
133 United Nations, "Strategy for the Advancement of Women in Iraq."
134 Alicia Cohn, "How the Iraq War Has Affected Women," *Her.meneutics*, September 15, 2010, http://www.christianitytoday.com/women/2010/september/how-iraq-war-has-affected-women.html.

135 United Nations, "Strategy for the Advancement of Women in Iraq."
136 Farhad Chomani, "ISIS War Fuels Steep Rise in Number of Widows in Iraq," *Rudaw*, April 19, 2015, http://rudaw.net/english/middleeast/iraq/190420151.
137 Free Iraq Foundation, "Women in the Council of Representatives."
138 Stina Larserud and Rita Taphorn, *Designing for Equality: Best-Fit, Medium-Fit and Non-Favourable Combinations of Electoral Systems and Gender Quotas* (Stockholm, Sweden: International IDEA, 2007), http://www.idea.int/publications/designing_for_equality/index.cfm.
139 Global Justice Project, "Women's Political Representation."
140 Free Iraq Foundation, "Women in the Council of Representatives."
141 CBS News, "Diverse Iraqi Women Seek Political Parity."
142 Iraq Foundation, "Women Leaders in an Era of Change."
143 All Iraq News (AIN), "AIN Political News," July 31, 2013.
144 Alfarat News Agency, "MP Jawari Demands IHEC to Repeat Sorting and Counting of Salah Il-Din Polling."
145 All Iraq News (AIN), "AIN Political News," September 18, 2012.
146 Donna Pankhurst, "The 'Sex War' and Other Wars: Towards a Feminist Approach to Peace Building," *Development in Practice* 13, no. 2/3 (May 1, 2003): 154–77.
147 Ahmed, "Women in the Shadows of Democracy," Brown and Romano, "Women in Post-Saddam Iraq."
148 United Nations, "Strategy for the Advancement of Women in Iraq."
149 Ibid.
150 Transparency International, "Corruption by Country Profiles—Iraq."
151 al-Fatlawi, "The Dynamics of Parliamentary Life in a Free Iraq."
152 Haddad, "Iraq Elections."
153 Stanislav Andreski, *The African Predicament* (New York: Atherton Press, 1968).
154 Najm, "Electoral Commission Inquiry Not 'Political Revenge' MPs Say."
155 All Iraq News (AIN), "AIN Political News," April 11, 2013.
156 Iraq Directory, "Iraq Fails to Attract Domestic Capitals."
157 Free Iraq Foundation, "Women in the Council of Representatives."
158 Jim Michaels, "Iraq's Female Lawmakers Make Strides," *USA Today*, October 27, 2008, http://usatoday30.usatoday.com/news/world/iraq/2008-10-26-iraqwomen_N.htm.
159 al-Azzawi, "Decline of Iraqi Women Empowerment through Education under the American Occupation of Iraq 2003–2011."
160 Iraqi Women's Educational Institute, "Advancing Women's Rights: Two Years in Iraq" (Washington, DC: Independent Women's Forum, 2008).
161 Free Iraq Foundation, "Women in the Council of Representatives."
162 United Nations, "Strategy for the Advancement of Women in Iraq."

163 LarbiSadiki, Heiko Wimmen and Layla Al-Zubaidi, eds. *Democratic Transition in the Middle East: Unmaking Power* (New York: Routledge, 2013).
164 Mehdi Jaber Mehdi, "The Faltering Democracy in Iraq after 2003," *Modern Discussion Journal*, no. 3928 (2012): 11–31.
165 Sadiki, Wimmen and al-Zubaidi, *Democratic Transition in the Middle East*.
166 Missy Ryan, "Imagining Iraq, Defining Its Future," *World Policy Journal* 27, no. 1 (2010): 65–73.

7 Symbolic Representation: Legitimacy and Media Treatment of Women as Political Agents

1 Drude Dahlerup and Lenita Freidenvall, "Judging Gender Quotas: Predictions and Results," *Policy & Politics* 38, no. 3 (2010): 407–25.
2 Ibid.
3 Leslie A. Schwindt-Bayer and William Mishler, "The Nexus of Representation: An Integrated Model of Women's Representation," 2002.
4 Meier and Lombardo, "Towards a New Theory on the Symbolic Representation of Women."
5 Myra Marx Ferree, "Inequality, Intersectionality and the Politics of Discourse: Framing Feminist Alliances," in *The Discursive Politics of Gender Equality: Stretching, Bending and Policy-Making*, ed. Emanuela Lombardo, Petra Meier and Mieke Verloo (London: Routledge, 2009).
6 Meier and Lombardo, "Towards a New Theory on the Symbolic Representation of Women."
7 Kristian Stokke and Elin Selboe, "Symbolic Representation as Political Practice," in *Rethinking Popular Representation*, ed. Olle Tornquist, Kristian Stokke and Neil Webster (New York: Palgrave Macmillan, 2009).
8 Pierre Bourdieu and John B. Thompson, *Language and Symbolic Power* (Cambridge, MA: Harvard University Press, 1991).
9 Stokke and Selboe, "Symbolic Representation as Political Practice."
10 Bourdieu and Thompson, *Language and Symbolic Power*.
11 Stokke and Selboe, "Symbolic Representation as Political Practice."
12 Ibid.
13 Ibid.
14 Meier and Lombardo, "Towards a New Theory on the Symbolic Representation of Women."
15 Ferree, "Inequality, Intersectionality and the Politics of Discourse."
16 Meier and Lombardo, "Towards a New Theory on the Symbolic Representation of Women."

17 Ferree, "Inequality, Intersectionality and the Politics of Discourse."
18 Shirin Rai, *The Gender Politics of Development: Essays in Hope and Despair* (London: Zed Books, 2008).
19 Meier and Lombardo, "Towards a New Theory on the Symbolic Representation of Women."
20 Ariel I. Ahram, "Symbolic Frames: Identity and Legitimacy in Iraqi Islamist Discourse," *Rhetoric & Public Affairs* 11, no. 1 (2008): 113–32.
21 Ibid.; Ofra Bengio, *Saddam's Word* (New York: Oxford University Press, 1998), 182, https://global.oup.com/academic/product/saddams-word-9780195151855.
22 Sarah Smiles, "On the Margins: Women, National Boundaries, and Conflict in Saddam's Iraq," *Identities* 15, no. 3 (2008): 271–96.
23 Perri Campbell, "Gender and Fundamentalism in the New Iraq: Women's Rights and Social Change in Cyberspace," *Outskirts: Feminisms Along the Edge* 16 (2007): 1–9.
24 Ibid.
25 Moghadam, *Modernizing Women*.
26 Stokke and Selboe, "Symbolic Representation as Political Practice."
27 Lonna Rae Atkeson, "Not All Cues Are Created Equal: The Conditional Impact of Female Candidates on Political Engagement," *The Journal of Politics* 65, no. 4 (2003): 1040–61.
28 Ibid.
29 Raquel Pastor and Tania Verge, "Women's Political Firsts and Symbolic Representation" (XII Congreso Espanol de Ciencia Politica y de la Administración, Donosti, 2015).
30 Helena Stensöta and Lena Wängnerud, "Gender and Corruption: The Mediating Power of Institutional Logics," *Governance* 28, no. 4 (2015): 475–96.
31 Atkeson, "Not All Cues Are Created Equal."
32 Ibid.
33 Ibid.
34 Ibid.
35 Sarah Childs, *Women and British Party Politics: Descriptive, Substantive and Symbolic Representation* (London: Routledge, 2008).
36 Pastor and Verge, "Women's Political Firsts and Symbolic Representation."
37 Meier and Lombardo, "Towards a New Theory on the Symbolic Representation of Women."
38 Ibid.
39 Monroe E. Price, Ibrahim al-Marashi and Nicole A. Stremlau, "Media in the Peace-Building Process: Ethiopia and Iraq," in *Public Sentinel: News Media and Governance Reform*, ed. Pippa Norris (Washington, DC: The World Bank Communication for Governance and Accountability Program, 2009), 221–75.

40 Hana Noor al-Deen, "Changes and Challenges of the Iraqi Media," *Global Media Journal* 4, no. 6 (2005): 1–17.
41 Benjamin Isakhan, "The Post-Saddam Iraqi Media: Reporting the Democratic Developments of 2005," *Global Media Journal* 7 (2008): 1–23.
42 al-Deen, "Changes and Challenges of the Iraqi Media."
43 William A. Rugh, *Arab Mass Media: Newspapers, Radio, and Television in Arab Politics*, First (Westport, CT: Praeger Publishers, 2004), 35.
44 al-Deen, "Changes and Challenges of the Iraqi Media."
45 Rugh, *Arab Mass Media*, 38.
46 Isakhan, "The Post-Saddam Iraqi Media," 1–23.
47 Baltic Media Centre et al., "A New Voice in the Middle East: A Provisional Needs Assessment for the Iraqi Media" (Svaneke, Denmark: Baltic Media Centre, 2003).
48 Jacqueline Sutton, Personal interview, March 27, 2015.
49 al-Deen, "Changes and Challenges of the Iraqi Media."
50 Ibrahim al-Marashi, "The Dynamics of Iraq's Media: Ethno-Sectarian Violence, Political Islam, Public Advocacy, and Globalization," *Cardozo Arts & Entertainment Law Journal* 25, no. 6 (2008 2007): 95–130.
51 Deborah Amos, "Confusion, Contradiction and Irony: The Iraqi Media in 2010," Joan Shorenstein Center on the Press, Politics and Public Policy Discussion Paper Series D-58 (Cambridge, MA: John F. Kennedy School of Government, Harvard University, 2010).
52 Ibid.
53 Ibid.
54 Ahmed K. al-Rawi, "The US Influence in Shaping Iraq's Sectarian Media," *International Communication Gazette* 75, no. 4 (2013): 374–91.
55 Ibid.
56 Price, al-Marashi and Stremlau, "Media in the Peace-Building Process."
57 al-Marashi, "Dynamics of Iraq's Media."
58 al-Rawi, "The US Influence in Shaping Iraq's Sectarian Media."
59 Ahmed Khalid al-Rawi, "Iraqi Women Journalists' Challenges and Predicaments," *Journal of Arab & Muslim Media Research* 3, no. 3 (2010): 223–36.
60 Price, al-Marashi and Stremlau, "Media in the Peace-Building Process."
61 al-Marashi, "Dynamics of Iraq's Media."
62 Amos, "Confusion, Contradiction and Irony."
63 al-Deen, "Changes and Challenges of the Iraqi Media"; Amos, "Confusion, Contradiction and Irony."
64 Amos, "Confusion, Contradiction and Irony."
65 Ahmed K. al-Rawi and Barrie Gunter, "Political Candidates' Coverage in the 2010 Iraqi General Elections," *Journal of Middle East Media* 19, no. 1 (2013): 69–94.
66 Price, al-Marashi and Stremlau, "Media in the Peace-Building Process."

67 Ibid.
68 Azza M. Karam, *Strengthening the Role of Women Parliamentarians in the Arab Region: Challenges and Options* (Kingston, Ontario, Canada: Queen's University School of Politics, 1998).
69 Ibid.
70 Zeina Zaatari, "No Democracy without Women's Equality: Middle East and North Africa," in *Conflict Prevention and Peace Forum* (Waterloo, Ontario, Canada: Social Science Research Council, 2015).
71 Ibid.
72 Ibid.
73 Leila Nicolas Rahbani, "Women in Arab Media: Present but Not Heard" (California: Stanford University Press, 2010).
74 Zaatari, "No Democracy without Women's Equality."
75 Global Media Monitoring Project, "Initial GMMP Findings Show Almost No Improvement in Women's Visibility" (Mexico City, Mexico: Global Media Monitoring Project, June 1, 2015), http://whomakesthenews.org/articles/initial-gmmp-findings-show-almost-no-improvement-in-women-s-visibility.
76 Rahbani, "Women in Arab Media."
77 Maurice Odine, "Role of Social Media in the Empowerment of Arab Women," *Global Media Journal* (Spring 2013): 1–30.
78 Rahbani, "Women in Arab Media."
79 Sutton, Personal interview.
80 Riverbend, *Baghdad Burning: Girl Blog from Iraq*, vol. 1, 2 vols. (New York: The Feminist Press at CUNY, 2005).
81 Campbell, "Gender and Fundamentalism in the New Iraq."
82 Ibid., 3.
83 Ibid.
84 Human Rights Watch, "Iraq: New Guidelines Silence Media" (Baghdad: Human Rights Watch, July 3, 2014), https://www.hrw.org/news/2014/07/03/iraq-new-guidelines-silence-media.
85 Ibid.
86 Iraq Foundation, "Women Leaders in an Era of Change" (Amman, Jordan: Woodrow Wilson International Center for Scholars, 2013).
87 Ibid.
88 Global Justice Project, "Women's Political Representation."
89 Free Iraq Foundation, "Women in the Council of Representatives."
90 CBS News, "Diverse Iraqi Women Seek Political Parity."
91 Free Iraq Foundation, "Women in the Council of Representatives."
92 Ibid.
93 Frances Guy, Personal interview, February 2016.

94 Sutton, Personal interview.
95 Iraq Foundation, "Women Leaders in an Era of Change."
96 Ibid.
97 Free Iraq Foundation, "Women in the Council of Representatives"; Global Justice Project, "Women's Political Representation"; Guy, Personal interview.
98 Odine, "Role of Social Media in the Empowerment of Arab Women."
99 Ibid.
100 Guy, Personal interview.
101 Free Iraq Foundation, "Women in the Council of Representatives."
102 Ibid.
103 Ibid.
104 Ibid.
105 Karam, *Strengthening the Role of Women Parliamentarians in the Arab Region*, 14–15.
106 Fischer-Tahir, "Competition, Cooperation and Resistance."
107 Free Iraq Foundation, "Women in the Council of Representatives."
108 Zaatari, "No Democracy without Women's Equality."
109 Shelly Inglis et al., "CEDAW and Security Council Resolution 1325: A Quick Guide" (New York: United Nations Development Fund for Women (UNIFEM), 2006).
110 Guy, Personal interview.
111 Zaatari, "No Democracy without Women's Equality."
112 Ibid.
113 Michael S. Schmidt and Yasir Ghazi, "Iraqi Women Feel Sidelined Despite Parliament Quota—NYTimes.com," *The New York Times*, March 12, 2011, http://www.nytimes.com/2011/03/13/world/middleeast/13baghdad.html?_r=0.
114 Zaatari, "No Democracy without Women's Equality."
115 Rahbani, "Women in Arab Media."
116 Free Iraq Foundation, "Women in the Council of Representatives."
117 United Nations, "Strategy for the Advancement of Women in Iraq" (UNIFEM, 2012).
118 Free Iraq Foundation, "Women in the Council of Representatives."
119 Ibid.
120 United Nations, "Strategy for the Advancement of Women in Iraq."
121 Ibid.
122 Iraq Foundation, "Women Leaders in an Era of Change."
123 Ibid.
124 Ibid.
125 Global Justice Project, "Women's Political Representation."
126 Guy, Personal interview.

127 al-Fatlawi, "The Dynamics of Parliamentary Life in a Free Iraq."
128 Iraqi Constitution, Article 38 states, "The State shall guarantee in a way that does not violate public order and morality: A. Freedom of expression using all means. B. Freedom of press, printing, advertisement, media and publication. C. Freedom of assembly and peaceful demonstration, and this shall be regulated by law."
129 By this statement, she refers to the fact that there were others in her bloc who took responsibility for interacting with the press.
130 International Telecommunications Union, "The World in 2015: ICT Facts & Figures" (Geneva, Switzerland: ITU, 2015).
131 Andrea Beccalli, "The Internet and Freedom of Expression in Iraq" (Paris, France: Internews Europe: United Nations Educational, Scientific and Cultural Organization (UNESCO), November 2012).
132 Ibid.
133 Ibid., 2.
134 Beccalli, "The Internet and Freedom of Expression in Iraq."
135 Mustapha Ajbaili, "How ISIS Conquered Social Media," *al-Arabiya News*, June 24, 2014, http://ara.tv/wxs4f.
136 Atkeson, "Not All Cues Are Created."
137 Free Iraq Foundation, "Women in the Council of Representatives."
138 United Nations, "Strategy for the Advancement of Women in Iraq."
139 UN Women, "Women in Iraq Factsheet," United Nations (2013), http://www.jauiraq.org/documents/1864/Woman-Factsheet.pdf.
140 Free Iraq Foundation, "Women in the Council of Representatives."
141 CBS News, "Diverse Iraqi Women Seek Political Parity."
142 Iraq Foundation, "Women Leaders in an Era of Change."
143 Zaatari, "No Democracy without Women's Equality."
144 United Nations, "Strategy for the Advancement of Women in Iraq."
145 Frances Guy, Personal interview.
146 Nicola Pratt and Nadje al-Ali, "Women's Organizing and the Conflict in Iraq since 2003," *Feminist Review*, 2007.
147 For example, when in March 2004 the United States announced its $10 million "Women's Democracy Initiative" in Iraq, the grants were distributed to seven US-based organizations or coalitions including the neoconservative Independent Women's Forum, Johns Hopkins School of Strategic and International Studies, and Kurdish Human Rights Watch (which despite its name was headquartered in the United States). See Ibid.
148 Zaatari, "No Democracy without Women's Equality."
149 Fischer-Tahir, "Competition, Cooperation and Resistance."
150 Pratt and al-Ali, "Women's Organizing and the Conflict in Iraq since 2003."
151 Zaatari, "No Democracy without Women's Equality."

152 Ibid.
153 Bourdieu and Thompson, *Language and Symbolic Power*, 503–4.

8 The Iraqi Political Situation and Women's Representation Post-2014: An Update on Case Study MP Activities since 2014

1. Christopher Davidson, "ISIS and the Iraq War: Regional and International Dimensions," CNN iReport (Washington, DC: CNN, June 21, 2014); Lizzie Dearden, "Former US Military Adviser David Kilcullen Says There Would Be No ISIS without Iraq Invasion," *The Independent*, March 4, 2016, http://www.independent.co.uk/news/world/middle-east/iraq-war-invasion-caused-isis-islamic-state-daesh-saysus-military-adviser-david-kilcullen-a6912236.html; Toby Dodge, "Can Iraq Be Saved?," *Survival* 56, no. 5 (2014): 7–20; International Crisis Group, "Déjà vu All over Again.".
2. Luisa Dietrich and Simone E. Carter, "Gender and Conflict Analysis in ISIS Affected Communities of Iraq" (Oxford, UK: OXFAM International, May 2017).
3. Muhamed H. Almaliky, "Mending Iraq: Can Abadi Bridge the Country's Sectarian Divide?," *Foreign Affairs*, January 16, 2015, https://www.foreignaffairs.com/articles/middle-east/2015-01-16/mending-iraq.
4. Jared Malsin, "Iraqi Prime Minister Haider Al-Abadi Says the End Is Nigh for 'Fake' Islamic State," *Time*, June 29, 2017, http://time.com/4839617/mosul-isis-mosque-haider-al-abadi/.
5. Ayman El-Dessouki, "The Internal and External Roles of Iraqi Popular Mobilization Forces," *African Journal of Political Science and International Relations* 11, no. 10 (2017): 274–83; Munqith M. Dagher, "ISIL in Iraq: A Disease or Just the Symptoms? A Public Opinion Analysis" (The National Consortium for the Study of Terrorism and Responses to Terrorism, University of Maryland: IIASS, 2014).
6. USAID, "Iraq—Complex Emergency" (Washington, DC: USAID, November 3, 2017).
7. Iraq Constitutional Committee, "Iraqi Constitution."
8. Maria Fantappie and Cale Salih, "The Politics of the Kurdish Independence Referendum: How the Vote Could Provoke Crises and Silence Dissent," *Foreign Affairs*, September 19, 2017, https://www.foreignaffairs.com/articles/2017-09-19/politics-kurdish-independence-referendum.
9. Christiane Baumeister and Lutz Killan, "Understanding the Decline in the Price of Oil since June 2014," *Journal of the Association of Environmental and Resource Economists* 3, no. 1 (2016): 131–58.
10. Fantappie and Salih, "The Politics of the Kurdish Independence Referendum."

11 Martin Chulov, "More than 92% of Voters in Iraqi Kurdistan Back Independence," *The Guardian*, September 27, 2017, https://www.theguardian.com/world/2017/sep/27/over-92-of-iraqs-kurds-vote-for-independence.
12 Haider al-Abadi, "Iraq Will Remain United," *The New York Times*, October 18, 2017, sec. Opinion Editorials.
13 Ahmed Rasheed and Raya Jalabi, "Iraqi Court Rules Kurdish Independence Vote Unconstitutional," *Reuters*, November 20, 2017, https://www.reuters.com/article/us-mideast-crisis-iraq-kurds/iraqi-court-rules-kurdish-independence-vote-unconstitutional-idUSKBN1DK0Q6.
14 Al-Ghad Press, "Parliament Is Campaigning to Amend the Law of Rafha and Pay the Dues of Martyrs and Displaced People," *Al-Ghad Press*, July 30, 2017, https://www.alghadpress.com/news/111683.
15 The Baghdad Post, "Abadi to Oust Corruption Parties after Liberating Iraq from ISIS," August 17, 2017, http://www.thebaghdadpost.com/en/story/15815/Abadi-to-oust-corruption-parties-after-liberating-Iraq-from-ISIS-MP.
16 The Baghdad Post, "MP Says Sectarian Iraqi Constitution Must Be Burned," *The Baghdad Post*, October 26, 2017, http://www.thebaghdadpost.com/en/story/18762/Video-MP-says-sectarian-Iraqi-constitution-must-be-burned.
17 Alwaght News & Analysis, "Iraq Irked by Saudi Envoy's Provocations, Meddling," *Alwaght News & Analysis*, June 19, 2016, http://alwaght.com/en/News/58183/Iraq-Irked-by-Saudi-Envoy's-Provocations,-Meddling.
18 Shafaaq, "Haider Abadi Rejects a Request to Hanan Al-Fatlawi Belongs to the Participants in the Referendum," *Shafaaq*, September 27, 2017, http://www.shafaaq.com/ar/Ar_NewsReader/7057d106-ba98-46b7-9d6f-b913d642a48c.
19 Asharq Al-Awsat, "Baghdad Questions Tillerson's Remarks on PMF, Brands Them Meddling in Internal Affairs," *Asharq al-Awsat*, October 23, 2017, https://aawsat.com/english/home/article/1061201/baghdad-questions-tillerson's-remarks-pmf-brands-them-meddling-internal-affairs.
20 Dinar Speculator, "The Claim of Kurdistan Issued Arrest Warrants against 11 Individuals, Including Qais Al-Khazali and Hanan Al-Fatlawi," *Dinar Speculator*, October 23, 2017, http://www.dinarspeculator.com/showthread.php/82975-The-claim-of-Kurdistan-issued-arrest-warrants-against-11-individuals-including-Qais-al-Khazali-and-Hanan-al-Fatlawi.
21 The Baghdad Post, "Hanan Fatlawi: Mullah's New Tool to Fracture Iraq," *The Baghdad Post*, October 10, 2017, http://www.thebaghdadpost.com/en/story/18063/Hanan-Fatlawi-Mullah-s-new-tool-to-fracture-Iraq.
22 Ashraf News, "MP Al-Jaf to Ashraf News: Supporting the MKO Terrorist Organization Has Political Reasons," *Ashraf News*, July 29, 2016, http://www.ashraf-news.com/en/3510/MP-AlJaf-to-Ashraf-News-supporting-the-MKO-terrorist-organization-has-political-reasons.

23. The Baghdad Post, "KDP: Accusing Us of Cooperating with Turkey Is Political Bankruptcy," *The Baghdad Post*, April 27, 2017, http://www.thebaghdadpost.com/en/story/9853/KDP-Accusing-us-of-cooperating-with-Turkey-is-political-bankruptcy.
24. Oumayma Omar, "Iraq's Children, a Generation Deprived of Education," *The Arab Weekly*, July 31, 2016, http://www.thearabweekly.com/Opinion/5952/Iraq's-children,-a-generation-deprived-of-education.
25. The I.Q.D.Team Connection, "Deputy Reveals a Proposal to Pay the Salaries of Editors from the Grip of Dahesh," *The I.Q.D. Team Connection*, June 29, 2017, http://www.theiqdteam.com/blog/deputy-reveals-a-proposal-to-pay-the-salaries-of-editors-from-the-grip-of-dahesh.
26. Karima Al-Jawari, Member of the Parliament Karima al-Jawari—an Interview, Arab News Broadcasting, December 3, 2015, https://www.youtube.com/watch?v=kDT7GGIK54E.
27. Suhad Al-Obaidi, Face to Face with Suhad Al-Obaidi, January 16, 2014, https://www.youtube.com/watch?v=w30X5-PW3vc.
28. Mariam Al-Rayyis, Live Interview with Mariam Al-Rayyis, AFAQ TV, February 26, 2014, https://www.youtube.com/watch?v=0CPpOSXmYoE; Mariam Al-Rayyis, Iraqi Future… Where to?, Al Mayadeen Programs, August 12, 2014, https://www.youtube.com/watch?v=vUUpVsdDqcg.
29. Huda Sajjad, Face to Face with Huda Sajjad, AFAQ TV, March 28, 2017, https://www.youtube.com/watch?v=tt2ZEIBTpq0.
30. All Iraq News, Safia al-Suhail—First Woman Ambassador to Iraq in Jordan, October 30, 2015, sec. Political, http://www.alliraqnews.com/modules/news/article.php?storytopic=41&storyid=19610.
31. SafeDinar.com, "Iraqi Ambassador Hails Jordan's Economic Support," *SafeDinar.Com*, March 2, 2016.
32. Iraq TradeLink, "Hopes to Open Treibel Route with Jordan," *Iraq TradeLink*, May 22, 2016, http://www.iraqtradelinknews.com/2016/05/hopes-to-open-treibel-outlet-with-jordan.html.
33. Iraq TradeLink, "No Extra Fees on Jordanian Exports to Iraq," *Iraq TradeLink*, August 11, 2016, http://www.iraqtradelinknews.com/2016/08/no-extra-fees-on-jordanian-exports-to.html.
34. Adnkronos International, "Iraq: Appeal for a Solution to Rising Suicide Rate among Women" (Baghdad: Adnkronos International, May 26, 2017), http://www1.adnkronos.com/AKI/English/Security/?id=1.0.2197664177.
35. Dinar Updates, "Alaa Talabani Reveal the Nature of the Relationship between Israel and the Iraqi Kurd," *Dinar Updates*, September 5, 2016, http://www.dinarupdates.com/showthread.php?40322-Alaa-Talabani-reveal-the-nature-of-the-relationship-between-Israel-and-the-Iraqi-Kurd.

36 Al-Jazeera, "Iraq's Former President Jalal Talabani Dead," *al-Jazeera*, October 3, 2017, http://www.aljazeera.com/news/2017/10/iraq-president-jalal-talabani-dead-171003140521896.html.
37 Alaa Talabani, Heated TV Debate between Alaa Talabani and Tamim Mohammed, Around the World, September 27, 2017, https://www.youtube.com/watch?v=zPx4A4r0pJ4.
38 Ibrahim Malazada, "Iraq's Kurds Question Motives behind Independence Vote," *Iraqi Economists Network*, June 27, 2017, http://iraqieconomists.net/en/2017/06/29/iraqs-kurds-question-motives-behind-independence-vote-by-ibrahim-malazada/.
39 Talabani, Heated TV Debate between Alaa Talabani and Tamim Mohammed.
40 Scott Lucas, "Essential Guide: The Battle for Kirkuk in Northern Iraq," *EA Worldview*, October 18, 2017, http://eaworldview.com/2017/10/why-is-there-a-battle-for-kirkuk-in-northern-iraq/.
41 Dinar Guru Recap, "Majida Al-Tamimi: The Real Budget Deficit 53 Trillion Dinars," *Dinar Guru Recap*, August 26, 2015, http://www.dinargururecap.com/2015/08/majida-al-tamimi-the-real-budget-deficit-53-trillion-dinars/.
42 Leyla H. Sherwani, "Iraq Spent $1,000 Billion in 13 Years, Wasting Most of It: MP," *BasNews*, January 8, 2017, http://www.basnews.com/index.php/en/reports/367725.
43 Ibid.
44 Ban Abd Alkarem, Majida al-Tamimi Interrogating the Speaker of the House of Representatives (Baghdad, 2017), https://www.youtube.com/watch?v=EnUuYi5yjic.
45 Al-Ghad Press, "Majida Al-Tamimi Talks about a 'Month Period' Regarding the Dismissal of the Electoral Commission," *Al-Ghad Press*, May 13, 2017, https://search4dinar.wordpress.com/2017/05/13/majida-al-tamimi-talks-about-a-month-period-regarding-the-dismissal-of-the-electoral-commission/.

9 Conclusion

1 For example, S. E. Finer, *Comparative Government* (London, Pelican, 1970), 441.
2 For example, Mehran Kamrava, "Conceptualising Third World Politics: The State-society See-saw," *Third World Quarterly* 14, no. 4 (1993): 710.
3 Michael C. Hudson, "The Political Culture Approach to Arab Democratization: The Case for Bringing it Back In, Carefully," in Rex Brynen, Baghat Korany, and Paul Noble (eds.), *Political Liberalization and Democratization in the Arab World* (Boulder and London: Lynne Rienner Publishers, 1995), vol. 1, 61–76.
4 United Nations, "Strategy for the Advancement of Women in Iraq."
5 Inglis et al., "CEDAW and Security Council Resolution 1325."

Bibliography

Primary Sources

Case Study Broadcast Interviews[1]

Baghdadia, al- Television. "Talk/Interview with an Official." Series of interviews with Iraqi policy-makers. Programs aired during Ramadan (July–August), 2012.
Iraqiya, al- Television. "Talk/Interview with an Official." Series of interviews with Iraqi policy-makers. Programs aired during Ramadan (July–August), 2013.

Additional Broadcast and Online Interviews

Baghdadia, al- Television. "Live TV." 2015. http://wwitv.com/tv_channels/b5964.htm.
Fatlawi, Hanan al-. "The Dynamics of Parliamentary Life in a Free Iraq." Oral presentation. In *Iraq and Its Politics*. Boston University, Boston, MA: Institute for Iraqi Studies, 2013. http://www.youtube.com/watch?v=vwbHprj3PJ4, al-Fatlawi Hanan, September 16, 2013. http://www.youtube.com/watch?v=d1eiKmHIL2I, al-Fatlawi Hanan, Free Sound Iraq/Dialogue, November 27, 2012.
Fayhaa, al-. "Al-Fayhaa Satellite Channel." *Al-Fayhaa TV*, 2015. http://www.alfayhaa.tv/en/.
Iraqiya, al- Television. "Aliraqiya." *al-Iraqiya*. Accessed August 23, 2014. http://www.aliraqiya.com.
http://www.youtube.com/watch?v=8foQr3VCfiI, Ashwaq al-Jaf, July 13, 2013.
http://www.youtube.com/watch?v=aaSEtt-G69o, Suhad al-Obaidi, August 3, 2012.
http://www.youtube.com/watch?v=HsMZhMQmjHQ, Alaa' al-Talabani, June 30, 2012.
http://www.youtube.com/watch?v=JF8YoErAOQ8, July 28, 2012.
http://www.youtube.com/watch?v=luLDSS90BqU, Mariam al-Rayyis, July 24, 2012.
http://www.youtube.com/watch?v=mgeYCNV_5fw, Noura al-Bajari, August 2, 2013.
http://www.youtube.com/watch?v=oFHxBUS5rw, Majida al-Tamimi, August 5, 2012.
http://www.youtube.com/watch?v=tweUFlyhiMc, Interview with Minister of Environment Narmeen Othman, December 1, 2010.

---

[1] These videotaped interviews, originally posted by the television channels on the video sharing site YouTube, have since been removed and therefore no online links are currently available. However, the author retains audio recordings of the interviews, which were transcribed and translated for analysis.

http://www.youtube.com/watch?v=uN4zPIK5qQ4, Suhad al-Obaidi, August 3, 2012.
http://www.youtube.com/watch?v=wKSjqqGgOR4, Etab al-Douri, July 28, 2012.
http://www.youtube.com/watch?v=x3yb7j2NC44, Karima al-Jawari, al-Fayhaa TV, October 21, 2011.
http://www.youtube.com/watch?v=Xn6PNkqn6Yo, Karima al-Jawari, July 15, 2013
https://www.facebook.com/jinan.mubarak.35, Jinan Mubarak, Facebook.com. Accessed November 17, 2015.
https://www.youtube.com/watch?v=0CPpOSXmYoE,New Live Interview with Mariam al-Rayyis, AFAQ TV, February 26, 2014.
https://www.youtube.com/watch?v=b9Jih2LwixQ, Interview with Minister of Environment Narmeen Othman, January 6, 2010.
https://www.youtube.com/watch?v=EnUuYi5yjic New, Majida al-Tamimi interrogating the Speaker of the House of Representatives, Ban Abd Alkarem, Baghdad, 2017.
https://www.youtube.com/watch?v=IXYdx5cy7NE, Huda Sajjad, July 11, 2013.
https://www.youtube.com/watch?v=IXYdx5cy7NE, Safia al-Suhail, August 2, 2013.
https://www.youtube.com/watch?v=kDT7GGIK54E, Interview with Karima al-Jawari, Arab News Broadcasting, December 3, 2015.
https://www.youtube.com/watch?v=Pwio5C1sfvo. al-A'hed Satellite Channel, Interview with Japook, August 30, 2013.
https://www.youtube.com/watch?v=tt2ZEIBTpq0, T.V. Interview with Huda Sajjad, AFAQ TV, March 28, 2017.
https://www.youtube.com/watch?v=Vq87j702po0, Jinan Mubarak, May 5, 2010.
https://www.youtube.com/watch?v=vUUpVsdDqcg, Future of Iraq—T.V. Interview with Mariam al-Rayyis, August 12, 2014.
https://www.youtube.com/watch?v=w30X5-PW3vc, Face to Face T.V. Interview with Suhad al-Obaidi, January 16, 2014.
https://www.youtube.com/watch?v=zPx4A4r0pJ4, Heated TV Debate between Alaa Talabani and Tamim Mohammed, Around the World, September 27, 2017.
Mariam al-Rayyis, Al Mayadeen Programs, August 12, 2014.

Reports and Interviews about Security Issues in Iraq

https://www.youtube.com/watch?v=tGU9S8sH_JY, ONTV, Interview with al-Ameri Khlood, Journalist, al-Hayat Newspaper, London, Security Issues in Iraq, December 10, 2014.
https://www.youtube.com/watch?v=HtcOY9G5TW98, AlAnn TV, Interview with al-Ameri Khlood, Journalist, al-Hayat Newspaper, London, Human Organs Trades in Iraq, November 19, 2013.
https://www.youtube.com/watch?v=Igd5Nu-_glw

Iraqi Centre for Women's Rehabilitation and Employment—The Way Program

https://www.youtube.com/watch?v=m_zQ9OofVUU, Iraqi Centre for Women's Rehabilitation and Employment—The Way (under the supervision of Jinan Mubarak), July 23, 2013.
https://www.youtube.com/watch?v=4iC0lphQjkU, Iraqi Women between Inclusion and Exclusion, Jinan Mubarak, October 29, 2011.

Personal Interviews

Guy, Frances (Head of Region, Middle East, Christian Aid, 35 Lower Marsh, Waterloo, London UK; former representative, UN Women in Iraq). Personal interview. February 17, 2016.
Sutton, Jacqueline (former Acting Iraq Director, Institute for War and Peace Reporting [IWPR]; former scholar of Iraqi media, Australian National University, Canberra AU; former journalist, BBC UK). Personal interview. March 27, 2015.

Official Documents

Free Iraq Foundation. "Women in the Council of Representatives: Lessons Learned and Case Studies Report." Washington, DC: Wilson Center, 2013.
Global Justice Project. "Women's Political Representation: Achieving the Iraqi Constitutional Objective." Salt Lake City, UT: S.J. Quinney College of Law, University of Utah, 2009.
Inter-Agency Information and Analysis Unit. "Women in Iraq." United Nations, March 2012. www.iauiraw.org/documents/1628/Women in Iraq Fact Sheet—English.pdf.
Inter-Parliamentary Union. "Iraq: Council of Representatives of Iraq." Geneva: Inter-Parliamentary Union, October 10, 2014.
Inter-Parliamentary Union. "Parline Database: Women in National Parliaments." Accessed December 10, 2013. http://www.ipu.org/wmn-e/classif.htm.
Iraq Constitutional Committee. "Iraqi Constitution." 2005. http://www.iraqinationality.gov.iq/attach/iraqi_constitution.pdf.
Iraq Legal Development Project (ILDP). "The Status of Women in Iraq: Update to the Assessment of Iraq's de Jure and de Facto Compliance with International Legal Standards." American Bar Association, 2006.
Iraqi Parliament. "Iraqi Parliament Guide." Accessed December 29, 2014. http://www.iraqiparliament.info/en.
Iraqi Women's Educational Institute. "Advancing Women's Rights: Two Years in Iraq." Washington, DC: Independent Women's Forum, 2008. http://www.iwf.org/files/c45cf4cdaac5f237475227839b40369d.pdf.

Iraqi Women's League, June 15, 2015, http://www.iraqiwomensleague.com/.
United Nations. "Strategy for the Advancement of Women in Iraq." New York: United Nations Development Fund for Women, 2012.
United Nations. "The United Nations Fourth World Conference on Women: Platform for Action." Beijing, China: United Nations, September 1995. http://www.un.org/womenwatch/daw/beijing/platform/decision.htm.
United Nations, Entity for Gender Equality and the Empowerment of Women. "Convention on the Elimination of All Forms of Discrimination against Women." United Nations Development Fund for Women, 2003. http://www.un.org/womenwatch/daw/cedaw/.

Secondary Sources

Books

Abdullah, Thabit A. J. *A Short History of Iraq: From 636 to the Present*. 2nd ed. New York: Routledge, 2013.
Ágoston, Gábor, and Bruce Alan Masters. *Encyclopedia of the Ottoman Empire*. New York: Infobase Publishing, 2009.
Ahmed, Leila. *Women and Gender in Islam: Historical Roots of a Modern Debate*. New Haven, CT: Yale University Press, 1993.
Ali, Nadje Sadig al-. *Iraqi Women: Untold Stories From 1948 to the Present*. London: Zed Books, 2007.
Andreski, Stanislav. *The African Predicament*. New York: Atherton Press, 1968.
Arkin, William M., Damian Durrant, and Marianne Cherni. *On Impact: Modern Warfare and the Environment: A Case Study of the Gulf War*. Washington, DC: Greenpeace, 1991.
Arnold, James R. *Saddam's Iraq*. Minneapolis, MN: Twenty-First Century Books (CT), 2008.
Azzawi, Souad N. al-. *Deterioration of Iraqi Women's Rights and Living Conditions under Occupation*. Brussels: Brussels Tribunal, 2007.
Batatu, Hanna. *The Old Social Classes and the Revolutionary Movements of Iraq: A Study of Iraq's Old Landed and Commercial Classes and of Its Communists, Ba'thists, and Free Officers*. Princeton, NJ: Princeton University Press, 1978.
Bengio, Ofra. *Saddam's Word*. New York: Oxford University Press, 1998. https://global.oup.com/academic/product/saddams-word-9780195151855.
Bourdieu, Pierre, and John B. Thompson. *Language and Symbolic Power*. Cambridge, MA: Harvard University Press, 1991.
Carothers, Thomas. *Aiding Democracy Abroad: The Learning Curve*. Washington, DC: Carnegie Endowment for International Peace, 1999.

Ceylan, Ebubekir. *Ottoman Origins of Modern Iraq: Political Reform, Modernization and Development in the Nineteenth Century Middle East.* New York: I.B. Tauris, 2011.

Chapin Metz, Helen. *Iraq: A Country Study.* Country Studies. Washington, DC: GPO for the Library of Congress, 1988.

Childs, Sarah. *Women and British Party Politics: Descriptive, Substantive and Symbolic Representation.* London: Routledge, 2008.

Cleveland, William L., and Martin Bunton. *A History of the Modern Middle East.* 5th ed. Boulder, CO: Westview Press, 2012.

Cockburn, Andrew, and Patrick Cockburn. *Out of the Ashes: The Resurrection of Saddam.* 2nd ed. New York: HarperCollins, 2000.

Cockburn, Cynthia. *From Where We Stand: War, Women's Activism and Feminist Analysis.* London: Zed Books, 2007.

Dahlerup, Drude. *Women, Quotas and Politics.* New York: Routledge, 2006.

Daud, Sahiba al-Shaikh. *Awwal Al-Tariq Lil Nahda Al-Nisa'iyya Fi Al-Iraq.* Baghdad: Matba at al-Rabitah, 1958.

Davidson, Christopher M. *The United Arab Emirates: A Study in Survival.* Boulder, CO: Lynne Rienner Publishers, 2005.

Diamond, Larry. *Squandered Victory: The American Occupation and the Bungled Effort to Bring Democracy to Iraq.* New York: Henry Holt and Company, 2007.

Dodge, Toby. *Inventing Iraq: The Failure of Nation Building and a History Denied.* New York: Columbia University Press, 2005.

Efrati, Noga. *Women in Iraq: Past Meets Present.* New York: Columbia University Press, 2012.

Eickelman, Dale F., and James Piscatori. *Muslim Politics.* Princeton, NJ: Princeton University Press, 1996.

Escobar, Arturo. *Encountering Development: The Making and Unmaking of the Third World.* Princeton, NJ: Princeton University Press, 2011.

Esposito, John L., and John Obert Voll. *Islam and Democracy.* Oxford, NY: Oxford University Press, 1996.

Faruqi, Ismail Raji al-. *Al Tawhid: Its Implications for Thought and Life.* 2nd ed. Herndon, VA: International Institute of Islamic Thought, 1992.

Finer, Samuel Edward. *Comparative Government.* Harmondsworth, UK: Penguin Books, 1970.

Graham-Brown, Sarah. *Sanctioning Saddam: The Politics of Intervention in Iraq.* London: I.B. Tauris, 1999.

Guilhot, Nicolas. *The Democracy Makers: Human Rights and the Politics of Global Order.* New York: Columbia University Press, 2005.

Hendrickson, David C., and Robert W. Tucker. *Revisions in Need of Revising: What Went Wrong in the Iraq War.* Carlisle, PA: Strategic Studies Institute, December 2005.

Hussein, Saddam. *Social and Foreign Affairs in Iraq.* 1st ed. London: Routledge, 2009.

Inglehart, Ronald. *Modernization and Postmodernization: Cultural, Economic, and Political Change in 43 Societies.* Princeton, NJ: Princeton University Press, 1997.

International Digital Library, Iraqi Books and Archive House. "Leila, No. 4, January 15, 1924." Library of Congress, 1924. https://www.wdl.org/ar/item/342/.

International Institute for Democracy and Electoral Assistance (IDEA). *The Arab Quota Report: Selected Case Studies*. Quota Report Series. Stockholm: International Institute for Democracy and Electoral Assistance, 2007.

Ismael, Tareq Y., and Jacqueline S. Ismael. *Iraq in the Twenty-First Century: Regime Change and the Making of a Failed State*. 1st ed. New York: Routledge, 2015.

Jawaheri, Yasmin Husein al-. *Women in Iraq: The Gender Impact of International Sanctions*. Boulder, CO: Lynne Rienner Publishers, 2008.

Kandiyoti, Deniz. *Women, Islam and the State*. Philadelphia, PA: Temple University Press, 1991.

Karam, Azza M. *Strengthening the Role of Women Parliamentarians in the Arab Region: Challenges and Options*. Kingston, Ontario, Canada: Queen's University School of Politics, 1998.

Larserud, Stina, and Rita Taphorn. *Designing for Equality: Best-Fit, Medium-Fit and Non-Favourable Combinations of Electoral Systems and Gender Quotas*. Stockholm: International Institute for Democracy and Electoral Assistance, 2007. http://www.idea.int/publications/designing_for_equality/index.cfm.

Law Library of Congress. *Iraq: Legal History and Traditions*. Washington, DC: Global Legal Research Center, June 2004.

Linz, Juan J., and Alfred Stepan. *Problems of Democratic Transition and Consolidation: Southern Europe, South America, and Post-Communist Europe*. Baltimore, MD: Johns Hopkins University Press, 1996.

Lovenduski, Joni, and Pippa Norris. *Gender and Party Politics*. London; Thousand Oaks, CA: Sage Publications, 1993.

Makiya, Kanan. *Republic of Fear: The Politics of Modern Iraq, Updated Edition*. Berkeley: University of California Press, 1998.

Marr, Phebe. *The Modern History of Iraq*. 3rd ed. Boulder, CO: Westview Press, 2012.

Mernissi, Fatema. *Islam and Democracy: Fear of the Modern World*. Translated by Mary Jo Lakeland. Cambridge, MA: Perseus Publishing, 1992.

Moghadam, Valentine M., ed. *From Patriarchy to Empowerment: Women's Participation, Movements, and Rights in the Middle East, North Africa, and South Asia*. Syracuse, NY: Syracuse University Press, 2007.

Moghadam, Valentine M., *Globalization and Social Movements: Islamism, Feminism, and the Global Justice Movement*. 2nd ed. Globalization. Lanham, MD: Rowman & Littlefield, 2013.

Moghadam, Valentine M., *Modernizing Women: Gender and Social Change in the Middle East*. 2nd ed. Boulder, CO: Lynne Rienner Publishers, 2003.

Nohlen, Dieter, Florian Grotz, and Christof Hartmann. *Elections in Asia and the Pacific: A Data Handbook*. 2nd ed. Volume I of II. Oxford, NY: Oxford University Press, 2002.

Nussbaum, Martha C. *Women and Human Development: The Capabilities Approach*. New York: Cambridge University Press, 2000.

NVivo Qualitative Data Analysis Software (version 11). London: QSR International, 2014.

Pappé, Ilan. *The Modern Middle East*. New York: Routledge, 2005.

Paulus, Trena, Jessica Lester, and Paul Dempster. *Digital Tools for Qualitative Research*. Thousand Oaks, CA: Sage Publications, 2014.

Paxton, Pamela, and Melanie M. Hughes. *Women, Politics and Power: A Global Perspective*. 3rd ed. Thousand Oaks, CA: Sage Publications, 2017.

Phillips, Anne. *The Politics of Presence*. Oxford: Oxford University Press, 1998.

Piscatori, James P. *Islam in a World of Nation-States*. Cambridge, MA: Cambridge University Press, 1986.

Rabinovich, Itamar, and Haim Shaked, eds. *Middle East Contemporary Survey, 1984–1985*. Vol. 9. Tel Aviv, Israel: The Moshe Dayan Center for Middle Eastern and African Studies, 1987.

Rai, Shirin. *The Gender Politics of Development: Essays in Hope and Despair*. London: Zed Books, 2008.

Rajaee, Farhang. *The Iran-Iraq War: The Politics of Aggression*. Gainesville, FL: University Press of Florida, 1993.

Rajagopal, Balakrishnan. *International Law from below: Development, Social Movements and Third World Resistance*. Cambridge, UK: Cambridge University Press, 2003.

Rawi, Ahmed Khalid al-. *Media Practice in Iraq*. Houndmills, Basingstoke, UK: Palgrave Macmillan, 2012.

Riemer, Neal, Douglas W. Simon, and Joseph Romance. *The Challenge of Politics: An Introduction to Political Science*. 3rd ed. Thousand Oaks, CA: CQ Press, 2010.

Riverbend. *Baghdad Burning: Girl Blog from Iraq*. Vol. 1 of 2. New York: The Feminist Press at CUNY, 2005.

Rugh, William A. *Arab Mass Media: Newspapers, Radio, and Television in Arab Politics*. 1st ed. Westport, CT: Praeger Publishers, 2004.

Sadiki, Larbi, Heiko Wimmen, and Layla Al-Zubaidi, eds. *Democratic Transition in the Middle East: Unmaking Power*. New York: Routledge, 2013.

Saikal, Amin, and Albrecht Schnabel. *Democratization in the Middle East: Experiences, Struggles, Challenges*. Tokyo, Japan: United Nations University Press, 2003.

Scahill, Jeremy. *Dirty Wars: The World Is a Battlefield*. New York: Nation Books, 2013.

Sharabi, Hisham. *Neopatriarchy: A Theory of Distorted Change in Arab Society*. New York: Oxford University Press, 1992.

Tripp, Charles. *A History of Iraq*. 3rd ed. Cambridge, UK: Cambridge University Press, 2007.

Visser, Reidar. *A Responsible End?: The United States and the Iraqi Transition, 2005–2010*. Charlottesville, VA: Just World Books, 2010.

Weldon, S. Laurel. *When Protest Makes Policy: How Social Movements Represent Disadvantaged Groups*. Ann Arbor, MI: University of Michigan Press, 2011.

Zedalis, Rex J. *The Legal Dimensions of Oil and Gas in Iraq: Current Reality and Future Prospects*. New York: Cambridge University Press, 2009.

Book Chapters

Abu Rumman, Saddam. "The Women's Quota in Jordan: Crowning Three Decades of Support for Female Political Participation." In *The Arab Quota Report: Selected Case Studies*, 42–50. Stockholm: International Institute for Democracy and Electoral Assistance, 2007.

Ali, Nadje al-, and Nicola Pratt. "The United States, the Iraqi Women's Diaspora and Women's 'Empowerment' in Iraq." In *Women & War in the Middle East*, edited by Nadje al-Ali and Nicola Pratt, 65–98. London: Zed Books, 2009.

Ballington, J., and D. Dahlerup. "Gender Quotas in Post-Conflict States: East Timor, Afghanistan and Iraq." In *Women, Quotas and Politics*, edited by D. Dahlerup, 249–58. New York: Routledge, 2006.

Chemali Khalaf, Mona. "Lebanon." In *Women's Rights in the Middle East and North Africa: Progress amid Resistance*, edited by Sanja Kelly and Julia Breslin, 249–81. New York: Freedom House, 2010.

Dahlerup, Drude. "Gender Balance in Politics: Goals and Strategies in a Global Perspective." In *The Arab Quota Report: Selected Case Studies*. Cairo, Egypt: International Institute for Democracy and Electoral Assistance, 2007.

Ferree, Myra Marx. "Inequality, Intersectionality and the Politics of Discourse: Framing Feminist Alliances." In *The Discursive Politics of Gender Equality: Stretching, Bending and Policy-Making*, edited by Emanuela Lombardo, Petra Meier, and Mieke Verloo, 18. London: Routledge, 2009.

Fleischmann, Ellen L. "The Other 'Awakening': The Emergence of Women's Movements in the Modern Middle East, 1900–1940." In *A Social History of Women & Gender in the Modern Middle East*, edited by Margaret L. Meriwether and Judith E. Tucker, 89–140. Boulder, CO: Westview Press, 1999.

Harrison, Graham. "Democratization and Liberalism." In *Encyclopedia Britannica Online*, 2015. http://www.britannica.com/EBchecked/topic/157304/democratization/307651/Democratization-and-liberalism.

Hudson, Michael C. "The Political Culture Approach to Arab Democratization: The Case for Bringing It Back In, Carefully." In *Political Liberalization and Democratization in the Arab World, Volume 1: Theoretical Perspectives*, edited by Rex Brynen, Bahgat Korany, and Paul Noble. Boulder, CO: Lynne Rienner Publishers, 1995.

Husseini, Rana. "Jordan." In *Women's Rights in the Middle East and North Africa: Progress amid Resistance*, edited by Sanja Kelly and Julia Breslin, 193–221. New York: Freedom House, 2010.

Jaza'iri, Zuhair al-. "Ba'thist Ideology and Practice." In *Iraq since the Gulf War*, edited by Fran Hazelton, 44. London: Zed Books, 1994.

Joseph, Suad. "Elite Strategies for State Building: Women, Family, Religion, and the State in Iraq and Lebanon." In *Women, Islam, and the State*, edited by Deniz Kandiyoti, 185. Philadelphia, PA: Temple University Press, 1991.

Kamp, Martina. "Fragmented Citizenship: Communalism, Ethnicity and Gender in Iraq." In *Women & War in the Middle East*, 193–216. London: Zed Books, 2009.

Kuku, Niemat. "Women's Political Participation: Legislated Quotas and Special Measures in Sudan." In *The Arab Quota Report: Selected Case Studies*, 32–42. Stockholm: International Institute for Democracy and Electoral Assistance, 2007.

Lorber, Judith. "Strategies of Feminist Research in a Globalized World." In *Analyzing Gender, Intersectionality, and Multiple Inequalities: Global, Transnational and Local Contexts*, edited by Esther Ngan-ling Chow, Marcia Texler Segal, and Lin Tan, 1–14. Bingley, UK: Emerald Group Publishing, 2011.

Price, Monroe E., Ibrahim Al-Marashi, and Nicole A. Stremlau. "Media in the Peace-Building Process: Ethiopia and Iraq." In *Public Sentinel: News Media and Governance Reform*, edited by Pippa Norris, 221–75. Washington, DC: The World Bank Communication for Governance and Accountability Program, 2009.

Rassam, Amal. "Revolution within the Revolution? Women and the State in Iraq." In *Iraq: The Contemporary State*, edited by Tim Niblock, 88–99. London: Croom Helm, 1982.

Rohde, Achim. "Opportunities for Masculinity and Love: Cultural Production in Ba'thist Iraq during the 1980s." In *Islamic Masculinities*, edited by Lahoucine Ouzgane, 184–201. London: Zed Books, 2006.

Sabbagh, Amal. "Overview of Women's Political Representation in the Arab Region: Opportunities and Challenges." In *The Arab Quota Report: Selected Case Studies*, 7–18. Stockholm: International Institute for Democracy and Electoral Assistance, 2007.

Schmitter, Philippe. "Civil Society East and West." In *Consolidating the Third Wave Democracies: Themes and Perspectives*, edited by Larry Diamond, Marc F. Plattner, Yun-Han Chu, and Hung-Mao Tien, 239–62. Baltimore, MD: Johns Hopkins University Press, 1997.

Schulze, Kristen. "Communal Violence, Civil War and Foreign Occupation: Women in Lebanon." In *Women, Ethnicity and Nationalism: The Politics of Transition*, edited by Rick Wilford and Robert L. Miller. London: Routledge, 1998.

Shvedova, Nadezhda. "Obstacles to Women's Participation in Parliament." In *Women in Parliament: Beyond Numbers. A Revised Edition*. Stockholm: International Institute for Democracy and Electoral Assistance, 2005.

Stokke, Kristian, and Elin Selboe. "Symbolic Representation as Political Practice." In *Rethinking Popular Representation*, edited by Olle Tornquist, Kristian Stokke, and Neil Webster. New York: Palgrave Macmillan, 2009.

Tohidi, Naheran. "Iran." In *Women's Rights in the Middle East and North Africa: Progress amid Resistance*, edited by Sanja Kelly and Julia Breslin. New York: Freedom House, 2010.

Journal Articles and Conference Papers

Ahmed, Huda. "Women in the Shadows of Democracy." *Middle East Report* 36, no. 239 (2006): 24–26.

Ahram, Ariel I. "Symbolic Frames: Identity and Legitimacy in Iraqi Islamist Discourse." *Rhetoric & Public Affairs* 11, no. 1 (2008): 113–32.

Alexander, Amy C. "Big Jumps in Women's Presence in Parliaments: Are These Sufficient for Improving Beliefs in Women's Ability to Govern?" *Advancing Women in Leadership* 35 (2015): 82–97.

Alexander, Amy C., and Christian Welzel. "Empowering Women: The Role of Emancipative Beliefs." *European Sociological Review* 27, no. 3 (2011): 364–84.

Ali, Nadje al-. "Reconstructing Gender: Iraqi Women between Dictatorship, War, Sanctions and Occupation." *Third World Quarterly* 26, no. 4–5 (2005): 739–58.

Ali, Nadje al-, and Nicola Pratt. "Women in Iraq: Beyond the Rhetoric." *Middle East Report* 36, no. 239 (2006).

Ali, Nadje al-, Mubejel Baban, and Sundus Abass. "Iraq Women's Rights under Attack: Occupation, Constitution and Fundamentalisms." Occasional Paper. London: Women Living Under Muslim Laws, December 2006.

Almaliky, Muhamed H. "Mending Iraq: Can Abadi Bridge the Country's Sectarian Divide?" *Foreign Affairs*, January 16, 2015.

Amos, Deborah. "Confusion, Contradiction and Irony: The Iraqi Media in 2010." Joan Shorenstein Center on the Press, Politics and Public Policy Discussion Paper Series D-58. Cambridge, MA: John F. Kennedy School of Government, Harvard University, 2010.

Atkeson, Lonna Rae. "Not All Cues Are Created Equal: The Conditional Impact of Female Candidates on Political Engagement." *The Journal of Politics* 65, no. 4 (2003): 1040–61.

Azzawi, Souad al-. "Decline of Iraqi Women Empowerment through Education under the American Occupation of Iraq 2003–2011." Paper presented at the International Seminar on the Situation of the Iraqi Academics, Ghent University, Belgium, March 9, 2011.

Baldez, Lisa. "Elected Bodies: The Gender Quota Law for Legislative Candidates in Mexico." *Legislative Studies Quarterly* 29, no. 2 (2004): 231–58.

Baldez, Lisa. "The Pros and Cons of Gender Quota Laws: What Happens When You Kick Men out and Let Women in?" *Politics & Gender* 2 (2006): 102–9.

Batatu, Hanna. "Class Analysis and Iraqi Society." *Arab Studies Quarterly* 1, no. 3 (July 1, 1979): 229–44.

Baumeister, Christiane, and Lutz Killan. "Understanding the Decline in the Price of Oil since June 2014." *Journal of the Association of Environmental and Resource Economists* 3, no. 1 (2016): 131–58.

Bellin, Eva. "The Iraqi Intervention and Democracy in Comparative Historical Perspective." *Political Science Quarterly* 119, no. 4 (May 2004): 595–608.

Brown, Lucy, and David Romano. "Women in Post-Saddam Iraq: One Step Forward or Two Steps Back?" *NWSA Journal* 18, no. 3 (2006): 51–70.

Bussey, Kay, and Albert Bandura. "Social Cognitive Theory of Gender Development and Differentiation." *Psychological Review* 106 (1999): 676–713.

Cainkar, Louise. "The Gulf War, Sanctions and the Lives of Iraqi Women." *Arab Studies Quarterly* 15, no. 2 (1993): 15–51.
Campbell, Perri. "Gender and Fundamentalism in the New Iraq: Women's Rights and Social Change in Cyberspace." *Outskirts: Feminisms along the Edge* 16 (2007): 1–9.
Caprioli, Mary, and Kimberly Lynn Douglass. "Nation Building and Women: The Effect of Intervention on Women's Agency." *Foreign Policy Analysis* 4, no. 1 (2008): 45–65.
Childs, Sarah, and Mona Lena Krook. "Critical Mass Theory and Women's Political Representation." *Political Studies* 56, no. 3 (2008): 725–36.
Cochrane, Paul. "The 'Lebanonization' of the Iraqi Media: An Overview of Iraq's Television Landscape." *Transnational Broadcasting Studies Journal* 16 (2006): 1–11.
Cockburn, Cynthia. "Gender Relations as Causal in Militarization and War." *International Feminist Journal of Politics* 12, no. 2 (2010): 139–57.
Cohn, Alicia. "How the Iraq War Has Affected Women." *Her.meneutics*, September 15, 2010. http://www.christianitytoday.com/women/2010/september/how-iraq-war-has-affected-women.html.
Coleman, Isobel. "The Payoff from Women's Rights." *Foreign Affairs* May–June (2004): 80.
Coleman, Isobel. "Women, Islam, and the New Iraq." *Foreign Affairs* 85, no. 1 (January 1, 2006): 24–38.
Dagher, Munqith M. "ISIL in Iraq: A Disease or Just the Symptoms? A Public Opinion Analysis." The National Consortium for the Study of Terrorism and Responses to Terrorism, University of Maryland, College Park, MD: IIASS, 2014.
Dahlerup, Drude, and Lenita Freidenvall. "Judging Gender Quotas: Predictions and Results." *Policy & Politics* 38, no. 3 (2010): 407–25.
Dahlerup, Drude, and Lenita Freidenvall. "Quotas as a 'Fast Track' to Equal Representation for Women." *International Feminist Journal of Politics* 7, no. 1 (2006): 26–48.
Davidson-Schmich, Louise K. "Implementation of Political Party Gender Quotas: Evidence from the German Lander 1990–2000." *Party Politics* 12, no. 2 (2006): 211–32.
Davis, Eric. "The Uses of Historical Memory." *Journal of Democracy* 16, no. 3 (2005): 54–68.
Dawisha, Adeed. "The Unraveling of Iraq: Ethnosectarian Preferences and State Performance in Historical Perspective." *Middle East Journal* 62, no. 2 (2008): 219–30.
Dawisha, A.I. "Democratic Institutions and Performance." *Journal of Democracy* 16, no. 3 (2005): 35–49.
de Castro Santos, Maria Helena, and Ulysses Tavares Teixeira. "Is It Possible to Export Democracy by the Use of Force? Military Interventions in Iraq and Libya." Paper presented at the FLACSO-ISA Joint International Conference, Buenos Aires, Argentina, 2014.
Deeb, Lara. "Piety Politics and the Role of a Transnational Feminist Analysis." *Journal of the Royal Anthropological Institute* 15 (2009): S112–26.

Deen, Hana Noor al-. "Changes and Challenges of the Iraqi Media." *Global Media Journal* 4, no. 6 (2005): 1–17.
Democratic Principles Working Group of the Iraqi Opposition. "Iraqi Opposition Report on the Transition to Democracy." *Journal of Democracy* 14, no. 3 (2003): 14–29.
Dessouki, Ayman El-. "The Internal and External roles of Iraqi Popular Mobilization Forces." *African Journal of Political Science and International Relations* 11, no. 10 (2017): 274–83.
Dodge, Toby. "Can Iraq Be Saved?" *Survival* 56, no.5 (2014): 7–20.
Efrati, Noga. "Negotiating Rights in Iraq: Women and the Personal Status Law." *Middle East Journal* 59, no. 4 (2005): 577–95.
Efrati, Noga. "The Other 'Awakening' in Iraq: The Women's Movement in the First Half of the Twentieth Century." *British Journal of Middle Eastern Studies* 31, no. 2 (November 1, 2004): 153–73.
European Parliament Committee on Women's Rights and Gender Equality. "Spring Forward for Women Conference Program." Brussels: European Parliament, November 5, 2014.
Fantappe, Maria and Cale Salih. "The Politics of the Kurdish Independence Referendum: How the Vote Could Provoke Crises and Silence Dissent." *Foreign Affairs*, September 19, 2017.
Farouk-Sluglett, Marion, and Peter Sluglett. "The Transformation of Land Tenure and Rural Social Structure in Central and Southern Iraq, C. 1870–1958." *International Journal of Middle East Studies* 15, no. 4 (1983): 491–505.
Fischer-Tahir, Andrea. "Competition, Cooperation and Resistance: Women in the Political Field in Iraq." *International Affairs* 86, no. 6 (2010): 1381–94.
Graham-Brown, Sarah. "Intervention, Sovereignty and Responsibility." *Middle East Report* 25, no. 193 (1995).
Graham-Brown, Sarah, and Chris Toensing. "Timeline of Iraq." *openDemocracy*, January 22, 2003.
Helou, Marguerite. "Lebanese Women and Political Parties: History, Issues and Options for Reform." *Emerging Voices: Young Women in Lebanese Politics*. International Alert, 2011: 16.
Hughes, Melanie M. "Armed Conflict, International Linkages, and Women's Parliamentary Representation in Developing Nations." *Social Problems* 56, no. 1 (2009): 174–204.
Hughes, Melanie M. "Intersectionality, Quotas, and Minority Women's Political Representation Worldwide." *American Political Science Review* 105, no. 3 (2011): 604–20.
Inhetveen, Katharina. "Can Gender Equality Be Institutionalized? The Role of Launching Values in Institutional Innovation." *International Sociology* 14, no. 4 (1999): 403–22.

Inglehart, Ronald, Mansoor Moaddel, and Mark Tessler. "Xenophobia and In-Group Solidarity in Iraq: A Natural Experiment on the Impact of Insecurity." *Perspectives on Politics* September, no. 3 (2006): 495–505.
Isakhan, Benjamin. "The Post-Saddam Iraqi Media: Reporting the Democratic Developments of 2005." *Global Media Journal* 7 (2008): 1–23.
Joseph, Suad. "Gender and Citizenship in Middle Eastern States." *Middle East Report* 26, no. 198 (1996): 4–10.
Joseph, Suad. "Women and Politics in the Middle East." *Middle East Report* 16, no. 138 (February 1986).
Kamrava, Mehran. "Conceptualising Third World Politics: The State-society See-saw." *Third World Quarterly* 14, no. 4 (1993): 703–16.
Kandiyoti, Deniz. "Fear and Fury: Women and Post-Revolutionary Violence." *openDemocracy*, January 14, 2013. http://www.opendemocracy.net/5050/deniz-kandiyoti/fear-and-fury-women-and-post-revolutionary-violence.
Kassem, Fatima Sbaity. "Can Women Break through? Women in Municipalities: Lebanon in Comparative Perspective." *Women's Studies International Forum* 35, no. 4 (July 2012): 233–55.
Keddie, Nikki R. "Women in the Middle East: Progress and Backlash." *Current History* 107, no. 713 (2008): 432–38.
Khatib, Lina. "Gender, Citizenship and Political Agency in Lebanon." *British Journal of Middle Eastern Studies* 35, no. 3 (2008): 437–51.
Kingston, Paul. "Women and Political Parties in Lebanon: Reflections on the Historical Experience." *Emerging Voices: Young Women in Lebanese Politics.* International Alert, 2011: 10.
Krook, Mona Lena. "Gender Quotas, Norms, and Politics." *Politics & Gender* 2 (2006): 110–18.
Krook, Mona Lena. "Studying Political Representation: A Comparative-Gendered Approach." *Perspectives on Politics* 8, no. 1 (2010): 233–40.
Krook, Mona Lena, and Diana Z. O'Brien. "The Politics of Group Representation: Quotas for Women and Minorities Worldwide." *Comparative Politics* 42, no. 3 (2010): 253–72.
Krook, Mona Lena, Diana Z. O'Brien, and Krista M. Swip. "Military Invasion and Women's Political Representation." *International Feminist Journal of Politics* 12, no. 1 (2010): 66–79.
Lee-Koo, Katrina. "Gender-Based Violence against Civilian Women in Postinvasion Iraq: (Re)politicizing George W. Bush's Silent Legacy." *Violence Against Women* 17, no. 12 (2011): 1619–34.
Lijphart, Arend. "Consociational Democracy." *World Politics* 21, no. 2 (January 1, 1969): 207–25.
Mansbridge, Jane. "Should Blacks Represent Blacks and Women Represent Women? A Contingent 'Yes.'" *The Journal of Politics* 61, no. 3 (1999): 628–57.

Marashi, Ibrahim al-. "The Dynamics of Iraq's Media: Ethno-Sectarian Violence, Political Islam, Public Advocacy, and Globalization." *Cardozo Arts & Entertainment Law Journal* 25, no. 6 (2007)(): 95–130.

Mehdi, Jaber Mehdi. "The Faltering Democracy in Iraq after 2003." *Modern Discussion Journal*, no. 3928 (2012): 11–31.

Moon, Bruce E. "Long Time Coming: Prospects for Democracy in Iraq." *International Security* 33, no. 4 (2009): 115–48.

Morlino, Leonardo. "What Is a 'Good' Democracy? Theory and Empirical Analysis." Paper Presented at the Conference on "The European Union, Nations State, and the Quality of Democracy. Lessons from Southern Europe." University of California, Berkeley, November 2, 2002.

Nanivadekar, Medha. "Are Quotas a Good Idea? The Indian Experience with Reserved Seats for Women." *Politics & Gender* 2 (2006): 101–28.

Natarajan, Usha. "Creating and Recreating Iraq: Legacies of the Mandate System in Contemporary Understandings of Third World Sovereignty." *Leiden Journal of International Law* 24, no. 4 (2011): 799–822.

Neshat, Saeid N. "A Look into the Women's Movement in Iraq." *Farzaneh* 6, no. 11 (2003): 54–65.

Norris, Pippa. "Opening the Door: Women Leaders and Constitution Building in Iraq and Afghanistan." *Gender Quotas and Electoral Democracy II*. Fukuoka, Japan: IPSA, 2007.

Norris, Pippa, and Ronald Inglehart. "Women and Democracy: Cultural Obstacles to Equal Representation." *Journal of Democracy* 12, no. 3 (2001): 126–40.

Odine, Maurice. "Role of Social Media in the Empowerment of Arab Women." *Global Media Journal* (Spring 2013): 1–30.

Omar, Safa' Saleh al-. Parliamentary Election in Iraq 1980–2000. Al-Gardenia, 2014

Pankhurst, Donna. "The 'Sex War' and Other Wars: Towards a Feminist Approach to Peace Building." *Development in Practice* 13, no. 2/3 (May 1, 2003): 154–77.

Pastor, Raquel, and Tania Verge. "Women's Political Firsts and Symbolic Representation." *Donosti*, 2015. https://aecpa.es/files/view/pdf/congress-papers/12-0/1379/

Pratt, Nicola, and Nadje al-Ali. "Women's Organizing and the Conflict in Iraq since 2003." *Feminist Review* 88, no.1 (April 2008): 74–85,

Qazzaz, Ayad al-. "Power Elite in Iraq – 1920–1958: A Study of the Cabinet." *The Muslim World* 61, no. 4 (1971): 267–83.

Rassam, Amal. "Political Ideology and Women in Iraq: Legislation and Cultural Constraints." *Journal of Developing Societies* 8 (January 1992): 82.

Rawi, Ahmed Khalid al-. "Iraqi Women Journalists' Challenges and Predicaments." *Journal of Arab & Muslim Media Research* 3, no. 3 (2010): 223–36.

Rawi, Ahmed Khalid al-, "The US Influence in Shaping Iraq's Sectarian Media." *International Communication Gazette* 75, no. 4 (2013): 374–91.

Rawi, Ahmed K. al-, and Barrie Gunter. "Political Candidates' Coverage in the 2010 Iraqi General Elections." *Journal of Middle East Media* 19, no. 1 (2013): 69–94.

Ryan, Missy. "Imagining Iraq, Defining Its Future." *World Policy Journal* 27, no. 1 (2010): 65–73.

Saadeh, Sofia. "Women in Lebanese Politics: Underlying Causes of Women's Lack of Representation in Lebanese Politics." *Emerging Voices: Young Women in Lebanese Politics*. International Alert, 2011: 14.

Salamey, Imad, and Rhys Payne. "Parliamentary Consociationalism in Lebanon: Equal Citizenry vs. Quotated Confessionalism." *The Journal of Legislative Studies* 14, no. 4 (2008): 451–73.

Shepherd, Laura J. "Veiled References: Constructions of Gender in the Bush Administration Discourse on the Attacks on Afghanistan Post-9/11." *International Feminist Journal of Politics* 8, no. 1 (2006): 19–41.

Smiles, Sarah. "On the Margins: Women, National Boundaries, and Conflict in Saddam's Iraq." *Identities* 15, no. 3 (2008): 271–96.

Stahnke, Tad, and Robert C. Blitt. "The Religion-State Relationship and the Right to Freedom of Religion or Belief: A Comparative Textual Analysis of the Constitutions of Predominantly Muslim Countries." *Georgetown Journal of International Law* 36 (2005):106.

Stensöta, Helena, and Lena Wängnerud. "Gender and Corruption: The Mediating Power of Institutional Logics." *Governance* 28, no. 4 (2015): 475–96.

Tados, Mariz. "Introduction: Quotas: Add Women and Stir?" *IDS Bulletin* 41 (2010): 1–10.

Tessler, Mark A., Mansoor Moaddel, and Ronald Inglehart. "What Do Iraqis Want?" *Journal of Democracy* 17, no. 1 (2006): 38–50.

Tønnessen, Liv. "Beyond Numbers? Women's 25% Parliamentary Quota in Post-Conflict Sudan." *Journal of Peace, Conflict and Development* 17 (2011): 43–62.

Walby, Sylvia. "Gender, Globalisation, and Democracy." *Gender and Development* 8, no. 1 (2000): 20–28.

Wängnerud, Lena. "Women in Parliaments: Descriptive and Substantive Representation." *Annual Review of Political Science* 12, no. 1 (2009): 51–69.

Waylen, Georgina. "Constitutional Engineering: What Opportunities for the Enhancement of Gender Rights?" *Third World Quarterly* 27, no. 7 (2006): 1209–21.

Wong, LP. "Data Analysis in Qualitative Research: A Brief Guide to Using NVivo." *Malaysian Family Physician* 3, no. 1 (2008): 14.

Yuval-Davis, Nira. "Women, Citizenship and Difference." *Feminist Review* 57 (Autumn 1997): 4–27.

Zaatari, Zeina. "No Democracy without Women's Equality: Middle East and North Africa." In *Conflict Prevention and Peace Forum*. Waterloo, Ontario, Canada: Social Science Research Council, 2015.

Reports and Scholarly Papers

Amnesty International. "Iraq: Systematic Torture of Political Prisoners." London: Amnesty International, 2001.

Amnesty International. "Ongoing Hunger Strikes Spotlights Rights Abuses in Tunisia." London: Amnesty International, October 29, 2010.

Baltic Media Centre, Index on Censorship, Institute for War & Peace Reporting, and International Media Support. "A New Voice in the Middle East: A Provisional Needs Assessment for the Iraqi Media." Svaneke, Denmark: Baltic Media Centre, 2003.

Basham, Patrick. "Can Iraq Be Democratic?" Text. Policy Analysis No. 505. Washington, DC: Cato Institute, 2004. http://www.cato.org/publications/policy-analysis/can-iraq-be-democratic-0.

Beccalli, Andrea. "The Internet and Freedom of Expression in Iraq." Paris: Internews Europe; United Nations Educational, Scientific and Cultural Organization, November 2012.

Borovsky, Gabriella and Asma Ben Yahia. "Women's Political Participation in Tunisia after the Revolution." Washington, DC: National Democratic Institute for International Affairs, May 2012.

Castillejo, Clare and Helen Tilley. "The Road to Reform: Women's Political Voice in Morocco." London: Overseas Development Institute, April 21, 2015.

Cherif, Nedra. "Tunisian Women in Politics: From Constitution Makers to Electoral Contenders." FRIDE Norwegian Ministry of Foreign Affairs, Norway, November 2014.

Davidson, Christopher. "ISIS and the Iraq War: Regional and International Dimensions." CNN iReport. Washington, DC: CNN, June 21, 2014.

Davis, Eric. "Strategies for Promoting Democracy in Iraq." Special Report. Washington, DC: United States Institute of Peace, October 2005.

Development Progress. "Progress on Women's Political Empowerment in Morocco." London: Overseas Development Institute, April 2015.

Dietrich, Luisa and Simone E. Carter. "Gender and Conflict Analysis in ISIS Affected Communities of Iraq." Oxford, UK: OXFAM International, May 2017.

The GlobalEconomy.com "Iran—Women in Politics, Female Parliament Members." TheGlobalEconomy.com. Accessed August 5, 2013. http://www.theglobaleconomy.com/Iran/indicator-SG.GEN.PARL.ZS/.

The GlobalEconomy.com "Iraq—Women in Politics, Female Parliament Members." TheGlobalEconomy.com, 2012. http://www.theglobaleconomy.com/Iraq/indicator-SG.GEN.PARL.ZS/.

The GlobalEconomy.com "Jordan—Women in Politics, Female Parliament Members." TheGlobalEconomy.com, 2012. http://www.theglobaleconomy.com/Jordan/indicator-SG.GEN.PARL.ZS/.

The GlobalEconomy.com "Lebanon—Women in Politics, Female Parliament Members." TheGlobalEconomy.com, 2012. http://www.theglobaleconomy.com/Lebanon/indicator-SG.GEN.PARL.ZS/.

The GlobalEconomy.com "Sudan—Women in Politics, Female Parliament Members." TheGlobalEconomy.com, 2012. http://www.theglobaleconomy.com/Sudan/indicator-SG.GEN.PARL.ZS/.

The GlobalEconomy.com "USA Women in Parliament." TheGlobalEconomy.com, 2012. http://www.theglobaleconomy.com/USA/Women_in_parliament/.

Global Media Monitoring Project. "Initial GMMP Findings Show Almost No Improvement in Women's Visibility." Mexico City, Mexico: Global Media Monitoring Project, June 1, 2015. http://whomakesthenews.org/articles/initial-gmmp-findings-show-almost-no-improvement-in-women-s-visibility.

GlobalSecurity.org. "Lebanon (Civil War 1975–1991)." Accessed May 23, 2014. http://www.globalsecurity.org/military/world/war/lebanon.htm.

Human Rights Office of the High Commissioner for Human Rights. "Report on Human Rights in Iraq: July–December 2012." Baghdad: United Nations Assistance Mission for Iraq, 2013.

Human Rights Watch. "At a Crossroads: Human Rights in Iraq Eight Years after the US-Led Invasion." New York: Human Rights Watch, February 21, 2011. https://www.hrw.org/report/2011/02/21/crossroads/human-rights-iraq-eight-years-after-us-led-invasion.

Human Rights Watch. "Background on Women's Status in Iraq Prior to the Fall of the Saddam Government." New York: Human Rights Watch, November 2003.

Human Rights Watch. "Iraq: New Guidelines Silence Media." Baghdad: Human Rights Watch, July 3, 2014. https://www.hrw.org/news/2014/07/03/iraq-new-guidelines-silence-media.

Hussein, Nahid. "Iraqi Parliament Set to Strengthen Its Oversight of National Budget." United Nations Development Program. November 16, 2014. http://www.iq.undp.org/content/iraq/en/home/presscenter/pressreleases/2014/11/16/workshop-to-support-the-iraqi-parliament-on-the-management-revision-and-the-analysis-of-the-of-the-national-budget/.

Inglis, Shelly, Maha Muna, Aina Iiyambo, Vina Nadjibulla, Lee Waldorf, and Anne Marie Goetz. "CEDAW and Security Council Resolution 1325: A Quick Guide." New York: United Nations Development Fund for Women, 2006.

International Crisis Group. "Deja vu All over Again: Iraq's Escalating Political Crisis." Middle East Report. Baghdad: International Crisis Group, July 30, 2012.

International Crisis Group. "Iraq's Secular Opposition: The Rise and Decline of Al-Iraqiya." Brussels: International Crisis Group, July 31, 2012.

International Labour Organization. "ILOSTAT Database." May 22, 2014. http://www.ilo.org/ilostat/faces/home/statisticaldata;jsessionid=p5LQT2hQKBrFxkNwmJ31YwxvGv2fWNnhHzy4TgsLcxfZsDy3Jh0j!1924909119?_afrLoop=893768200015683#%40%3F_afrLoop%3D893768200015683%26_adf.ctrl-state%3D10o0l63mzc_4.

International Telecommunications Union. "The World in 2015: ICT Facts & Figures." Geneva: International Telecommunications Union, 2015.

Katzman, Kenneth. "Iraq: Politics, Governance, and Human Rights." Washington, DC: Congressional Research Service, October 29, 2014.

Meier, Petra, and Emanuela Lombardo. "Towards a New Theory on the Symbolic Representation of Women." Rochester, NY: Social Science Research Network, 2010. http://papers.ssrn.com/abstract=1643961.

Mithaq. "The Charter of Cooperation between Public Authorities and NGOs for the Development of Iraqi Society." Iraqicharter.org, April 2013. http://iraqicharter.org/en/.

Na'im, Abdullahi an-. "Forced Marriage." Commissioned white paper, Department of International Law, Emory University, Atlanta, Georgia, 2000.

Nauphal, Naila. "Women and Other War-Affected Groups in Post-War Lebanon." *Gender and Armed Conflicts: Challenges for Decent Work, Gender Equality and Peace Building Agendas and Programs*, 57–62. Focus Program on Crisis Response and Reconstruction, Working paper 2. Geneva: Recovery and Reconstruction Department, 2001.

Norris, Pippa, and Mona Lena Krook. "One of Us: Multilevel Models Examining the Impact of Descriptive Representation on Civic Engagement." Social Science Research Network (SSRN) Scholarly Paper. Rochester, NY: Social Science Research Network, 2009. http://papers.ssrn.com/abstract=1451149.

Ohman, Magnus. "Political Finance and the Equal Participation of Women in Tunisia: A Situation Analysis." The Hague, The Netherlands: Netherlands Institute for Multiparty Democracy, 2016.

Pina, Aaron D. "Women in Iraq: Background and Issues for US Policy." CRS Report for Congress. Washington, DC: Congressional Research Service, The Library of Congress, March 13, 2006.

quotaProject: Global Database of Quotas for Women. "About Quotas | quotaProject: Global Database of Quotas for Women." Accessed October 5, 2013. http://www.quotaproject.org/aboutQuotas.cfm.

quotaProject: Global Database of Quotas for Women. "South Sudan." 2014. http://www.quotaproject.org/uid/countryview.cfm?id=253.

quotaProject: Global Database of Quotas for Women. "Sudan." 2014. http://www.quotaproject.org/uid/countryview.cfm?CountryCode=SD.

Rahbani, Leila Nicolas. "Women in Arab Media: Present but Not Heard." California: Stanford University Press, 2010.

Schwindt-Bayer, Leslie A., and William Mishler. "The Nexus of Representation: An Integrated Model of Women's Representation." American Political Science Association (ASPA), August 2002.

Thomson Reuters Foundation. "Reuters Foundation Alertnet.org Iran." 2013. http://www.trust.org/country/iran/.

Transparency International. "Corruption by Country Profiles—Iraq." 2013. http://www.transparency.org/country#IRQ.

United Nations Development Program, Arab Fund for Economic and Social Development. "Arab Human Development Report 2002: Creating Opportunities for Future Generations." New York: United Nations Development Program, 2002.

United Nations Office for the Coordination of Humanitarian Affairs (UNOCHA). "Humanitarian Bulletin: Middle East and North Africa." UNOCHA, February 2014.

United Nations Office of the Iraq Program. "Oil-for-Food: About the Program." United Nations, November 4, 2003. http://www.un.org/Depts/oip/background/.

United States Agency for International Development (USAID). "Iraq—Complex Emergency." Washington, DC: USAID, November 3, 2017.

United States Government Accountability Office. "Report to Congressional Committees: Rebuilding Iraq: US Assistance for the January 2005 Elections." Washington, DC: United States Government Accountability Office, September 7, 2005.

UN Women. "Iraq—Women, War, and Peace." 2007.

UN Women. "With Some Electoral Gains in Iraq, Women Candidates Work towards Change." *headQuarters*, May 16, 2014. http://www.unwomen.org/en/news/stories/2013/5/with-some-electoral-gains-in-iraq-women-candidates-work-towards-change.

UN Women. "Women in Iraq Factsheet." United Nations, 2013. http://www.jauiraq.org/documents/1864/Woman-Factsheet.pdf.

UN Women. "Women in Power and Decision-Making: Strengthening Voices for Democracy." *headQuarters*, June 27, 2014. http://www.unwomen.org/en/news/stories/2014/6/women-in-power-and-decision-making.

Unrepresented Nations and Peoples Organization. "Election Observation Mission Report." The Hague, The Netherlands: Unrepresented Nations and Peoples Organization, July 2014.

US Department of State. "Iraqi Women under Saddam's Regime: A Population Silenced." March 20, 2003. http://2001–2009.state.gov/g/wi/rls/18877.htm.

US Energy Information Administration. "Country Analysis Brief: Iraq." Washington, DC: US Energy Information Administration, January 30, 2015.

Walk Free. "Forced Child Marriage in Iraq." *Arab Human Rights Academy*, April 30, 2014. http://www.walkfree.org/iraq-child-marriage/.

World Bank, The. "Middle East and North Africa—Middle East and North Africa : Gender Equality and Empowerment." Accessed June 26, 2013. http://go.worldbank.org/PWOKKK10B0.

Zuhur, Sherifa D. "Iraq, Women's Empowerment, and Public Policy." Carlisle, PA: Army War College, Strategic Studies Institute, 2006.

Online Articles

Abadi, Haider al-. "Iraq Will Remain United." *The New York Times*. October 18, 2017, sec. Opinion Editorials. https://www.nytimes.com/2017/10/18/opinion/iraq-will-remain-united.html.

Abu-Lughod, Lila. "Do Muslim Women Need Saving?" *Time*. November 1, 2013. http://ideas.time.com/2013/11/01/do-muslim-women-need-saving/.

Administrator. "Iraq: Women's Rights in Iraq Compromised: Women Reclaiming and Redefining Cultures." *The Middle East Times.* July 13, 2006. http://www.wluml.org/node/3086.

Administrator. "Iraqi Officials Confirm Saddam's Execution." *CRI News.* December 30, 2006. http://english.cri.cn/2947/2006/12/30/189@179166.htm.

Administrator. "Magda Tamimi: 2015 Budget and Fake like Formulated in Another World." *All Iraq News.* January 21, 2015. http://iraqidinarchat.net/?p=32904.

Administrator. "Magda Tamimi: 2015 Budget Will Reduce the Level of Corruption." *Al-Baghdadia News.* December 21, 2014. http://iraqdinar.us/magda-tamimi-2015-budget-2/.

Administrator. "Widespread Corruption Paralyses Investment in Iraq, MP Forms Committee." Parliament. *Iraq Parliament Guide*, November 20, 2012. http://www.iraqiparliament.info/en/node/1516.

Adnkronos International. "Iraq: Appeal for a Solution to Rising Suicide Rate Among Women." *Adnkronos International.* May 26, 2017. http://www1.adnkronos.com/AKI/English/Security/?id=1.0.2197664177.

AFP. "Al-Sadr Ministers Leave Government." *Taipei Times.* April 17, 2007. http://www.taipeitimes.com/News/front/archives/2007/04/17/2003356980.

AFP. "Iraq Ration Card Reform Sparks Anger." *Breitbart.* November 12, 2012. http://www.breitbart.com/news/cng-31155d745f32809d18cd13234c1f32c4-2a1/.

AFP. "World Leaders Hail Iraq Vote." *Theage.com.* January 31, 2005, sec. Features. http://www.theage.com.au/news/Iraq/World-leaders-hail-Iraq-vote/2005/01/31/1107020303303.html.

Ahmad, Laila. "Palestinian Refugees Calling for Help." *NSNBC International.* June 9, 2012. http://nsnbc.me/2012/06/11/palestinian-refugees-calling-for-help/.

Ajbaili, Mustapha. "How ISIS Conquered Social Media." *Al-Arabiya News.* June 24, 2014. http://ara.tv/wxs4f.

Allam, Hannah. "Complicated Quota System Helps Put Iraqi Women in Parliament." *McClatchy DC.* March 23, 2010, sec. World. http://www.mcclatchydc.com/2010/03/23/90932_complicated-quota-system-helps.html?rh=1.

All Iraq News. "Safia al-Suhail—First Woman Ambassador to Iraq in Jordan." *All Iraq News.* October 30, 2015, sec. Political. http://www.alliraqnews.com/modules/news/article.php?storytopic=41&storyid=19610.

Alwaght News and Analysis. "Iraq Irked by Saudi Envoy's Provocations, Meddling." *Alwaght News & Analysis.* June 19, 2016. http://alwaght.com/en/News/58183/Iraq-Irked-by-Saudi-Envoy's-Provocations,-Meddling.

Ashraf News. "MP Al-Jaf to Ashraf News: Supporting the MKO Terrorist Organization Has Political Reasons." *Ashraf News.* July 29, 2016. http://www.ashraf-news.com/en/3510/MP-AlJaf-to-Ashraf-News-supporting-the-MKO-terrorist-organization-has-political-reasons.

Assir, Serene. "Invisible Lives: Iraqis in Lebanon." *Assyrian International News Agency.* April 9, 2007. http://www.aina.org/news/2007049133807.htm.

Associated Free Press. "'We Can't Walk Freely.'" *News24*. September 27, 2005. http://www.news24.com/World/News/We-cant-walk-freely-20050924.

Associated Press. "Iraqis Eyeing Bahrain Protests with Anger, Caution." *Associated Press*. March 17, 2011. http://www.foxnews.com/world/2011/03/17/iraq-shiites-rally-saudi-troops-bahrain/.

Awsat, Asharq al-. "Baghdad Questions Tillerson's Remarks on PMF, Brands them Meddling in Internal Affairs." *Asharq al-Awsat*. October 23, 2017. https://aawsat.com/english/home/article/1061201/baghdad-questions-tillerson's-remarks-pmf-brands-them-meddling-internal-affairs.

Baghdadiabian. "Majida al-Tamimi: Because the Ministry of Finance to His Predecessor Percent Salary and Loans Is out of Cash in a Bank and Rafidain." *Baghdadiabian News*. September 18, 2012. http://www.dinarrecaps.com/iraqi-news-recaps/majida-al-tamimi-because-the-ministry-of-finance-to-his-predecessor-percent-salary-and-loans-is-out-of-cash-in-a-bank-and-rafidain.

Baghdad Post, The. "Abadi to Oust Corruption Parties after Liberating Iraq from ISIS." *The Baghdad Post*. August 17, 2017. http://www.thebaghdadpost.com/en/story/15815/Abadi-to-oust-corruption-parties-after-liberating-Iraq-from-ISIS-MP.

Baghdad Post, The. "Hanan Fatlawi: Mullah's New tool to Fracture Iraq." *The Baghdad Post*. October 10, 2017. http://www.thebaghdadpost.com/en/story/18063/Hanan-Fatlawi-Mullah-s-new-tool-to-fracture-Iraq.

Baghdad Post, The. "KDP: Accusing Us of Cooperating with Turkey Is Political Bankruptcy." *The Baghdad Post*. April 27, 2017. http://www.thebaghdadpost.com/cn/story/9853/KDP-Accusing-us-of-cooperating-with-Turkey-is-political-bankruptcy.

Baghdad Post, The. "MP Says Sectarian Iraqi Constitution Must Be Burned." *The Baghdad Post*. October 26, 2017. http://www.thebaghdadpost.com/en/story/18762/Video-MP-says-sectarian-Iraqi-constitution-must-be-burned.

BBC. "Shot Iraq Council Member Dies." *BBC*. September 25, 2003, sec. Middle East. http://news.bbc.co.uk/2/hi/middle_east/3131424.stm.

BBC News. "Iraq's Women Scientists." *BBC*. September 22, 2004, sec. Middle East. http://news.bbc.co.uk/2/hi/middle_east/3679040.stm.

BBC News. "Profile: Iraq's 'Mrs Anthrax.'" *BBC*. September 22, 2004, sec. Middle East. http://news.bbc.co.uk/2/hi/middle_east/3002103.stm.

Bennett, Brian, and Michael Weisskopf. "The Sum of Two Evils." *Time*. May 25, 2003. http://www.time.com/time/magazine/article/0,9171,454453,00.html.

Berwani, Hawar. "MP Jawari Survives Assassination." *Iraqi News*. January 31, 2013. http://www.iraqinews.com/iraq-war/urgent-mp-jawari-survives-assassination/.

Bradley, Matt. "Iraqi Parliament Breaks Deadlock to Elect Speaker: Election Marks Small Step Toward Resolving Leadership Impasse." *Wall Street Journal*. July 15, 2014, sec. World. http://www.wsj.com/articles/iraqi-parliament-breaks-deadlock-to-elect-speaker-1405426884.

Bush, Sarah, and Amaney Jamal. "Does Western Pressure for Gender Equality Help?" *The Washington Post*. July 30, 2014. https://www.washingtonpost.com/news/monkey-cage/wp/2014/07/30/does-western-pressure-for-gender-equality-help/.

CBS News. "Diverse Iraqi Women Seek Political Parity." *CBSNews*. March 3, 2010. http://www.cbsnews.com/news/diverse-iraqi-women-seek-political-parity/.

Chomani, Farhad. "ISIS War Fuels Steep Rise in Number of Widows in Iraq." *Rudaw*. April 19, 2015. http://rudaw.net/english/middleeast/iraq/190420151.

Chulov, Martin. "More than 92% of Voters in Iraqi Kurdistan Back Independence." *The Guardian*. September 27, 2017. https://www.theguardian.com/world/2017/sep/27/over-92-of-iraqs-kurds-vote-for-independence.

Ciezadlo, Annia. "Iraqi Women Raise Voices—for Quotas." *Christian Science Monitor*, December 17, 2003. http://www.csmonitor.com/2003/1217/p01s02-woiq.html.

Constable, Pamela. "Iraqi Women Decry Move to Cut Rights." *The Washington Post*. January 16, 2004. https://www.washingtonpost.com/archive/politics/2004/01/16/iraqi-women-decry-move-to-cut-rights/74decc2e-6724-470e-b521-8df09ec30fd2/.

Cross, George. "George Galloway Interview." *The Independent on Sunday*, 2003. Accessed September 8, 2015. https://www.independent.co.uk/news/uk/politics/generalelection/george-galloway-interview-you-are-here-because-you-want-to-find-something-to-attack-me-with-10219504.html.

Dearden, Lizzie. "Former US Military Adviser David Kilcullen Says There Would Be No ISIS without Iraq Invasion." *The Independent*. March 4, 2016. http://www.independent.co.uk/news /world/middle-east/iraq-war-invasion-caused-isis-islamic-state-daesh-saysus-military-adviser-david-kilcullen-a6912236.html.

Dinar Guru Recap. "Majida Al-Tamimi: The Real Budget Deficit 53 Trillion Dinars." *Dinar Guru Recap*. August 26, 2015. http://www.dinargururecap.com/2015/08/majida-al-tamimi-the-real-budget-deficit-53-trillion-dinars/.

Dinar Speculator. "The Claim of Kurdistan Issued Arrest Warrants against 11 Individuals, Including Qais Al-Khazali and Hanan Al-Fatlawi." *Dinar Speculator*. October 23, 2017. http://www.dinarspeculator.com/showthread.php/82975-The-claim-of-Kurdistan-issued-arrest-warrants-against-11-individuals-including-Qais-al-Khazali-and-Hanan-al-Fatlawi.

Dinar Updates. "Alaa Talabani Reveal the Nature of the Relationship between Israel and the Iraqi Kurd." *Dinar Updates*. September 5, 2016. http://www.dinarupdates.com/showthread.php?40322-Alaa-Talabani-reveal-the-nature-of-the-relationship-between-Israel-and-the-Iraqi-Kurd.

Dinarvets. "Majda al-Tamimi Threatened to Disclose Private Financial Oversight Reports Corrupt Ministries." *Iraqi Dinar News*. October 30, 2012. http://dinarvets.com/forums/index.php?/topic/132588-majda-al-tamimi-threatened-to-disclose-private-financial-oversight-reports-corrupt-ministries/.

Epstein, Susan B., Nina M. Serafino, and Francis T. Miko. "Democracy Promotion: Cornerstone of US Foreign Policy?" CRS Report for Congress. Washington, DC: Congressional Research Service, December 26, 2007, https://fas.org/sgp/crs/row/RL34296.pdf

Forat, al- News Agency. "MP Jawari Demands IHEC to Repeat Sorting and Counting of Salah Il-Din Polling." May 25, 2014. http://en.alforatnews.com/modules/news/article.php?storyid=7645.

Forat, al- News Agency. "Maliki's Advisor Expects Holding Wide Alliances after Elections." Accessed February 14, 2015. http://en.alforatnews.com/modules/news/article.php?storyid=3512.

Forat, al- News Agency. "MP Demands Residents of Areas under Occupation of ISIL to Help in Liberating Their Areas." *Alforat News*. February 3, 2015. http://en.alforatnews.com/modules/news/article.php?storyid=15755.

Foust, Joshua, and Melinda Haring. "Who Cares How Many Women Are in Parliament?" *Democracy Lab*, June 25, 2012. http://foreignpolicy.com/2012/06/25/who-cares-how-many-women-are-in-parliament/.

Ghad, al- Press. "Majida Al-Tamimi Talks about a 'Month Period' Regarding the Dismissal of the Electoral Commission." *Al-Ghad Press*. May 13, 2017. https://search4dinar.wordpress.com/2017/05/13/majida-al-tamimi-talks-about-a-month-period-regarding-the-dismissal-of-the-electoral-commission/.

Ghad, al- Press. "Parliament Is Campaigning to Amend the Law of Rafha and Pay the Dues of Martyrs and Displaced People." *Al-Ghad Press*. July 30, 2017. https://www.alghadpress.com/news/11683.

Glenewinkel, Klaas. "Role of women and religion in the Constitution." *Niqash*. July 18, 2005, sec. Politics. http://www.niqash.org/en/articles/society/691/.

Gordon, Eleana. "Our Friend in the Gallery: Safia Al-Suhail and the New Iraq." *National Review Online*. February 4, 2005. http://www.nationalreview.com/articles/213575/our-friend-gallery/eleana-gordon.

Haddad, Fanar. "Iraq Elections: Marred by Corruption?" *Al-Jazeera*. April 26, 2014. http://www.aljazeera.com/indepth/opinion/2014/04/iraq-elections-marred-corruptio-201442116043642713.html.

Haitami, Meriem El. "Women in Morocco: Political and Religious Power." *50.50: Gender, Sexuality and Social Justice*, January 31, 2013, sec. Gender Politics Religion, https://opendemocracy.net/5050/meriem-el-haitami/women-in-morocco-political-and-religious-power.

Hamoudi, Haider Ala. "Decision 88: Balance of Power under the Iraq Constitution." *Jurist*. March 18, 2011, sec. Opinion Editorials. http://jurist.org/forum/2011/03/decision-88-checks-and-balances-in-iraq.php.

Hunt, S. and C. Posa. "Where Are the Women in the New Iraq?" *Boston Globe*. June 22, 2004.

Hussein, Ahmed. "Fatlawi Withdraws from Presidency Race—Iraqi News." *Iraqi News*. July 24, 2014. http://www.iraqinews.com/baghdad-politics/fatlawi-withdraws-from-presidency-race/.

Hussein, Ahmed. "IS MP Calls Maliki to Reveal Involved Officials in Terrorist Actions." *Iraqi News*. May 24, 2013. http://www.iraqinews.com/baghdad-politics/is-mp-calls-maliki-to-reveal-involved-officials-in-terrorist-actions/.

Hussein, Ahmed. "Meetings among Political Leaders to Settle Crisis, Says MP." *Iraqi News*. July 21, 2012. http://www.iraqinews.com/baghdad-politics/meetings-among-political-leaders-to-settle-crisis-says-mp/.

Hussein, Ahmed. "MP Reveals Corrupt Contractors Associated to Maliki's Office." *Iraqi News*. June 13, 2013. http://www.iraqinews.com/baghdad-politics/mp-reveals-corrupt-contractors-associated-to-maliki-s-office/.

iKNOW Politics. "Ala Talabani." December 11, 2013. http://iknowpolitics.org/en/knowledge-library/interview/ala-talabani.

Institute for Inclusive Security. "Ala Talabani." *Search for Women Peace Experts*, March 2006. http://www.inclusivesecurity.org/network-bio/ala-talabani/.

Institute for Inclusive Security. "Zakia Hakki." Washington, DC: Institute for Inclusive Security, May 2006. https://www.inclusivesecurity.org/network-bio/zakia-hakki/.

I.Q.D. Team Connection, The. "Deputy Reveals a Proposal to Pay the Salaries of Editors from the Grip of Dahesh." *The I.Q.D. Team Connection*. June 29, 2017. http://www.theiqdteam.com/blog/deputy-reveals-a-proposal-to-pay-the-salaries-of-editors-from-the-grip-of-dahesh.

I.Q.D. Team Connection, The. "Majida Al-Tamimi: Ground Is Prepared for the Process of Lifting the Zeros from the Currency in 2013." *Voice of Iraq*. December 15, 2012. http://www.theiqdteamconnection.com/iraq-news/majida-al-tamimi-ground-is-prepared-for-the-process-of-lifting-the-zeros-from-the-currency-in-2013.

Iraq Directory. "Iraq Fails to Attract Domestic Capitals." *Iraq Directory*. January 1, 2014. http://www.iraqdirectory.com/en/print.aspx?sid=25947.

Iraq TradeLink. "Hopes to Open Treibel Route with Jordan." *Iraq TradeLink*. May 22, 2016. http://www.iraqtradelinknews.com/2016/05/hopes-to-open-treibel-outlet-with-jordan.html.

Iraq TradeLink. "No Extra Fees on Jordanian Exports to Iraq." *Iraq TradeLink*. August 11, 2016. http://www.iraqtradelinknews.com/2016/08/no-extra-fees-on-jordanian-exports-to.html.

Jawad, Layth. "Iraqi Minister Dismisses Claims of Female Prisoner Abuse." *Al-Monitor*. December 5, 2012. http://www.al-monitor.com/pulse/fa/politics/2012/12/iraqi-politicians-dismiss-female-prisoner-abuse-charges.html.

Jazeera, al-. "Iraq's Former President Jalal Talabani Dead." *Al-Jazeera*. October 3, 2017. http://www.aljazeera.com/news/2017/10/iraq-president-jalal-talabani-dead-171003140521896.html.

Jazeera, al-. "Protests in Iraq Continue amid New Killings." *Al-Jazeera*. February 22, 2013. http://www.aljazeera.com/news/middleeast/2013/02/2013222124151982737.html.

Khalil, Ashraf. "Women Call for Equal Representation in Iraq." *Womens eNews*. February 6, 2004, sec. Politics & Influence. http://womensenews.org/story/the-world/040206/women-call-equal-representation-iraq#.UtwyLbTTmUk.

Klein, Naomi. "Baghdad Year Zero: Pillaging Iraq in Pursuit of a Neocon Utopia." *Harper's Magazine*. September 2004.

Latif, Nizar. "Iraqis Step up Protest in Job and Food Crisis." *The National*. February 6, 2011, sec. World. http://www.thenational.ae/news/world/middle-east/iraqis-step-up-protest-in-job-and-food-crisis.

Latif, Nizar. "Sultan Hashim's Death Sentence Underscores Iraq's Deep Divisions." *The National*. July 23, 2011, sec. World. http://www.thenational.ae/news/world/middle-east/sultan-hashims-death-sentence-underscores-iraqs-deep-divisions.

Lejeune, Pauline. "FairVote.org | Iraq's 2010 Parliamentary Election—Part 4: Iraqi Women's Political Reality." *FairVote*. March 22, 2010. http://fairvote.org/iraq-s-2010-parliamentary-election4.

Lucas, Scott. "Essential Guide: The Battle for Kirkuk in Northern Iraq." *EA Worldview*. October 18, 2017. http://eaworldview.com/2017/10/why-is-there-a-battle-for-kirkuk-in-northern-iraq/.

Mada, al-. "Constitution Update." *Al-Mada News*. June 2, 2005. http://iraqthemodel.blogspot.com/2005/06/constitution-update.html.

Mail Online. "What Are the UN Sanctions on Iraq?" *Mail Online*. 2013. http://www.dailymail.co.uk/news/article-180046/What-UN-sanctions-Iraq.html.

Malazada, Ibrahim. "Iraq's Kurds Question Motives behind Independence Vot." *Iraqi Economists Network*. June 27, 2017. http://iraqieconomists.net/en/2017/06/29/iraqs-kurds-question-motives-behind-independence-vote-by-ibrahim-malazada/.

Malsin, Jared. "Iraqi Prime Minister Haider Al-Abadi Says the End Is Nigh for 'Fake' Islamic State." *Time*. June 29, 2017. http://time.com/4839617/mosul-isis-mosque-haider-al-abadi/.

Mamoun, Abdelhak. "MP Hanan Al-Fatlawi Survives Assassination Attempt upon Return from Salahuddin." *Iraqi News*. March 10, 2015. http://www.iraqinews.com/features/mp-hanan-al-fatlawi-survive-assassination-attempt-upon-return-salahuddin/.

Michaels, Jim. "Iraq's Female Lawmakers Make Strides." *USA Today*, October 27, 2008. http://usatoday30.usatoday.com/news/world/iraq/2008-10-26-iraqwomen_N.htm.

Mitchell, Andrea. "Iraq Diaspora Is 'Humanitarian Crisis.'" *Msnbc.com*. March 21, 2007. http://www.nbcnews.com/id/17726836/ns/nbcnightlynews/t/report-iraq-diaspora-humanitarian-crisis/.

Mohammed, Kareem." International Support for Women Economic Endeavour." Iraqi Programs File. *IraqHurr.org*, August 2, 2012, http://www.iraqhurr.org/content/article/24477362.html.

Mubarak, Jenan. "ICWRE." *Iraqi Center for Women Rehabilitation & Employment*, 2007. http://icwre.org/default_en.aspx.

Mustafa, Hamza. "Iraq: Army Advances as Al-Qaeda Militants Open New Fronts." *Asharq al-Awsat*. February 22, 2014, sec. Middle East. http://www.aawsat.net/2014/02/article55329244/iraq-army-advances-as-al-qaeda-militants-open-new-fronts.

Naji, Zainab. "Baghdad Awaits New Security Plan." *International Relations and Security Network*. February 12, 2007. http://www.isn.ethz.ch/Digital-Library/Articles/Detail/?lng=en&id=52914.

Naji, Zainab. "Iraq's Jobless Female Students Losing Hope." *Middle East Online*. April 25, 2008. http://www.middle-east-online.com/english/?id=25568.

Naji, Zainab. "Will Iraq's New Quota System Give Women More Political Power?" *Alternet*. January 24, 2009. http://www.ora.tv/homepage/2015/12/15/1.

Naji, Zainab. "Women's Rights Candidate Keen to Make Impact." *Institute for War and Peace Reporting)*. March 5, 2010. http://www.ecoi.net/local_link/135064/235149_en.html.

Naji, Zainab. "Women Set to Take More Power Locally." *Institute for War and Peace Reporting*, January 20, 2009. https://iwpr.net/global-voices/women-set-take-more-power-locally.

Najm, Haider. "Electoral Commission Inquiry Not 'Political Revenge' MPs Say." *Niqash*. April 21, 2011. http://www.niqash.org/en/articles/politics/2824/.

National Democratic Institute. "National Platform for Women Launched in Lead up to Iraqi Elections." February 23, 2010. https://www.ndi.org/National_Platform_for_Women_Launched.

Nobel Women's Initiative. "Shirin Ebadi—Nobel Women's Initiative." *Meet the Laureates*, 2003. http://nobelwomensinitiative.org/meet-the-laureates/shirin-ebadi/.

OCHA. "Iraq Drafts First Policy on Civil Society." Text. *ReliefWeb*. September 16, 2012. http://reliefweb.int/report/iraq/iraq-drafts-first-policy-civil-society.

O'Leary, Brendan, and David Bateman. "Article 140: Iraq's Constitution, Kirkuk and the Disputed Territories." Washington, DC, 2008.

Omar, Oumayma. "Iraq's Children, a Generation Deprived of Education." *The Arab Weekly*. July 31, 2016. http://www.thearabweekly.com/Opinion/5952/Iraq's-children,-a-generation-deprived-of-education.

Otterman, Sharon. "IRAQ: The Interim Government Leaders." *Council on Foreign Relations*. June 2, 2004. http://www.cfr.org/iraq/iraq-interim-government-leaders/p7664.

Rasheed, Ahmed and Raya Jalabi. "Iraqi Court Rules Kurdish Independence Vote Unconstitutional. *Reuters*. November 20, 2017. https://www.reuters.com/article/us-mideast-crisis-iraq-kurds/iraqi-court-rules-kurdish-independence-vote-unconstitutional-idUSKBN1DK0Q6.

Reid, Robert H. "Sunni Leader Open to Coalition Government." *The Guardian*. December 19, 2005, sec. World Latest. https://web.archive.org/web/20051219104151/ http://www.guardian.co.uk/worldlatest/story/0,1280,-5485174,00.html.

Reuters. "Baghdad to Exclude Oil Firms with KRG Deals." *TradeArabia*. November 15, 2007. http://www.tradearabia.com/news/OGN_133962.html.

Rubin, Alissa J., and Asmaa Waguih. "Fighting to Preserve Women's Rights in Iraq." *Los Angeles Times*. August 7, 2005. http://articles.latimes.com/2005/aug/07/world/fg-women7.

rudaw.net. "Baghdad Sells Kirkuk's Oil as It Stalls Article 140." *Ekurd Daily*. June 3, 2012. http://ekurd.net/mismas/articles/misc2012/6/kirkuk739.htm.

SafeDinar.com. "Iraqi Ambassador Hails Jordan's Economic Support." *SafeDinar.com*. March 2, 2016. https://www.safedinar.com/news/article/iraqi-ambassador-hails-jordans-economic-support/.

Santana, Rebecca. "At Least 17 Killed as Iraq Voting Begins." *Huffington Post*. May 4, 2010. http://www.huffingtonpost.com/2010/03/04/at-least-17-killed-as-ira_n_485398.html.

Schmidt, Michael S., and Yasir Ghazi. "Iraqi Women Feel Sidelined Despite Parliament Quota—NYTimes.com." *The New York Times*, March 12, 2011. http://www.nytimes.com/2011/03/13/world/middleeast/13baghdad.html?_r=0.

Semple, Kirk. "US Makes Largest Move into Shiite District since 2004." *The New York Times*. March 4, 2007, sec. International/Middle East. http://www.nytimes.com/2007/03/04/world/middleeast/04cnd-iraq.html.

Serrano, Alvaro, and Janet Jensen. "Adult Education Offers New Opportunities and Options to Iranian Women." *UNFPA News*. March 7, 2006. http://www.ungei.org/infobycountry/iran_550.html.

Shafaaq. "Haider Abadi Rejects a Request to Hanan Al-Fatlawi Belongs to the Participants in the Referendum." *Shafaaq*. September 27, 2017. http://www.shafaaq.com/ar/Ar_NewsReader/7057d106-ba98-46b7-9d6f-b913d642a48c.

Sharq, al-, al-Awsat Online. "The Archive." *Al-Sharq Al-Awsat Online*. October 29, 2006. http://archive.aawsat.com/default.asp.

Shawqi, Afrah. "Iraq: Nearly 3,000 female candidates expected in Parliament elections." *Asharq al-Awsat*. March 8, 2014. http://english.aawsat.com/2014/03/article55329789/iraq-nearly-3000-female-candidates-expected-in-parliament-elections.

Sherwani, Leyla H. "Iraq Spent $1,000 Billion in 13 Years, Wasting Most of It: MP." *BasNews*. January 8, 2017. http://www.basnews.com/index.php/en/reports/367725.

Singleton Press. "Iraq's Amnesty and De-Baathification Laws." *Dinar Recaps*. January 5, 2015. http://www.dinarrecaps.com/1/post/2015/01/iraqs-amnesty-and-de-baathification-laws-by-singleton-press.html.

SourceWatch. "Ala Talabani." *Center for Media and Democracy*. 2003. http://www.sourcewatch.org/index.php/Ala_Talabani.

SourceWatch. "Iraqi Media Network." *Center for Media and Democracy*. February 21, 2006. http://www.sourcewatch.org/index.php/Iraqi_Media_Network.

Staff Writer. "'Dark' Message from Al-Zawahiri's Wife Draws Condemnation in Iraq." *Mawtani Al-Shorfa.com*. June 19, 2012, sec. Terrorism. http://al-shorfa.com/en_GB/articles/meii/features/main/2012/06/19/feature-02?format=mobile.

Staff Writer. "Iraq Needs to Deter pro-Terrorism Countries, Says Obaidi." *Alforat News*. June 6, 2014. http://en.alforatnews.com/modules/news/article.php?storyid=8014.

Staff Writer. "Iraqi Parliament Elects New President." *Arab News Express*. July 24, 2014. http://arabpressreleases.qa/general/19607/iraqi-parliament-elects-new-president/.

Staff Writer. "Majida Al-Tamimi: Next June Will See the Distribution of Surplus Oil Revenues to the People." *Iraqi Gazette*. April 3, 2013. http://www.dinarspeculator.com/showthread.php?67433-Majida-al-Tamimi-next-June-will-see-the-distribution-of-surplus-oil-revenues-to-the-people.

Staff Writer. "Rights Group Condemns Iraq Trials." *Al-Jazeera English*. January 8, 2007. http://www.aljazeera.com/news/middleeast/2007/01/2008525143032353532.html.

Staff Writer. "Suhad Al-Obeidi Reveals the Agreement between Maliki and Najafi and Barzani to Postpone Parliamentary Elections." *Dinarvets.com*. October 13, 2013.

Stevenson, Struan. "Iraq's Revolution." *The Huffington Post*, June 16, 2014. http://www.huffingtonpost.co.uk/struan-stevenson-mep/iraqs-revolution_b_5491818.html.

Sūdānī, Ittiḥād al-Waṭanī lil-Shabāb al-. "Sudan People's Liberation Army, Sudan People's Liberation Movement, and IGAD Secretariat on Peace in the Sudan." *The Comprehensive Peace Agreement between the Government of the Republic of the Sudan and the Sudan People's Liberation Movement, Sudan People's Liberation Army*. National Federation of Sudanese Youth, 2005, https://fas.org/irp/world/para/spla.htm

Taie, Khalid al-. "Iraqi Ports Introduce Modern Inspection Equipment." *Mawtani Al-Shorfa.com*. January 31, 2014, sec. World. http://mawtani.al-shorfa.com/en_GB/articles/iii/features/2014/01/31/feature-01.

Taie, Khalid al-. "Public Buses Promote Iraqi Election Participation." *Mawtani Al-Shorfa.com*. February 28, 2014, sec. World. http://mawtani.al-shorfa.com/en_GB/articles/iii/features/2014/02/28/feature-01.

Tamimi, Aymenn Jawad al-. "No confidence in Maliki?" *The American Spectator*. June 19, 2012, sec. At Large. http://spectator.org/articles/35299/no-confidence-maliki.

Tarabay, Jamie. "Amid Iraq Turmoil, Kurds Seize Kirkuk, a Long Disputed Prize." *Al-Jazeera America*. June 12, 2014. http://america.aljazeera.com/articles/2014/6/12/rise-of-the-kurds.html.

Tarabay, Jamie. "Political Struggle for Kirkuk Intensifies." *NPR.org*. Washington, DC: National Public Radio, June 11, 2007. http://www.npr.org/templates/story/story.php?storyId=10931833.

Telegraph, The. "Aqila al-Hashimi." *The Telegraph*. September 26, 2003, sec. Obituaries. http://www.telegraph.co.uk/news/obituaries/1442475/Aqila-al-Hashimi.html.

Thawra, al- News. *al-Thawra News*, 1984. http://www.althawranews.net/.

UN News. "UN Security Council Eases Some Sanctions on Iraq over 1990 Invasion of Kuwait." *UN News Service Section*. June 27, 2013. http://www.un.org/apps/news/story.asp?NewsID=45287&Cr=iraq&Cr1=kuwait#.UtxghLTTmUl.

UN Office for the Coordination of Human Affairs. "Women's Rights Activists Increasingly Targeted by Militants." *IRIN Humanitarian News and Analysis*. July 24, 2007. http://www.irinnews.org/Report/73392/IRAQ-Women-s-rights-activists-increasingly-targeted-by-militants.

Windrem, Robert. "The World's Deadliest Women?" *NBC World News*, 2004.

Wolfowitz, Paul. "Women in the New Iraq." *The Washington Post*. February 1, 2004, sec. Opinion. http://2001-2009.state.gov/g/wi/28686.htm.

Zubaidi, Hassan Latif al-. "Why Iraq's Ration Card Can't Be Scrapped." *Niqash*. November 15, 2012. http://www.niqash.org/en/articles/economy/3156/.

Zurutuza, Karlos. "Iraqi Women Face Widespread Abuse and Discrimination." *Deutsche Welle*. September 30, 2012, sec. World. http://www.dw.de/iraqi-women-face-widespread-abuse-and-discrimination/a-15799850.

Index

Abass, S. 237
abayas 23, 194, 237
Abdul-Latif, W. 43
Abdullah, Thabit A. J. 236, 237, 239
Abu Hatem, Kareem Khalaf Muhammad 99
Afkhami, M. 50
Ahmadinejad, M. 51
Ahmed, H. 243
Ahmed, L. 236
Ahram, Ariel I. 271
Al Ahd 15
Alexander, Amy C. 84, 254, 255
al-Ali, Nadje Sadig 40, 42, 149, 231, 233, 234, 237, 241
al-Alousi, Manal Younis 67
al-Azzawi, Souad N. 240, 267, 269
al-Baghdadia TV 89–91, 94–6, 99, 102, 121–3, 125, 131, 132, 133, 135, 160, 161, 165, 169, 190, 200, 201, 204, 257
al-Bajari, Noura 94–8, 164, 212–13
al-Bakr, A. H. 23, 25, 129
al-Damaluji, M. 43
al-Douri, Etab 98–102, 143, 214
al-Dulaimi, N. 22, 32, 62
al-Fatlawi, Hanan 91, 102–5, 214–16
   constitutional reform 147
   gender quota 140
   media reports 200
   multinational intervention, Saddam 167
   NGOs 162
   Oil and Gas Law 156
al-Fayhaa TV 91, 129, 149, 153, 163, 168, 169
al-Furat (Shi'a) 190
al-Hashimi, A. 74, 200
al-Hurria (Kurdish) 190
al-Iraqiya TV 89, 90, 106, 108–14, 116, 126, 128, 136, 137, 138, 140, 152, 160, 161, 172, 188, 196, 200, 204
al-Ittihad al-Nisai (Women Union, 1949) 20

al-Jaf, A. 89, 106–8, 151, 152, 155, 156, 160, 162, 164, 167, 171, 177, 195, 200, 216–17
al-Jawaheri, H. 33, 241
al-Jawari, K. 108–13, 217–18
Al-Khafaji, S. 40–1, 244
al-Khufaji, S. 74
al-Khuzaai, Raja Habib 74
al-Khuzaiye, K. 115
Allawi, A. 43, 76, 77, 80, 95, 112, 123, 128
al-Maliki, N. 7, 51, 82, 91, 95, 97, 100, 102, 105, 108, 110, 112, 123, 125, 126, 127, 128, 133, 136, 138–9, 164, 172, 178, 192, 200, 210
Almaliky, Muhamed H. 276
al-Mara al-Haditha (Modern Woman, 1936) 20
Al-Marashi, I. 271, 272
al-Obaidi, S. 120–5, 218–19
al-Obeidi, J. 44
al-Qazzaz, A. 61, 249
al-Rawi, Ahmed K. 190, 257, 272
al-Rayyis, Mariam 125–8, 219–20
   Assembly of the Coalition Movement 163
   Resolution 137, 149
al-Rihab (1946) 20
al-Sabaah 90, 188
al-Sharifi, S. 74
al-Sharqiya (Sunni) 190
al-Sheikhli, A. 44
al-Suhail, S. 37, 42, 89, 91, 129–30, 149, 151, 153, 154, 157, 163, 164, 167, 168, 177, 201, 221
al-Sumariyya 190
al-Talabani, Alaa' 130–5, 162, 222–3
al-Tamimi, Layla Abd al-Latif 74–5
al-Tamimi, Majida 135–40, 223
al-Umm wa-l-Tifl (Mother and Child, 1946) 20
al-Zahawi, Asma' 16
Al-Zubaidi, L. 270

Ammash, Huda Salih Mahdi 71
American Bar Association 13
American National Democratic Institute (NDI) 80–1
Amnesty International 28, 56
Amos, D. 189, 272
Andreski, S. 178, 269
Arab Quota Report 9
Arab Spring 45, 49, 56, 166
Arnold, James R. 256
Atkeson, L. R. 186, 271, 275
attenuated autocracy 14
authenticity 5
authoritarianism 71
authoritarian paternalism 15

Ba'athist Party 21–4, 26, 28
  descriptive representation, during 1920–79 63–4
Ba'athist Provisional Constitution 2
Ba'athist regime 23–4, 63–4
Baban, M. 237
Baghdadia, al- television 89–91
  al-Bajari, Noura 94–6, 161, 165, 201
  al-Douri, Etab 99, 102, 160
  al-Obaidi, Suhad 120–3, 125, 169
  al-Talabani, Alaa' 131–3, 135, 165, 200
  al-Tamimi, Majida 139
Baldez, L. 37
Ballington, J. 2–3, 40, 231, 234, 244, 252, 253
Barwari, N. 42, 74, 75, 148
Barzani, M. 69, 110, 123, 125, 211, 216, 222
Basham, P. 37
Batatu, H. 15, 234, 235, 236, 237, 250, 268
Ben Ali, Zine El Abidine 55–6
Bint al-Rashid (al-Rashid's Daughter, 1948) 20
Bourdieu, P. 205, 270, 276
Bourguiba, H. 55
Bradley, M. 254
Bremer, L. Paul 41, 42, 73, 153
British invasion and colonization
  British-style governance 16
  constitutional monarchy 16
  Iraqi constitutions 1925–present 16–19
  Layla, Iraqi women's magazine 20
  Ottoman reforms 15–16

  Tribal Criminal and Civil Disputes Regulations (TCCDR) 15, 21
  Women's Awakening Club 20
Bush, George W. 90, 129, 167, 175

centralized administrative system 14
Chapouk, S. 74
Chemali Khalaf, M. 247
Childs, S. 3, 4, 231, 271
Coalition Provisional Authority (CPA) 6, 42, 74, 188
Cochrane, P. 256
Coleman, I. 40, 83, 233, 243, 244, 254, 255, 264, 265, 267
consociationalism 52
constituents, substantive representation 159–61
constitutional monarchy 16, 60
Constitution and Electoral Law 21
Constitution Drafting Committee 56
Convention to End All Forms of Discrimination against Women (CEDAW) 29, 37, 166, 228
corruption 178–9
Council of Representatives 36

Dahlerup, D. 2–3, 38–40, 183, 231, 232, 234, 242, 243, 244, 252, 253, 255, 256, 270
Daud, Sabihah al-Shaikh 20, 236
Davidson, Christopher M. 237, 266, 276
De-Ba'athification Law 76, 84, 153
decentralized rule 14
decision-making process 8, 36
Democratic Patriotic Alliance of Kurdistan (DPAK) 76–7
democratization theory 4, 10, 61, 64, 72, 169–70
descriptive representation 9, 38, 226
  De-Ba'athification Laws 84
  definition 87
  early Ba'athist regime 63–4
  gender equality values 83
  global theoretical discourses 87
  Hashemite monarchy 60–2
  historical and sociopolitical context 59
  Hughes's theoretical framework 85
  interim national assembly 83
  Inter-Parliamentary Union 83
  Iran-Iraq conflict (*see* Iran-Iraq war)

policy-making 59
political agenda 60
post-2003 invasion 72–5
post-occupation 2005–14 (*see* post-occupation 2005–14, descriptive representation)
public activities 60
religious organizations 84
under Saddam 64–6
sanctions era (*see* sanctions era, descriptive representation)
symbolic effects 86
Dinarvets 125

Ebadi, S. 50, 247
economic supports 163–4
educational supports 167–8
Efrati, Noga 16, 234, 235, 236, 238, 239, 240, 242, 249, 265
egalitarianism 22
egalitarian political cultures 37
Elections Law 2
electoral gender quotas 35–40, 150
  adoption 37–8
  Convention to End All Forms of Discrimination against Women (CEDAW) 37
  Council of Representatives 36
  decision-making process 36
  descriptive representation 38
  egalitarian political cultures 37
  "fast track" 39
  global politics 35–6
  "incremental track" 39
  International Institute for Democracy and Electoral Assistance (IDEA) 37
  legal candidate quotas 36
  nongovernmental organizations (NGOs) 37
  patronage politics, Saddam era 40
  political party quotas 36
  post-conflict transition and reconstruction 36
  reserved seats 36
  socioeconomic condition 39
  substantive representation 38
  symbolic representation 38
  types 36
  voluntary quotas 37

electoral law 61
electoral reform 157
"emancipation" 24
Empowerment of Women 24, 73
Entity for Gender Equality 24
Erbil Agreement 95, 110
Ethnosectarian schisms 229

Fatat al-Arab (Young Arab Woman, 1937) 20
Fatat al-Iraq (Young Iraqi Woman, 1936) 20
Fayhaa, al-television 91, 129, 149, 153, 163
Feda'iyye 30
Female members of parliament
  al-Bajari, Noura 94–8
  al-Douri, Etab 98–102
  al-Fatlawi, Hanan 102–5
  al-Jaf, Ashwaq 106–8
  al-Jawari, Karima 108–13
  al-Obaidi, Suhad 120–5
  al-Rayyis, Mariam 125–8
  al-Suhail, Safia 129–30
  al-Talabani, Alaa' 130–5
  al-Tamimi, Majida 135–40
  Mubarak, Jinan 116–20
  Sajjad, Huda Mahmoud 113–16
feminist theory 61, 144, 225
Ferree, M. M. 270
Fleischmann, E. L. 235
forced marriage 32
Fourth World Conference on Women 5, 36
Free Iraq Foundation 152, 157, 162, 193
  constituents 159–60
  economic challenges 175
  educational supports 168
  gender quota 157
  human rights 153
  international influences 166
  media barriers 198
  media supports 193–4
  NGO support 162
  patriarchy 179
  political infighting 174
  security 172
  voter attitudes 196, 203
"Free Officers" Movement 21
Freidenvall, L. 38–9, 232, 242, 243, 253, 270

gender
  conservatism 28
  discrimination 4
  egalitarian trends 1, 4
  equality values 83
gender quotas, Middle East
  Coalition Provisional Authority (CPA) 42
  constitutional design 41
  electoral (*see* electoral gender quotas)
  female politicians 45–6
  High Commission for Human Rights (HCHR) 41
  Iran 50–1
  Iraqi Higher Women's Council 41
  Jordan 46–7
  Lebanon 51–5, 57
  Morocco 49–50
  policy-making roles 40
  post-conflict society 45
  Provincial Councils 44
  regional politics, factors 46
  Sudan 47–9
  tight-knit communities 43
  Transitional Provisional Authority 42
  Tunisia 55–6
  US military invasions 45
  women's rights 40
General Federation of Iraqi Women (GFIW) 24–5, 64–5, 70, 72
General Foundation of Iraqi Women (GFIW) 24–5, 64
Global Justice Project 195
Global Media Monitoring Project (GMMP) 191
governmental budget funds 154–5
Grotz, F. 249, 250, 251
"guardians of tradition" 185
1991 Gulf War 29, 131, 168
Guy, Frances 82, 194–5, 197, 204

Hakki, Z. 62
harems 49
Hare quota 77
Hartmann, Christof 249, 250, 251
Hashemite monarchy 16, 20–2, 34
  descriptive representation, during 1920–1979 60–2
Hassun, P. 20
Helou, M. 52

High Commission for Human Rights (HCHR) 41
Hudson, Michael C. 279
Hughes, M. M. 83, 85, 241n.1, 255n.153, 255n.163, 255n.174, 256n.178
Human rights violations 72–3
Human Rights Watch 41, 172–3, 192, 237, 238, 244, 268, 273
Hunt, S. 42, 244
Husseini, R. 245

Independent High Electoral Commission (IHEC) 43, 79, 102, 157
infrastructural laws 185
1970 Interim Constitution 25
interim government 73–5
interim national assembly 83
International Foundation for Electoral Systems (IFES) 41
International Institute for Democracy and Electoral Assistance (IDEA) 9, 37–8, 243, 245
International Labour Organization 7
International Labour Union 62
International Organization for Migration (IOM) 166
International Telecommunications Union 201
Inter-Parliamentary Union 7, 67, 83
interventionist democracy promotion 227
Iran-Iraq war 27
  1980 elections 66–7
  1984 elections 67–8
  Amnesty International 28
  financial and legitimacy crises 28
  gender conservatism 28
  moral authority 29
  Revolutionary Command Council (RCC) 66
  Sunni support 29
  vocational training 27
  women employment 27
Iraq battle 209–11
Iraq Communist Party 21, 22, 61
2005 Iraq electoral law 42–3
Iraq Foundation analysis 150
Iraqi Centre for Women's Rehabilitation and Employment (ICWRE) 117–18, 162, 218

Iraqi constitutions 1925–present 16–19
Iraqi Governing Council (IGC) 74, 148
Iraqi Higher Women's Council 41
Iraqi Independent High Electoral
    Commission (IHEC) 79
Iraqi Interim Government (IIG) 74
Iraqi Journal of Agriculture 74
Iraqi Media Network (IMN) 90, 188
Iraqi media post-2003
    Ba'athist political elite 188
    Coalition Provisional Authority (CPA)
        188
    Global Media Monitoring Project
        (GMMP) 191
    intercommunal violence 189–90
    Maliki government 192
    media gender inequalities 191
    satellite television channels 190
Iraqi National Communications and
    Media Commission (INCMC) 90
Iraqi National Movement (INM) 80
Iraqi Provisional Constitution 24
Iraqi Reconstruction Development
    Council 62
Iraqi Security Forces (ISF) 210
Iraqi Women's League (IWL) 22, 61
Iraqi Women's Organization (IWO) 74
Iraqiya, al- television 89–90, 188–9
    al-Jaf, Ashwaq 106, 108, 160, 196
    al-Jawari, Karima 109–13
    al-Rayyis, Mariam 126, 128
    al-Tamimi, Majida 136–8, 140, 200, 204
    Sajjad, Huda Mahmoud 114, 116, 152, 169
Iraq Legal Development Project (ILDP)
    group 13
Iraq National Assembly 25–6
Iraqi Hashemite Monarchy 60
Islamic Consultative Assembly 50
Islamic Republic of Iran 50, 51
Islamic State of Iraq and Levant 116
Islamic State of Iraq and Syria (ISIS)
    209–12
Islamist Party of Justice and Development
    (PJD) 49
Istiqlal (Independence) Party 21, 22

Jacqueline, S. 194, 272
Jaf, Ashwaq al- 106–8, 216–17
Jawaheri, Yasmin Husein al- 33, 241

Joseph, S. 232, 233, 238, 249, 250, 252, 267

Kamp, M. 233
Kandiyoti, D. 5, 72, 171, 233, 251, 264, 268
Karam, Azza M. 94, 197, 273, 274
Kassem, F. S. 55
Khatib, Lina 53
King Abdullah 46
Kingston, P. 52
kleptocracy 178
Krook, Mona Lena 38, 45, 231, 233, 234,
    242, 243, 244
Kuku, N. 241, 245, 246
Kurdish society 26
Kurdistan Democratic Party (KDP) 69,
    106, 211
Kurdistan Regional Government (KRG)
    155
Kurdistan Revolutionary Party 66–7

"lawmaker" 8
Layla, Iraqi women's magazine 20
legal candidate quotas 36
legitimacy, political institutions 3
Lijphart, A. 52
Lorber, J. 252
Lovenduski, J. 37, 53, 242, 248

Maliki government 192
marginalization and monopolization
    policies 154
Marr, P. 22, 235, 236, 237, 239, 250, 256
Maternal Law of 1971 25
"Media barriers" 170, 198–202
media supports, symbolic representation
    abayas 194
    Free Iraq Foundation 193
    gender balance 193
    parliamentary achievements 194
    social media 195–6
    Woodrow Wilson International Center
        for Scholars 193
Mernissi, F. 3, 232, 252
Middle East and North Africa (MENA)
    45, 55, 166, 172, 198
Moghadam, V. M. 4, 45, 52, 232, 240, 245,
    247, 252, 267, 271
Moumin, M. 74–5
Mubarak, Jinan 116–20, 218

National Congress Party (NCP) 47
National Constituent Assembly (NCA)
    elections 56
National Democratic Party 21, 22
National Endowment for Democracy
    (NED) 41
Nauphal, N. 54
Nohlen, D. 65, 249, 250, 251
nongovernmental organizations (NGOs)
    10, 30, 37, 62
    support 161–3
Norris, P. 37, 83, 242, 244, 248, 249, 255,
    256, 271
Nussbaum, Martha C. 255

O'Brien, D. Z. 38, 233, 242, 243, 244
occupational training 25
Oil-for-Food Program 151–2, 155
Organization of Women's Freedom in Iraq
    (OWFI) 162
Othman, N. 74–5
Ottoman Empire 1, 13–15
    agricultural populations 13
    authoritarian paternalism 15
    centralized administrative system 14
    decentralized rule 14
    legacy 13, 15
    shari'a law 14
    Tanzimat Reforms 14
    "Turkification" policy 14–15

Pappé, I. 246, 247
parliamentary gender quota 168–9
Parsawas, F. 50
patriarchal systems 170
patriarchy 179–80
Patriotic Union of Kurdistan 131,
    141, 211
Paxton, P. 83, 255
Payne, R. 52
Peace Agreement 47–8
Personal Status Law (1959) 23, 24, 29,
    31–3, 62, 118, 148–50, 171, 204
policy legislation, substantive
    representation
    electoral gender quota 150
    electoral reform 157
    governmental budget funds 154–5
    human rights 153–4

hydrocarbon-related political disputes
    156
infrastructure and social services 151–3
Iraq Foundation analysis 150
Kurdistan Regional Government (KRG)
    155
legislative committees 151
Oil-for-Food Program 155
women's issues 157–8
political agency 225
political efficacy 224
political party quotas 36
political situation and women's
    representation post-2014
    al-Bajari, Noura 212–13
    al-Douri, Etab 214
    al-Fatlawi, Hanan, 214–16
    al-Jaf, Ashwaq 216–17
    al-Jawari, Karima 217–18
    al-Obaidi, Suhad 218–19
    al-Rayyis, Mariam 219–20
    al-Suhail, Safia 221
    al-Talabani, Alaa' 222–3
    al-Tamimi, Majida 223
    Mubarak, Jinan 218
    Sajjad, Huda Mahmoud 220–1
Posa, C. 42, 244
post-Ba'athist media 206
postcolonial feminist theory 11
post-invasion reconstruction 2
post-occupation 2005–2014, descriptive
    representation
    2010 elections 79–81
    2014 elections 81–3
    December 2005, elections under new
        constitution 76–8
    electoral results 75
    January 2005 transitional elections 75–6
Pratt, N. 40, 42, 149, 233, 234, 241, 243,
    244, 245, 251, 252, 255, 265, 275
Price, Monroe E. 190, 271, 272
Provincial Councils 44
public policy-making 2

Qasim, Abd al-Karim 21–3
Qazzaz, Ayad al- 61
quotaProject 36

Rabinovich, I. 250, 251

Radio Sawa 90
Rai, S. 271
Rajaee, F. 238
Rajagopal, B. 249
rentier political marketplace 178
reserved seats 36
Revolutionary Command Council (RCC) 66
Riverbend 192, 273
Rohde, A. 239
Rugh, William A. 188, 272

Saadeh, S. 55
Sabbagh, A. 9, 234, 264, 267, 268
Sabri, N. 74
Saddam Hussein 25, 34, 237
  Ba'athist Party 26
  descriptive representation 64–6
  Iran-Iraq war 27–9
  Iraq National Assembly 25–6
  Kurdish society 26
  Qadissiyah 69
  systematic rape and sexual assault 26
  women objectification, political tools 29–31
Sadiki, L. 270
Saikal, A. 169
Sajjad, Huda Mahmoud 113–16, 220–1
Salomey, I. 52
sanctions era, descriptive representation
  1996 elections 69–70
  2000 elections 70–1
  authoritarianism 71
  Ba'ath Party 68
  biological warfare 71
  democratization theory 72
  enfranchisement 71–2
  liberal concept of citizenship 72
  National Progressive Patriotic Front 68
  parliamentary seats 71
  Sha'aban Intifada 69
  weapons of mass destruction 71
Sawt al-Mara (Women's Voice, 1943) 20
Scahill, J. 264
Schnabel, A. 169
Schulze, K. 53, 247, 248
Security Council Resolution 28, 197, 228
Selboe, E. 270, 271
Sha'aban Intifada 69

Shah, Mohammad R., 50
Shaked, H. 250, 251
Sharabi, H. 267
shari'a law 6–7, 14, 32, 47, 72, 107, 146, 148, 162, 172, 179, 192
Shvedova, N. 268
Single Transferable Vote (STV) systems 77
social media 195–6, 227
sociopolitical fractionalization 153
Stokke, K. 270, 271
Stremlau, Nicole A. 271, 272
substantive representation 9, 38, 144
  autocracy 181
  Coalition Provisional Authority (CPA) 145
  constituents 159–61
  Constitution Drafting Committee 145
  constitutional document 145
  corruption 178–9
  democratization 144, 169–70
  economic challenges 174–6
  economic supports 163–4
  educational supports 167–8
  electoral influences 176–7
  exclusion 178
  factors 158–9
  feminist theory 144
  high-profile male figures 164–5
  international influences 165–7, 177–8
  "Media barriers" 170
  NGO support 161–3
  parliamentary gender quota 168–9
  patriarchy 179–80
  Personal Status Law 148–50
  policy legislation (*see* policy legislation, substantive representation)
  political infighting 173–4
  Provincial Council 147
  qualitative analysis 144
  security 170–3
  self-efficacy 180
  sociopolitical concept, gender quota 144
  Transitional National Assembly (TNA) 144
  tribalism and patriarchy 143
  United Iraqi Alliance (UIA) 146
  "Voter attitudes" 170
  "Western agenda" 170

women's political empowerment 170–1
Sudan People's Liberation Movement (SPLM) 47
Sunni insurgent force 209
Sutton, Jacqueline 194
symbolic representation 9, 38, 183, 227
   autocracy 185
   content analysis 184
   definition 183
   gender quota effects 184
   "guardians of tradition" 185
   "independent media" 187
   infrastructural laws 185
   Iraqi media post-2003 (see Iraqi media post-2003)
   legitimate authority 184
   media barriers 198–202
   media supports 193–6
   NGO barriers 204–5
   NGO supports 197
   peace-building and national unity 205
   political agent 197
   political roles 186
   post-Ba'athist media 206
   post-conflict interventionist state 187
   qualitative analyses 184
   "rules of the game" 184
   social identity 207
   Transitional Coalition and Constitution 185
   voter attitudes 196, 202–4
   "Western" ideology 186

Taha, Dr. Rihab Rashid 71
Tahrir al-Mara (Women Liberation, 1947) 20
Tanzimat Reforms 14
Tohidi, N. 246, 247
Tønnessen, L. 48, 246
Transitional Administrative Law (TAL) 41, 77
Transitional Coalition and Constitution 185
Transitional National Assembly (TNA) 144
Transitional Provisional Authority 42
Tribal Criminal and Civil Disputes Regulations (TCCDR) 15, 21
Tripp, C. 236
"Turkification" policy 14–15

United Iraqi Alliance (UIA) 76–7, 136, 146
United Nations Development Fund for Women (UNIFEM) 24
United Nations Development Program 7
United States Agency for International Development (USAID) 41, 166
US Department of Defence 166

Visser, R. 264
vocational training 27
voluntary quotas 37
voter attitudes 170, 196, 202–4

Warda, Pascale Isho 74–5
weapons of mass destruction (WMD) 1, 33, 71
Weldon, S. Laurel 4
Welzel, C. 84, 255
"Western agenda" 170
"Western" ideology 186
Western representative democracy 3
Western-style political system 62
Wimmen, H. 270
"window dressing" 225
Wolfowitz, P. 73, 252
women employment 27
Women's Empowerment Organization (WEO) 162
women objectification, political tools 29–31
Women's Awakening Club 20
women's political participation
   Ba'athist regime 23–4
   British invasion and colonization 15–20
   egalitarianism 22
   "emancipation" 24
   gender equality 22
   General Foundation of Iraqi Women (GFIW) 24–5
   Hashemite monarchy 20–2
   Iraq Legal Development Project (ILDP) group 13
   maternity benefits and transportation 25
   occupational training 25
   Ottoman Empire 13–15
   Personal Status Law 31–3

Saddam Hussein regime (*see* Saddam Hussein)
United Nations Development Fund for Women (UNIFEM) 24
war and sanctions, long-term impact 33–4

Women's Society for Combating Fascism and Nazism 61
Woodrow Wilson International Center for Scholars 193

Zedalis, Rex J. 266

www.ingramcontent.com/pod-product-compliance
Lightning Source LLC
Chambersburg PA
CBHW070015010526
44117CB00011B/1579